Day by Day with the English Puritans

Day by Day with the English Puritans

Compiled and Edited by

Randall J. Pederson

© 2004 by Hendrickson Publishers, Inc.
P. O. Box 3473
Peabody, Massachusetts 01961-3473

ISBN 1-56563-834-4

Printed in the United States of America

First Printing — June 2004

Unless otherwise noted, all Scripture quotations are taken from the KING JAMES VERSION OF THE BIBLE.

Cover Art: Freeman, Samuel (1773–1857). "John Bunyan, c1670–c1688." Plate 3 from *Lives of Eminent and Illustrious Englishmen, from Alfred the Great to the Latest Times,* Vol. 5. Glasgow & Edinburgh, 1834–1837. (613.i.5–8) British Library, London. Used with permission. Photo Credit: HIP/Scala /Art Resource, NY.

Library of Congress Cataloging-in-Publication Data

Day by day with the English Puritans / [edited by] Randall J. Pederson.
    p. cm.
    Includes bibliographical references.
    ISBN 1-56563-834-4 (alk. paper)
    1. Devotional calendars. 2. Puritans. I. Pederson, Randall J., 1975–
    BV4810.D347 2004
    242'.2—dc22

                              2004009610

Table of Contents

Foreword

W onderful things!" So said the awestruck Egyptologist Howard Carter when his colleagues asked him what the light he was shining round the newly discovered tomb of King Tutankhamen was showing him. His words came to my mind as I leafed through the Puritan extracts that make up this book. They are wonderful in the way that all good devotionals are—that is, they enlarge your sense of God's greatness, goodness, and closeness to you, and so make you praise and pray. Randall Pederson has done a great job in selecting them (some of the titles of the books he drew on are devotionals in themselves!), and I am sure that receptive readers will be greatly energized by them in faith and hope and love.

Historically, the influence of the English Puritans extended over a century and a half, approximately 1560–1710. Publicly and politically they campaigned for many reforms in church and state, and ended up losing every battle that they fought. During that time, however, by preaching, teaching, personal lifestyle and patience under persecution, they crystallized and communicated a glorious ideal of heart-holiness expressed in conscientious, well-ordered, doxological behavior—the authentic biblical ideal of a godly life, which in due course became basic to the Great Awakening and to Britain's Evangelical Revival. Clear-headed about biblical authority, justification by faith, and the covenantal framework of God's grace, they were equally clear on the realities of the Christian life— communion with the triune God, biblical morality, and the pilgrim perspective. In spiritually decadent days like ours they can help us to recover the wisdom and power of this ideal, as we all surely need to do.

"But the Puritans are so, well, *old-fashioned!*" Don't say that; it is not a Christian way to think. You would not speak that way about the apostles Paul and John, or about Augustine and Luther, all of whom antedated the Puritans; nor, I hope, would you thus put down Whitefield and Wesley and Edwards and Spurgeon, all of whom valued the Puritans enormously. Why would you not? Because you see these men as carriers of eternal truth and reality, and you know that truth and reality do not date. Now the Puritans convey eternal truth and reality also. Their grasp of godliness remains unrivaled, and we today, who lack it, need to learn it from them. This volume will help us to do that.

So, happy reading—and praying—and praising—with profit!

J. I. Packer
Regent College, Vancouver, B.C.

Preface

Spend one year with these English Puritans and see if you are not the better for it. They have a way of stripping life to its bare essentials and presenting us with a rich, lively, and untainted Christianity. The best Puritan streams were pure and living fountains, full of the sincere milk for the soul. Read them with delight and treasure them above fine jewelry; as Solomon says, "the mouth of the righteous is a well of life" (Prov. 10:11).

The devotional readings in this book have been carefully selected from over eighty Puritan manuscripts. Most are here reprinted for the first time. Each selection has been carefully edited to conform to modern usage while preserving the author's original meaning. All Scripture references are from the King James Version, except where the Puritan seems to have quoted from memory. Ellipses (. . .) have been used for purposes of clarity. In addition, the back of the book contains biographical sketches of each of the Puritans. I hope you will find these readings to be powerful and persuasive inducements to make Christianity "serious business."

I am grateful to Dr. James Ernest, previous Associate Editorial Director for Hendrickson Publishers, for helping get this project afoot; to Dr. Don Kistler for his endearing friendship; to Dr. J. I. Packer, for kindly writing the foreword; and to Stephen J. Hendrickson, in particular, for giving this project the go-ahead. I am also thankful for my wife, Sarah, and remain under an obligation, which I here acknowledge but can scarce repay.

Randall J. Pederson
April 2004

Introduction to the English Puritans

A BRIEF HISTORY

English Puritanism began as a reform movement in the early years of Queen Elizabeth's reign. Having been driven out of England under the Catholic Queen Mary, Protestant exiles returned to an atmosphere of political, cultural, and spiritual reform. These Protestants sought further reformation of government and of church liturgy, earning the derogatory epithet "Puritan."

However, while not inflexible, Elizabeth was modest with her reformist ideas. Her religious settlements consisted of The Acts of Uniformity and Supremacy and *The Prayer Book* in 1559 and the Thirty-Nine Articles in 1563. She was content with the climate of British Protestantism and strove to subdue dissident voices. Those who fought too much for change were persecuted and deprived of their livings. Thomas Cartwright, for instance, was formally censured because he demanded the removal of episcopacy in favor of Presbyterian polity.

Not until 1603, when James VI of Scotland succeeded as James I of England, did Puritan hopes for national reform revive. But James' program of reform was not what the most idealistic Puritans expected. It was true; James was more tolerant than Elizabeth, and he did grant a hearing of Puritan disputes at the Hampton Court Conference of 1604, but ultimately reformation efforts amounted to little. At the conference, Bishops portrayed the Puritans as "schismatic scholars," and James, for the most part, accepted this assessment.

Nevertheless, one of the Puritans at the conference gained James' ear with his simple and eloquent request: "May your Majesty be pleased that the Bible be new translated?" In some respects, the suggestion from John Reynolds attacked the standard Elizabethan Bible, "The Bishop's Bible." Even so, James agreed to the petition, but stated that no marginal notes be inserted, a reference to the extensive and interpretive notations of the Geneva Bible that Puritans had used for half a century. The finished work issued in 1611 as the Authorized, or King James Bible.

After James' death in 1625, succession fell to his twenty-five year old son Charles. The young monarch inherited a kingdom fraught with severe financial stress. Parliament, which in the past had served the monarchy with respect, refused to raise funds for a king who neglected the wishes of his nobility. Increasingly Puritan in their persuasions, the nobles felt suspicious of Charles' ability to manage the nation well. When he decided to marry Henrietta Maria, the Catholic daughter of France's King Henry IV, Puritans and Parliament became incensed. They viewed the new Queen as a meddling woman, who preferred the welfare of her Catholic friends over the well-being of her Protestant realm.

In October 1636, Charles fueled the controversy by attempting to force use of the Anglican Prayer Book on Scotland. A year later, three Puritans—Prynne, Burton, and Bastwick—were publicly mutilated for criticizing the Church of England under the leadership of Archbishop William Laud. There followed a riot against the new prayer book in St. Giles Cathedral, Edinburgh, and in February 1638, the Scottish church drafted the Scottish National Covenant, a document rallying for defense against the inroads of Anglicanism. Charles, however, considered the document a symbol of national rebellion and sent troops to Scotland in May of the succeeding year. This precarious situation forced him to summon Parliament because he was unable to financially sustain his army. At first Parliament refused to support Charles, but concessions were eventually made that allowed Parliament to impeach Laud for high treason in 1640.

Just when things seemed to be agreed upon between Charles, Parliament, and the Scots, Ireland erupted in rebellion. Charles returned to Parliament for aid, but instead Parliament issued a "grand remonstrance," detailing all of Charles' political and religious abuses. Four months later, Parliament raised a military force and the following August (1642), with Charles' call for all loyal subjects to support him, the English Civil War ensued.

Throughout the war, the Long Parliament, deriving its name from its twenty-year tenure, continued to meet under the leadership of Oliver Cromwell. In 1643, it gathered a company of theologians to propose reforms for the Church of England. Known as the Westminster Assembly because it met in Westminster Abbey over the next decade, this group drafted three major documents, *The Larger and Shorter Catechisms, Westminster Confession,* and *Directory of Public Worship.* While predominantly Presbyterian, the Assembly did allow Erastians, Episcopalians, and Independents to voice their opinions. Its final documents stand as a synthesis of British Puritan theology.

Oliver Cromwell eventually defeated Charles's forces and was instrumental in ending the royalist threat. He supported the army's belief that Charles should stand for his crimes against the English. Not surprisingly, Charles refused to acknowledge the authority of those who charged him. He was convicted of high treason and executed in 1649. Among his last words were, "I go from a corruptible to an incorruptible crown, where no disturbance can be, no disturbance in the world." For the first time in British history, a reigning monarch was executed by his own people.

Cromwell, on the other hand, was elected Lord Protector over all Britain. Averse to the concept of supreme power, he sought to work with and through a Council of State and to meet Parliament regularly. He committed to a wide measure of religious liberty for those who did not threaten the general liberty, though Roman Catholics were suppressed. There was a state church under Cromwell, but attendance was optional. It was during this time of toleration that a number of radical religious groups emerged, including the Levelers, the Diggers, Fifth Monarchy Men, and the Quakers.

When Cromwell's health steadily declined in 1658, the demise of the English Commonwealth seemed to loom. Cromwell died on September 3, 1658, and was buried in Westminster Abbey. His son and chosen successor, Richard, served as Lord Protector for less a year. In May of 1659, the Rump Parliament, a reinstated version of the Long Parliament, forced him to abdicate, and he fled to France to escape creditors. There he lived for a time as John Clarke, returning to England in 1680 to live out the remainder of his life in seclusion.

After Richard Cromwell's departure, Parliament officially invited Charles II to return from exile. He did so, promising religious toleration for dissenters. When Charles arrived in London on his birthday, May 20, 1660, crowds roared with applause. Charles, who favored his mother's Catholicism, wanted to pursue toleration for Catholics among others, but the new Parliament still held the majority of power and passed the Clarendon Code, a series of acts that ensured Anglicanism as the state religion and persecuted religious dissidents. The most famous of these acts, the Act of Uniformity, was enforced on St. Bartholomew's Day, 1662, and resulted in the expulsion of over two-thousand nonconforming clergy, mostly Puritans, from the Church. Puritanism as an ecclesiastical reform movement ended. As a cultural and spiritual force, it lasted well into the eighteenth century, only bowing to changing political and cultural climates with the entrance of the Enlightenment.

PURITAN LIFE AND PRACTICE

The Puritans were more than a political party in the Church of England. They were also a major cultural and spiritual force. Puritan life and practice in the sixteenth and seventeenth centuries was important in several ways.

First, the Puritans were *simple* people. In contrast to the more elegant Anglican churches, which often contained huge pipe organs and stained-glass windows portraying biblical events, they strove to worship in unadorned churches. Common Puritan objections to Anglican worship included the use of clerical vestments (particularly the surplice, a white wide-sleeved gown worn to officiate in church services), making the sign of the cross at baptism, kneeling to receive communion, bowing at the name of Jesus, the use of wedding rings in marriage services, and church bells. Puritans also held to a strict Sabbatarian view, demanding that members cease from unnecessary labor on the Christian Sabbath.

Second, the Puritans were a *working* people. The modern distinction between the sacred and the secular held no sway in the Puritan worldview. For them, all of life was sacred, and especially the field of work. John Dod and Robert Cleaver, for instance, wrote that "the great and reverend God despiseth no honest trade . . . but crowneth it with his blessing."

Third, the Puritans were a *familial* people. Great emphasis was placed on the family as "a little church," in which the father was to act as minister. Preachers admonished Puritan men to love their wives as Christ had loved the church, and the women, in turn, were told to reverence their husbands. In his *Christian Directory,* Richard Baxter confessed, "It is a mercy to have a faithful friend that loveth you entirely . . . whom you may open your mind and communicate your affairs."

Fourth, the Puritans were a people of the *Word*. Early in the 1550s, preaching the Scripture became central to the Puritan cause. Perceived to be the primary means of God's working in the individual heart, Puritan sermons tended to address the mundane, everyday occurrences of daily living and avoided the more philosophical discourses of Anglican divines.

No introduction to the Puritans would be complete, however, without mentioning their faults. At times, Puritans could be an intolerant and fearful people. Dissenting voices were often either exiled or oppressed, and practices such as the witch trials still mar the Puritan past. However, not every Puritan condoned harsh methods. Ministers like Samuel Willard publicly detested them. Others like Roger Williams opposed them in spite of the consequent persecution. Even judges like Samuel Sewall, who was prominent in the trials, later repented of their involvement.

Yet in spite of the careful studies and correctives of modern historians— secular as well as religious—the word Puritan is still employed to stand for harshness, rigidity, superstition, blindness to the beauty of the world, and various psychological abnormalities. While it is true that they lived strict lives, they nevertheless had a profound sense of God's mercy and forgiveness. What the Puritans disdained was worldly thinking, living as though time and eternity were insignificant to the human soul. However, the classic picture of the Puritan as the *pilgrim* or *traveler to Zion* is only a partial view. The Puritans blended otherworldly aspiration with this-worldly usefulness. Each one strove to be the best husband, the best wife, the best son, the best daughter, the best worker. In short, each one strove to be the best citizen of both worlds.

FOR FURTHER READING

Beeke, Joel R., and Randall Pederson. *Meet the Puritans.* Edinburgh: Banner of Truth Trust, forthcoming.

Crampton, W. Gary. *What the Puritans Taught: An Introduction to Puritan Theology.* Morgan: Soli Deo Gloria, 2003.

Hulse, Errol. *Who Are the Puritans . . . And What Did They Teach?* Darlington: Evangelical Press, 2000.

Lake, Peter. "Defining Puritanism—Again?" Pages 3–29 in *Puritanism: Transatlantic Perspectives on a Seventeenth-Century Anglo-American Faith.*

Edited by Francis J. Bremer. Boston: Northeastern University Press, 1993.

Lewis, Peter. *The Genius of Puritanism*. Morgan: Soli Deo Gloria, 2003.

Lloyd-Jones, D. M. *Puritans: Their Origins and Successors*. Edinburgh: Banner of Truth Trust, 1987.

Morgan, Edmund S. *Puritan Family*. New York: Perennial, 1942.

Packer, J. I. *A Quest for Godliness: The Puritan Vision of the Christian Life*. Wheaton: Crossway, 1990.

Ryken, Leland. *Worldly Saints: The Puritans As They Really Were*. Grand Rapids: Zondervan, 1990.

Seed of the Church

Jeremiah Burroughs

The power of God is glorious, not only in preserving His church, in raising the spirits of His servants in their greatest affliction, but in increasing His church by them. If it is a wonder to be upheld in them, it is much more a wonder to be increased by them. "The more we are cut down, the more we persist," says Tertullian. The church never grew so fast as when it was under the most affliction. Sulpitius says of the Christians in the primitive times, that they were then as greedy of martyrdom, as in his time men were greedy of the bishopric. The blood of martyrs was the seed of the church. Pliny reports of the lily, that it is increased by its own juice that drops from it, and so is the church, which is the lily that grows among the thorns; the very blood that drops from it, multiplies it; the sufferings of one beget many to the love of the truth. John Knox . . . reports of a gentleman, one John Lindsay, familiar to Bishop James Bettoune, that he said to the Bishop upon the occasion of the burning of Patrick Hamilton: "My Lord, if you burn any more, you will destroy yourselves; if you will burn them, let them be burnt in hollow cellars, for the smoke of Mr. Patrick Hamilton has infected as many as it blew upon." It is reported of one Cecilia . . . that her constancy and exhortations, before and after her martyrdom, were the means to convert four hundred people. "By blood and prayer the church converts the whole world," says Luther.

And I say also unto thee that thou art Peter, and upon this rock I will build my church; and the gates of hell shall not prevail against it.
Matthew 16:18

> The sufferings of one beget many to the love of the truth.

Precious Promises

William Spurstowe

*Whereby are given
unto us exceeding
great and precious
promises; that by these
ye might be partakers
of the divine nature,
having escaped the
corruption that is in
the world through
lust.*

2 Peter 1:4

Meditate thoroughly and frequently upon the promises, and . . . deal with them as the Virgin Mary did with the things that were spoken concerning Christ: "She kept all these things, and pondered them in her heart" (Luke 2:19). The distiller does not put any virtue into the herbs, but it distills and extracts whatever is efficacious and useful from them. The bee does not provide any sweetness to the flower, but by its industry it sucks the latent honey from it. Meditation conveys nothing of worth unto the promise, but it draws forth the sweetness, and discovers the beauty of it, which otherwise would be little crafted and discerned. I have sometimes thought that a believer's looking upon a promise is not unlike a person's beholding of the heavens in a full and serene evening, who when he first casts up his eye, sees happily a star or two only to peep, and with difficulty to put forth a feeble and disappearing light; but by and by he looks up again, and both their number and luster are increased. A while later he views the heavens again, and then the whole firmament, from every quarter, full of a numberless multitude of stars, is richly enameled as with so many golden studs. So when Christians first turn their thoughts towards the promises, the appearances of light and comfort which shine from them, do oft-times seem to be as weak and imperfect rays which neither scatter fears nor darkness; when again they set themselves to ripen and improve their thoughts upon them, then the evidence and comfort which they yield to the soul, is both more clear and distinct. But when the heart and affections are fully fixed in the meditation of a promise, Oh! What a bright mirror is the promise then to the eye of faith? What legions of beauties do then appear from every part of it, which both ravish and fill the soul of a believer with delight? . . . One promise thoroughly ruminated and meditated upon, is like to a morsel of meat well chewed and digested, which distributes more nourishment and strength to the body, than great quantities taken down whole.

Helps to Prayer

Gervase Babington

Surely goodness and mercy shall follow me all the days of my life: and I will dwell in the house of the LORD forever.
Psalm 23:6

ave an eye to the sweet promises of God, concerning the suits of His children to Him, which are so many and so entire, as no heart, if it be not flint or steel, but must receive comfort and courage to speak unto such a Lord. "Ask, and it shall be given you; seek, and ye shall find; knock, and it shall be opened unto you. Whatsoever ye shall ask the Father in my name, He will give it you" (Matt. 7:11; John 16:23), and a thousand such like. Muse upon them until the fire kindle within you, and then speak with a spirit to so sweet a God as so cheers His children to pray heartily. And remember it often what once was said: "I will come into thy house even upon the multitude of thy mercy, and in thy fear will I worship toward thy holy temple" (Ps. 5:7). The multitude of God's mercies make a sweet entrance into the house of prayer: yes, say you with David joyfully and comfortably, "In God's word will I rejoice, in the Lord's word will I comfort myself, in God have I put my trust, I will not fear what man can do unto me" (Ps. 56:10–11). Sometimes our weakness is great and our minds begin to strap from our prayer conceived in silence, and then it shall be good to speak out, yes even to cry out that which we but thought before, to the end that so we may stay a straying mind and bring it to the sound of the tongue. This has been the wisdom of the godly ever, and a means as we read to help them. The prophet David says, "I cried to the Lord with my voice, and I said, thou art my hope and my portion in the land of the living" (Ps. 142:1, 5). So that he uses the pronunciation of words happily even for this cause that we speak of. Augustine says, "Our devotion and affection is stirred up and quickened by the voice." And experience serves for longer proof in this matter. The gestures of body, as kneeling, lying prostrate upon the earth, knocking of the breast, and covering the face, or turning to the wall, lifting up the eyes, and such like, they are helps also of affection. Yea, then are they lawful, and right in deed, when they serve to this purpose in sincerity, and not to any outward show in hypocrisy.

The Saint's Life

John Durant

*And to know the love
of Christ which
passeth knowledge.*
Ephesians 3:19

Christ's love is the saint's life. Paul tells you he was dead to the law that he might live to God. And the ground thereof was this, that he lived by faith in Christ, who loved him (Gal. 2:20). As the life, so likewise the comfort of the saints is wrapped up in the love of Christ. A believer can neither live nor rejoice if the Lord Jesus smiles not upon the soul. But if Jesus Christ will but smile, and shine in the light of His love, believers know, not only how to live, but also how to rejoice, in all, even the worst of times. Hence it was, that this apostle, praying to the Father of our Lord Jesus, for the Ephesians, that they might not faint at his tribulations, he entreats that to this purpose they might know the love of Christ which passes knowledge . . . the love of Christ to believers is transcendent, it being above expression. Those who enjoy Christ's love, they know not how to express it, such is the transcendence of the love, that is passes their knowledge how to express it in any language. The Scripture sets out the height of things by this, that they are unspeakable; so when it would heighten, and declare the transcendence of the rapture in which Paul was (when wrapped up on the third heaven) and the glory of that which he then heard, it sets it down by this, that it was unutterable. He heard unutterable words (which may be a Hebraism for things, *word* and *thing* being in the Hebrew changeable) which it was not possible for a man to utter (2 Cor. 12:14) . . . the transcendence of Christ's love to believers is such that no one (no, though they had the tongues of men and angels) knows how to express it . . . The most spiritual mathematician is not able to commensurate Christ's love in all its dimensions. It is as possible for that little crevice of the body (the eye) to let in all the light of the sun, as it is for that great eye of the soul (knowledge) to let in the luster of Christ's love.

Godly Sorrow

Thomas Doolittle

Leave not the reins loose upon your affections, lest they carry you to sin in your sorrow. Lavish not those tears in washing your dead, which should be kept for lamenting your sins. Let there be a difference between your sorrow and the sorrow of others, as there should be between those that have hope and those that have no hope of a joyful resurrection to eternal, glorious life. . . . "I would not have you to be ignorant." Others are, and therefore mourn to excess; but I would not have you to be, that you may not sorrow as they do. Did you know, think, and believe, that their death is but a sleep, out of which they shall certainly awake; their graves . . . out of which, when the morning of the resurrection shall come, they shall arise, and that their souls in the mean time are with God, and Christ, and the Eternal Spirit, admitted into that glorious society of angels and saints above, perfectly loving, constantly delighting, perpetually praising and triumphing in that God that did choose them, in that Jesus that did redeem them with His blood, in that Holy Spirit that made them meet to be partakers of that inheritance of yonder saints in light, and life, and love. Would you groan while they rejoice? Would you mourn while they sing songs of praise? Are you grieved because they are exalted? . . . Could you hear them speak to you, they would say, "you are in daily trouble, we in everlasting rest, and peace, and triumph; you are in the field, we have got the victory; you are in danger of sin and Satan, we are freed from them forever; your love unto our Lord and yours, is imperfect love, while ours wants no degree; you know not what we do know of God, and Christ, and Glory; you see not what we do see, nor enjoy so much as we enjoy, therefore spend your tears upon yourselves, and not for us; weep for yourselves, and not for us. . . . You pray, and wait, and hope to be where we are, but we have no desire to be where you are. We have a better house than you live in, better company, and better work, and sweeter employment; therefore, sorrow for your selves, and not for us."

I would not have you to be ignorant, brethren, concerning them which are asleep, that ye sorrow not, even as others which have no hope.
1 Thessalonians 4:13

Christ's Scepter

Obadiah Sedgwick

But unto the Son he saith, Thy throne, O God, is for ever and ever: a sceptre of righteousness is the sceptre of thy kingdom.
Hebrews 1:8

True faith . . . takes Christ and Him only to be its Lord. . . . Many will come to Christ to find a feast, but few come to Christ to bear His scepter. Some would come under the safety of His blood, but disdain the authority and dominion of His sword; they like Christ the Priest, but not Christ the Lord. I will briefly show you two things . . . unbelievers will not accept Christ to be their Lord only, because their heart has another Lord. . . . He is our Lord to whom we give service, and we His servants *who obey him.* . . . Let the commands of profit or pleasure and Christ come into competition and you shall see that the unbelieving heart will go after its Lord; it will not hearken to Christ, for it prefers sin before Him. The unbelieving heart will easily adventure Christ's displeasure to fulfill its own lusts. Again, the unbelieving heart cannot choose Christ; it cannot like Him for a Lord. Why? Because the dominion of Christ is holy and heavenly; it is directly opposite to the sordid principles and affections, and ways of an unbelieving heart. Secondly, every believer admits Christ to be their Lord as Thomas said, "My Lord, and my God" (John 20:28) . . . and so (1) Faith sets up the scepter of Christ, and sweetly frames the soul to a willing subjection, (2) Again, faith takes the whole Christ, and therefore Christ is the only King and Lord to faith, (3) Again, faith knows that the whole person is Christ's purchase, His blood has bought us, and so passed us into the entire dominion of Christ: "ye are bought with a price; ye are not your own," said the apostle, 1 Cor. 6:19–20. Now then try yourself in this: who is your Lord? If by faith you have sworn fidelity to Christ, then though all temptations beset you, to captivate, or to alienate your heart from the service of Christ, yet amidst all oppressions, yes, under all the knocks and buffetings, and interruptions by sin, the heart cries out, I acknowledge no Lord but Christ; Him I would obey; Him I honor, I love; His I am, and I yet hate those sins which yet I cannot conquer.

Meeting God

Samuel Bolton

To have to do with any matter which concerns the worship and service of God is to draw near to God. And in other places it is called a coming before God, a treading His courts, an approaching to God, a meeting of God, all which languages imply thus much: that who ever has to do with God in any ordinance, draws near to God. You tread His courts, you come into His presence, you approach unto God, you meet God, you have communion with God; no, you have to do with God's Name. God's ordinances are part of His Name. No, you have to do with God Himself. He that has to do with any ordinance, with any part of His worship, has to do with God Himself. When you have to do with the Word, when you go to prayer, when you have to do with the sacraments, you have to do with God Himself in them. What could the Word do, either in commands to engage us, in promises to comfort us, in threatening to terrify us, if we had not to do with God in them? What is prayer, but a distracted seriousness, a religious madness, if we had not to do with God in it? What were the sacraments, but gaudy pageants, no, empty fancies, beggarly elements, if we had not to do with God in them? It is God that we have to do with in the ordinances, that sheds a glory, casts a majesty, and puts an efficacy into all the ordinances we have to do withal. It is God who makes the promises of the Word rocks of stay and support, that makes the commands of the Word full of authority, that makes the threatening of the Word exceeding terrible. It is God that makes a little handful of water, a little bit of bread, and sup of wine, exceeding glorious and efficacious. What empty, what poor, what contemptible things would these be (and are to unbelieving men) if we had not to do with God in them?

I will be sanctified in them that come nigh me, and before all the people I will be glorified.
Leviticus 10:3

> It is God that sheds a glory into all the ordinances we have to do withal.

A Tender Heart

Timothy Cruso

enderness of heart supposes deep conviction, as that which must go before, in order to the producing of such a frame. The sword in Christ's mouth must pierce (as it were) between the joints and marrow, divide the soul and spirit asunder, and make such kind of wounds as the regardless sinner never felt before. . . . Where the word does not enter thus, the heart will remain hard still, and wonderfully insensible both of sin and duty. A sound which only passes by the ear signifies nothing more than a feather drawn over the skin, until the commandment comes with power, for the raising of men's stupid faculties out of their deep sleep. Christ told Judas that he had a devil, and would betray Him, yet conscience never stirred, so as to execute its office to any purpose. So long as people are alive and vigorous, cheerful and confident (as Paul was once in his natural condition [Rom. 7:9]) without the law, this disposition of holy tenderness is not likely to spring up in them, and they may be truly said to be without the law, though they have the outward dispensation of it, so long as they are not thoroughly convinced and humbled by it. . . . Such high mountains, as our hearts natural are, like vast heaps of filth cast up in the way of the Lord, will not slow down at any presence but His. None is able of these stones to rise up believing children, spiritual seed, to Abraham, but only He. He against whom sin is committed, must give saving repentance for sin; He that pressed under us metaphorically must also cause us to feel the load of our own defilements really; the God in whose sight we are most abominable, must bring us to loath ourselves. He fashioned the heart at first and He can turn it which way He pleases. It was formed by His hand originally, and it is in His hand still, that is, it is under His sovereign power, which He can successfully exert in any case.

The Perfect Path

Richard Alleine

You should level at perfection of holiness, and no mark short of perfection should limit or bound your aims: "Having these promises, let us cleanse ourselves from (all) filthiness of flesh and spirit, perfecting holiness in the fear of God" (2 Cor. 7:1). Though perfect holiness cannot be attained, yet it must be aimed at; though we cannot reach into it, yet we must be reaching towards it; though we cannot obtain, yet we must be still following after. Because we cannot obtain all that is desirable, but there will be still while we live, something that is before, which we are yet short of; therefore our motion in religion must be constantly a progressive motion; we must still be going forward, and reaching out to that which is before, that our works may be more, and our hearts may be better at last than at first (Prov. 4:18). The path of the just must shine more and more unto perfect day; grace must be growing up till it be swallowed up of glory.

And when Abram was ninety years old and nine, the LORD appeared to Abram, and said unto him, I am the Almighty God; walk before me, and be thou perfect.
Genesis 17:1

Though perfect holiness cannot be attained, yet it must be aimed at.

Holy Fidelity

Richard Vines

A bundle of myrrh is my well-beloved unto me; he shall lie all night betwixt my breasts.
Song of Solomon 1:13

I f you are married to Jesus Christ, you like Him and His love better than all the world. Therefore, it is said, "His love is better than wine," that is, than all the excellency of the creature; that there is not any other grape that yields such sweetness and comfort as His love; no grape of pleasure, or credit, or profit, in all the vineyard of the world that is like it, to your spouse-like taste. Jesus Christ is better than all, even as wine exceeds all other liquors whatsoever. What then is it that fills up your heart, which takes up the chief place and room there? What is it that sits highest and possesses the first room of your liking, the top of your love? Is it the world or is it Jesus Christ . . . If you are near unto Christ, as the wife to the husband, then you take Him for better or for worse, and you keep Him for better or for worse . . . that is, not only for His crown, but also for His cross; not only for health and wealth, and good report, but for sickness, and poverty, and evil report; not only for what He has, but for what He wants, to share with Him alike in all conditions.

Jesus Christ is better than all, even as wine exceeds all other liquors.

Better Things

William Jenkyn

It should be the Christian's chief care to obtain from God the choicest mercies. The worldly are indeed easily put off with the meanest, because their inquiry is only who will show them any good. But O Christian! Let nothing please or satisfy you, but the light of God's countenance and do so receive from God here, as that you may be received to God hereafter. Desire not gifts, but mercies from God; not pebbles but pearls, and always labor for that which God never bestows but in love. Luther, when he had a rich present sent to him, professed with a holy boldness to God that such things should not serve his turn. Always desire the favor of God rather than outward felicity. O desire from God that your portion may not be in this life, but that what you enjoy here may be a pledge of better things hereafter.

And whatsoever ye shall ask in my name, that will I do, that the Father may be glorified in the Son.
John 14:13

> **Let nothing please or satisfy you, but the light of God's countenance.**

Always Near

Richard Vines

Thou art near, O LORD; and all thy commandments are truth.

Psalm 119:151

Though God stands far off, yet He is near, though not sensibly, yet really and truly; the essence of the nearness remains still, though the sense and influence is somewhat cut off. Even as it is with the sun, when it is covered with a cloud, the body of the sun is as near as when the cloud was not before it, though the heat and light, its influence, are somewhat cut off. A man is still as near the sun in a cloudy day as in a clear day; so, too, a man is as near God, that once is truly near Him, even when He hides Himself under a cloud of trial . . . The relation to the substance holds firm, as a son is as much a son when he is a thousand miles off from his father, as when he is in the same room, in his father's presence; so, too, a son of God is as much a son, for the essence and truth of the relation, and as much a spouse, when God is hidden from him under the distance of affliction, as when He was joyous and at peace.

When it is covered with a cloud, the sun is as near as when the cloud was not before it.

False Anticipations

Daniel Dyke

Our hearts deceive us in promising I know not what contentment and happiness in the fruition of these outward blessings, when yet the event answers not our expectation. O says the deceitful heart, "If I might have this or that which I desire, so much living, such or such an office, or preferment, how comfortable and salacious a life should I lead?" Well, when it has its wish, it fares with it almost, as with the Israelites in their quails: it finds more vanity and vexation of spirit in its presence than it did before in the want of this its so much desired good. Hence also that phrase of the "deceitfulness of riches," because they do not perform that which our hearts promise us concerning them. In the same regard all worldly honors are called "lies" by David: "O ye sons of men, how long will ye follow after lies?" (Ps. 4:2). The lie indeed is in our own false hearts. We make them liars, in that we promise such great matters to ourselves of them. . . . The rich fool promised himself a little heaven in his riches: "Soul, take thine ease" (Luke 12:19), but alas how soon did God disease him? "O fool, this night shall they take away thy soul," and then where is thy ease? The reason of this deceit is that we, in our expectation of these outward things, before they come, apprehend only the good and the sweet, abstracted from the sour, the pleasure divided from the pain, but in the fruition we feel both, yes, more of the sour than of the sweet, and hence it comes to pass that nothing pleases us so well in the fruition, as in the expectation. Nay, almost nothing pleases us as much when had as when hoped for. Nothing, I mean, of these temporal things; as for eternal things, they are more loved by us when possessed than when desired.

And the cares of this world, and the deceitfulness of riches, and the lusts of other things entering in, choke the word, and it becometh unfruitful.
Mark 4:19

God Will Deliver

John Dod and Robert Cleaver

I sought the LORD, and he heard me, and delivered me from all my fears.
Psalm 34:4

Whatever misery God's children are in, yet in the best time God will deliver them. . . . The Israelites were under a long and strong affliction for many years, under tyrants that whipped their bodies, and scourged them, and put them to labor above their strength, and (which was a most intolerable vexation) made the parents drown their own children. No one ever treated any so spitefully as they were used; yet we see that God delivered them. So in the Psalm He says, "Many are the troubles of the righteous, but God delivers them out of all" (34:19). It is not their wealth, nor money, for of that they are often bare enough; nor friends, for sometimes they have none; nor their strength, for they are often weak and brought low. But God will deliver them. Let them get righteousness, and faith, and the spirit of prayer, and though they were in an iron furnace under Pharaoh, in a house of bondage, let them but cry, and from thence God will deliver them. So in Esther's time, a wonderful affliction it was, that the day of execution was appointed, when all the godly should be put to the sword, not one to be left alive. But now, when they could cry to God, and had no one else to go to but only to Him, and Him they would go to, and stay upon, knowing that He could help them if He would, and would also for His promise's sake deliver them, then we see, the day that was appointed for their sorrow, turned to their joy; that which was purposed to bring destruction upon them, brought destruction upon their enemies; and the day of their most extreme misery, proved to be a day of their most joyful deliverance.

> **No one ever treated any so spitefully; yet we see that God delivered them.**

Desiring God

Samuel Annesley

Were phylacteries in use among Christians, I would recommend this Scripture to be bound about your necks, or written upon the table of your hearts. This is a Scripture whereon we may well say "Amen" to Augustine's *Confessions:* "O, the wonderful depth, my God, the wonderful depth of thy Word! Though there be an outside sweetness, tempting us to taste it, there is an inside excellency forcing us to admire it." "Whom have I in heaven but thee," that is, who is there in heaven for me to trust in, or call upon besides God? Or this, what is there, that is precious in heaven, which I desire without thee, or before thee? "And there is none upon earth that I desire besides thee," that is, so much as I can wish, I will not dote upon any thing on earth; nothing less, my acquiescence in God renders all things without Him worth nothing.

Whom have I in heaven but thee? And there is none upon earth that I desire besides thee.
Psalm 73:25

An outside sweetness, tempting us to taste it — an inside excellency forcing us to admire it.

Trace God's Mercies

Richard Steele

Whoever would be wise should read the Proverbs; whoever would be holy should read the Psalms. Every line in this book breathes peculiar sanctity. Psalm 18, though placed among the first, was penned among the last (as the preface assures us) and is left as the epitome of the general history of David's life. It is twice recorded in the Scriptures (2 Sam. 22, and in this book of Psalms) for the excellence and sweetness thereof; surely, we should take notice of it. Holy David, being near the shore, here looks on his former dangers and deliverances with a thankful heart, and writes this psalm to bless the Lord. As if each of you that are grown in years should review your lives and observe the wonderful goodness and providence of God towards you, and then sit down and write a modest memorial of His most remarkable mercies, for the comfort of yourselves and posterity. An excellent practice: what a comfort would it be for you to read how good your God was to your father, or grandfather, that is dead and gone? So would your children rejoice in the Lord, upon the reading of His goodness to you, and you cannot have a better pattern for this, than holy David who wrote this psalm when he was threescore and seven years old, when he had outlived most of his troubles and almost ready for his journey to his Father in heaven, he resolves to leave this good report of Him on earth.

> **Write a modest memorial of His mercies, for the comfort of yourselves and posterity.**

The Easy Yoke

Nathanael Vincent

For my yoke is easy, and my burden is light.
Matthew 11:30

Since Christ is so compassionate, surely it is unreasonable to quarrel at and refuse to submit unto His yoke? The yoke of such a merciful one must be an easy yoke, and his burden a light burden (Matt. 11:30). The kingdom of heaven is like a marriage and as the wife's subjection unto a tender and indulgent husband is sweet and pleasant, so, and much more pleasant, is the believer's subjection unto Christ. Ungodly ones are strangely prejudiced against the scepter and government of Jesus; but indeed it is without cause. They say, "We will not have this Lord to reign over us." It is a mercy to be translated into the kingdom, for then you are freed from other lords, which are so imperious, so cruel, and will reward with death all the service which you do for them. All the precepts of Christ are for your profit and He forbids you nothing, but what He sees will harm you. I think that at the reading of this, the most stubborn should yield and say, "We stood outside against the Lord of life, but it was upon a mistake; we did not think His service was so near a kin to freedom; we once imagined His commands grievous, therefore we cast them behind our backs, but now they are to be esteemed above gold, nay, the finest gold, and are sweeter than the honey and the honeycomb."

It is a mercy to be translated into the kingdom, for then you are freed from other lords.

The Best Duty

Christopher Nesse

Then shall ye call upon me, and ye shall go and pray unto me, and I will hearken unto you.

Jeremiah 29:12

As faith is called the best of graces, so prayer is called the best of duties. If other duties are pennies, this is a pound in many respects. First, it gives God the glory of His three great attributes. 1. It gives Him the glory of His omniscience, that He knows all your wants, that He, whose throne is in heaven, yet hears all your petitions presented to Him upon earth, yes, even when you pray only heart prayer (which man hears not, and knows not) as Moses in Exod. 14:15. The Lord said, wherefore do you cry unto me, when Hannah spoke not a word (1 Sam. 1:13). And David said, "all my desire is before thee, and my groaning is not hid from thee" (Ps. 38:9). 2. It gives Him the glory of His omnipotence; it presupposes that God is able to supply all your wants, which you spread before Him (Eph. 3:20). The very act of prayer says to God as Job, "I know that thou canst do every thing" (Job 42:2). 3. It gives Him the glory of His merciful goodness, or bountiful benevolence, that He is willing as well as able to supply your wants. Divine might and divine mercy are the two pillars that the house of prayer stands upon, as the temple of Solomon stood upon Joachim and Boaz, which signified stability and strength.

> The very act of prayer says to God, "I know that thou canst do every thing."

The All-Sufficient

Jeremiah Burroughs

God is a being that is all-sufficient. He stands in no need of any creature. He has need of nothing, of none of us. He has enough within Himself before the world was; God was as blessed in Himself as now He is. There can be nothing added to Him; there is such an excellency even in God's being itself, that there can be nothing added to Him. We are poor creatures that stand in need of a thousand things continually, the air to breathe in, the earth to bear us, fire to warm us, clothes to cover us, meat and drink, a thousand things; we stand in need of the meanest creature, and if God should take away the use of it, our lives would be made miserable to us. But that is the excellency of God's being that He has need of nothing; He has all within Himself; all the creatures in heaven and earth cannot add to Him; no, if there were then thousand worlds more, although God did possess them all, yet they would not add one whit to what is in God Himself; therefore, though the Lord has made the heaven and earth, and all things therein, yet we must not think that God is ever a whit the better for these things, or has the more glory. He had as much glory and blessedness as now He has, or can have. When all the angels and saints shall be eternally blessing God in heaven, yet they can add nothing to God's glory. We say the sun is a glorious creature, but does that add any light to the sun? So for saints and angels to be praising and blessing God, what does that add to God? And in this the Name of God is excellent.

God that made the world and all things therein, seeing that he is Lord of heaven and earth, dwelleth not in temples made with hands. Neither is worshipped with men's hands, as though he needed any thing, seeing he giveth to all life, and breath, and all things.
Acts 17:24–25

> All the creatures in heaven and earth cannot add to Him.

Little Faith

John Rogers

If ye have faith as a grain of mustard seed, ye shall say unto this mountain, Remove hence to yonder place; and it shall remove; and nothing shall be impossible unto you.
Matthew 17:20b

Little faith is true faith, as well as great. A little man is a man as well as a great man; a little water is as truly water as the ocean sea. The disciples had true faith, and yet very weak, weak in knowledge, though they believed that Jesus was the Messiah that should save the world, yet how, they could not tell. They were ignorant of His death, for when He told them of His sufferings, it is said they understood not that word. And Peter took his Master aside and counseled Him not to go to Jerusalem to die. They were ignorant also of His resurrection. For when Mary told them of it, they believed it not. Of His ascension, when He spoke of a little tarrying with them, and then of His going away, they understood it not, they knew not where He went, they said, and knew not the way. Now how weak was this their knowledge, to be ignorant of such main articles? . . . But weak faith may prove strong in time: the most learned clerk was in his grammar book, the greatest giant was in swaddling clothes, the tallest oak was a twig, and faith grows from a grain of mustard seed to a tall tree. As from a child to a man, so corn grows from a weak blade to a stalk and ear, and ripe corn therein. The disciples, so weak before, afterwards when the Holy Spirit was sent upon them, they were exceedingly strong, and feared not the face of tyrants.

But weak faith may prove strong in time.

Forgotten Sins

John Shower

There are many sins that we have forgotten, for which we were never humbled in particular. And yet if we truly repent of those we do know, and call to mind, our forgotten sins shall be forgiven. For God will pardon us like Himself; He will forgive us like a God, not according to our knowledge, but according to His own. And as He is greater than our hearts, to know much more against us, than we can remember against ourselves, yet He is greater than our hearts, to forgive even those faults which our hearts and consciences do not recollect. He knows the value of Christ's blood and merits, to forgive all our sins. And by unfeigned faith, we are interested in the virtue of it. God has more thoughts of mercy in Him than we have had of rebellion against Him. His thoughts have been from everlasting, and reach to everlasting; whereas, it is but as of yesterday that the oldest sinner began to rebel against God.

Many, O LORD my God, are thy wonderful works which thou hast done, and thy thoughts which are to us-ward: they cannot be reckoned up in order unto thee: if I would declare and speak of them, they are more than can be numbered.
Psalm 40:5

> God has more thoughts of mercy in Him than we have of rebellion against Him.

The Saint's Beauty

Thomas Watson

Deck thyself now with majesty and excellency; and array thyself with glory and beauty.

Job 40:10

How worldly beauty is courted by all, and what is it? "Beauty is vain" (Prov. 31:30). The bravest features of the body and the loveliest complexion are no other than well-colored earth. But a righteous person has a celestial beauty shining in him. He is embellished with knowledge, love, and meekness, which are of such oriental splendor as to allure the very angels. A good Christian has some idea and resemblance of that sparkling holiness which is the Deity. Christ is infinitely taken with the spiritual beauty of His church. "Thou art beautiful, O my love, as Tirzah, comely as Jerusalem" (Song 6:4). Tirzah was a map of pleasure; Jerusalem was the metropolis of Judea, the star and light of all the eastern world. This was symbolic, to set forth the radiance of the church's glory. "Turn away thine eyes from me for they have overcome me" (v. 5). It is as if Christ had said, "Oh, My spouse, such a resplendent luster is in your visage that I can hardly bear it. I am wounded with the delightful darts of your beauty!" One eye of a believer draws Christ's heart to it: "Thou hast ravished my heart with one of thine eyes," (Song 4:9). A saint's beauty never withers; it outlives death. True grace is like colors laid in oil which cannot be washed off.

> Christ is infinitely taken with the spiritual beauty of His church.

Table Blessings

Thomas Gouge

orget not to pray unto God for a blessing on the things you are to partake. For as the apostle says, "Every creature of God is good, being sanctified by the Word of God, and prayer" (1 Tim. 4:4–5). By the Word, as it does show, and warrant our right thereunto; and by prayer, as it is a means appointed by God for obtaining His blessing upon our food, without which it will do us little good. "For man liveth not by bread only, but by every word that proceedeth out of the mouth of God" (Matt. 4:1); that is, bread does not nourish by its own power, but by the appointment and blessing of God. And therefore it was the usual practice of our Savior to lift up His eyes and crave a blessing upon the creatures, before He did partake of them, which has been the usual practice of the saints and people of God, before and since Christ's time (1 Sam. 9:13; Acts 27:30). Having therefore such worthy patterns and precedents, follow them, not daring to partake of any of God's good creatures, until you have lifted up your heart to God and craved His blessing upon them, for otherwise how justly might you expect from God a curse rather than a blessing? The things on your table are God's things, and therefore you must need be more bold than welcome, if you make use of them without asking His blessing.

What shall I render unto the LORD for all his benefits toward me?
Psalm 116:12

> Bread does not nourish by its own power, but by the appointment and blessing of God.

The Saint's Pastime

Robert Dingley

I will meditate also of all thy work, and talk of thy doings.
Psalm 77:12

editation . . . is a saint's pastime. It recreates and perfumes the tired spirits. It is a ladder by which the soul climbs to heaven. It is a duty ever at hand (Prov. 6:22), when you are alone, nay, in the dark, when traveling, and so on. On all occasions you may let out your soul in meditation, when other duties cannot be performed. Nay, when you sleep you may be meddling with this duty. For having communion with God in the day, and closing your eyes with some meditation, even your dreams may be of the love of God, and the glory of heaven, as the experiences of the saints can witness. Meditation brings us to the first degrees of those heavenly joys, and imparts to us some beginnings of the vision and fruition of God. It enables us with Moses to discern, as we are able, some glimpses of God, that our faces shine with purity and divine splendor. By this we are ravished with Paul, and are caught up into paradise, and in the twinkling of an eye are driven (as in a fiery chariot) into heaven. By this with holy Stephen we see the heavens opened, and Jesus sitting at the right hand of God. Indeed admirable are the effects of divine meditation. It confirms our knowledge (Ps. 119:99). It strengthens our memory (Ps. 63:6). It enflames our love (Ps. 119:97). It cherishes time with God (Ps. 119:148). It maintains a true and childlike fear of God (Ps. 4:4). It hushes and quiets the soul in afflictions (Ps. 119:23). . . . It promotes prayer (Ps. 143:5–6). . . . What shall I say? Meditation is the very life of our life, as a heathen could say and see by the light of nature. It is the food of our souls, the fuel of our zeal, the spur of our devotion; the soul that can meditate on God is never less alone than when alone, for its fellowship is then with the Father and His Son, Jesus Christ.

Room for Babes

John Collinges

For all Christians, especially those that are most sensible of the weakness of their faith, there have been and are more dwarfs besides you. Perfection is a white that was never hit; the best archers prove a handful short. It is indeed the mark at which every one sets out to level his arrows, but all the souls of Christians, like the arrows of Jonathan, have flown, some over into glory, some short, some on this hand, some on that, but none have hit the mark. Be of good comfort, weak faith is faith; little ones are true children of the Father, who casts none away that comes (though creeping) to Him. Heaven has room for babes as well as adults. A child may pull the latch of heaven's door, and go in, and be welcome to the knee of the King of Glory, to His bosom, "Who feeds His flock like a shepherd" (Isa. 40:11) and carries the lambs in His bosom. Jesus Christ has His arms full of tender sucking lambs, or at least, that were so upon the earth. The youngest Christian, if an heir, is of age to take land in heaven; youth is no bar. The garden of God has more slips than old stocks in it. Now indeed they are to become stocks in heaven, but here on earth they were but tender slips when Christ took them up to the land of grace and transplanted them.

In that hour Jesus rejoiced in spirit, and said, I thank thee, O Father, Lord of heaven and earth, that thou hast hid these things from the wise and prudent, and hast revealed them unto babes: even so, Father; for so it seemed good in thy sight.
Luke 10:21

Be of good comfort. Weak faith is faith.

Enduring Adversity

Samuel Shaw

Behold, thou hast made my days as an handbreadth; and mine age is as nothing before thee: verily every man at his best state is altogether vanity.
Psalm 39:5

I do not know of any one temptation that in all ages has more solicited and perplexed the minds of good men, than that which springs from the prosperity of the wicked; a scandal that the best of men have been ever apt to take against the dispensations of God Himself. It has therefore pleased God, in compassion to the suffering, frequently to obviate this temptation, by causing many parts of holy Scripture to be written purposely upon this argument, among which the thirty-ninth Psalm is one, the main proposition of which is an exhortation that we, beholding the prosperity of the wicked, do not doubt of the divine care and providence. We must not be broken in our minds, nor murmur against God, or fall away from Him, but patiently endure adversity, and hold fast our profession.

We, beholding the prosperity of the wicked, do not doubt of the divine care and providence.

The Most Beautiful

Thomas Vincent

Christ is the most amiable person and the most suitable object for your love. If you ask of the days which are past, which were before you since the day that God created man upon the earth; if you seek from one side of heaven to the other; if you make enquiry into all the parts of the earth, you will never find that there ever was or is to be found any person so lovely, so beautiful and so in every way deserving of your love, as the Lord Jesus Christ. There is a matchless, transcendent, and incomparable beauty and excellency in Him. How passionately are some foolish men in love with the external beauty which they see in some women . . . the lovely mixture of colors in the face, the beauty of the eyes, their spirit, their quick and graceful motions, and amorous glances; how this ravishes the hearts of some fond lovers! Although, the most beautiful body in the world is no better than painted clay, dirt and corruption, enclosed in fair skin, which sickness will cause to look pale, and death will mar and spoil. But the amiableness and beauty of Christ is more transcendent and permanent, and therefore a more fit object for your love. Christ is fairer than the children of men; He is all fair, without any spot, altogether lovely, without any blemish or deformity.

One thing have I desired of the LORD, that will I seek after; that I may dwell in the house of the LORD all the days of my life, to behold the beauty of the LORD, and to inquire in his temple.
Psalm 27:4

Christ is fairer than the children of men.

Work Made Light

William Gurnall

The divine assistance which Christians have in their work alleviates the labor of it. Consider the Christian's work without this help. It is heavy indeed, yes, too heavy to stand under. But God's helping hand put to it makes this heavy work light. The ship, which when lying on ground, all the teams in the country could not draw off, how easily is it set afloat when the tide comes in? Thus the heart can rise out of its dullness and indisposition to duty. Oh how soon is it elevated and inspired when God flows in with His secret aspirations and excitations of His blessed Spirit and grace! He who confessed that he could do nothing of himself, not so much as think a good thought, tells us that he is able to do all things through Christ who strengthens him. Now this help from the Lord is promised, but it comes not till the Christian's hand is put to work. Let us be up and doing, and then God will not fail to be with us. . . . It is easy working while God holds our hand, yes, and puts strength into it. Are you tempted? While you are fighting in the valley below, Christ's hands are lifted up in heaven above for your victory. "I have prayed that thy faith fail not" (Luke 22:32); yes, He does not only pray above for you, but will be in the field with you, and in you, by the secret succors of His Spirit. "My grace is sufficient for thee" (2 Cor. 12:9), which is not meant of grace inherent in us, that indeed is insufficient of itself, but the auxiliary grace, which He sends in to assist us in a time of need.

> It is easy working while God holds our hand.

Walk in Humility

Thomas Gataker

Walk in humility . . . take heed of pride. It is a deadly poison that spoils and kills all where it comes; so dangerous that another poison was used as a counter-poison to preserve St. Paul from it. And we are never more in danger of it than when we have done most, and made greatest progress in the profession and practice of piety. For it is as the spleen in the body, that grows most when the other parts waste. It grows fast often, when other evils decay, and out of the decay of them, sucks matter to feed and foster itself with. This therefore must be carefully cast out and avoided. When we have done well, we must take heed how in that regard we begin to think highly of ourselves. If we do so, all is gone; we are undone. Be affected rather as Paul was. After he had gone so far, and done so much, "I make account, that I come not short," says he, "of the very chief apostles" (2 Cor. 11:5). Yea, "I have labored more than them all" (1 Cor. 15:10). For, "from Jerusalem round about, even unto Illyricum (that is, from Syria to Slovenia) have I plentifully preached the gospel" (Rom. 15:19). Yet, "I forget what is past" (Phil. 3:13). That is, I regard no more what I have done than as if yet I had done nothing, or had clean forgotten what I did. "And I put on toward to what is before, pressing on toward the high calling of God in Christ Jesus" (v. 14). He did as men in a race that look not back to see how many they have passed, or how far they have progressed, but have their eyes fixed on those that have gained ground on them, and on the ground before them, that they are to measure, ere they can come to the mark. Let us not consider so much how far we have gone, and how many others come short of us, but how far we are to go, and how far we come short of that Christian perfection that we should all strive and contend to attain unto.

By humility and the fear of the LORD are riches, and honour, and life.
Proverbs 22:4

> He did as men in a race that look not back to see how many they have passed.

Cause of Discontent

Edward Lawrence

And having food and raiment let us be therewith content.
1 Timothy 6:8

Discontent arises from being so very sensible of the evil of affliction and senseless of the evil of sin. People's bodies are tender, and their senses quick, and therefore even the biting of a flea or the scratching of a pen is presently felt. People are so tender of their reputation, profits and delights, that the least touch in these is a cross to them. Their hearts are so hard, and consciences seared, that they can lie securely under all the curses of God's book, have mountains of wrath abide on them, and feel nothing. Therefore afflictions lie so heavy because sin lies so easy. Whereas, if a person knew what sin is, and saw at night what wrath he had treasured up all day, he would rather wonder why he was out of hell than murmur that he was in trouble.

If a person knew what sin is, he would rather wonder why he was out of hell.

The Sin of Atheism

Richard Capel

We are much assaulted to atheism and blasphemy; to atheism, as the greatest sin that is, in that it smites at the root of all; for to say the truth, all sin comes from atheism (for who would sin, did he then verily think that there were a God that saw all, and would punish all) and such a God, God must be, or no God. And all sin tends to atheism (for when we have sinned, sin draws us towards atheism exceedingly, and wipes out all notions of a deity as much as it can); and when we are in sin, we must be either willing to get out of it by repentance, or else we shall be willing to become atheists; the best of our play then, being to feed ourselves with a conceit, that all is but talk to hold men in awe, and that there is indeed neither heaven nor hell; no place of torment, that when we die all is gone, that it is with us not otherwise than with a beast. Thus when the conscience will not get quiet by turning to God by repentance, then it will seek to quiet itself by unbelief bearing itself in hand, that there is no such place as hell to torment people in. Consider, however, that Satan does all he can to make people atheists, because when there is no fear of God before their eyes, they will sin all manner of sins that the devil would have them sin. So Ps. 14, "The fool hath said in his heart, There is no God." What follows? "They are corrupt," they have done abominable works; thus then, when once men take to atheism, they grow most corrupt and do abominable works. There is no restraint in sinning then, for what should or can keep the wit and will of man, when once he conceives that there is no such thing as God? The devil cannot be a flat atheist, for he believes and trembles; and were it nothing but the sense he has of the wrath of God tormenting, why that is enough to prove that Satan does fully and undoubtedly acknowledge a divine power. He is not an atheist because he cannot, because he shall not, but yet he bears good will to atheism, because that sin does much advantage his kingdom.

The fool hath said in his heart, There is no God.
Psalm 14:1a

Richest Foundation

Nicholas Byfield

Can a woman forget her sucking child, that she should not have compassion on the son of her womb? yea, they may forget, yet will I not forget thee.

Isaiah 49:15

The love and favor of God . . . is the foundation of the Christian's happiness. If we could order our own heart aright, we would easily see that we could not be miserable so long as we were in favor with our God. If the favor of great persons be so much accounted of, what reckoning is to be made of God's favor, who is Lord of lords? Yea, King of kings, and the more should Christians fill their hearts with joining in this prerogative, if they consider three properties in the love of God. For first, it is a free love. He is gracious, looking upon His own goodness, and not on ours (Hos. 14:4). Secondly, it is an eternal love, and unchangeable. God will never be weary of loving us (Jer. 31:3). His loving-kindness is better than life, for it lasts unto eternity, without alteration. The favor of individuals in this world is mutable. Kings might extremely loathe those they used to love with their entire affection. But in God there is no shadow of changing; He loves with an everlasting love. Thirdly, it is infinitely immense, and great. No affection in any, or in all the creatures of this world, if they could be fastened upon one person, can reach to the thousandth part of God's love to us (Eph. 2:4–7). This light of God's countenance shining upon us makes us at all times more rich than those that are increased most in corn, wine, and oil (Ps. 4:7–8).

What reckoning is to be made of God's favor, who is Lord of lords?

Seeking Jehovah

Nathaniel Vincent

he bent of Isaiah's very soul was towards God, and his desires were kept up in vehemence both night and day. The Lord humbles Himself to behold things done in heaven, yet He looks down upon the children of men upon the earth to see if there is any that understand and seek Him. And if He seeks after these seekers, how ready is He to be found of them! The command is that we should seek the Lord, His strength, and His face evermore (Ps. 105:4). God is to be sought unto for Himself. When the all-sufficient Jehovah gives Himself to any, He gives infinitely more than if He gave them many thousand such worlds as this is. His strength is of absolute necessity, to secure us from evil and to assist us in the doing of good. And the shining of His face makes our work easy and pleasant. It makes our life, and even death itself, comfortable. No wonder, therefore, when God said, "Seek ye my face," one of His attendants heard presently, as the echo answers the voice, said, "Thy face, Lord, will I seek" (Ps. 27:8). To seek to any else is vain. It is seeking for water in a broken cistern that can hold none. Those of low degree, though never so great a multitude, are vanity, and those of highest degree are a lie (Ps. 62:9). But God's power, mercy, and truth are an evident proof that He is forward and sufficient to satiate the souls of all that charge their souls to wait only upon Him, and to have their expectations from Him.

With my soul have I desired thee in the night, yes with my spirit will I seek thee early.
Isaiah 26:9

> If He seeks after these seekers, how ready is He to be found of them!

Barking Dogs

Thomas Taylor

He was despised and rejected of men; a man of sorrows, and acquainted with grief: and we hid as it were our faces from him; he was despised, and we esteemed him not.

Isaiah 53:3

We must consider that if we are rejected of men, so was the Chief Builder, and the master builders, the apostles themselves. If we speak words of truth and wisdom out of the book of God, in the name of God, out of the place of God, some dare say we will lie as fast as a dog will run. If our innocence were as bright as the sun, some dog will bark against us. The servant is not above the Master. Our Master, as innocent as He was, some few said that He was a good man, but many that He was a devil. Some said that He was a very vile man. Well, this is the comfort of faith: it shall break out of all clouds and darkness, and shine in the face of all adversaries one day. For as it frets the enemy that he cannot withhold God's gracious blessing from His faithful servants here, so much more shall it break the hearts of all adversaries, that they cannot resist the glorious light of faith hereafter.

> It frets the enemy that he cannot withhold God's gracious blessing from His faithful servants.

Sovereignty

Nathaniel Taylor

Consider the absolute sovereignty and dominion of God. This divine attribute is displayed when He closes His right hand to hide these stars, wherein they were formerly held (Rev. 3:1). Or, when He seals them up in a sudden and so a thick darkness that we can neither see them, nor receive any further influences from them. And if we had nothing else to urge in the case, even this alone were enough to stop all our mouths. Shall we not allow God that which we challenge to ourselves, namely, to do with His own what He pleases? "Be still and know that I am God" (Ps. 46:10). And the exercise of this attribute about good people, even when it seems to bear a little hard upon them, should least of all be regretted by them, because it has been employed about them in vastly greater instances, so much for their advantage. For it was divine sovereignty that selected them out of the common mass of mankind, when others were passed by, and crowned them with all those gifts and graces wherein they did excel. Now if the same hand that frames them into vessels of honor breaks them into pieces with one single stroke, it becomes us to bow our heads, and humbly adore Him, crying out, "How unsearchable are His judgments, and His ways past finding out, who yet works all things according to the counsel of His own will!"

And unto the angel of the church in Sardis write; These things saith he that hath the seven Spirits of God, and the seven stars; I know thy works, that thou hast a name that thou livest, and art dead.

Revelation 3:1

> Shall we not allow God to do with His own what He pleases?

To Rightly Use

Robert Dingley

And God saw every thing that he had made, and, behold, it was very good.
Genesis 1:31a

In the first creation all was very good, but all things changed with us and we became vain. Sin put chinks into the creatures, whereby very much of their sweetness and goodness leaked out: "The creature was made subject to vanity" (Rom. 8:20), which before was free from it. And by reason of our corruption, we reap nothing but vanity out of these things, as a spider that draws poison from the sweetest flower. "Every creature of God is good (not only was good) and nothing to be refused, if it be received with thanksgiving; for it is sanctified by the word of God and prayer" (1 Tim. 4:4–5). So then, it is because the creatures are not rightly received or used that they become vain to us; our filthy spider-like nature sucks poison from them. We love them too much, or we trust in them, or we abuse them. "Unto the pure all things are pure, but unto them that are defiled and unbelieving nothing is pure, but even their mind and conscience is defiled" (Titus 1:15). They are as pure water that runs into a filthy channel, or as a rich garment received with muddy hands.

Sin put chinks into the creatures, whereby very much of their goodness leaked out.

Prayer's Acceptance
Henry Scudder

As the prayers of a true child of God differ from the prayers of the unregenerate, so their acceptance with God is also different. Their difference is seen in three ways. First, a true child of God in prayer calls God "Father" with faith and holy confidence, with the affections of a child. When we ask forgiveness for sin, it is with grief that we have by our sin offended our Father, and it is with a hearty purpose not to offend Him again. Also, when we pray for health, liberty, grace, or for any other good thing, it is with a desire that in the enjoyment of them, we may better please and honor our Heavenly Father. In contrast, the wicked calls God "Father" only for form. . . . Secondly, the child of God prays chiefly and most heartily for spiritual things, such as faith, forgiveness of sins, holiness, God's favor, and those things which concern God's kingdom and glory. In contrast, the unregenerate prays chiefly and most heartily for corn and wine, for temporal things. It may be for heaven and happiness (with Balaam) in general wishes, but not particularly and unfeigned for grace to forsake their beloved sin, and to live holily unto the end of their days. Thirdly, the prayers of the godly, when they are made in sincerity, are like all of their other good works; they have a supernatural goodness in them, being acts of the regenerate through the Spirit, and are performed to a supernatural end. In contrast, the prayers of the wicked, though in some ways unfeigned, at best are but natural desires, not intended as a service to God, but only as a means to serve themselves in those things which they know can be obtained by no other means. Now as to the acceptance of prayers with God, those which His children make, though they are not without much imperfection, because they are the prayers of men reconciled to God by Christ, and proceed from hearts purified by faith, and because they are in the name of Christ, become acceptable through Him, so far as to procure not only temporal good things, but also spiritual and eternal.

For ye have not received the spirit of bondage again to fear; but ye have received the Spirit of adoption, whereby we cry, Abba, Father.
Romans 8:15

Love's Object

David Clarkson

That which we love, we worship as our God. For love is an act of soul-worship. To love and to adore are sometimes both one. That which one loves, he worships. This is undoubtedly true, if we hereby love that which is superlative and transcendent. For to be loved above all things is an act of honor, worship, which the Lord challenges as His due in peculiar (Deut. 6:5). In this the Lord Christ comprised all that worship which is required of man (Matt. 22:37). Other things may be loved, but He will be loved above all other things. He is to be loved transcendently, absolutely, and for who He is; all other things are to be loved in Him, and for Him. He looks upon us as not worshipping Him at all, not taking Him for a God, when we love other things more, or as much as God. Those that are lovers of pleasure make their pleasures and their bellies their God. Those that love their riches, the things of the world, more than, or equally with God, make these their gods, and worship a golden calf. . . . Those that love themselves more than God, idolize themselves. Love, whenever it is inordinate, is an idolatrous affection.

> To be loved above all things is an act of honor, which the Lord challenges as His due in peculiar.

About His Business

John Rogers

They that love God would that all others did so, and draw as many to God as they can, as Philip drew Nathanael, and rejoice to see any come home to God by repentance, as the angels of heaven do. They will grieve when they see Him wronged or dishonored, as Moses, when he threw down the tables of the Law, and Phineas, when he ran through Zimri and Cozbi. Lot's righteous soul was vexed at the unclean conversation of the Sodomites. They that love God will love His Word, being holy and pure as He is, and containing His good will. They love His faithful ministers, His children, and His image, wherever they see it. They will take pains in His service, as Jacob did night and day in Laban's, for the love of Rachel. They will be at cost as David was towards the building of the temple, and Mary with her box of precious ointment poured on our Savior Christ. Yea, and speedily those that love God will go about what God calls them to do.

And he said unto them, How is it that ye sought me? wist ye not that I must be about my Father's business?
Luke 2:49

They will take pains in His service, as Jacob did night and day in Laban's, for the love of Rachel.

Untold Glories

John Shower

Eye hath not seen, nor ear heard, neither have entered into the heart of man, the things which God hath prepared for them that love him.
1 Corinthians 2:9

How excellent a change will death make upon the soul's leaving the body, if it pass into a glorious paradise, and hear a voice from Him that sits upon the throne, "Enter into thy Master's joy" (Matt. 25:21). Poor Lazarus was lately very miserable at the rich man's door; now very happy in Abraham's bosom. Lately covered with sores and ulcers; now clothed with glory. Lately pining with hunger; now all his wants are supplied. His extreme poverty made him the other day despised by the rich man; he could find no entrance at his gates, no admission, no relief. But now he is envied for his happiness. The difference which departed souls will feel of their happy state, from what they lately were, and the sense they have of the evils they are delivered from, will give an account of their happiness. The fresh remembrance of what they were in this world will help their joyful sense of the happy change. And to compare their own condition with that of lost, miserable souls; to think of the hell they deserved, and others suffer; and they themselves did sometimes fear; and compare it with the rest, and peace, and joy, and glory that they now partake of, will add to their felicity. And who can tell how great that is, even before the resurrection?

> **The fresh remembrance of what they were in this world will help their joyful sense of the happy change.**

Behold the Crown

Richard Alleine

Keep the crown in your eye, and let that word be ever in your ear from Rev. 3:11: "Hold fast what thou hast, that no man take thy crown." Run from your colors and you lose the crown. He who has heaven in his eyes will not fear to have holiness in his life. The hope of the victory will encourage us in the fight; the hope of the crown will make the cross to be easy, and make us faithful in the covenant. Therefore, remember that word from Rev. 2:10: "Be thou faithful unto death, and I will give thee a crown of life." Christians, if you would not lose the crown, then be faithful; be faithful to the death in the covenant of your Lord. Whatever difficulties or discouragements you may meet with in your way; whatever hardships or tribulations may befall you, if you can yet say with the church, "though all this be come upon us, yet have we not forgotten thee, neither have we dealt falsely in thy covenant; our heart is not turned back, neither have our steps declined from thy way" (Ps. 44:17–18); if you can but say this, your Lord will say also to you, "Whatever I have done or brought upon you, yet I have not forgotten you; the covenant of My peace shall never be removed. Fight the good fight, keep the faith, till you have finished your course, and then know that there is laid up for you a crown of righteousness, which I will surely give you at that day."

And I put a jewel on thy forehead, and earrings in thine ears, and a beautiful crown upon thine head.
Ezekiel 16:12

> "Whatever I have done or brought upon you, yet I have not forgotten you."

Sacred Dignity

William Gouge

For ye have not received the spirit of bondage again to fear; but ye have received the Spirit of adoption, whereby we cry, Abba, Father.

Romans 8:15

The dignity of God's children is having such a familiarity with God, as face to face to speak to Him. For this title, "Father" is so set down as directed to God Himself in His own presence. David excellently sets forth this privilege, where he says, "Lord, I pour my whole desire before thee." All have not this liberty, as an evidence whereof they have not ability thus to come into God's presence. Upon whom God pours the Spirit of grace, He pours also the Spirit of supplication, but upon no other. It is therefore a gift appropriated to the saints to call upon God in faith. . . . Others may use this word, and with their lips say to God, "O Father," but their supposed prayers are but mere lip-labor. At the best their inward desires are but wishes. Now there is a great difference between wishing and praying. A wish may intimate some sense of that which someone wants, and some desire of having it, but small care in using the means to get it, and less faith in obtaining it. But the faithful prayers of the saints are full of sense, desire, care, faith and all. Balaam could wish and say, "Let me die the death of the righteous" (Num. 23:10). Like to whom were they that said, "Who will show us any good?" But David goes directly to God, and thus expressly prays to Him, "LORD, lift thou up the light of thy countenance upon us" (Ps. 4:6). We know that any man may in any place wish and say, "I would the King would grant me this or that suite," but at all times to have a free access to the King's presence, and to say unto Him, "O my Liege, I beseech thee grant me this suite," is a great privilege, appertaining only to the King's favorites. And so much the greater when there is assurance of prevailing by this free access as there is assurance of that free access which saints have to God's presence. For it makes us after a manner presume that we shall obtain what we ask when before we ask, we receive so great a privilege as to be suffered to say, "Our Father," to God.

Bearing Reproaches

Jeremiah Burroughs

Cast out the scorner, and contention shall go out; yes, strife and reproach shall cease.
Proverbs 22:10

We are to bear reproaches wisely . . . There is a great deal of wisdom required in the bearing of reproaches and the evils that some are accused of. Though we should not be insensible, yet we should not take too much notice of every reproach that is cast upon us. It was the speech of a philosopher when one was reproaching him, some told him he was being derided, but said he, "I am not derided; I will not take to myself that which is cast upon me." It is wisdom for people to go away, and take but little notice of anything that is cast upon them, and therefore when upon every idle reproach, there come a company tattling, and say, such a one says thus and thus, such should be sent away with angry countenance, it is a dishonor to you to receive them, as if you would take notice of every word, and as if you had no other things to take up your thoughts. Dionysius, having not very well used Plato at the court, when he was gone, feared lest he should write against him, therefore he sent after him, to bid him not to write against him. Plato replied, "Tell Dionysius I have not so much leisure to think of him." So we should let those that reproach us to know that we have not leisure to think of them. As Saint Paul, when the viper came upon his hand he shook it off; some would have swelled, and almost died at the very sight of such a thing, but he did but shake it off and so should we do to our reproaches; when reproaches are opposed they do grow, as hair the more it is cut the more it grows; when they are despised they will vanish away; there is a great deal of evil that comes by making much ado about reproaches.

> It is wisdom for people to take but little notice of anything that is cast upon them.

Faithful Seekers

Jeremiah Burroughs

This is the generation of them that seek him, that seek thy face, O Jacob.
Psalm 24:6

Surely it is not in vain to seek God. For there never were any faithful seekers that ever would leave off, but would continue as long they lived seeking God. They would seek His face evermore. If it had been in vain, they would have left off. When we see a bee stick on a flower, and will not be driven off, or if she be driven off, she will come again, we conclude certainly that she finds honey there. So all the saints of God that have ever sought God truly, would never be beaten off this way. Let the world do what it will, persecute them, set spies to watch them in their prayer meetings; let it punish and imprison them, let all the malice and rage of men be against them, yet they cannot hinder them either from praying in their closets, or from enjoying the benefit of the communion of saints in prayer. Daniel had rather lose his life than be kept from his prayers, though but for a day, yes, three times a day, as he was accustomed. He would not forbear one time. He did stick to prayer finding honey and sweetness in it. Oh how unlike are we to Daniel, though the performance of this duty was exceeding hazardous to him; yet he would not be deterred from it.

> When we see a bee stick on a flower, and will not be driven off, we conclude that she finds honey there.

Looking unto Jesus

Isaac Ambrose

By looking unto Jesus we mean an inward experimental knowing, desiring, hoping, believing, loving, calling on Jesus, and conforming to Jesus. It is not a bare swimming knowledge of Christ; it is not a bare thinking of Christ. As Christ has various excellences in Himself, so has He formed the soul with a power of diverse ways of apprehending, that so we might be capable of enjoying these diverse excellencies that are in Christ; even as the creatures having their several uses. God has accordingly given us several senses, that so we might enjoy the delights of them all. What the better had we been for pleasant odiferous flowers, or sweet perfumes, if we had not possessed the sense of smell? Or what good would language, or music, have done us, if God had not sent us the sense of hearing? Or what delight should we have found in meats or drinks, or sweetest things, if we had been deprived of the sense of tasting? So what pleasure should we have had even in the goodness and perfection of God in Christ, if we had been without the faculty and power of knowing, desiring, hoping, believing, loving, and enjoying? As the senses are to the body, so are these spiritual senses, powers, and affections to the soul the very way by which we must receive sweetness and strength from the Lord Jesus.

Looking unto Jesus the author and finisher of our faith; who for the joy that was set before him endured the cross, despising the shame, and is set down at the right hand of the throne of God.
Hebrews 12:2

> As the senses are to the body, so are these spiritual senses, powers, and affections to the soul.

The Lord's Supper

Jeremiah Dyke

*Give ear to my words,
O LORD, consider my
meditation.*
Psalm 5:1

The duty to be done at the sacrament of the Lord's Supper is to offer up ourselves to God, in a holy and spiritual disposition in receiving the Supper. . . . There must be a heart enlarged with godly sorrow for sin; there must be compunction and contrition of spirit. It is meditation that must fit for it, and bring that, and lay that to the heart which must bruise it. Meditation gives a sight and knowledge of self, of sins, and of the riches of God's mercies in Christ, and such knowledge is it which works compunction of spirit. We are to be taken up in duties of thanksgiving, and to be more than ordinarily enlarged therein. There is no such way to enlarge the heart in that duty, as by meditation, to heat and warm our hearts. So Ps. 104:33–34: "I will sing unto the Lord as long as I live. I will sing praise unto my God while I have my being; my meditation of Him shall be sweet; I will be glad in the Lord." There is nothing that so feeds spiritual joy, and so maintains and holds up that holy frame that should be in the heart in the duty of thanksgiving, as meditation. That is the oil and the fuel that keeps such fire burning. The sweeter our meditation is, the more is the heart prepared and enlarged to praises, thanksgiving, and joy in the Lord. Therefore a special duty to be done at the Lord's Supper is to take up our hearts with serious meditation. And for the better raising and feeding of meditation, it is good, when we are come to the Lord's Table, to do as Solomon wishes us to do in that case: "When thou sittest to eat with a ruler, consider diligently what is before thee" (Prov. 23:1).

> The sweeter our meditation is, the more is the heart prepared and enlarged.

Children of God

Jeremiah Burroughs

In the beginning of 1 John, the blessed state of the saints of the most High God is proclaimed before all the world: "Behold what manner of love the Father hath bestowed upon us!" We may well with a kind of astonishment and amazement of spirit admire at this, but the eloquence of men and angels is not able fully and effectually to express it. We must be some time in heaven before we can take a due survey of all the dimensions of this eternal, fatherly love of God in Christ to His adopted ones. "That we should be called sons of God"; that we, wretched, base, vile sinners; that we, not angels, but we should be called, not servants, not friends only, but that we should be called the children of God. Even we that were the children of the devil, as firebrands of hell in ourselves, that we should not only be plucked out of the fire, but be called the children of God . . . this excellent and blessed state of ours is spiritual, hidden from the world; the world knows us not, and good reason, for it knows not God; the world knows not our Father, knows not Christ, and therefore we cannot marvel that they do not know us, nor know the blessed condition we are in, in being the children of God.

Behold, what manner of love the Father hath bestowed upon us, that we should be called the sons of God: therefore the world knoweth us not, because it knew him not.

1 John 3:1

We should not only be plucked out of the fire, but be called the children of God.

Repentance

Robert Bolton

But go ye and learn what that meaneth, I will have mercy, and not sacrifice: for I am not come to call the righteous, but sinners to repentance.
Matthew 9:13

Augustine wrote twelve books of repentance. To whom much is forgiven, they love much. And this is a fountain of evangelical repentance. As a traitor who has been condemned to die but receives a pardon would wonderfully break his heart, and wonder why he should have been so villainous to so gracious a prince, so it is with a Christian that beholds God's mercy. Christians, after their conversion, desire to see their sins to the utmost, with all the circumstances that make them hateful, as the object, nature, person, time, and age, in which and how they were done, so that they may be more humbled for them. If it be not so, then such troubles as these usually seize on them: First, they are often afflicted that their conversion is not thorough and sound, and so do not with such heartiness and cheerfulness perform the duty of godliness. Second, they are many times haunted with listlessness and coldness in their progress of Christianity.

> God has ends in all His works, known only to Him.

Third, they are visited with some cross or other that sticks by them, to make them lay a greater load upon sin. Fourth, they are more subject to be overtaken with their sweet sin, because they have no more sorrow for it; the less it is sorrowed for, the more it ensnares them. Fifth, some of them have been assaulted upon their death-bed with sorrowful and strong temptations. Not that people should conceive this is always the reason of it, for God has ends in all His works, known only to Him . . . but this may be in great mercy to make a weak conversion more strong.

Fire in the Soul

Simeon Ashe

Be zealous.
Revelation 3:19b

hat zeal for which Phineas is recorded to his ever-lasting commendation, did comprehend the great-ness, both his grief and anger, as the history clearly evidences. And the apostle thus reports his fears of the Corinthians' apostasy: "I am jealous (or zealous) over you, with godly jealousy" (2 Cor. 11:2). That which the philosopher speaks of natural fire, is therefore applicable to this spiritual fire. As natural fire has various operations upon things of a different nature, either to congregate or separate, in like manner spiritual fire works holy zeal in those bosoms wherein God has kindled it, into much heat for good and against evil. And as fire which burns up with wood warms the whole room, in like manner the flame of holy zeal in the soul is influential in its operations, through the Christian's whole life. That which the prophet Jeremiah speaks concerning God's Word, being like fire in his bones . . . is true concerning the fire of zeal, for "out of the abundance of the heart the mouth speaketh" (Matt. 12:34).

> **As fire which burns up wood warms the whole room, the flame of holy zeal warms the soul.**

Psalm 119

Edmund Calamy

*Great peace have they
which love thy law.
Psalm 119:165a*

This psalm exceeds all the other psalms, not only in length but in excellency, so far (in the judgment of Ambrose) as the light of the sun excels the light of the moon. As the book of Psalms is styled by Luther, "An epitome of the Bible, or a little Bible," so this psalm may fitly be called an epitome of the book of Psalms. It was written (as is thought) by David in the days of his banishment under Saul, but so penned, that the words thereof suit the condition of all saints. It is a public storehouse of heavenly doctrines, distributing fit and convenient instructions to all the people of God, and therefore should be in no less account with those who are spiritually alive, than is the sun, air, and fire, with those who are naturally alive. It is divided into twenty-two sections, according to the Hebrew alphabet, and therefore fitly called, "A holy alphabet for Zion's scholars," and the ABC's of godliness. Sixtus Senensis calls it, "An alphabetical poem." The Jews are said to teach it to their little children the first thing they learn, and therein they take a very right course, both in regard of the heavenly matter, and plain style fitted for all capacities. The chief scope of it is to set out the glorious excellencies of the law of God. There is not a verse in this long psalm, wherein there is not mention made of the law of God, under the name of law, or statutes, or precepts, or testimonies, or commandments, or ordinances, or word, or promises, or ways, or judgments, or name, or righteousness, or truth.

The words thereof suit the condition of all saints.

In the Morning

Henry Scudder

In the instant of awakening let your heart be lifted up to God with a thankful acknowledgment of His mercy to you. For it is He that gives His beloved sleep (Ps. 127:2), and who keeps you both in soul and body, while you sleep. He renews His mercies every morning (Lam. 3:22–23). While you sleep, you are as it were out of actual possession of yourself, and all things else. Now, it was God that kept you and all that you had, and restored them again, with many new mercies, when you awoke. Arise early in the morning (if you are not necessarily hindered) following the example of our Savior Christ (John 8:2), and of the good matron in the Proverbs (Prov. 31:15). For this will usually much conduce to the health of your body, and the prosperity, both of your temporal and spiritual state. For you will have the day before you, and will gain the best, and the fittest times for the exercises of religion and for the works of your calling. In the time between your awaking and arising (if other suitable thoughts offer not themselves) it will be useful to think upon some of these: I must awake from the sleep of sin, to righteousness (Eph. 5:14), as well as out of bodily sleep unto the labor of my calling. The night is far spent, the day is at hand; I must therefore cast off the works of darkness and put on the armor of light (Rom. 13:11–13). I must walk honestly as in the day. I am, by the light of grace and knowledge, to arise and walk in it, as well as by the light of the sun to walk by it. Think also of your awaking out of the sleep of death, and out of the grave; at the sound of the last trumpet, even of your blessed resurrection unto glory, at the last day. It was one of David's sweet thoughts (speaking to God): "When I awake, I shall be satisfied with thy likeness" (Ps. 17:15).

Cause me to hear thy lovingkindness in the morning; for in thee do I trust: cause me to know the way wherein I should walk; for I lift up my soul unto thee.

Psalm 143:8

The night is far spent. The day is at hand.

Careful Faithfulness

Gervase Babington

And God remembered Noah, and every living thing, and all the cattle that was with him in the ark: and God made a wind to pass over the earth, and the waters assuaged.

Genesis 8:1

It is said, "The Lord remembered Noah," wherein is discovered to us the most faithful care and careful faithfulness that is in Almighty God for His true servants. He looks upon their perils, He sees their dangers, and in His due time He remembers to relieve and release them, as He did here Noah and his family. Can the bride forget her ornaments? Can the mother forget her child? These things are not easily done, but they might be done, but the Lord cannot forget His, who making Him their God, He has made His servants, and written them in His hand, and has made them as signets on His right finger, that He may never forget them. "O Lord," said David, "what is man that thou art mindful of him, or the son of man that thou so regardest him?" (Ps. 8:4). Wait then upon God's leisure as Noah did, and be sure of remembrance in due time as he had.

Wait then upon God's leisure, and be sure of remembrance.

Evidence of Heaven

Edmund Calamy

aith is the grace, and the only grace, whereby we are justified before God; by it we eat of the Tree of Life (Jesus Christ) and live forever. It is therefore the fittest grace of all to satisfy conscience in this weighty matter and to make up conclusions from and about our eternal estate. This Satan knows full well, and therefore when he would flatter someone to hell, he persuades them that their faith is right good, when indeed there is no such matter, and when he would overthrow all hope of heaven in them, and drag them into despair, he persuades them that their faith, though never so good, is but a feigned and counterfeit thing, and the poor soul is ready to say, Amen. It mainly concerns all persons therefore, that would here get a good evidence for heaven, thoroughly to try their faith, whether it be a shield of gold, or but a shield of brass; whether it be a justifying, or but a temporary faith; whether it be a faith that justifies before God, or but only before the populace.

Wherefore the rather, brethren, give diligence to make your calling and election sure: for if ye do these things, ye shall never fall.
2 Peter 1:10

> It concerns all that would here get a good evidence for heaven, thoroughly to try their faith.

One Father

Thomas Manton

Our Father which art in heaven.
Matthew 6:9b

As the Lord's Prayer shows us what brotherly love we should express in prayer, so it checks many carnal dispositions which we are guilty of, and Christ would remind us of them. It checks strife and contention; we are brethren—we have one common Father. Everywhere we should live in meekness and love: it is a qualification for prayer. "Let the husband live with his wife according to knowledge, that their prayers be not hindered" (1 Pet. 3:7). If there be such brawls in the family, how can the husband and wife call upon God with such a united heart as is requisite? So 1 Tim. 2:8: "I will that men pray everywhere, lifting up holy hands, without wrath and doubting." Not only lift up "pure" hands to God, and that "without doubting"; there must be confidence in our prayers. But that is not all—but "without wrath." There must be nothing of revenge and passion mingled with your supplication. And then it checks pride and disdain. Christ teaches all, in all conditions, whether masters or servants, fathers or children, kings or beggars, all to say "Our Father"; for we have all one Father. You do not have a better Christ, or a better Father in heaven, than they have. The rich and the poor were to give one ransom under the law, to show they had all the same Redeemer. The weak should not despise nor disdain the strong, nor the rich be ashamed to own the poor as brethren. We should never be ashamed to own him as a brother whom God will own as a son.

> Christ teaches all, whether kings or beggars, all to say "our Father."

Multitude Pardoned

John Collinges

It is the same thing with God to pardon multitudes of sins as it is to pardon a few; yes, He never pardons the sins of any one soul but He pardons a multitude. God must forsake His justice, and deny Himself in His vindictive justice to pardon but one sin. There is no single sin, but that it has a kind of infiniteness in it, or rather contracts an infinite guilt. Every sin which we commit is against an infinite God, against infinite justice and goodness, and nothing but infinite goodness can remit it and pass it by. And an infinite remission as easily extends to a multitude of sins as to a few, so that as that good prince said unto God in the recognition of His power, "It is easy with thee to save by many as by few," so we may say in the case before us, "It is as easy with God to save from many, from the guilt of many, many thousands of sins, as from the guilt of a few." Especially considering that there is also infiniteness in the redemption price that is paid. If indeed that had been scant, something might have been objected, but that is proportionate to the goodness that is in God. The person that died for our sins was the God-man, an infinite person; His blood was of infinite virtue as to satisfaction.

Speak ye comfortably to Jerusalem, and cry unto her, that her warfare is accomplished, that her iniquity is pardoned: for she hath received of the LORD's hand double for all her sins.
Isaiah 40:2

An infinite remission as easily extends to a multitude of sins as to a few.

Faith Conquers All

Thomas Adams

And this is the victory that overcometh the world, even our faith.
1 John 5:4b

By faith Christ is made ours; by love we are made His. It was a piece of the philosopher's meditation that man has all in himself that has himself. The believer adds, he has himself that has Christ, and he has Christ that has true faith. This is the victory that overcomes the world, even our faith; yes, more, it overcomes Christ Himself. The world is overcome by faith because it cannot withstand it; Christ is overcome by faith because He will not withstand it. Christ in a duel overcame the devil (Matt. 4). A Canaanite woman so overcame Christ Himself; He yielded, "O woman, great is thy faith, be it unto thee even as thou wilt" (Matt. 15:28). This is able to smooth His countenance though it is frowning, to tie His hands though they are striking. The lion of this world raged long, and still rages, seeking whom he may devour. The Lion of the tribe of Judah conquered him; now faith conquers the Conqueror. How great is the power of faith that overcomes Him who overcame all! Thus is God pleased to let faith have a holy victory over Himself; He loves this sanctified violence, and bids faith wrestle courageously with Him, like Jacob, permitting His Almighty Self to be conquered and moved from executing deserved vengeance. So Job: "Albeit thou kill me, yet will I trust in thee" (Job 13:15), and because (says God) thou dost trust in me, I will not kill thee. It was honor enough for faith to subdue kingdoms, but to achieve the kingdom of heaven! Enough to stop the mouths of lions, but to vanquish that roaring lion, and to resist him! Enough to quench the violence of elementary fires, but to deliver from the eternal fire of hell! Enough to escape the edge of men's swords, but to escape the sword of God's justice! O the matchless virtue of faith!

> It was honor enough for faith to subdue kingdoms, but to achieve the kingdom of heaven!

Straight to God

Samuel Annesley

Our communion with God in heaven shall be immediate, without so much as a mediator. We shall go straight unto God, and immediately participate in His glory and happiness. There can be no immediate communion between God and the creature while sin or any of its effects remain. But when sin shall be abolished, then God shall be all in all, as before Christ was all in all. Christ shall deliver up the kingdom to God the Father, when He shall have put all enemies under His feet (1 Cor. 15:24) . . . And when all things shall be subdued to Him, then shall the Son also Himself be subject unto Him that put all things under Him, that God may be all in all. Christ as man constitutes a part of the church . . . but there will be no further need of a mediator. Suppose you saw a company of crystal globes, placed in a parallel line, and a single globe in the middle of them to transmit the sunbeams unto them, because their posture will not admit the sun's immediate beams. But when the sun shall so come about, as that they may immediately receive its beams, there is no further use of the single globe. So here, while we through our distance from God are incapable of immediate enjoyment, there is a necessity of Christ's mediation; but when all things that cause that distance are removed, and we are brought into the presence chamber where God dwells, there will be no such necessity of a mediator.

Thou wilt shew me the path of life: in thy presence is fulness of joy; at thy right hand there are pleasures for evermore.

Psalm 16:11

> When sin shall be abolished, then God shall be all in all, as before, Christ was all in all.

Truly Wise

William Bates

The fear of the LORD is the beginning of wisdom.

Psalm 111:10

Let me press upon you this eminent grace of fearing God, a grace that in this respect has a special prerogative and singularity that attends it. Whereas many other graces of the Christian life are but respective graces, they only concern some persons, some conditions, and some states of life, the fear of God . . . respects all persons in all states, and at all times. It is not a greater absurdity for a carpenter to be without his rule, than for a Christian to be without the fear of God. This is that grace which is the director of all other graces; therefore let us fear Him. But especially upon this account, the fear of the Lord is the best preservative against sin; the love of God is that which constrains us to service, but the fear of God is that which checks and restrains us from disobedience. This will preserve the soul in the midst of snares; lay but this fear aside and you will fall to the ground. . . . Therefore as you desire to keep yourselves spotless, so let the fear of God reign in you. Remember our whole lives are a continued temptation; we walk in the midst of snares. O consider, that although the enemy is outside us, yet there is a traitor within us, I mean our deceitful hearts. Therefore fear God with a fear of reverence, and fear your hearts with a fear of jealousy; if this grace do but take its regency in the soul, the devil may surround us, but he cannot surprise us. . . . Remember this, if every grace of the soul should languish, yet the fear of God last of all remains; that is the bond of the new covenant: "I will put my fear into their hearts that they shall not depart from me" (Jer. 32:40); this is that grace that is of most universal use and influence in the Christian's life. Therefore let us exercise this duty, this affection, that so we may be truly wise, we may be wise for ourselves, and wise towards God.

> If this grace do but take its regency in the soul, the devil may surround us, but he cannot surprise us.

The New Birth

Isaac Ambrose

If the new birth is necessary, how should we labor to be born again? I do not mean as Nicodemus, to enter into our mother's womb again and be born. It is not the seed of man in the womb of our mother, but the seed of grace in the womb of the church, that makes us blessed. And if we are thus born by grace, then are we sanctified, made children of God, heirs with Christ, over whom Satan can have no power at all. Now then, as you tender your souls, and desire heaven at your ends, endeavor to attain this one thing necessary. Lift up your hearts unto God that you may be washed, justified, and sanctified in the Name of the Lord Jesus; and that by the Spirit of God you may walk in new ways, talk with new tongues, as being new creatures, created unto good works. Thus if you wait on God in His way, I trust the Lord in mercy will remember you, and His Spirit will blow upon you, and then you will find and feel such a change within you, that you will bless God forever that you were thus born again. Otherwise, how woeful are you, considering this bar in heaven's door, to keep out the unregenerate: "Except a man be born again, he cannot see the kingdom of God."

Ye must be born again.
John 3:7b

> His Spirit will blow upon you, and then you will find and feel such a change within you.

Shortness of Life

Thomas Watson

Remember how short my time is: wherefore hast thou made all men in vain?

Psalm 89:47

It is "but a vapor," saith James (4:14). Life is a wheel ever-running. The poets painted time with wings to show the volubility and swiftness of it. Job compares it to a swift runner (Job 9:25); our life rides past; he likens it to a day, not to a year. It is indeed like a day. Infancy is as it were the day-break, youth is the sun-rising, full growth is the sun in the meridian, old age is sun-setting, sickness is the evening, then comes the night of death. How quickly is this day of life spent! Oftentimes this sun goes down at noon-day; life ends before the evening of old age comes. Nay, sometimes the sun of life sets presently after sun-rising. Quickly after the dawning of infancy the night of death approaches. O, how short is the life of man! The consideration of the brevity of life may work the heart to contentment. Remember thou art to be here but a day; thou hast but a short way to go, and what needs a long provision for a short way? If a traveler hath but enough to bring him to his journey's end he desires no more. We have but a day to live, and perhaps we may be in the twelfth hour of the day; why if God gives us but enough to bear our charges till night, it is sufficient; let us be content. If a man had the lease of a house, or farm, but for two or three days, and he should fall a building and begin planting, would he not be judged very indiscreet? So, when we have but a short time here, and death calls us presently off the stage, to thirst immoderately after the world, and pull down our souls to build up an estate, is an extreme folly. Therefore, as Esau said once, in a profane sense, concerning his birthright, "Lo, I am at the point to die, and what profit shall this birthright do to me?" (Gen. 25:32), so let a Christian say in a religious sense, "Lo, I am even at the point of death, my grave is going to be made, and what good will the world do me? If I have but enough till sun-setting, I am content."

Knowing God

James Janeway

I f there is acquaintance with God, then gross wicked- ness drops off, as scales from an ulcerated body when the constitution of the body is mended. Acquain- tance with God will be your only true comfort in this life, and the perfection of it is the very happiness of heaven. Let us then behold, till our hearts earnestly desire, till our souls are drawn out after acquaintance with God. If God is to be known, to be approached unto, to be conversed with by me, will He communicate Himself to me, and I to Him? Oh that He would love me, that I might love Him! Oh, blessed are they that know Him, as they are known of Him! "It is good for me to draw nigh to Him" (Ps. 73:28). "A day in His court is better than a thousand elsewhere" (Ps. 84:10). "My soul longeth, yes fainteth for the courts of the Lord; my heart and my flesh crieth out for the living God" (Ps. 84:2). Oh that I were received into conversation with God! That I might hear His voice and see His countenance, for His voice is sweet and His countenance comely! Oh that I might communicate myself to God, and that He would give Himself to me! Oh that I might love Him! That I were sick of love! That I might die in love! That I might lose myself in His love, as a small drop in the un- fathomable depth of His love! That I might dwell in the eternal love of Him! This is ac- quaintance with God.

Acquaint now thy- self with him, and be at peace: thereby good shall come unto thee.
Job 22:21

His voice is sweet and His countenance comely!

Our Best Affections

John Rogers

The LORD preserveth all them that love him: but all the wicked will he destroy.

Psalm 145:20

We ought to love God because He is goodness itself, which is most worthy of all love. And wherever we see any part of this image, it should draw our hearts to it. God has created us after His own image, redeemed us by His dear Son, preserved us always, and multiplied upon us . . . innumerable mercies for soul and body. Should not these challenge all our best affections? Thus have the worthy servants of God done in their several generations. The holy martyrs, who have forsaken all for His love, and counted their lives as nothing for His Name's sake; yes, they chose rather to endure the utmost tortures that their persecutors could inflict upon them rather than do anything to God's dishonor. Those who are far from this love of God are no better than haters of God.

They chose rather to endure the utmost tortures rather than do anything to God's dishonor.

Close with God

Jeremiah Burroughs

When God sets Himself before the soul by way of covenant, He not only tells those He takes into covenant that He will do mighty things for them, but that He would have them to close with Himself: "I will be your God" (Exod. 6:7). The Lord told Abraham that He would be his exceeding great reward, but that was not enough to satisfy Abraham. "What wilt thou give me?" he says, (Gen. 15:2) having an eye to Christ, and the enjoyment of God in Him. When God says that He will do such and such things for a gracious heart it is not enough, unless God Himself is the portion of the soul, for the soul cannot be satisfied with anything that God does. If God should say to one whose heart He has enlarged with grace, "I will give you all the world to possess, you shall have all the glory, all the pomp, all the sweetness, and all the comforts of the world; no, more than that I will make ten thousand worlds more, and give you them all, and they shall have all of them more excellency than this present world has." Why, all this would not satisfy a heart that has been enlarged by grace. Though such a one sees itself unworthy of the least crumb of bread, yet it cannot be satisfied with all the world. What then will satisfy the gracious heart? Only God Himself, for so God gives Himself unto His people by way of covenant: "I will be thy God, I will be your portion," and upon this, those that are in covenant with Him . . . do rejoice to see God manifesting Himself in all His Names . . . for the beholding so much as they do of Him in His works, but the thing that their hearts are most upon is God Himself, the excellency that there is in God above all His works.

The LORD is the portion of mine inheritance and of my cup.
Psalm 16:5a

> **What then will satisfy the gracious heart? Only God Himself.**

Final Perseverance

Gervase Babington

The Father's giving us to Christ . . . implies the certainty and assurance of our salvation. For, if the constancy of Christ's love to all that come unto Him be such that He never casts any of them away, judge in your own self, if once you find the assurance of your coming, whether your safety is not sealed in the word of God's truth, that you can no more perish than He can be untrue. Let us lay this truth next to several texts that most comfortably deliver this doctrine to us, for instance, the first Psalm, which says that the blessed of the Lord that once comes to Christ by a true belief in His Name and life, as God enables, according to faith, is like a tree planted by the rivers of water, whose leaf shall never, never, wither for want of moisture. Also the thirty-second of Jeremiah, where the promise is made that the covenant with such as are come unto Him shall be everlasting, that He will never turn away from doing good to them, but will put His fear in their hearts, that they shall not depart from Him. This text Augustine often urges to be set up as a wall of brass against doubt in anyone. And the text in Matthew, where it says that the elect should be deceived (if that were possible), again I say, if that were possible, and ever remember it. Another is the tenth of John, where our Savior says, "I will give my sheep eternal life, and they shall never perish, neither shall any pluck them out of my hands" (John 10:28). We may be shaken, and dangerously tempted, as God shall think good, but perish we cannot, if these Scriptures are true. Peter is a pattern of what may befall us, and Peter is a proof of God's goodness towards us. Tertullian said of him, "The strength of his faith was shaken, but not shattered in pieces; moved it was, but not removed; it began to dry, but it never withered; with his mouth he denied God, but his heart did not fully and finally let Him go." Thus far we may fall (which yet God forbid) and by the mercy that raised him, rise again.

To Persuade God

William Fenner

mportunate prayer is prayer that is full of strong arguments. And hence it is that Job says, "I will fill my mouth with arguments" (Job 23:4), like an importunate man, who will bring all reasons and arguments to effect his cause. Even so the importunate person at the throne of grace will bring all arguments to persuade God. . . . You cannot expect to prevail with God, unless you purpose to do it. How did Jacob come to prevail with God, but by wrestling? Prayer is called fighting; it is a holy kind of violence. You cannot obtain a mercy from God's hand, unless you use all your force to get it. Even as a Father who has an apple in his hand, and his child would have it; he first opens one finger, then another, till the apple drops out. So it is with a poor sinner at the throne of grace. The Lord opens His hands, and fills all things living with plenty. What are the means that are used? Why, the prayers of His children, who by their prayers open God's hand, and so make the blessings to descend. Go for grace and the Lord will say to you, "You are proud, you must be humble," and so open that finger. "You are careless, you must go quicken yourself," and so open that finger. God says, "You will not make much of this grace when you have it, but you will turn it into wantonness; you must learn to mortify your members," and so open that finger. You cannot get grace from God's hand unless you open all His fingers, and then it will fall down. There is much power in the prayers of God's children; some have more, some have less, and yet all must be powerful at the throne of grace, else none can prevail with God.

Come now, and let us reason together, saith the LORD.
Isaiah 1:18a

> There is much power in the prayers of God's children.

Two Cups

Robert Dingley

I call heaven and earth to record this day against you, that I have set before you life and death, blessing and cursing: therefore choose life, that both thou and thy seed may live.

Deuteronomy 30:19

here is a cup in God's right hand that is ten thousand times sweeter than nectar. Of this He invites you to taste, and many will not. But then there is a cup of trembling in His left hand, into which the dregs of His fury are wrung out, and of this cup they shall taste and drink deep to eternity. You must all have to do with God one way or another, as children with a father, or as traitors with a judge. God can raise Himself glory out of your ashes. If you will forsake your own mercies, and shut the door against the offers of grace, justice shall break in upon you as an armed soldier, and deliver you to the tormenters. Behold, I set life and death, hell and heaven, sweet and bitter, before you this day, you must taste of one. Make therefore (with Mary) a wise and judicious choice; taste and see how good the Lord is, and then you shall never taste and see how terrible He is, how just He is, how powerful He is for the destruction of the creature, yet so that it may ever live to feel what infinite power, justice, and wisdom can inflict upon it to all eternity.

All have to do with God as children with a father, or as traitors with a judge.

Living Grace

Jeremiah Dyke

t is a point that concerns us at all times to look to the growth of our grace, as that which much evidences the truth of it. For where there is no growth of grace, there is no truth of grace. True grace is growing grace. There is a growing in knowledge (2 Pet. 3:18), a growing in wisdom (Luke 2:40), and a growing in faith (2 Thess. 1:3). All true grace grows. There are counterfeit and false graces, and this is the main thing that differentiates between true and counterfeit ones: true grace grows, counterfeit grace grows not. There is a great deal of differences between a true tree and a pictured tree, between a true child, and the statue or image of a child. A true child grows, but the image grows not—it is no taller or bigger at a hundred years old than it was the first day it was made. Where there is truth of grace, there is life of grace, and life will put forth itself and cause a growth, as we see in living trees, and living children that are not yet come to their full growth—they grow because they live.

The righteous shall flourish like the palm tree: he shall grow like a cedar in Lebanon.
Psalm 92:12

> There is a great deal of differences between a true tree and a pictured tree.

The Way Home

Samuel Doolittle

O death, where is thy sting? O grave, where is thy victory?
1 Corinthians 15:55

Do you ask why the righteous must die? They die that sin might be destroyed. As sin brought death into the world, so death shall forever abolish sin. Though death had its sting, strength, power, nay, its very being from sin, yet it proves by the ordination of God the destruction of it. Those arrows of death which kill the Christian, strike through the very heart of his sins, and lusts, and they both die together. A saint puts off the garments of mortality, and filthy raiment at once; the sin that was born with them, and lived with them, and accompanies them from place to place, in their last moments takes leave of them forever. The Christian dies that sin may do so too. The righteous are strangers and pilgrims; this is their character, and it is expressive of their frame and temper. While they live they are in a strange place, among a strange people, and at a distance from their own. Oh! How do they wish, long, pant, desire, and groan to be elsewhere! They are born from heaven, belong to it, and wish to be there. They are citizens of the new Jerusalem; in it are mansions designed, purchased, prepared, and standing empty for them; but they must dip their feet in the cold fatal stream that runs between this world, and that, before they can get there. Faith may, and very often does, give them refreshing, ravishing, and transporting prospects of heaven. Oh! How often after such a view does the soul flutter in the Christian's breast, clap its wings, and would be gone, but death only can carry us over to and give us the possession of it. In short, God's children die that they may go home.

> Faith may give them refreshing, ravishing, and transporting prospects of heaven.

Growth by Degree

John Flavel

t is true, indeed, that Christ is perfectly and completely applied to the soul in the first act for righteousness. "Justification being a relative change, properly admits no degrees, but is perfected together, and at once, in one only act; though as to its manifestation, sense, and effects, it has various degrees," says William Ames. But the application of Christ to us, for wisdom and sanctification, is not perfected in one single act, but rises by many, and slow degrees to its just perfection. And though we are truly said to have come to Christ when we first believe (John 6:35), yet the soul after that is still coming to Him by further acts of faith: "To whom [coming] as unto a living stone" (1 Pet. 2:4). The participle notes a continued motion, by which the soul gains ground, and still gets nearer and nearer to Christ; growing still more inwardly acquainted with Him. The knowledge of Christ grows upon the soul as the morning light, from its first spring to the perfect day (Prov. 4:18). Every grace of the Spirit grows, if not sensibly, yet really; for it is in discerning the growth of sanctification, as it is in discerning the growth of plants, which we perceive to have grown, rather than grow. And as it thrives in the soul, by deeper movements of the habits, and more promptitude and spirituality in the acting; so Christ, and the soul proportionally, close more and more inwardly and efficaciously, till at last it is wholly swallowed up in Christ's full and perfect enjoyment.

Those that be planted in the house of the LORD shall flourish in the courts of our God.
Psalm 92:13

> The knowledge of Christ grows upon the soul as the morning light, from its first spring to the perfect day.

Heavens Declare

Nathaniel Vincent

The heavens declare the glory of God; and the firmament sheweth his handywork.
Psalm 19:1

The works of God, though in Himself invisible, show forth the Worker's wisdom, power, and goodness. The heavens preach to those on earth, and plainly declare their Creator's glory; they utter a voice which all of all languages may understand. Here are such lines, in which every eye may read the eternal power and goodness of Him, of whom, and through whom, and to whom are all things, and who is to be glorified forevermore. Among the other works of God, the Psalmist takes special notice of the sun in the firmament, whose light and influence is so great and beneficial, and then makes a transition to the law and Word of God, whose light in a sense obscures that glorious luminary, giving forth such clear manifestation, and affecting knowledge to man, concerning his Maker, as turns his heart to Him, though naturally blind and foolish, alienated and estranged.

The heavens preach to those on earth, and plainly declare their Creator's glory.

Sin is Forgiven

John Shower

You ought to consider that if sin is forgiven all things shall work for good. "Take away all iniquity (says the church) and receive us graciously, or do us good" (Hos. 14:2). Every providence shall be sanctified, if sin is forgiven. "For peace I had great bitterness," says Hezekiah, "but in love to my soul, thou hast delivered it from the pit of corruption; for thou hast cast all my sins behind thy back" (Isa. 37:17). You have a similar instance in Jer. 33:6–8. But if you had all the plenty, peace, health, riches and grandeur of the world, yet the guilt of one sin on the conscience, under the apprehension of God's deserved wrath, will spoil the relish of all. Where sin is forgiven, other mercies will be sweet, and the burden of affliction tolerable; but without this, and under the apprehensions of the contrary, every temporal calamity is double. For this is wormwood and the gall in every bitter cup. We shall not under the troubles and disappointments of this world cry out, "We are undone," if we can think that God has forgiven us. No more than a man, who has just received his prince's pardon, can be thought, if he lose his glove or handkerchief in the way home, that he will wring his hands, and weep, and take on for such a loss, when he had so lately his life graciously given him. Besides, here is a foundation laid for a life of thankful love and obedience to God. Conscience, being purged of dead works, we serve the living God without fear, in hope of His acceptance, with the promise of His hearing our prayers, and that He will be well pleased with our services, and overlook our infirmities. We may therefore well bear the trials of this life with patience and resignation, and in a dying hour shall be able to commend our souls with faith and hope, into the hands of Christ, who will take care of us as His own when we leave the world; and at last publicly acknowledge and absolve us in the great Day. Oh how many mercies accompany this one, of this forgiveness of sin!

In whom we have redemption through his blood, the forgiveness of sins, according to the riches of his grace.

Ephesians 1:7

Most Gloriously

Francis Roberts

When I consider thy heavens, the work of thy fingers, the moon and the stars, which thou hast ordained. What is man, that thou art mindful of him? and the son of man, that thou visitest him?
Psalm 8:3–4

In the work of creation, God's freedom, wisdom, power, and goodness shine most gloriously. First, freedom in that He "hath done whatsoever He pleased" (Ps. 115:3). He made one world and no more; such creatures and no other, and such sort and not otherwise because He so pleased. None may control His work. "Shall the thing formed say to Him that formed it, why hast thou made me thus?" (Rom. 9:20). Second, wisdom, for He "worketh all things according to the counsel of His own will" (Eph. 1:11). How many ways has God discovered His wisdom herein! As in the order of creation He made all things in six days. He could have made them in one day, in one hour as easily, but He would show Himself a God of order. He first made the . . . lesser creatures and proceeded to the greater creatures. . . . There is one glory of the sun, another glory of the moon, another glory of the stars, and one star differs from another star in glory. Some of the elements are hot, some cold, some moist, some dry, some light, some heavy. The virtues of plants and fruits are innumerable. In the sweet harmony of the whole universe, the wisdom of God wondrously appears. Third, power, that He could frame all things of nothing, without any preexistent matter, and all most easily, by His Word. He said, "Let there be light," and there was light (Gen. 1:3). He spoke works more easily than we can speak words. He spoke, and it was done. He commanded and it stood fast. He commanded and they were created. It was but a word, and a work. Fourth, goodness, in that God (though infinitely happy and satisfied) was pleased to create the world, especially men and angels, to communicate His goodness to them.

> He spoke, and it was done. He commanded and it stood fast. He commanded and they were created.

The Desirable Life

Matthew Lawrence

Life of all things is most sweet. And therefore the tree of life was placed in the midst of paradise, as if it were the perfection of all other comforts. How sweet is then the sweetest life? In comparison all other life is but death. Luke 15:32 says, "Thy brother was dead, and is alive"—O, that we had eyes to see, and hearts to consider the excellency of this life! Look how much difference there is between the life of a child in the womb, and the life when it is come abroad into the world, where it has freedom of breathing, hearing, seeing, and exercising all the senses, so great a difference there is between the life of nature and grace, as also between the life of grace and glory. We do no more know what is reserved for us in heaven than a child in the womb knows what is reserved for it when it enters the world. Only as there is a natural instinct in the child to go forth of the prison of the womb into a better life, so there is a spiritual and supernatural instinct in all God's children to be made partakers of a better life. "For as the whole creation groans, so we ourselves groan within ourselves," says the Apostle (Rom. 8:22). In the mean time, before we come to enjoy the life of glory to the full, glorious things in their degree are spoken of the life of grace, in regard of the nature, principle, and comforts of it. To all which we might add its excellency in regard of operations, that is, the crucifying our corruptions, overcoming the world, and all opposite powers, making us more than conquerors in Christ. Therefore, it is an excellent life and thus most desirable.

And I will bring the blind by a way that they knew not; I will lead them in paths that they have not known: I will make darkness light before them, and crooked things straight. These things will I do unto them, and not forsake them.
Isaiah 42:16

> There is a spiritual instinct in all God's children to be made partakers of a better life.

Reverent Fear

George Swinnock

Let all the earth fear the LORD: let all the inhabitants of the world stand in awe of him.

Psalm 33:8

When you pray, put up your petitions to God with awful apprehensions of Him. The Latin Vulgate reads Ps. 84:10 this way: "I have chosen to be cast upon the earth, to lie prostrate in the house of God." The eastern Christians, when they called on God, threw themselves to the ground. Luther prayed with confidence as to a father, but with reverence as to a God. Remember that when you speak to the Lord, you are but dust and ashes. You are at best but a beggar, and a proud heart will not suit a beggar's purse. "The poor must use entreaties" (Prov. 18:23). The twenty-four elders fell on their faces and worshipped (Rev. 4:16). So did Jesus Christ in prayer (Matt. 26:30). "O come, let us worship and bow down; let us kneel before the Lord our Maker" (Ps. 95:6). The elephant that could not bow nor kneel was no fit beast for a sacrifice.

Luther prayed with confidence as to a father, but with reverence as to a God.

Grace Not Gifts

Richard Sibbes

We must know that Christianity is more a matter of grace rather than gifts, of obedience than of playing a part. Gifts may come from a more common work of the Spirit; they are common to castaways, and are more for others than for ourselves. Grace comes from a peculiar favor of God and especially for our own good. In the same duty where gifts and grace are both required, as in prayer, it is more important to perform it with evidence of great grace than with great skill. Moses (a man not of the best speech) was chosen before Aaron, to speak to God, and to strive with Him by prayer, while Israel fought with Amalek with the sword. It is a business more of the heart than of the tongue, more of groans, than of words, which groans and sighs the Spirit will always stir up, even in the worst condition. Yet for parts there is no member, but it is fitted with some abilities, to do service in the body, and by faith may grow up to a greater measure. For God calls none to that high condition but whom in some measure He fits to be a useful member, and endues with a public spirit.

Even so ye, forasmuch as ye are zealous of spiritual gifts, seek that ye may excel to the edifying of the church.
1 Corinthians 14:12

> God calls none to that high condition but whom in some measure He fits to be a useful member.

Holiness

Henry Scudder

*Who is like unto thee,
O LORD, among the
gods? who is like thee,
glorious in holiness,
fearful in praises,
doing wonders?*
Exodus 15:11

When Christ (in the Lord's Prayer) signified that God was to be esteemed and acknowledged with the most absolute honor that could be, He said "hallowed," that is, "let Thy Name be known and acknowledged to be holy." We may infer from this that holiness is the highest title of honor and glory that can belong to any person, yes, to the most high God. If any person or thing is holy, is it honorable. When the seraphims would give God the greatest honor and glory, they cried, "Holy, holy, holy is the Lord of hosts" (Isa. 6:3). The four living creatures said, "Holy, holy, holy, Lord God almighty" (Rev. 4:8). It was the honor of Jerusalem to be a holy city. It is the glory of the third heaven to be the high and holy place (Isa. 57:15). David counted holy men to be excellent (Ps. 16:3). And when Christ Jesus will present His church unto Himself as a glorious church, He will sanctify it and present it holy and without blemish.

The more they partake of holiness, the more like they are to God.

Holiness in God is the rectitude and perfection of His power, mercy, justice, and all of His other attributes, which, if they were not all holy, could not be good, much less goodness. God could not be God if He were not holy, yes, holiness itself. And as for other creatures, the more they partake of holiness, the more like they are to God, and are therefore the more glorious. Man at the first was therefore the most glorious of all creatures here below, because he was made according to God's image, most holy.

In Christ's Bosom

Isaac Ambrose

Rest in the LORD, and wait patiently for him.
Psalm 37:7a

Communion with Christ is a foretaste of heaven. Here we enjoy His person and all the sweet relations to His person. We enjoy His death and all the saving fruits, privileges, and influences of His death. We are also brought into Christ's banqueting house, held in His galleries, His banner over us being love. We are carried up to the mount with Christ, that we may see Him (as it were) transfigured, and may say with Peter, "Master, it is good for us to be here; and let us here build tabernacles" (Matt. 17:4). Oh, it is a happy thing to have Christ dwelling in our hearts, and to lodge in Christ's bosom! It is a happy thing to maintain communion between Christ and our souls! He took our sins; we take His healing; He endured wounds for us; we drink the spiritual balsam that sprang from His wounds; He took upon Him our unrighteousness; we clothe ourselves with His righteousness. He endured pains for us; we come to Him and take His rest to our souls. He embraced our curse and condemnation; we embrace His blessing, justification, and salvation. To this end we look on Jesus. Now, if He hides His face by desertion, do not rest until you find Him. And when you find Him, hold fast to Him, do not let Him go, nor drive Him from your heart through your corruptions. If you would prize the presence of Christ, how comfortably would you maintain and increase your communion with Him.

> He endured pains for us; we come to Him and take His rest to our souls.

Our Morning Cry

Jeremiah Burroughs

For this corruptible must put on incorruption, and this mortal must put on immortality.
1 Corinthians 15:53

Philip, the king of Macedon, would have a man come and cry to him every morning, "You are mortal"; this is that which I would rather choose, that you might daily hear a voice that "You are immortal." The better part of you must live eternally. If eternity were presented to us in the reality of it, how mightily would it work to draw our hearts to eternal things? Certainly our thoughts are not upon eternity; the thoughts of eternity are mighty prevailing thoughts, they are over-awing thoughts, soul-humbling thoughts that would ballast our hearts. They are infinite pertinent thoughts that do infinitely concern us. You that have had a company, of slight thoughts, and have set the strength of our spirits in thinking of light things; oh this day here is an object presented to you, to help against slight thoughts. This one word eternity, and the thoughts of this word, may be enough for you to banish vain and vexing thoughts away forever.

> You are immortal. The better part of you must live eternally.

Acknowledge God

John Dod and Robert Cleaver

"God spake all these words and said, I am the Lord thy God which brought thee out of the land of Egypt, out of the house of bondage" (Exod. 20:1–2). These words contain a preparation, to stir us up with all care and conscience to keep the law of God, which partly concerns the observing of all the commandments in general, and more specially, the keeping of the first. That preparation which pertains to all, is in these words "God spake," that is, that seeing they have God for their Author, and immediate teacher of them, even by His own voice; therefore we must settle ourselves to obey them without resistance, or gainsaying. That which belongs to the first is drawn from the nature of God, being Jehovah, which signifies His essence and being, incommunicable to any creature; and secondly, from His benefits, either general in these words "thy God," that is, one that have bound myself in covenant with thee, to be thine, to deliver thee from all evils of soul and body, and to do thee all good for this life, and that which is to come; or else special in the last words "which have brought thee out of the land of Egypt," whereby is signified, that He had brought them out of that place, which was wholly addicted to idolatry and superstition; and out of that condition and state which was full of misery and bondage. Since then this wonderful deliverance does abundantly testify of His love and goodness towards them, therefore they should wholly submit themselves to Him, and acknowledge Him, and Him only, to be their God.

The law of his God is in his heart; none of his steps shall slide.
Psalm 37:31

This wonderful deliverance does abundantly testify of His love and goodness.

To Weep Properly

Christopher Love

In his neck remaineth strength, and sorrow is turned into joy before him.
Job 41:22

Christians should not be excessive in worldly sorrow; they should weep as if they did not weep. Then this reproves those that can mourn for every cross that befalls them, but yet cannot shed a tear for any sin they commit. Many complain of small inconsiderable troubles and affliction, but yet never complain of their sins and corruptions; these never trouble them, nor come near their hearts. They can mourn for that which can but at most prejudice the body, and yet never grieve for that which can prejudice and destroy their souls. I beseech you, beloved, take heed of being lavish of your tears for worldly crosses and afflictions; it is a pity to wash a foul room with sweet water. I must tell you, tears are too precious to shed for every trifle; it would be a great deal better if you would keep this precious water to wash away your sins; for though it is Christ's blood alone that can wash away the guilt of sin, yet your tears may much conduce to wash away the filth and power of sin. When you mourn for worldly crosses, then weep as if you wept not; but when you mourn for sin, mourn as much as you can. Be like the sun, that will soon melt and convert into water; you that are the children of God know that you have greater things, of higher concern, to bestow your tears upon, than any outward troubles. You have daily failings, and many sins and corruptions that are not mortified and not subdued, and the loss of the light of God's countenance to mourn for; your sorrows never run aright, but when they run in this channel, when your tears run into the mill-pond, to grind your lusts and corruptions to consume and weaken them, then are your sorrows right and regular.

> *Tears are too precious to shed for every trifle.*

Prayer's Wing

Edmund Calamy

he promises are the wings of prayer. Prayer is a divine cordial to convey grace from heaven into our souls. It is a key to unlock the bowels of mercy, which are in God. The best way to obtain holiness is upon our knees; the best posture to fight against the devil is upon our knees. Therefore prayer is not put as a part of our spiritual armor, but added as that which must be an ingredient in every part, and which will make every part effectual. But now the promises are the wings of prayer. Prayer without a promise is as a bird without wings. Therefore we read both of Jacob and Jehosaphat, how they urged God in their prayer, with His promises. And certainly the prayers of the saints, winged with David's promises, will quickly fly up to heaven, and draw down grace and comfort into their souls. And upon this account it is that the promises are so useful to a Christian, because they are so helpful in prayer. When we pray, we must urge God with His promises, and say, "Lord, hast thou not said, Thou wilt circumcise our hearts to love thee, thou wilt subdue our sins, thou wilt give the Spirit to those that ask it? Lord! Thou art faithful. Fulfill thine own promises," and we must remember this great truth, "That the promises God makes to us to mortify our sins for us, are greater helps against sin than our promises to God to mortify sin." Many people in the day of their distress vow and promise to leave sin, and fight against it in the strength of these promises, and instead of conquering sin, are conquered by sin. But if we fight against sin in the strength of Christ and of His promises, if we urge God in prayer with His own Word, we shall at last get victory over it, for He has said that sin shall not have dominion over us (Rom. 6:14).

Turn again, and tell Hezekiah the captain of my people, Thus saith the LORD, the God of David thy father, I have heard thy prayer, I have seen thy tears: behold, I will heal thee: on the third day thou shalt go up unto the house of the LORD.
2 Kings 20:5

> **Promises are so useful to a Christian, because they are so helpful in prayer.**

Security

Samuel Slater

*And thou shalt be se-
cure, because there is
hope; yes, thou shalt
dig about thee, and
thou shalt take thy
rest in safety.*
Job 11:18

Secret prayer is a choice and excellent means of security; would a man be safe when he is alone, then
let him pray when he is alone. On this side of
heaven there is no place to be found, in which a person
may rationally look upon himself as quite out of the
reach of danger. I heard one once wittily say that he did
not venture upon the road for fear of robbers, so long as
he was alone. But there are other enemies from whom
we may apprehend mischief when we are most alone.
The subtle serpent wringed himself into paradise, and
there he did mortally sting our first parents, and undid
them and all their posterity in them. Holy Paul was perfectly safe while he continued in the third heaven for the
malicious tempter could not come at him there; since the
tempter came down from that blessed place, he never yet
could, and for the future never shall make a reentry; nor
is his arm strong enough to shoot an arrow, or throw a
fiery dart so high; but no sooner had that eminent apostle
come down again, but he was desperately set upon,
worse than the Philistines were; there was a thorn stuck
in his flesh, which could not but put him to pain, and a
messenger of Satan was sent to buffet him. . . . One
would conclude a person safe enough when nobody is
with him; as there is none to help, so there is none to
hurt. But even then he may be in danger, for though there
is no man with him, yet there is a devil with him; yes,
more than one, possibly more than a legion. It might have
been rationally concluded that David walking upon the
top of his house did not stand in need of his life-guard
about him. Who was there that should or could do the
king mischief? Yet even there a naked woman conquered
that man of war, and a malicious devil let fly one of his
envenomed arrows, and wounded him to the very heart
of the eye. It had been well for that good man if, instead
of gazing about, and viewing every object that presented,
he had been looking up to his God and praying in secret.

Life and Heart

Thomas Vincent

The life of Christianity consists very much in our love to Christ. Without love to Christ, we are as much without spiritual life as a carcass when the soul is fled from it is without natural life. Faith without love to Christ is a dead faith; and a Christian without love to Christ is a dead Christian, dead in sins and trespasses. Without love to Christ, we may have the name of Christians, but we are wholly without the nature. We may have the form of godliness, but are wholly without the power. "Give me thine heart" is the language of God to all the children of men (Prov. 23:26). And "give me thy love" is the language of Christ to all His disciples. Christ knows the command and influence which love to Him, in the truth and strength of it, has. It will engage all the other affections of His disciples for Him, that if He have their love, their desires will be chiefly after Him. Their delights will be chiefly in Him, their hopes and expectations will be chiefly from Him; their hatred, fear, grief, anger, will be carried forth chiefly to sin, as it is offensive to Him. He knows that love will engage and employ for Him all the powers and faculties of their souls . . . If they have much love to Him, they will not think much of denying themselves, taking up His cross, and following Him wherever He leads them; love to Christ then being essential to true Christianity, so earnestly looked for by our Lord and Master, so powerfully commanding in the soul and over the whole man, so greatly influential on our duty.

So when they had dined, Jesus saith to Simon Peter, Simon, son of Jonas, lovest thou me more than these?
John 21:15a

> **Without love to Christ, we may have the name of Christians, but we are wholly without the nature.**

Christian Prize

Richard Alleine

Wherefore seeing we also are compassed about with so great a cloud of witnesses, let us lay aside every weight, and the sin which doth so easily beset us, and let us run with patience the race that is set before us.

Hebrews 12:1

Christ is a Christian's prize, and a Christian's pattern. He is the prize which a Christian runs for; what would you have as the fruit of all your labors and sufferings? O Christ, Christ, that Christ may be mine; and He is their pattern, the pattern that God has set before them, and that they also have set before themselves, that their eye and their heart is set upon. What is your aim? What is it that you are reaching towards, and working up yourselves unto? What manner of person would you be? How would you live? If you may have your wish, or your desire, what is it? What would you be? How would you live? O let me be made conformable to Christ. We may find both these in the apostle's eye, in comparison of which he counted all things but loss and dung (Phil. 3:8–10), that he may win Christ, and that he may be conformable to Christ. "For whom I have suffered the loss of all things, and do count them but dung, that I may win Christ, and be found in Him"; and v. 10, "that I may know Him, and the power of His resurrection, and the fellowship of His sufferings, and be made conformable to His death." Every Christian is of the same mind; all is dung in comparison to Him, and it is not only to be found in Christ, that He so earnestly desires, but also to be made conformable to Him. They would live as He lived, and as He would have them live; they would not only, that they may be blessed in Christ, but that Christ may be pleased in them. They never have their wills, but when Christ has His will of them. It does not suffice me, says a Christian, that I have hopes of getting to heaven by Christ at last, I must be more holy here; I would live so, that my ways may please Christ. O that I might hold me close by Him, that I might in my whole course please the Lord. I would fain be a more exact and perfect Christian. All this the apostle follows so hard after: "Not as though I had already obtained, or were already perfect, but I follow after, if I may apprehend" (Phil. 3:12).

Strength in Trouble

Jeremiah Burroughs

They that are afflicted understand Scripture, says Luther, but those who are secure in their prosperity read them as a verse in Ovid. Among others, this is one special means whereby an afflicted condition comes to be useful for the increase of grace, because in it the soul gains much experience of God and of His ways. It experiences the goodness and faithfulness of His Word, as we read in Ps. 107. Those who go down into the sea see the wonders of the Lord; much more do those who come into the seas of troubles and afflictions. How do they see the wonders of the Lord? They can tell their friends much of the wonders of the Lord towards them. Israel in the time of trouble cried out "My God, we know thee" (Hos. 8:2). They knew God more then than before affliction and experiencing of the evil of sin. It was a speech of Caspar Olevianus in his sickness: "In this disease I have learned how great God is, and what the evil of sin is; I never knew what God was to purpose before, or what sin meant." When God spoke to Job out of the whirlwind, Job answered "Behold I am vile; what shall I answer thee? I will lay mine hand upon my mouth" (Job 40:3–4). . . . It is very observable, that of all the seven churches that Christ wrote to in the second and third chapters of Revelation, that there are only two which He charges no evil upon, the Church of Smyrna and the Church of Philadelphia. These two were exercised with much trouble. The Church of Smyrna is said to have endured much tribulation (Rev. 2:9) and to have been in poverty, yet Christ commends her, and says, "She is rich." Her poverty made her rich; her tribulations made her glorious in the eyes of Christ. The Church of Philadelphia had little strength (Rev. 3:8–10); she was in a low, poor, afflicted, and contemptible condition. Yet she denied not the name of Christ, she kept the word of Christ's patience, that word for which she suffered much, being strengthened by the patience she received from Jesus Christ.

Therefore being justified by faith, we have peace with God through our Lord Jesus Christ: By whom also we have access by faith into this grace wherein we stand, and rejoice in hope of the glory of God. And not only so, but we glory in tribulations also: knowing that tribulation worketh patience; And patience, experience; and experience, hope: And hope maketh not ashamed; because the love of God is shed abroad in our hearts by the Holy Ghost which is given unto us.
Romans 5:1–5

Law and Conscience

Robert Bolton

For we must all appear before the judgment seat of Christ; that every one may receive the things done in his body, according to that he hath done, whether it be good or bad.

2 Corinthians 5:10

When we shall come to judgment, and appear before God's tribunal (and we little know how near it is) two books shall be laid open to us; the one, of God's law, and the other, of our own conscience. The former will tell us what we should have done, for the Lord has revealed it to the world, to be the rule of our faith, and of all our actions. The other will tell us what we have done, for conscience is a register, light, and power in our understanding, which treasures up all our peculiar actions against the day of trial, discovers to us the equity, or iniquity of them, and determines of them, either for us or against us. Now we must not take any exception against the first, that is, the law of God: "The law of the LORD is perfect, converting the soul: the testimony of the LORD is sure, making wise the simple" (Ps. 19:7). We cannot against the second, that is, the book of our conscience, for it was ever in our custody and keeping; no one could corrupt it, there is nothing writ in it but with our own hands.

Conscience is a register, light, and power in our understanding.

Esteem God's Will

William Gouge

God's will is to be preferred before all others. This Joseph, Daniel and his three companions, the apostles, and many others well observed, when they refused to yield to man's will against God's. And David, Paul, and Christ, when they submitted their own wills to God's in such things as if it had been the will of God, they could have desired to have been otherwise. Among others, the example of Christ is to be observed, because He was a Son, and we are but servants. If the Son yielded to do the will of His Father, how much more ought the servant to yield to the will of his Master. Both the supreme sovereignty of God, and also the absolute perfection of His will require as much. As for our own wills, they are subject to much error, and often prove very harmful. . . . we are taught always to have one eye on God's will, and not on our own. For in our will there are many contradictions, but in the Lord's will there is always life and goodness.

Behold, my master wotteth not what is with me in the house, and he hath committed all that he hath to my hand; . . . how then can I do this great wickedness, and sin against God?
Genesis 39:7–9

> How much more ought the servant to yield to the will of his Master.

Consider the Glory

William Whittaker

For I reckon that the suffering of this present time are not worthy to be compared with the glory which shall be revealed in us.

Romans 8:18

Consider the glory that this inheritance contains in reference to the souls of the saints. Bernard breaks out into this high expression: "How great shall the glory of God's people be when their very bodies shall be as glorious as the sun, and they shall shine as the sun in the firmament." Concerning the glory of the souls of the saints, I shall not be large in treating of that. All the faculties of their souls shall then be more enlarged and widened to receive in more of God, to take in more of happiness than now they are capable of. Our souls now are but narrow vessels in comparison of what they shall be then. The soul of man is too big a vessel for the world to fill. . . . But then it shall be widened and shall have a larger capacity than now it has. Our understandings shall know more of God; knowledge is one of the great accomplishments of man. It sets him in a higher rank of being than other creatures. And that there is a very great excellency in knowledge appears because this was the bait Satan made use of: "So shall you be as God, knowing good and evil" (Gen. 3:5). That subtle adversary knew no bait more taking. Knowledge in itself is a most lovely and amiable thing, but in comparison to spiritual knowledge, the knowledge of God and of ourselves, all other knowledge is but poor and mean. The philosopher when he had been much admiring the knowledge of nature did wonder that any would give way to sensual and brutish pleasures, which they by the light of nature so much condemned. But what is this knowledge in comparison of the knowledge of Christ? All knowledge whether natural or divine, is now but weak, and feeble, scant and narrow. How little does anyone know themselves! How many things are there in nature that to this day do remain a mystery and riddle to the wisest individual! How little do we know of God! But then our knowledge shall be widened. Our wills and affections are now but narrow and weak things; they can hold but a little. But then they shall be enlarged.

Grafted into Christ

Joseph Caryl

A crab tree will never yield pleasant fruit, until you change the nature of it. Take a crab tree and plant it in the best soil that you have, and water it, and dress it, and prune it as much as you can, yet this crab tree will bear nothing but crabs, sour fruit, until you come to graft it; and then your grafting of it changes the nature of the stock, and it has another principle, and so then it brings forth good fruit. . . . Take the best natured person in the world and plant him in the best soil, in the best ground, in church ground; plant him in the house of God, and there let him be watered by holy doctrine, and let him be cultivated every day, but still he will bring forth nothing but unsavory fruit, until he himself is changed. Though he is under all those spiritual means, yet until those means have wrought effectually in him, his actions are all unsavory. It is only by our implantation into Jesus Christ that we become fit to do good that is acceptable to God. It is this that makes the change. For as in nature the graft changes the stock, so in grace, the stock changes the grafted branch. As we are grafted into Christ, He changes the branch; being planted into Christ, by the power of the Spirit, we are then made like Him, and then we shall bring forth fruits of righteousness, which are to the glory of God.

I am the vine, ye are the branches: He that abideth in me, and I in him, the same bringeth forth much fruit: for without me ye can do nothing.
John 15:5

> Being planted into Christ, by the power of the Spirit, we are then made like Him.

Make Haste

Nathaniel Vincent

Conversion that is true is present. Delaying to turn is indeed no turning at all. There is a deceitfulness to hide the unwillingness to turn, with a seeming willingness to turn later. The Apostle tells us, "Behold now is the accepted time, behold now is the day of salvation" (2 Cor. 6:2). The note of attention "behold," is used, and again repeated, and the instant of time, "now," is also twice mentioned. God is pleased *now* to call, it concerns us, in point of duty, wisdom, and safety, *now* to turn. When the Holy Ghost says, "To day if ye will hear His voice, harden not your hearts" (Heb. 3:7–8), He plainly signifies that no sinner in the world, when he or she hears the gospel call, should defer conversion so much as one day longer. When the Psalmist turned, "He made haste, and delayed not" (Ps. 119:60), which showed that he turned indeed. To make haste in conversion, is to resemble a condemned man, who quickly takes the offered pardon, because every moment he is in danger of having the sentence pass upon him that will put him to the execution. Genuine conversion resembles a man that makes haste out of a city that is all in flames.

> To make haste in conversion, is to resemble a condemned man, who quickly takes the offered pardon.

Blessed Union

Thomas Watson

We shall so behold Christ as to be made one with Him. What nearer or sweeter thing is there than union? Union is the spring of joy, and the ground of privilege. By virtue of this blessed union with Christ all those rare beauties that the human nature of the Lord Jesus is bespangled with shall be ours. Let us compare two Scriptures: "Father, I will that they also whom thou hast given me, be with me, where I am, that they may behold my glory" (John 17:24), that is, the glory of the human nature; but that is not all, "The glory that thou hast given me, I have given them" (v. 22). Christ does not have His glory only for Himself, but for us; we shall shine by His beams. Here Christ puts His grace upon His spouse, and in heaven He will put His glory upon her. No wonder then the king's daughter is all glorious within, and her clothing of wrought gold (Ps. 45:13). How glorious will the spouse be when she has Christ's jewels upon her! Judge not the saints by what they are, but by what they shall be. "It doth not yet appear what we shall be" (1 John 3:1). What shall we be? We shall be like Him. The spouse of Christ shall not only be made one with Christ, but she shall be made like Christ. In other marriages the spouse changes her condition, but here she changes her complexion. Not that the saints in glory shall receive of Christ's essence. They shall have as much glory, as the human nature is capable of, but though Christ conveys His image, yet not His essence. The sun shining upon a glass leaves a print of its beauty there, and it is hard to distinguish between the glass and the sunbeam. But the glass is not the beam; the sun conveys only its likeness, not its essence.

Who shall also confirm you unto the end, that ye may be blameless in the day of our Lord Jesus Christ.

1 Corinthians 1:8

Union is the spring of joy and the ground of privilege.

Excellent Pattern

Isaac Ambrose

*Be ye therefore follow-
ers of God, as dear
children.*
Ephesians 5:1

If Christ's life is ours, then we shall walk even as He walked. Such is the efficacy of Christ's life, that it will work suitably, and make our life in some sort like His life. The apostle observes that our communion with Christ works on our very lives: "He that abideth in Him walks even as He walked" (1 John 2:6). And to this purpose are those holy admonitions "Walk in love, as Christ also loved us" (Eph. 5:2), and "I have given you an example, that you should do as I have done unto you" (John 13:15), and, "As He which hath called you is holy, so be ye holy in all manner of conversation" (1 Pet. 1:15). Then is Christ's life mine, when my actions refer to Him as my copy, when I transcribe the original of Christ's life, to my life. Alas! What am I better to observe in the life of Christ: His charity to His enemies, His reprehensions of the Scribes and Pharisees, His subordination to His heavenly Father, His ingenuousness towards all, His effusion of love to all the saints, if there be no likeness of all this in my own actions? The life of Jesus is not described to be like a picture in a chamber of pleasure, only for beauty and entertainment of the eye, but like the Egyptian hiero-glyphics whose every feature is a precept, whose images converse with men sense and signification of excellent discourses. To this purpose Paul says, "We all, with open face, beholding as in a glass the glory of the Lord, are changed into the same image from glory to glory" (2 Cor. 3:18). Christ is the image of His Father, and we are the image of Christ. Christ is God's masterpiece, the most ex-cellent device, and work, and frame of heaven that ever was, or ever shall be. Now Christ being the top excellency of all, He is most fit to be the pattern of all excellencies whatsoever, and therefore He is the image, the idea, the pattern, the platform of all our sanctification. Come then, O my soul, look unto Jesus, and look into yourself, yes, look and look, till you are more transformed into His likeness.

To Have Tasted

Robert Dingley

When you have tasted the goodness of God, you will esteem God above all earthly things, preferring celestial before sublunary sweetness. All will be counted dirt and dung to Christ, or as some render it, dog's meat to Christ (Phil. 3:8), that is, coarse and contemptible food after such junkets. You will esteem Christ as the people did David, worth more than ten thousand, or as Naomi did Ruth, better than seven sons. "None but Christ, none but Christ," said Lambert, lifting up such hands as he had and his fingers' ends flaming. A good heart prizes God in Christ above all the world. For as the shining of the sun drowns the stars, so the inconceivable sweetness of Christ turns other sweets (which you admired before) into bitterness. And if you meet with any sweetness, any content in earthly things, it still admires God and cannot but infer, that if the creature be so sweet, how sweet the Creator must be? If the viaticum is so pleasant in my journey, how glorious will the feast be at home? Have you such thoughts of Christ? You indeed have tasted the goodness of God.

My son, eat thou honey, because it is good; and the honeycomb, which is sweet to thy taste.
Proverbs 24:13

> If the viaticum is so pleasant in my journey, how glorious will the feast be at home?

Wanting Fully

Jeremiah Dyke

They that are whole need not a physician; but they that are sick.

Luke 5:31

In the sacrament of the Lord's Supper, we go to Christ Jesus to have Him help us in our wants and necessities. Now Christ Jesus will first have us to know our wants, and be particularly sensible of them, before He will supply them. He counsels the church of Laodicea "to buy of Him gold, raiment, and eye-salve" (Rev. 3:18), but first He convinces her of her wants, of her poverty, nakedness, and blindness, that when she comes to Him in a particular sense of those wants, thus (making her errand to Him) she may have those wants supplied. It was, one would think, a strange question that our Savior put to that man in John 5:6: "Wilt thou be made whole?" Was there any question to be made of it, whether or not that man, who had been sick thirty-eight years, would be willing to be made whole? It is certain that he desired nothing more. When then did Christ ask him that question? He does so to affect him with the sense of his want, and to make him the more sensible of His necessity. So will Christ have His people affected with the sense of their wants . . . The blind man that heard Christ pass by, cried out, "Have mercy on me, O Lord, thou Son of David" (Mark 10:47), and he cried so again. At last, Christ calls to him, "What wilt thou that I should do unto thee?" Did not Christ see that he was blind? Yes, without question, but yet He would first have him particularize his wants, and in what particular it was He would have Him show him mercy, before He would do it. . . . They then that come to Christ to receive any thing from Him, who have a sense of their wants, are most likely to receive what they desire to have from Christ.

What wilt thou that I should do unto thee?

The Life of Joy

James Janeway

So comfortable a Friend is God that those who love Him can rejoice in times when others would be weeping and wringing their hands. God's company is so refreshing, that it turns a prison into a palace; it brings joy and pleasure into a dungeon. Stand forth, O ye suffering saints, and speak your experiences! The world sees your state as sad, that you have good reason to accuse God, and if any have anything to say against the comfortableness of a religious life, it is you. Well then, will you promise, O sinners, to stand to the judgment of the greatest sufferers? We will inquire of them that have been sawn asunder, tormented, and roasted for God's sake. Look into that little *Book of Martyrs,* and you shall find that as uncomfortable as their state was, yet they would not accept deliverance. None of them would open his mouth against this Friend for all this. What say you, O Paul and Silas, now that your backs are raw, and your feet are in the stocks? Their singing speaks significantly enough for them that they were not over sad, and they are so busy in crying Hallelujahs that they cannot attend to give an answer to so sorry a question. What say the martyrs out of the flames? Does not their love burn as hot as ever? Did any of them from Abel to the least that suffered in Christ's cause ever say that God was an uncomfortable Friend? Do not all the children of wisdom, from first to last, justify wisdom, and say, that all her ways are ways of pleasantness, and all her paths, peace? Of those that have God for their Friend and know it, bring me any of them that complain of God. How He comes and cheers them up when all the world is against them! (John 16:33). The holy man in Ps. 23 says that though he should walk through the valley of the shadow of death, he would fear no evil. What, no fear then? . . . This the saint can do, and more too: he can look infinite justice in the face with a cheerful heart, he can hear of hell with joy and thankfulness, and he can think of the Day of Judgment with great delight and comfort.

Behold, God is my salvation; I will trust, and not be afraid: for the LORD JEHOVAH is my strength and my song; he also is become my salvation. Therefore with joy shall ye draw water out of the wells of salvation.
Isaiah 12:2–3

Incomparably Sweet

John Durant

My meditation of him shall be sweet: I will be glad in the LORD.
Psalm 104:34

It has been the design of the enemy of our salvation, Satan, to keep souls from closing with the Author and Captain of our salvation, Jesus Christ. Now for the advancement of this design, he still endeavors (among his other wiles) to raise and nourish in the hearts and minds of poor souls very hard thoughts of Jesus Christ. If Satan cannot keep souls in his slavery by representing himself to them as terrible, he will (if possible) keep them from entering into Christ's service by persuading them that Christ is not merciful. Indeed it is the devil's main design to detain a poor soul away under his own yoke, and to this end he would fain delude the soul, making it believe it is all golden, but if he miss in this, his next method is to dissuade the soul from taking up Christ's yoke, and therefore he endeavors to deceive, by pressing the soul that it is all iron. And if souls desert him, and will serve Christ, they must look (so the Serpent insinuates) to meet with hard employment and a harsh Master, in whose service they must expect many sorrows, but few joys, great work and little wages. But in all this Satan acts like himself, a liar, and speaks of himself, lies. For surely never did a poor soul give up its name (and with that its heart) to the service of Jesus Christ, but found both in the Master and the service incomparable sweetness. It was but a slanderous and slender excuse of him in the parable, which said, he knew Christ was an austere Master. The faithful servants found Christ's bounty fully confuting that slander. Indeed, Christ is a Lion and so knows how to be angry, and tear in pieces such as forget Him, and themselves, and forsake their own mercies, by hearkening to lying vanities, preferring Satan's slavery before His service. But Jesus is also a Lamb (and so fitted to be kind) and He knows how to follow such poor souls with embraces of love, as love themselves by loving Him, and cleaving to Him, and forsaking all things else.

To Love Christ

Thomas Vincent

his Jesus Christ whom Christians love, is the eternal Son of God, the second Person in the glorious Trinity, who in time assumed our human nature, clothed himself with our mortal flesh, lived like a servant in a mean condition, died like a malefactor the cursed death of the cross, and all for our sakes, for our sins, rose again the third day for our justification, ascended up into heaven after forty days, and there is set down at the right hand of the throne of the majesty on high, to make intercession for us, and to make preparation there for our reception into the glorious mansions and eternal habitations, which are in the Father's house. He is called "Jesus," from the Hebrew word *yeshua,* which signifies "to save," because He "saveth His people from their sins" (Matt. 1:21). He is called Christ from the Greek word *christos,* which signifies to anoint, He being anointed by the Father with the Spirit and with power, to be Mediator between God and man, to be the great Prophet, and Priest, and King of the church. This Jesus Christ Christians have not seen with the eye of sense; indeed some Christians in the primitive times, as the apostles, who were of His family, and other disciples who conversed with Him frequently, did see Christ with the eye of sense, but it was in His state of humiliation, when He was here upon the earth, and not in His state of exaltation now in heaven. . . . It is this Jesus Christ whom Christians have not seen, that is the object of their love.

Whom having not seen, ye love; in whom, though now ye see him not, yet believing, ye rejoice with joy unspeakable and full of glory.
1 Peter 1:8

It is this Jesus Christ, whom Christians have not seen, that is the object of their love.

Refreshing Seasons

William Spurstowe

To every thing there is a season, and a time to every purpose under the heaven.
Ecclesiastes 3:1

In making use of the promises, direct the eye of your faith to the wisdom of God, by which the various blessings that are held in them, are dispensed and given to believers in the fittest and best season, and thereby become both the more remarkable, and the more useful. The works of God's providence have a beauty and luster set upon them, from the appointed time and season which He has allotted to them. The light of the day becomes more desirable by the interposition of the night, and the rest and darkness of the night is rendered more grateful by the labors and toils for the day. The former and the latter rain He gives in season (Jer. 5:24), the one to bring forth and cherish the newly sown seed, and the other to ripen and make fruitful the harvest. The summer and winter by an inviolable ordinance He has made to succeed each other, the one to be as a key to open the womb of the earth that it might discharge itself of its many births; the other as a key to shut it, that so it might not languish and grow barren by a perpetual travail. Now if the wisdom of God has to these common mercies wherein His enemies have a share (as well as others) set such appointed times, as may make them more useful and beneficial to His creatures, certainly He will not fail to perform to His people the promises of His free grace in that season and fullness of time, which may best suit their welfare and His glory.

> He will not fail to perform to His people the promises of His free grace in that season and fullness of time.

To Live Suitably

Thomas Gouge

Ye are the light of the world. A city that is set on an hill cannot be hid.
Matthew 5:14

Labor to live suitably to your prayers; it is to no purpose to begin the day with God and to keep the devil company all the day after, to be a saint in the morning and a swine all the day following. Therefore, having prayed against sin, be sure you set a watch against it, avoiding the occasions and temptations to it; for it is impossible to avoid any sin if we shun not the occasions and temptations that promote it. Having prayed for holiness of life, labor to live holily; having prayed for humility, labor to walk humbly; having prayed for sobriety and temperance, labor to live soberly and temperately. Having prayed in the Spirit, and to walk in the flesh, is a contradiction. The whole course of a Christian's life should savor of his or her prayers. He who has all his religion in his prayers has indeed no religion at all. . . . Look back upon your prayers and let the consideration of the manifold weakness and distractions, which have accompanied them, drive you to Christ. As this is one chief end why God suffers corruption to remain in His children, even after their regeneration . . . so it is the use we should make of it. And therefore, as often as you find your heart dead and dull, and your mind distracted with wandering thoughts in prayer, say within yourself, "Lord, what need have I of a Savior! I see Thou mayest condemn me for my best services; therefore with a disclaiming of all my own righteousness as filthy rags, I expect life and salvation freely upon the account of the righteousness of Jesus Christ, and by the merits of His death and passion."

> I expect life and salvation freely upon the account of the righteousness of Jesus.

Altogether Lovely

William Dyer

He is altogether lovely.
Song of Solomon
5:16

Out of the Lion of the Tribe of Judah comes better and sweeter honey than out of Samson's lion. That is the sweetest honey which we suck out of Christ's hive. For the face of none is so comely in a saint's eye, as the face of Christ; and the voice of none is so pleasant in a saint's ear, as the voice of Christ. O Christian! The God whom you serve is so excellent, that no good can be added to Him, and so infinite, that no good can be diminished in Him. He makes happy, and yet is not the less happy; He shows mercy to the full, and yet remains full of mercy; O come eat and drink abundantly! O Beloved! There is no fear of excess here, though one drop of Christ be sweet; the deeper the sweeter. The wine that Christ draws is the best wine that a Christian drinks. The whole book of Canticles is bespangled with the praises of Jesus Christ. The subject matter of this book is a declaration of the mutual intercourse of love and affection between Christ and His church; what spiritual entertainment is given on both sides, with the sweet content they have in each other's beauty. Here you may see the King in His glory, the spouse in her beauty; here you may see Christ giving her sweet promises, adorning her with sundry excellencies, communicating His love, and commending her graces. Here you may see the church even ravished with the consideration and contemplation of Christ's love and beauty; His beauty is taking; His love is ravishing; His voice is pleasing; His goodness is drawing; His manifestations are enrichening; He is the beloved Son; and the Son of love; He is nothing but love to those who are His love.

> **There is no fear of excess here, though one drop of Christ be sweet; the deeper the sweeter.**

Days of Visitation

John Rogers

I t is lamentable to see how precious time is spent by many in sinful courses and exercises. With most it is spent in eager pursuit of the world, the profits, honors, and pleasures thereof, as if they were the necessary things, and end of our being here, when the means of the knowledge of God, and the things that concern our own happiness, lie woefully neglected. Has God after the long night of superstition, ignorance, and idolatry, that our forefathers lay under, caused the day to arise, and the sun of righteousness to shine so long upon us and shall we yet love darkness and not light, be ignorant and grope at noon day? Has God set us up with those precious means of grace and life, and given us our full scope in them, when He has denied them to nations twenty times as great as ourselves? Shall we make slight of them? Oh, how many there are under the tyranny of antichrist that would skip at the crumbs that fall from our tables and would adventure their lives for the scraps and leavings of such things that we cast under our feet! They would and cannot; we may and will not. May we not justly fear, lest God before long snatch His Word from us, and bestow it upon those that will make better use of it? May the Lord awaken the people of this land, to know the day of their visitation, and to understand the things that belong to their peace, before the decree come forth and it be too late.

O Jerusalem, Jerusalem, thou that killest the prophets, and stonest them which are sent unto thee, how often would I have gathered thy children together, even as a hen gathereth her chickens under her wings, and ye would not!
Matthew 23:37

May the Lord awaken the people of this land.

Healing Stripes

Thomas Doolittle

By his stripes we are healed.
1 Peter 2:24

We should admire the wisdom and the grace of God that by the stripes inflicted upon Christ the wounds that sin had made in our souls should be healed. The wisdom of God is wonderful in this, to find out such a way, that the scourging of His Son should be the cure of our souls, and His wounding our healing. And the grace of God is in this to be admired, that when He might have laid the strokes of His revenging justice upon us, He would accept the scourging of His Son for the punishment of our sins, that we might not be scourged forever. We deserved to be broken into pieces with His iron rod, and to be beaten with the rod of His wrath, but we are saved and delivered by the stripes that were laid upon His Son. Our wounds were killing wounds, but the wounds of Christ are healing wounds. Oh what a surgeon is the Son of God that makes a balsam of His sores, to heal and cure ours! What manner of physician is this, that by His own blood fetched from His body, by cruel stripes and blows, makes a potion for diseased sinners, and thereby cures all their maladies! Oh think of this till you do admire the wisdom and grace of God.

> Oh what a surgeon is the Son of God that makes a balsam of His sores to heal and cure ours!

All Things Lawful

Thomas Watson

The lawful use of the world is yours. The gospel does somewhat enlarge our charter. We are not in all things so tied up as the Jews were; there were several sorts of meat that were prohibited them; they might eat of those beasts only that did chew the cud, and part the hoof. They were not allowed to eat the swine, because though it did divide the hoof, yet it did not chew the cud, nor of the hare, because it did chew the cud, yet it did not divide the hoof. But to Christians that live under the gospel, there is not this prohibition. The world is yours, the lawful use of it is yours; every creature being sanctified by the Word of God and prayer is good, and we may eat, asking no question for conscience's sake. The world is a garden; God has given us leave to pick of any flower. It is a paradise, we may eat of any tree that grows in it, but the forbidden, that is, sin; yet even in things lawful beware of excess. We are apt to offend most in lawful things. The world is yours to traffic in, only let them that buy, be as if they bought not (1 Cor. 7:30). Take heed that you do not drive such a trade in the world that you are like to fracture your trading for heaven.

All things are lawful unto me, but all things are not expedient: all things are lawful for me, but I will not be brought under the power of any.
1 Corinthians 6:12

> The world is a garden; God has given us leave to pick of any flower.

Pursue Patience

John Collinges

Wait on the LORD. Be of good courage, and he shall strengthen thine heart. Wait, I say, on the LORD.
Psalm 27:14

Beg of God a waiting frame of spirit. As there is nothing more sinful in itself, nor more tormenting to ourselves in an evil day, than an impatient, hasty spirit, so there is nothing more conducive to our glorifying of God, nor to the quiet of our own spirits, than a silent waiting spirit. This the God of heaven must give, and He gives it to them that ask Him. Beg of God those graces which may dispose you to this patient waiting. I might instance in many habits of grace necessary to bring the soul into this waiting temper, but I will touch only upon five. 1. Beg faith of God, faith in His Word and promise. He that believes does not make haste. The hastiness and impatience of the soul is the result of distrust in God. 2. Hope is another gracious habit which disposes the soul to waiting; we hope for what we see not, for what we see, why do we any longer wait for? 3. Humility is a third; the proud soul thinks much to wait; he looks upon mercy as his due, and thinks that God has wronged him while He withholds it from him; the humble soul believes that it deserves nothing, and is therefore willing upon the least crevice of hope to wait on God. 4. Pray for patience; a passive patience is necessary in order to the bearing of evils. 5. Pray for meekness; a forward spirit is always a hasty spirit, and does not know how to wait.

> There is nothing more conducive to the quiet of our own spirits, than a silent waiting spirit.

Hope's Voice

Thomas Adams

ope is the sweetest friend that ever kept a distressed soul company; she beguiles all the tediousness of the way, and all the miseries of our pilgrimage. . . . She tells the soul such sweet stories of the succeeding joys, what comforts there be in heaven; what peace, what joy, what triumphs, marriage-songs, and hallelujahs, there are in that country, toward which she is traveling; hope goes merrily her way with her present burden. She holds the head while it aches, and gives invisible drink to the thirsty conscience. She brings liberty to them that are in prison, and the sweetest medicine to the sick. Saint Paul calls her an anchor. Let the winds blow, and the storms beat, and the waves swell, yet the anchor stays the ship. She breaks through all difficulties and makes way for the soul to follow. She teaches Abraham to expect fruit from a withered flock, and Joseph, in a dungeon, to look for the sun's and stars' obeisance. She consoles the grieving, as Esdras did the woman, which having lost her son, would have died languishing in the disconsolate fields. "Go thy way into the city to thine husband." (2 Esd. 10:17) Mourn not, wretch, for the loss of some worldly and perishing delight; sit not down and die, though the fruit of your womb be swallowed into the earth, but go home to the city, the city of mercy, to thine husband, even thy husband Jesus Christ; let Him comfort you. This is the voice of hope.

Let Israel hope in the LORD from henceforth and for ever.
Psalm 131:3

> Go home to the city, the city of mercy, to thy husband Jesus Christ; let Him comfort you.

Grief's Dissipation

Peter Sterry

For his anger endureth
but a moment; in his
favour is life: weeping
may endure for a
night, but joy cometh
in the morning.
Psalm 30:5

When Jonah was in the bottom of the sea and belly of the fish, his soul fainting within him, then he remembered the Lord (Jonah 2:7). As pearls are found at the bottom of the sea, so frequently do the beauties of the Lord Jesus disclose themselves to us in the depths of grief, when we are sunk below the waters of this world, and are swallowed up into a spirit of darkness. It is St. James's advice, "Let patience have its perfect work, and it shall make you perfect" (Jas. 1:4). As one element stretched to the utmost passes into another, water into air, air into fire, and as a big cloud swelling dissolves itself upon the earth, so your griefs, if you wait calmly upon them as they swell, and grow, will at length dissolve themselves into God. As snow and frost cherish the seed in the ground, so do biting and binding sorrows both kill the weeds of vanity, and reap the seed of divinity in man. I can no more lack sorrows for my soul than the husbandman can lack winter seasons for his corn fields. As natural melancholy draws the soul deeply into herself, and her divine principles, whence she issues forth again, with the most great and glorious lights, so do sad things work upon a holy spirit sinking her into the depths of the Godhead, out of which she rises renewed to a fresh spring of life and joy.

> **Your griefs, if you wait calmly upon them as they swell and grow, will at length dissolve.**

Meditations

Matthew Lawrence

I f we would flatter ourselves that we have heavenly affections, and yet lack heavenly meditations, we do but deceive our own hearts, and bring ourselves into a fool's paradise. For it is most certain that where our affections are, there will our meditations also be. We cannot keep our thoughts from what we love, and prize dearly: "Where our treasure is, there will our heart be also" (Matt. 6:21). There will our minds be, where it loves, not where it lives. Is our meditation therefore, and contemplation in heaven? It is sweet indeed to contemplate the visible part of the heavens. For, "the heavens declare the glory of God and the firmament sheweth His handy work" (Ps. 19:1). But it is far sweeter to a gracious soul to contemplate the inside. The starry vault is but the pavement of God's house, and the clouds are the dust of His feet. And if there is so much glory without, what is there within? Oh! How sweet is it to a gracious soul, to look into the holy of holies, to take a turn with Christ every day in His banqueting house? For so is heaven called (Song 2:4). And this is the property of a soul espoused to Christ by faith: "The Spirit and the bride say, Come" (Rev. 22:17). And if Christ come not to her as soon as she desires, she will be sure to go to Him, at least, in her serious thoughts, and heavenly meditations. She lays out much of her soul in meditation; the meditation of Christ and heaven, is very sweet (Ps. 104:34). She says of heaven, as David of God's law, "Oh how do I love it, it is my meditation all the day" (Ps. 119:97).

My meditation of him shall be sweet: I will be glad in the LORD.
Psalm 104:34

> If there is so much glory without, what is there within?

Heaven's Paradise

William Bates

To him that overcometh will I give to eat of the tree of life, which is in the midst of the paradise of God.
Revelation 2:7

Heaven is represented to us in the Scripture under the notion of a place of pleasure, and so it is called a paradise. So you shall find our Savior speaking to the thief on the cross that prayed to Him, "Lord, remember me, when thou comest into thy kingdom" (Luke 23:42). Jesus said to him, "Verily, I say unto thee, today shalt thou be with me in paradise" (v. 43). The Apostle Paul tells us that he was caught up into paradise, and heard unspeakable words (2 Cor. 12:4). Now this expression is allegorical, and allusive to that first delicious garden that God prepared to be a seat for innocent humanity. The Garden of Eden was a place that had in it all things that were for the support, comfort, and pleasure of this life; and paradise is a word that signifies a garden of pleasure. Now heaven is represented to us by paradise, a place that was made for delight and joy, and it has this glorious privilege above this earthly paradise, that the earthly paradise was not exempted from the poison of the serpent, that infected man in his head and original, the woeful effect of which we feel to this day. But the paradise above is inaccessible to all evil, a place framed for delight, no thorns or briars there, nothing that can afflict or cause sorrow; no, it is the paradise of God, a paradise in the midst whereof is the Son of God in the tree of life, upon which the saints feed and live forever.

> The paradise above is inaccessible to all evil.

For You

Robert Dingley

hrist tasted gall for you, that you might taste ambrosia for Him. He tasted death for you, that you might taste life for Him, and drink of the heavenly Nepenthe, that ocean of pleasure. He did sweat and faint in His agonies, that He might stay you with flagons, and comfort you with apples. He fasted forty days that you might be feasted to eternity. He wore a crown of thorns, that you may wear a crown of glory. He suffered among base evil doers, that you may be blessed among those sweet companions in heaven. In a word, He endured the sorest pains, that you may enjoy the greatest pleasures. O therefore do not deceive His expectation, but let Him see the travail of His soul, and be satisfied. It is sad when Christ shall complain, as in Isa. 49:4: "Then I said, I have labored in vain, I have spent my strength for nought, and in vain: yet surely my judgment is with the LORD, and my work with my God." O make not His death to be of no effect to you; forbear to fetch any more sighs from that heart that is so full of love to you, and now at length be persuaded to give yourselves to Christ, to taste and see how good the Lord is.

Greater love hath no man than this, that a man lay down his life for his friends.
John 15:13

He suffered among base evil doers that you may be blessed among sweet companions.

Heaven and Earth

George Swinnock

*He will regard the
prayer of the desti-
tute, and not despise
their prayer.*
Psalm 102:17

The infinite and glorious God, though He is so high that He humbled himself to behold things in heaven, and so holy that "the heavens are unclean in His sight" (Job 15:15), is yet so gracious that He condescends to, and converses with, poor sinful dust and ashes. Among all those ways which He has appointed the children of men to walk with Him in, prayer is one of the fairest and pleasantest. In this duty, the children of God whisper Him in the ear, open their minds, and unbosom themselves to Him, as His intimate friends and favorites. He has been pleased to command it, not only out of His dominion over them, and for His own glory—"He that offereth praise glorifieth me" (Ps. 50:23)—but also out of His compassion to them, and for their good, that by prayers (as some far distant do by letters) there might be a constant and uninterrupted communication and correspondence between heaven and earth.

He has appointed
the children of
men to walk with
Him.

For the Cross

Thomas Vincent

he love of Christ is useful to fit you for the cross, and the greatest sufferings which you may be called to for the sake of Christ. If you have great love to Christ, you will be ready to suffer for Christ with patience and with cheerfulness. The heaviest cross will seem light, disgrace and shame will be accounted honor, losses will be esteemed gains, and pains, pleasures, or at least privileges. Prisons will seem like palaces, and death will be accounted life. O how have some run to the stake, and embraced the flames of fire kindled to burn them, when they have felt the fire of love to Christ burning strongly within them! Thus this love is useful in life. The love of Christ is also useful at death. Its strength will put a beauty upon the aspect of death which seems so grim and terrible to most. If you have much love to Christ, you will look upon death as Christ's messenger, sent for you to bring you out of the dark prison of the world and body, and to convey you into the mansions of glory, where your dear Lord is, and you will not be unwilling to leave the world that you may live with Christ.

And he that taketh not his cross, and followeth after me, is not worthy of me.
Matthew 10:38

> This love is useful in life. The love of Christ is also useful at death.

Labor for Hope

Samuel Doolittle

And thou shalt be secure, because there is hope; yes, thou shalt dig about thee, and thou shalt take thy rest in safety.

Job 11:18

That death is certain and unavoidable, near at hand and will quickly come, I suppose you take for granted. You are dying verily, my friends, you are dying men, and women; the time is coming, and how quickly will it be here? When you must breathe your last, when neither the tears of relations, the pity of friends, the skill of physicians, nor any virtue there is in medicine can prolong life or keep off death, lo, this is your motto: "Dust you are and to the dust shall you return" (Gen. 3:19). And should you not labor to be such persons while you live that you may have hope in your death? To be a stranger upon earth is your character; to get a hope of an abiding city should be your endeavor. And this cannot be had without gospel-righteousness. It is not a superficial sorrow, and slight repentance for your past sins; a few good thoughts or wishes, a few cold and lifeless prayers in the church or closet. It is not an escaping of the gross pollutions of the flesh or doing some acts of charity, and justice, sobriety, and temperance that will be a sufficient ground to hope in a dying hour. It is nothing short of a thorough, universal change of heart and life; nothing short of a supernatural principle in the heart, exerting itself in suitable actions in the life, will warrant and legitimate your hope, and oh how speedily, and diligently should everyone labor after it!

> To be a stranger upon earth is your character; to get a hope of an abiding city should be your endeavor.

Taste and See

Robert Dingley

If so be ye have tasted that the Lord is gracious.
1 Peter 2:3

A saint tastes God, and lives upon God in prayer. By this he or she draws out of the well of salvation, which is deep, but very sweet. David says that God is nigh, and Paul, "He is rich to all that call upon Him" (Rom. 10:12). And Christ says, "Your heavenly Father will give good things to them that ask Him" (Matt. 7:11), that is, by and in prayer, they shall taste of His goodness. For making their requests known to Him, the very peace of God which passeth understanding, shall keep their hearts and minds through Christ Jesus (Phil. 4:6–7). I here appeal to believers. Have you not known the time that you have touched the hem of Christ's garment, and tasted of the loves of heaven in prayer? Have you not known the holy enlargement of heart, when you have wrestled with God? Have you not seen heaven cleft, and Christ sitting at God's right hand? There is no believer but frequently tastes the goodness of God in and by prayer, for God says not, "Seek me in vain."

> Have you not known the time that you have touched the hem of Christ's garment?

Kept Afloat

William Spurstowe

And I will wait upon the LORD, that hideth his face from the house of Jacob, and I will look for him.
Isaiah 8:17

Be much in the use and application of promises, even though we do not find such visible effects either of grace or comfort issuing from them, as we expect or desire. Elijah when he went up to the top of Mount Carmel, and fell upon his face before the Lord to pray for rain, sent his servant seven times to look towards the sea, before he saw so much as the appearance of a cloud of an hand-breadth, yet he was not discouraged (Kgs. 18:43). So believers, though they have been much in musing upon the promises in their thoughts, frequent in pleading and spreading them before the Lord in prayer, and after all their looking toward heaven, say as the servant of Elijah when he looked towards the sea, "There is nothing." Yet must they not cast away their confidence in them, or neglect the daily use of them, because the promise, and the word that goes from God's mouth, shall not return to Him void, but shall accomplish that which He pleases, and it shall prosper in the thing whereunto He sent it (Isa. 55:11). The manner of the fulfilling of it may be various, but the performance of it is most certain. The blessing of the promise descends sometimes like rain in visible showers, producing the sensible effects of joy, and peace in the soul. Sometimes it falls like dew in a silent and imperceptible way, without making any discernable alteration in the heart of a believer. The virtue which it puts forth is real, but yet hidden and secret. As gold put and boiled in broth helps to make it strengthening and cordial, which if weighed afterwards in the scale, is found to lose little or nothing of its former weight, or to suffer any diminution of its substance, so the promise when much meditated on, when frequently applied by a believer to his present straits, yields a secret influence and support, though to his apprehension no virtue or quickening does appear to have issued from it. Then it is as the cork to the net to keep it floating in a sea of difficulties, when every moment we look for nothing else but a dismal and irrecoverable perishing amidst those many rolling waves and billows that pass over us.

Yours Forever

John Dod and Robert Cleaver

Is God the same forever and that in His dealings to His children? And has He before used His power for their defense, His wisdom for their direction, and His mercy for their comfort? Then He will do the same still to us. Therefore when any of His children have been brought into great misery, and that for their sins, as Manasseh was in most hard case for his great wickedness, yet when he repented, and took himself to prayer, we see that God heard him, and helped him both out of his sins and misery (2 Chron. 33:12–13). Did He deal so with him? Then He being Jehovah, the same forever without any change, He must deliver us also when we call upon Him. But are we sure to be delivered out of this trouble, and to be set out of this debt, or temptation, if we call upon God? This we are sure of, that if we cry to God, He will deliver us from our sin and from the punishment of it; or if the cross hangs still upon us, He will sweeten it with some spiritual comfort, and strengthen us, that we shall be able to endure it. And so recompense it with heavenly grace, that we shall gain more in the spirit than we lose in the flesh. But unless that we believe that God is Jehovah and immutable, all the histories of the Scriptures are made unprofitable to us; then we have no use nor comfort of those things which we hear and read, as how God blessed Abraham, and delivered Jacob, and did many wonderful things for His people in former times. But if we hold this firmly, that God is the same forever, this is sure, that whatsoever good thing He did for them, He will do the like for us, if we use the same means. So also if anyone have found in himself that at such a time I was in great troubles and terror, and then I prayed to God, and I know that He heard my prayer, and helped me, are you certain that God did hear you when you cried heretofore? Then you may be far more sure of this, that if you cry again, He will hear you again, else He should not be Jehovah. If He has been yours once, He is yours still, and will be yours forever.

Jesus Christ the same yesterday, and today, and for ever.
Hebrews 13:8

Hate Covetousness

William Gouge

Incline my heart unto thy testimonies, and not to covetousness.
Psalm 119:36

Covetousness is like a hell that can never be satisfied. For by abundance this desire is increased; the more it is filled, the less it is satisfied. Hereof our Lord advises to take heed and beware. For as it is an insatiable sin, so also it is a devouring sin. As Pharaoh's lean cows devoured the fat ones, so covetousness devours all of God's blessings and graces; it chokes the Word, and makes hearers thereof unfruitful. It so entangles men with the things of this world, as it makes it easier for a camel to go through the eye of a needle, than for a rich man to enter the kingdom of God. No sin more bewitches a man, drawing his heart from God the only true ground of confidence, and making him trust in vanity, which is plain idolatry. Yea, it is truly styled "the root of all evil" (1 Tim. 6:10). For it so blinds man's mind, and hardens his heart, as he makes conscience of no sin; no not of denying God, and renouncing true religion; nor of perjury, and blasphemy; nor of profaning and breaking the Sabbath; nor of rebelling against superiors, and neglect of inferiors; nor of murder or any other unkindness, nor of oppression, deceit, falsehood, or any other evil.

> As Pharaoh's lean cows devoured the fat ones, so covetousness devours all of God's blessings.

Conform to Christ

Jeremiah Burroughs

That which God aims at in the afflictions of His people is to make them conformable to Christ, their Head, that they may enter into their glory as Christ did into His. "Ought not Christ to have suffered these things, and to enter into His glory?" (Luke 24:26). We read of Paul in Phil. 3:10 that he earnestly desired to be a partaker of the fellowship of Christ's sufferings and to be conformable to His death. God will have conformity to the death of His Son. We read of Godfrey of Bullein, that he would not be crowned in Jerusalem with a crown of gold where Christ was crowned with a crown of thorns; because he would not have such a great disproportion between him and Christ. It is reported of Origen that when Alexander Severus, the emperor, sent for him and he appeared to be meanly clothed, there were diverse costly garments prepared for him. They were sent to him, but he refused them. When he came near to Rome, there was a mule and a chariot sent for him, that he might choose which liked him best, but he refused them also. He would not go in pomp to the emperor, saying that he was less than his Master Christ of whom he never read that He rode more than once.

Forasmuch then as the children are partakers of flesh and blood, he also himself likewise took part of the same; that through death he might destroy him that had the power of death, that is, the devil.

Hebrews 2:14

He would not have such a great disproportion between him and Christ.

The Triune God

Henry Scudder

And he that searcheth the hearts knoweth what is the mind of the Spirit, because he maketh intercession for the saints according to the will of God.
Romans 8:27

Everyone that would worship God aright must first learn to know Him to be the one only true God, distinguished into Father, Son, and Holy Ghost. However, much caution must be used so as not to probe into this mystery of mysteries to understand above what Scripture has revealed. It is an object of faith to be believed, and not able to be fully comprehended by reason. In considering the distinction of the three persons, beware of two extremes: First, we must not conceive that there is an essential difference between them, as if all three did not have the same nature. Secondly, we must not think that there is only an imaginary distinction. . . . In the same way as He exists He must be worshipped according to the direction of our Savior. Stephen directed his prayer to Christ upon beholding Christ Jesus standing at the right hand of God; it was a special and extraordinary occasion. This argues that it is not unlawful to direct prayer to the second or third person on special cause, but ordinarily this rule and order in worshipping God must be observed. First, we must direct prayer unto the Father of lights, the Giver of every good and perfect gift. Secondly, we must offer up prayer and praise by Christ Jesus, who offers up incense with the prayers of all saints, by whom we have access to the throne of grace, to find grace and help in time of need. Thirdly, we must use all means to obtain the Holy Spirit of grace and supplication. We must pray for Him to work, and hear the gospel (the ministry of the Spirit) preached, taking heed that we do not grieve or quench Him by any evil conversation. Let us get a holy acquaintance with Him, that He may make hearty requests for us. Prayers cannot be sweet incense if they are not mingled and anointed with holy oil, which is the anointing of the Spirit. He teaches all things, as John speaks (1 John 2:27), and especially He must teach us to pray aright. . . . I can assure whoever prays in this manner that he will always be able to offer up sighs and desires that please God, and prevail with Him.

Ill Requital

Isaac Ambrose

hrist is our friend, and in that respect He loves us, and bears us in His heart. Shall we not have Him in ours? Surely this is ill requital; this is a great contradiction to the law of friendship. But Christ is our Lord as well as friend, and if the Lord of glory can stoop so low as to set His heart on sinful dust, one would think we should easily be persuaded to set our hearts on Jesus Christ. Do you not perceive that the heart of Christ is set upon you? And that He is still minding you with tender love, even when you forget both yourselves and Him? Do you not find Him following you with daily mercies, moving on your souls, providing for your bodies, and preserving both? Does He not continually bear you in His arms of love, and promise that all shall work together for your good (Rom. 8:28)? Does He not give His angels charge over you, and suit all His dealings to your greatest advantage? And can you find it in your hearts to cast Him away? Can you forget the Lord who never forgets you?

Can a woman forget her sucking child, that she should not have compassion on the son of her womb? yes, they may forget, yet will I not forget thee.
Isaiah 49:15

> He is still minding you with tender love, even when you forget both yourselves and Him.

To Never Depart

Nathaniel Vincent

And I will make an ev-erlasting covenant with them, that I will not turn away from them, to do them good; but I will put my fear in their hearts, that they shall not depart from me.
Jeremiah 32:40

Conversion is true and lasting. No one ever totally and finally turned away from God, who was once turned to Him. Christ the Mediator has made such a lasting peace between God and those who believe. The enmity between Jews and Gentiles, and between them both and God, is slain by the cross of Christ. Upon our turning and believing, the Lord enters into a covenant that He will never break. As Christ by His death made atonement, and appeased His Father's displeasure, so His crucifixion is effectual to destroy the enmity that was naturally in us against God. Our flesh and its lusts are crucified: "They that are Christ's have crucified the flesh with the affections and lusts" (Gal. 5:24); and, "Knowing this, that our old man is crucified with Him, that the body of sin might be destroyed, that henceforth we should not serve sin" (Rom. 6:6). True converts shall persevere, for Christ has prayed that they may be established, kept from the evil of the world, and be with Him where He is, and behold (which does imply the enjoyment of) His glory (John 17:15, 24). Persevering grace is promised in the covenant of grace. God Himself engages for those who turn to Him in truth, that He will not suffer them to fall away and perish.

> God Himself engages for those who turn to Him in truth.

Christ's Kingship

Henry Scudder

t is by virtue of Christ's exaltation and dominion that, triumphing over His enemies, He ascended up on high, led captivity captive, and gave gifts to men, His officers which under Him would erect and perfect His kingdom of grace here upon earth. He gave some to be apostles, some evangelists, and some pastors and teachers, for the perfecting of the saints, for the work of the ministry, and for the edifying of the body of Christ, that we all may come into the unity of the faith. It is also that we may have knowledge of the Son of God. Christ Jesus being thus advanced, it belongs unto Him to reign as King until He has perfected the salvation of all the elect, put all His enemies under His feet, and delivered up this kingdom to God the Father. This kingdom of Christ differs from all other kingdoms, for though it is in the world, and above all the kingdoms of the world, yet it is not of the world; it is a spiritual and heavenly kingdom, bearing rule in and over the souls and consciences of men. It is directly opposite to the kingdom of darkness and of the devil, the prince of this world; for by His agents, through His ordinances, and by the power of His Spirit He puts down strongholds, casting down imaginations and every high thing that exalts itself against the knowledge of God. He brings into captivity every thought to His obedience, having readiness to avenge all disobedience when the obedience of His own subjects shall be fulfilled. This kingdom of Christ is an everlasting kingdom with no end to subjects or King. At the last day all that were subject unto Him in this world in the kingdom of grace shall with a holy and glorious subjection reign with Him in the world to come, in the kingdom of glory for evermore.

Wherefore God also hath highly exalted him, and given him a name which is above every name: That at the name of Jesus every knee should bow, of things in heaven, and things in earth, and things under the earth; And that every tongue should confess that Jesus Christ is Lord, to the glory of God the Father.
Philippians 2:9–11

Above All Things

John Rogers

And thou shalt love the LORD thy God with all thine heart, and with all thy soul, and with all thy might.

Deuteronomy 6:5

The love of God is a most precious and honorable esteeming and affecting of Him, with a chief delight in Him above all things. God is worthy to be loved immeasurably, because He is infinitely and immeasurably holy, pure, perfect, and good in Himself, and also because He has been immeasurably good to us, especially in giving His Son to the death for us. . . . We must love Him simply and absolutely for Himself and all other things for Him, in, and under Him. We must not love Him as we love other things, but above all other things in the world. . . . If we do not love Him above all other things, He is not our God.

> God is worthy to be loved immeasurably, because He is infinitely and immeasurably holy.

A Wonderful Sight

Jeremiah Burroughs

Christ shall in a wonderful manner come to judge the world, and shall come to be admired indeed. . . . Those that do believe in Christ see Him to be wonderful. Now they do admire at Him, but when He shall come again in glory at the great day, then He shall appear so wonderful, as they shall all stand admiring, and saying, "Well we indeed heard that our blessed Savior was the wonder of the world, and we saw so much as made us admire at His glory, but we never thought that we had such a glorious Savior, as now we see we have." Wonderful and glorious is Jesus Christ now, but when He shall come with His thousand thousands of angels, and when there shall be such a wonderful change in the world, the elements melt with fervent heat, and the heavens depart like a scroll, and the heavens and earth shaken, and all the princes and monarchs in the world, and all the children of men appearing before Him: Oh wonderful then shall He be in His attendance, and in His own person. Wonderful then shall He be in the manner of His proceedings, in bringing forth all the books of God's forbearance, and the books of conscience, and the book of the word to proceed with humans and angels for their eternal estate; in this Christ will appear then to be wonderful.

When he shall come to be glorified in his saints, and to be admired in all them that believe.
2 Thessalonians 1:10

> We never thought that we had such a glorious Savior, as now we see we have.

Only a Shadow

Robert Dingley

Lord, all my desire is before thee; and my groaning is not hid from thee.
Psalm 38:9

Nothing but God in Christ can satisfy the heart. To feed upon husks, and yet not have a belly-full of them, was the prodigal's misery. The world is but husks, hollow and deceitful food; or a feeding upon wind. With the dog in the fable, we catch at shadows; and embrace with Ixion a cloud instead of Juno. We dream that we eat, and when we awake, we find ourselves empty. This world is but the dream of a shadow; and the good things thereof are rather appearances than realities. The round world cannot fill the triangular heart; some nooks and corners will be empty, and there is restlessness in the soul after more. Whence arise distractions of heart, roving after variety, sparks of endless thoughts, and those secret flowings and ebbs, and tempests and estuations of the sea of corruption in the heart of man, because he cannot find a fullness and satisfaction in sublunaries. With Noah's dove, he sees no footing but on the Ark, Christ Jesus. Solomon says, "The eye is not satisfied with seeing, nor the ear with hearing" (Eccl. 1:8). Isaiah says, "Why do ye bestow your labor for that which satisfies not?" (Isa. 55:2). O but there is fullness in Christ, His flesh is meat indeed; and He will satisfy the longing soul with goodness. One compares this world to a king's palace; children and country people are taken with the pictures and fine hangings, but the wise and grave statesmen do pass by them, for their business is with the king. So most men stay in the out-rooms and low things of the world, while believers pass on, and have communion with the King of kings.

He will satisfy the longing soul with goodness.

Comfort in Prayer

Henry Scudder

Directing prayers to the Father, in the name of the Son, through the Holy Ghost, can remove the greatest discouragements that any Christian ever meets with when they pray. Neither God's majestic infinite justice, the greatness of the multitude of sins, the sense of unworthiness and insufficiency to think a good thought, nor the feeling that many times we do not know what nor how to pray can dishearten us, if we consider that we pray to God, who is God the Father, Son, and Holy Ghost. Also, we can be heartened that we may pray in this order, namely, to the Father of Christ who is our Father, in the name of Jesus Christ who has satisfied His Father for all our sins and daily makes intercession for us, and in the Spirit who helps our infirmities and makes requests for us, though it is sometimes with sighs and groans which are not distinctly uttered. These marks show that there is life and spirit in our prayers, and God will accept them. He knows the meaning of His Spirit, and will accept the work of His Spirit in us through Christ, though we have many imperfections.

Blessed be God, even the Father of our Lord Jesus Christ, the Father of mercies, and the God of all comfort; Who comforteth us in all our tribulation, that we may be able to comfort them which are in any trouble, by the comfort wherewith we ourselves are comforted of God.
2 Corinthians 1:3–4

> He knows the meaning of His Spirit, and will accept the work of His Spirit in us.

To Leave All

William Greenhill

If any man come to me, and hate not his father, and mother, and wife, and children, and brethren, and sisters, yes, and his own life also, he cannot be my disciple.

Luke 14:26

A sound heart may be known by its willingness to part with anything for the Lord's sake. A sound heart says, "What good will these things do me, if I lose my integrity, if I lose my sincerity, if I lose my fitness to do God service by defiling myself? What shall I get?" The young man comes to Christ and says, "Good Master, what shall I do to inherit eternal life?" Christ answers, "keep the commandments." "Why, all these things have I kept from my youth up." Christ says, "Go and sell all that thou hast and give to the poor, and come and follow me, and thou shalt have treasure in heaven" (Matt. 19:16–21). One would think that this promise, and treasure, would be enough for him, but he had rotten principles in him; he had the world in him, and his heart was for the world and nothing for God. Simon Magus went further than this man did; he was a professor, and had a relation to the church, but he brought out his bags of gold and silver, and would give them to the apostles, that he might have the power they had, to give the Holy Ghost. But Peter says, "Your heart is not right; therefore pray if it be possible that the thoughts of your heart may be forgiven you" (Acts 8:22). But a gracious heart will part with all. Paul says, "I account all things loss and dung" (Phil. 3:8), that is, all my privileges, all my learning, all that ever I have I account it loss for the excellency of the knowledge of Jesus Christ. As the disciples said, "We have left all to follow thee" (Mark 10:28) Galeatius left all for Christ's sake, and went to Geneva that he might enjoy the gospel. The martyrs left their lives (what is dearer than a man's life?). Yet they were ready to let go of their lives, rather than let go of their soundness.

> A gracious heart will part with all. Paul says, "I account all things loss and dung."

Unseen Love

Thomas Watson

When God hides His face from His child, His heart may be towards Him, as Joseph, when he spoke roughly to his brethren, and made them believe he would take them for spies; still his heart was towards them, and he was as full of love as ever he could hold. He was fain to go aside and weep. So God is full of love to His children, even when He seems to look strange at them. And as Moses' mother, when she put her child into the ark of bulrushes, and went away from it, yet still her eye was towards it; the babe wept, and the mother wept too. So God when He goes aside, as if He had forsaken His children, yet He is full of sympathy, and love towards them; God may change His countenance, but not His heart. It is one thing for God to desert, another to disinherit: "How shall I give thee up, O Ephraim?" (Hos. 8:11). This is a metaphor taken from a father going to disinherit his son, and while he is going to set his hand to the deed, his bowels begin to melt, and to yearn over him. Though he is a prodigal child, yet he is a child. So God says, "How shall I give thee up? Though Ephraim hath been a rebellious son, yet he is a son, I will not disinherit him." God's heart may be full of love, when there is a veil upon His face. The Lord may change His dispensation towards His children, but not His disposition. So that the believer may say, I am adopted, and let God do what He will with me, let Him take the rod, or the staff, it is all one, for He loves me.

For the LORD thy God is a merciful God; he will not forsake thee, neither destroy thee, nor forget the covenant of thy fathers which he sware unto them.
Deuteronomy 4:31

> So God says, "How shall I give thee up?"

Secret Mourners

Richard Alleine

I beheld the transgressors, and was grieved; because they kept not thy word.
Psalm 119:158

The churches' special complaints are of the churches' sins, of their own sins; they cast the first stone at themselves. Though we are—not Ishmael or Edom, or the Philistines—but the Israel of God, we are as an unclean thing. It is grievous to God's people to see and hear of the sins of others: "I was grieved because of the transgressors" (Ps. 119:158). That the uncircumcised among us, the open enemies of the gospel are so wicked, should be a grievous thing to us. The idolatries and adulteries, the drunkenness and shameful spewing, those floods of filthiness that overflow among such, should be a grief of heart to all the saints. It is not a thing to be made so light of, as it is by us, that there is such a vile generation risen up among us, even as if hell itself were broken loose to affront the God of heaven, to defile His holy name, and to disgrace the throne of His glory: this should go near the hearts of all that love Christ and the holiness of the gospel. And there is doubtless a great fault among us, and it is our great sin that we do not more lay it to heart. We tell stories one to another of the wickedness that is among us, but we do but tell it as matter of news; who among us are mourners in secret for all these abominations? If men's hatred of godliness, and the persecutions that they raise against it, do reach even to us, and touch ourselves in our own particulars, as far forth as we feel their rage to light upon ourselves, in our own persons or estates, so far forth we are apt enough to complain against them; but whilst we can escape, and sleep in a whole skin, all is but lightly passed over. This is our great sin, and a great argument that our hearts are not so much concerned for God, or religion, as for our own interest; 'tis what we ourselves suffer, not what religion suffers, that goes so near us.

> **Who among us are mourners in secret for all these abominations?**

Mutual Duties

Thomas Gouge

A mutual duty between spouses is the provident care of one another's souls. If a believing husband, or wife, is married to an unbeliever, they ought to use all the means they can to win the other. And if either of you shall be a means of the conversion of the other, how entirely will it knit your affections one to another. If both husband and wife are in the state of grace, they should be watchful one over the other, as to prevent sin in one another, so to redress it the best way they can when either of them are fallen into sin, by seasonable admonition, yes, and correction also. Here the husband and wife should more respect the mutual good of one another, than fear the giving of offense. And it is likewise a special duty incumbent upon husband and wife to help the growth of grace in each other, as by a frequent conferring together of good things, especially of what they hear in the public ministry of the Word, so likewise in constant performing of family duties, especially prayer.

Likewise, ye husbands, dwell with them according to knowledge, giving honour unto the wife, as unto the weaker vessel, and as being heirs together of the grace of life; that your prayers be not hindered.
1 Peter 3:7

Be watchful one over the other.

Supplied Wants

Thomas Manton

Your Father which is in heaven knoweth you have need of these things.

Matthew 6:12

A father will not let his child starve—certainly none so fatherly as God. You do not have such a Father as is ignorant or regardless of your condition; He takes an exact notice of all your wants and pressures. It is notable to observe how God condescends to express the particular notice that He takes of the saints: "Behold, I have graven thee upon the palms of my hands" (Isa. 49:16). As we tie things about our hands, that we may remember such a work and business; so God does, as it were, put a print and mark upon His hands, to speak after the manner of men. Nay, "The hairs of their heads are numbered" (Matt. 10:30). God has a particular notice of their necessities; and Jesus Christ is His remembrancer, one that ever appears before Him to represent their wants (Heb. 9:24). As the high priest in the law was to go in with the names of the tribes upon his breast and shoulder when He did minister before God, this is a type of how much we are in the heart of Christ, ever presenting Himself before the Lord on the behalf of such and such a believer.

> He takes an exact notice of all your wants and pressures.

Two Gardens

Thomas Doolittle

The heart of man cannot conceive, and the tongues of men and angels cannot express what Christ did endure in the garden. It is observed in the Scripture that Christ began His sufferings in a garden, and when He died He was buried in a garden (John 19:41). Now it is not without some mystery why Christ did choose the garden to suffer so much in. It was in the garden of paradise that our first parents did sin, and brought the wrath of God upon themselves and all their posterity, and there made themselves and all mankind obnoxious to the curse of the law and the pains of hell forever. There they were undone and became sinful and miserable. Therefore Christ would begin His last sufferings in a garden. In a garden man deserved the wrath of God, and in a garden Christ endured the wrath of God. In a garden man did sin, and when Christ came to satisfy for our sin, He suffered in a garden. Where the disease began, there the cure was provided. . . . Our first parents lost the image of God, and their righteousness in the garden, and when Christ comes to restore His image in us, and to bring in a righteousness in which we may be clothed, He suffers in the garden. The first Adam after he had sinned, stood trembling in the garden; and the second Adam taking upon Him our sin, was afraid and sorely amazed in the garden. The first Adam heard his sentence of condemnation in the garden, and the second Adam that we might have an absolution, suffered in the garden. The enmity between the seed of the woman and the seed of the serpent first began in the garden; there the serpent did bruise his heel, and there the seed of the woman did break the serpent's head. In the garden were the first promises of a Savior made, and when the Savior comes to recover lost souls, He betakes Himself unto the garden. Here is matter of meditation for you when you go into your gardens, to think that there man sinned, and there the Lord of glory suffered; there we fell, and there we were recovered.

And they heard the voice of the LORD God walking in the garden in the cool of the day: and Adam and his wife hid themselves from the presence of the LORD God amongst the trees of the garden.
Genesis 3:8

The Soul's Plague

Ralph Robinson

My son, if sinners entice thee, consent thou not.
Proverbs 1:10

Watch against sin as you watch against sickness. How cautious are many of their bodily health. They will eat and drink nothing that may prejudice their well-being. If they know anything that will disturb the quiet of their bodies, they will not meddle with it, though their affliction be never so much inclined to it. And why will you not be as cautious of sin? Take heed and remember that swearing is a sickness, lying is a disease; pride is a sickness, and so on. So avoid all occasions of sin, and all temptations to it. Pray against it, and watch against it. Sin is a sickness that will keep you out of heaven; it is a sickness that will provoke God to hate you. Keep sin out of your family. Let not liars, swearers, and drunkards, lodge a night under your roof (Ps. 101:7). No sickness is so catching as sin is. Everyone has the root of it, and an inclination to it in their hearts. Preserve your children from this sickness. It is worse than the small pox, worse than the plague. Other diseases will kill the bodies of your children, but sin will kill both body and soul. Therefore, keep watch and ward over your hearts and over your families that sin may not enter them, nor that any of your children may go where this catching sickness is.

> No sickness is so catching as sin is. Everyone has the root of it.

Prefer God's Glory

William Bates

All things are so wisely ordered, that God shall be glorified in them. It is the noblest disposition of a Christian to prefer the advancement of God's glory before all the comforts of this life, and life itself. Our blessed Savior in the forethoughts of His suffering was in distress and perturbation of mind, like the darkening of the sky before a great shower. But the short conflict of nature was soon at an end; He willingly gave himself up to be a sacrifice to the divine honor, and said, "Father, glorify thy name" (John 12:28). Moses and Paul, whose admirable zeal had only a parallel between them in the same degree of holy heat, desired the salvation of the Jews before their own, if God might be more glorified by it. This is the first petition in order and dignity, in that complete form of prayer composed by our Savior, as the rule of all our desires, "Thy name be hallowed and glorified in us, and by us." . . . If we were called to martyrdom for His truth, and our lives should bleed forth, as sacrifices on the altar, or our bodies be consumed as incense on the censer, it were an unjust and ungrateful complaint, to express passionate reluctance against His providence. If there were no other consequences of our present sufferings, but the glorifying of God, we should be content. That is the worthiest end which He proposes to Himself, and will accomplish: His divine excellencies will be illustrated by the wickedness of men, that at present obscures the glory of His government; His wisdom, power, holiness, mercy and justice will be acknowledged, admired and magnified at last.

All things work together for good.
Romans 8:28

> If there were no consequences of our sufferings, but the glorifying of God, we should be content.

Rich Comforts

George Swinnock

Oh, what a privilege you enjoy in having freedom of access to the throne of grace! The Persian kings enacted a rule upon pain of death that no one should come uncalled, but the gates of heaven are always open. You have liberty, night and day, of presenting your petitions in the name of Christ to the King of the whole earth, and you need not fear a chiding for your presumption. . . . If you are in doubts about your spiritual state and about your title to the inheritance of the saints in light, you may by prayer go to Him who is "marvelous in counsel" and have His advice for nothing. If any disease appears in your soul, which you fear may endanger its life or hinder its peace and health, you may by prayer knock up the true Physician at midnight, and prevail with Him to hasten to your help and cure. If you are surrounded with many and bloody enemies and know not what to do or where to go, you may by prayer send post to heaven, and you need not fear, for Christ will meet the messenger half-way, and come timely to your rescue. If you are bound with the bond of iniquity, and like Peter, watched narrowly night and day; though you are encompassed around with the black guard of hell so you cannot escape, yet "prayer without ceasing" would knock off your chains, break open the prison doors, and, in spite of all the legions of devils that kept you, set you at liberty. If you are overwhelmed with sorrow, like the Psalmist, this sighing into God's ears by prayer will ease your heart. When the glass of your soul is so full of those strong spirits, fear and grief, that it threatens to burst, you may give it vent by prayer to God, and there will be no danger. While you are in this valley of tears, you are encompassed with enemies and have many and urgent necessities, doubts, and dangers; but prayer will go before you like it did Moses. Engage Him on your side that will overcome them all and guide you all the way through the wilderness of this world to the very borders of Canaan and never leave you until you come to enter into the place of praise.

Honey from Christ

John Owen

he Father loves us, and "chose us before the foundation of the world," but in the pursuit of that love, He "blesseth us with all spiritual blessings in heavenly places in Christ" (Eph. 1:3–4). From His love, He sheds or pours out the Holy Spirit richly upon us, through Jesus Christ our Savior (Titus 3:6). In the pouring out of His love, not one drop falls beside the Lord Christ. The holy anointing oil was all poured on the head of Aaron (Ps. 133:2), and thence went down to the skirts of his clothing. Love is first poured out on Christ; and from Him it drops as the dew of Herman upon the souls of His saints. The Father will have Him to have "in all things the pre-eminence" (Col. 1:18); "it pleased Him that in Him all fullness should dwell" (v. 19); that "of His fullness we might receive, and grace for grace" (John 1:16). Though the love of the Father's purpose and good pleasure has its rise and foundation in His mere grace and will, yet the design of its accomplishment is only in Christ. All the fruits of it are first given to Him; and it is in Him only that they are dispensed to us. So that though the saints may, nay, do, see an infinite ocean of love unto them in the bosom of the Father, yet they are not to look for one drop from Him but what comes through Christ. He is the only means of communication. Love in the Father is like honey in the flower—it must be in the comb before it is fit for our use. Christ must extract and prepare this honey for us. He draws this water from the fountain, and we from the wells of salvation that are in Him.

If the LORD delight in us, then he will bring us into this land, and give it us; a land which floweth with milk and honey.
Numbers 14:8

> Love is first poured out on Christ; and from Him it drops upon His saints.

Self-Inflicted Harm

John Collinges

And be ye kind one to another, tenderhearted, forgiving one another, even as God for Christ's sake hath forgiven you.

Ephesians 4:32

If we would keep ourselves from Satan's assaults to harm us, we must make it our business to learn in all estates to be content, and to possess ourselves with patience, and arm ourselves against all manner of discontent. No soul satisfied and contented with his or her state and condition falls into this snare of the devil. It is always the effect of discontent. Now discontent is ordinarily bottomed in pride, but possibly not always. St. Paul tells us, "I have learned in whatsoever state I am, therewith to be content. I know how to be abased, and I know how to abound; everywhere, and in all things, I am instructed, both to be full, and to be hungry, both how to abound, and suffer need" (Phil. 4:11–12). There is no such antidote as this against the poison of this fiery dart. The temptation lies here: better be out of the world any way, than be exposed to this shame . . . But the soul that has possessed itself with patience, that has learned in every estate to be content, and has brought itself into a willingness that God should choose its lot, and carve its portion (for then it is armed as with a coat of mail), no dart of this nature can possibly penetrate such a soul.

> No soul satisfied and contented with his or her state and condition falls into this snare of the devil.

God Sees Us

Robert Dingley

The Lord's eyes will be on you . . . "Behold the eye of the Lord is upon them that fear Him" (Ps. 33:18). Indeed His eye of providence and omnipresence is upon all. By His eye of omniscience He views and sees and knows all things. But the Lord has a special and tender eye of love upon His people, an eye that opens His ear, heart and hand, for their good. "The eyes of the Lord are over the righteous, and His ears are open to their prayers, but the face of the Lord is against them that do evil" (Ps. 34:15–16). Nay, the Lord does not only afford His people a loving glance of His eye, but they are dear to Him as the apple of His eye, and as the signet on His right hand. The Lord will not silently see them injured, but says, "Touch not my anointed ones, and do my prophets no harm" (Ps. 105:15). Consider how much Christ is enamored with looking on His people: "Thou hast ravished my heart, my sister, my spouse; How much better is thy love then wine? And the smell of thy perfume than all spices? Turn away thine eyes from me, for they have overcome me!" (Song 4:9; 6:5). By which you see how deeply Christ stands affected to a true believer; He looks and looks again. He is not ashamed of His love! And if the Lord's eyes do yearn after the saints, you may conclude the eyes of angels are towards them. The curtains of the Tabernacles were pictured full of cherubims. Which way the eye of a great monarch goes, that way goes the eyes of His nobility, and followers. Therefore, seeing God looks upon us, it is not to be doubted the angels eye us. How safe, how comfortable then is the condition of God's people. . . . How then are believers esteemed, and how shall they be cherished, that have their Master's eye upon them for good, yes the eye of a Father and Husband, and an eye that cannot slumber? We cannot sigh, or pray in secret, but He sees us; we cannot lift up our eyes to Him at midnight, but He observes it. In all our services and sufferings He sees us, and will pity and help us.

For a thousand years in thy sight are but as yesterday when it is past, and as a watch in the night.
Psalm 90:4

Reasoning with God

Jeremiah Burroughs

Fear God, and keep his commandments: for this is the whole duty of man.
Ecclesiastes 12:13

The promise of God is, "What man is he that feareth the LORD? Him shall He teach in the way that He shall choose (Ps. 25:12)." The fear of God will put you into a teachable frame, and the Lord delights to teach such. Surely it is an unspeakable blessing of God, to be taught in the way of our choice. How happy would it be if the Lord put a reasoning frame into your hearts, that you might begin to ponder and weigh things, and if spiritual arguments cannot prevail, yet let us see whether you are reasonable creatures or not. Isaiah 46:8 says, "Remember this, and shew yourselves men: bring it again to mind, O ye transgressors." Come, let us reason together; is there not infinitely more reason for God's ways than those ways you have walked in? Is not God infinitely worthy of honor and praise from you, and of other manner of honor and praise than He has had from you? Your own consciences are judges. Has not God given you immortal souls? And are they not capable of better things than these things that you have chosen for your chief good? Has not God made you for a higher end than to eat, drink, and play? What! Did the blessed Trinity consult to make a glorious creature, "Come let us make man, according to our own image" (Gen. 1:26) and when this great work was done, was he made for no other end than to eat, drink, and commit wickedness?

> **Surely it is an unspeakable blessing of God, to be taught in the way of our choice.**

Blush Daily

Richard Alleine

Friends, whatever your faults are, do not mince the matter, do not count your errors little errors, your sins, little sins. Be sure of this, that mincing is not the way to mending. Shame yourselves before the Lord, abase yourselves in His sight; study the greatness of those you count your little sins; rip open your hearts, and find out what a nest of wickedness is there; ransack your ways, and see what a course of folly and vanity is to be found there, and do not go about to hide them. "He that covereth his sins shall not prosper" (Prov. 28:13). Do not go about to hide them, but confess them, and spread them before the Lord, till your soul is ashamed. O that this word might send us to our homes, every one of us with an aching heart, and a blushing face, that it might make us all fall down before God, with Ezra's words in our mouth, "O my God, I am ashamed, and blush to lift up my face to thee, my God, for our iniquities are increased over our head, and our trespasses are grown up unto the heavens" (Ezra 9:6). Let us blush at our hypocrisy, let us blush at our lukewarmness, let us blush at our worldliness and carnality; let us blush in our prayers, let us go blushing home, and weeping as we go; let us acknowledge we all are as an unclean thing, and our righteousness is as filthy rags.

If we confess our sins, he is faithful and just to forgive us our sins, and to cleanse us from all unrighteousness.
1 John 1:9

> Be sure of this, that mincing is not the way to mending.

The Golden Shield

Thomas Watson

Thou wilt keep him in perfect peace, whose mind is stayed on thee: because he trusteth in thee.

Isaiah 26:3

Contentment is the spiritual arc, or pillar of the soul; it fits a man to bear burdens; he whose heart is ready to sink under the least sin, by virtue of this hath a spirit invincible under sufferings. A contented Christian is like the chamomile; the more it is trodden upon the more it grows: as physic works disease out of the body, so doth contentment work trouble out of the heart. Thus it argues, "If I am under reproach, God can vindicate me; if I am in want, God can relieve me." "Ye shall not see wind, neither shall you see rain, yet the valley shall be filled with water" (2 Kgs. 3:17); thus holy contentment keeps the heart from fainting. In the autumn, when the fruit and leaves are blown off, still there is sap in the root: when there is an autumn upon our external felicity, the leaves of our estate drop off, still there is the sap of contentment in the heart: a Christian hath life inwardly, when his outward comforts do not blossom. The contented heart is never out of heart. Contentment is a golden shield that beats back discouragements. Humility is like the lead to the net which keeps the soul down when it is rising through passion; and contentment is like the cork which keeps the heart up when it is sinking through discouragements. Contentment is the great under-prop; it is like the beam which bears whatever weight is laid upon it; nay, it is like a rock that breaks the waves. It is strange to observe the same affliction lying upon two men, how differently they carry themselves under it. . . . Discontent swells the grief, and grief breaks the heart. When this sacred sinew of contentment begins to shrink, we go limping under our afflictions; we know not what burdens God may exercise us with; let us therefore preserve contentment; as is our contentment, such will be our courage. David with his five stones and his sling defied Goliath, and overcame him. Get but contentment into the sling of your heart; and with this sacred stone you may both defy the world and conquer it; you may break those afflictions, which else would break you.

Sincerity

John Bunyan

rayer is a sincere pouring out of the soul to God. Sincerity is such a grace as runs through all the graces of God in us, and through all the actings of a Christian, and has the sway in them too, or else their actings are not any thing regarded of God, and so of and in prayer, of which particularly David speaks, when he mentions prayer. "I cried unto Him (the Lord) with my mouth, and He was extolled with my tongue. If I regard iniquity in my heart, the Lord will not hear" my prayer (Ps. 66:17–18). Part of the exercise of prayer is sincerity, without which God looks not upon it as prayer in a good sense (Ps. 16:1–4). Then "ye shall seek me and find me, when ye shall search for me with all your heart" (Jer. 29:12–13). The lack of this made the Lord reject their prayers in Hos. 7:14, where He says, "They have not cried unto me with their heart," that is, in sincerity, "when they howled upon their beds." But for a pretense, for a show in hypocrisy, to be seen of men, and applauded for the same, they prayed. Sincerity was that which Christ commended in Nathaniel, when he was under the fig tree: "Behold, an Israelite indeed, in whom is no guile" (John 1:47). . . . And why must sincerity be one of the essentials of prayer which is accepted of God, but because sincerity carries the soul in all simplicity to open its heart to God, and to tell Him the case plainly, without equivocation; to condemn itself plainly, without dissembling; to cry to God heartily, without complimenting. "I have surely heard Ephraim bemoaning himself thus; Thou has chastised me, and I was chastised, as a bullock unaccustomed to the yoke" (Jer. 31:18). Sincerity is the same in a corner alone, as it is before the face of the world. It knows not how to wear two faces, one for an appearance before men, and another for a short snatch in a corner; but it must have God, and be with Him in the duty of prayer. It is not lip-labor that it regards, for it is the heart that God looks at, and that which sincerity looks at, and that which prayer comes from, if it be that prayer which is accompanied with sincerity.

Hear my cry, O God; attend unto my prayer.
Psalm 61:1

Absolute Obedience

William Perkins

And Samuel said, Hath the LORD as great delight in burnt offerings and sacrifices, as in obeying the voice of the LORD? Behold, to obey is better than sacrifice, and to hearken than the fat of rams.

1 Samuel 15:22

Our obedience must be absolute, for we must (as it were) shut up our own eyes, and simply, without any ado, trust God upon His bare and naked Word, and suffer ourselves to be led by it. In natural things experience is first, and then faith comes afterward. And Thomas following nature desired first to feel, before he would believe. But God must be trusted, though that which He says seems to be against reason and experience. Thus Abraham believed God against all human hope (Rom. 4:18). The second thing is, our obedience must be sincere. For we must trust God's Word for itself, because it is God's Word, all prejudice set apart. They which are as the stony ground receive God's Word and rejoice in it, and yet after a time of temptation go awry. The reason is because they receive the Word and rejoice in it not properly for itself, but in respect of honor, profit, or pleasure, which they look to reap thereby. John the Baptist was a burning candle, and the Jews rejoiced in his light, only in respect of the novelty of it, and therefore the Holy Ghost says, "They rejoiced in it but for a season" (John 5:35). We must trust God not in part, but in His whole Word; and therefore many fail in their faith, that are content to trust Him in His promises of mercy and salvation, but list not to believe Him in His commandments and threats. We must trust God in His Word with all our hearts, that it may take deep root and be an ingrafted Word. It is not sufficient for us to have a taste of the good Word of God and to receive it with joy, unless we thoroughly and soundly build and rely ourselves upon it. This trusting of God must be with an honest heart, that is, with a heart in which there is a distinct and settled purpose not to sin, but in all things to do the will of God. The good hearers are they which receive the Word with an honest and good heart. Without this none can possibly live by faith. Whoever puts away their good conscience makes shipwreck of their faith. It is godliness alone that has the promises of this life and the life to come. And none can live the life of faith but the just.

Deeper Principles

Joseph Caryl

hose works that flow from a good principle are pleasing to God . . . thus we see the necessity of regeneration. Christ says in John 3:3, "Verily, verily." There is a strong and double asseveration: "Verily, verily, I say unto you, except a man be born again, he cannot enter into the kingdom of God." We are not born with this pure heart, with this good conscience; with this faith unfeigned, which are the realities of a good work. We are not born with these, for who can bring a clean thing out of an unclean? Not one. Not one among the children of men (Job 14:4). A pure heart, a good conscience, and faith unfeigned are the issues of the new birth. Education cannot make the heart pure; it must be revelation which makes the heart pure. Good education may change the life and the conversation. As they say, to study arts and philosophy, it takes off the roughness that is in man's nature, and does smooth men, and frame them very much for excellent uses. Good literature and education may civilize, but it cannot spiritualize. It may change a man's course, but it cannot change his nature; that is only done by regeneration. Now I say, a man's state, his nature must be changed; he must have a pure heart, which we never have till our natures are changed. He must be good before he can do good spiritually. Mark that word of the Apostle, "We are His workmanship, created in Christ Jesus unto good works, which God hath before ordained that we should walk in them" (Eph. 2:10). Mark it, here are good works. But how do we come to these good works? Why, we are His workmanship, says He. God works in us before we can work for Him. He makes us good before we can do good. He says, "we are His workmanship." And then, created, or so created in Christ Jesus to do good works. We by union to Jesus Christ come to have a spiritual principle to carry us out in the doing of all good works. You must be new creatures, created in Christ Jesus unto good works, before you can do them.

That he may incline our hearts unto him, to walk in all his ways, and to keep his commandments, and his statutes, and his judgments, which he commanded our fathers.

1 Kings 8:58

Redemption Applied

John Flavel

But of him are ye in Christ Jesus, who of God is made unto us wisdom, and righteousness, and sanctification, and redemption.

1 Corinthians 1:30

He that enquires what is the just value and worth of Christ asks a question which puts all the people on earth, and angels in heaven, to an everlasting bewilderment. The highest attainment of our knowledge in this life is to know, that Himself and His love do pass knowledge (Eph. 3:19). But how excellent Christ is and what treasures of righteousness lie in His blood, and whatever joy, peace, and ravishing comforts, spring up to men out of His incarnation, humiliation, and exaltation, they all give down their distinct benefits and comforts to them, in the way of effectual application. For never was any wound healed by a prepared, but unapplied ointment; never any body warmed by the most costly garment made, but not put on; never any heart refreshed and comforted by the richest cordial compounded, but not received: nor from the beginning of the world was it ever known, that a poor, deceived, condemned, polluted, miserable sinner, was actually delivered out of that woeful state, until of God, Christ was made unto him, wisdom and righteousness, sanctification and redemption. For as the condemnation of the first Adam passes not to us, except (as by generation we are his; so grace and remission pass not from the second Adam to us, except (as by regeneration) we are His. Adam's sin hurts none but those that are in him: and Christ's blood profits none but those that are in Him: How great a weight therefore does there hang upon the effectual application of Christ to the souls of men! And what is there in the whole world so awfully solemn, so greatly important, as this is! Such is the strong consolation resulting from it, that the Apostle, in this context, offers it to the believing Corinthians, as a superabundant recompense for the despicable meanness and baseness of their outward condition in this world, of which he had just before spoken in vv. 27–28, telling them that though the world condemned them as vile, foolish, and weak, yet "of God Christ is made unto them wisdom and righteousness, sanctification and redemption."

Live to Persuade

Jeremiah Burroughs

You must walk and live so that by your walking you may draw others to be in love with the fellowship of Christ. God has made it to be glorious, so that you would show the glory of it to others, that all that go by you will say, "Surely they are blessed of the Lord, certainly God is with them, and therefore we will join with them." Oh what a blessed thing it would be if we could by our lives convince others that we are the plants of the Lord's own planting! The lives of men convince more strongly than their words. "The tongue persuades, but the life commands" is the speech of an ancient. We read in Rev. 14 that those that stood with the Lamb upon Mount Zion, enjoying communion there, had the Father's name written upon their foreheads, the glory of God shining there. God calls for a convincing conversation from you. Let the name of God be precious to you. Is it not a precious thing to live to bring honor to God? To show forth the honor of God is all the glory we can bring to God; let us be known to be those we profess ourselves to be, separated from the world by the holiness of our lives. Tertullian said of the Christians in his time that they were known to be Christians from the amendment of their former lives. You are joined near to Christ as a girdle about a man's loins, but take heed that you are not as the girdle in Jer. 13:10: "This evil people, which refuse to hear my words, which walk in the imagination of their heart, and walk after other gods, to serve them, and to worship them, shall even be as this girdle, which is good for nothing." A rotten girdle fit for nothing was the church of the Jews at that time. But you should be as that girdle of Christ found in Rev. 1—a golden girdle about His chest. In this way the beauty and glorious condition of the church is described.

Let your light so shine before men, that they may see your good works, and glorify your Father which is in heaven.

Matthew 5:16

> They were known to be Christians from the amendment of their former lives.

Heavenly Affection

William Bates

Let God be the supreme object of our esteem and affections; and whatsoever evils we sustain, will be made light and easy to us. The apostle assures us, "That all things," even the most afflicting, "work for the good of those that love God" (Rom. 8:28). That heavenly affection is not only the condition that entitles us to that promise, that by special privilege makes all the evils of this world advantageous to the saints; but it is the qualification by which it is accomplished. By love we enjoy God, and love will make us willing to do or suffer what He pleases, that we may have fuller communion with Him. In God all perfections are in transcendent eminence, they are always the same and always new. He gives all things without any decrease of His treasures; He receives the praises and services of the angels, without any advantage or increase of His happiness. By possessing Him, all that is amiable and excellent in the creatures, may be enjoyed in a manner incomparably better than in the creatures themselves. His infinite goodness can supply all our wants, satisfy all our desires, allay all our sorrows, and conquer all our fears. One beam of His countenance can revive the spirit dead in sorrow, and buried in despair.

> His infinite goodness can supply all our wants, allay all our sorrows, and conquer all our fears.

Meekness

Robert Harris

eekness is a grace that moderates anger, both in the affection itself and in the effects thereof; for it teaches a man when to be angry, how to be angry, and how far he must and must not be angry. And he who practically knows when, why, and how far to be angry is a meek man, and so a blessed man, which is here proved by this: he shall inherit the earth. As for heaven, he is sure of it, but as for earth, there is some question of that; and therefore the matter is here put out of doubt by our Savior that meek men shall also inherit the earth. Observe here that the blessing promised is suited to the grace, as it was in the two former beatitudes. To poor ones is promised a kingdom; to mourners, comfort. So here, to meekness is promised quietness upon earth, for our Savior presents an objection. Some might say, "If we should be meek, and take passively such wrongs as offered to us, we might soon have enough of it, be thrown out of our estates, and, by bearing one injury, invite another." To this He answered that there is no such matter, for meek ones shall inherit the earth. Their meekness shall be no prejudice to their estates; they shall have a quiet estate on earth, or at least quietness in their estate. Yea, such a man shall have the earth as an heir; he shall hold it by the right of adoption (as the word in the original here used signifies; as also the Hebrew word used in Ps. 37:11 from whence this promise seems to be taken). He shall have right unto it as an heir and fruition also of it, for he shall delight himself, said the Psalmist, in the abundance of peace. Another man may delight himself in the abundance of cattle, in the abundance of treasure, in the abundance of friends (as Augustine comments upon the passage), but the meek man delights himself only in the abundance of peace.

The meek shall eat and be satisfied: they shall praise the LORD that seek him: your heart shall live for ever.
Psalm 22:6

> The blessing promised is suited to the grace.

Crown of Rejoicing

Nicholas Byfield

Seek good, and not evil, that ye may live: and so the LORD, the God of hosts, shall be with you, as ye have spoken.

Amos 5:14

It is a special promise of God in the new covenant that He will write His laws in your heart, and He will make you to know the Lord. You may go boldly to the throne of grace to beg the further illumination of the Spirit of God. This is one of the suits that God cannot deny. He has promised to lead you by a way which you have not known. He will preserve you by His knowledge, though you are unacquainted with the way yourself. He that led His people from Babel to Zion, when they scarce knew a foot of that long way, will lead you in the straight way from earth to heaven, if you seek a way of God as they did (Isa. 42:16). We have such a High Priest as knows how to have compassion on the ignorant. He that required that property of the high priest in the law will much more express it Himself (Heb. 5:13). This must be your glory, and the crown of rejoicing, that though you might be ignorant of many things, yet you know God and Christ crucified, and this is eternal life (John 17:3).

We have such a High Priest as knows how to have compassion on the ignorant.

Chiefest of Works

Christopher Nesse

You must know that man is the masterpiece of the World's Maker. God calls (as it were) a council in heaven, saying, "Let us make man" (Gen. 1:26). Us, the whole wisdom of the Trinity was exercised in the making of man. The consultation and deliberation therein plainly demonstrates that there was then the bringing forth of a piece of work of greatest moment and importance; and therefore what is said of Behemoth, "He is the chief of the ways of God" (Job 40:19) may more eminently be said of man; he is the chiefest of the ways and of the works of God. The sun, moon, and stars are but the works of God's fingers (Ps. 8:3), but man is the work of His hands (Ps. 139:14–15). Hence David, speaking of man, first wonders and then speaks, and when he has done speaking, he has not finished wondering. Every creature of God is (indeed) a wonder, yes little creatures (those decimals of the creation) are great wonders (as well as the great Behemoth, and other large creatures), for the infinite wisdom and power of the Creator is manifest in couching up both life and motion in such a little compass, as in insects, flies, and ants. But man is the greatest wonder, as having the excellency of all other creatures in him; he is the abridgement of all wonders. You believe that God is a Spirit, and you see that the world is a body; man is an epitome of both, of God in respect of His Spirit, and of the world in the composition of His body, as if the great Jehovah (purpose to set forth a plain mirror of Himself and His work) designed to bring into this one narrow compass of man, both the infiniteness of His own nature, and the vastness of the whole world together.

So God created man in his own image, in the image of God created he him; male and female created he them.
Genesis 1:27

> Little creatures, those decimals of the creation, are great wonders.

The Heart's Fire

John Bunyan

As the hart panteth after the water-brooks, so panteth my soul after thee, O God.
Psalm 42:1

Prayer is . . . an affectionate pouring out of the soul to God. O the heat, strength, life, vigor, and affection, that is in right prayer! "I have longed after thy precepts" (Ps. 119:40). "I have longed for thy salvation" (v. 174). "My soul longeth, yes, even fainteth, for the courts of the Lord; my heart and my flesh crieth out for the living God" (Ps. 84:2). "My soul breaketh for the longing that it hath unto thy judgments at all times" (Ps. 119:20). Mark here, "My soul longeth," it longeth, it longeth, etc. O what affection is here discovered in prayer! The like you have in Daniel: "O Lord, hear; O Lord, forgive; O Lord, hearken and do; defer not, for thine own sake, O my God" (Dan. 9:19). Every syllable carrieth a mighty vehemency in it. This is called the fervent, or the working prayer, by James. And so again, "And being in an agony, he prayed more earnestly" (Luke 22:44). Or had his affections more and more drawn out after God for His helping hand. O how wide are the most of men with their prayers from this prayer, that is, prayer in God's account! Alas! The greatest part of men make no conscience at all of the duty; and as for them that do, it is to be feared that many of them are very great strangers to a sincere, sensible, and affectionate pouring out their hearts or souls to God; but even content themselves with a little lip-labor and bodily exercise, mumbling over a few imaginary prayers. When the affections are indeed engaged in prayer, then the whole man is engaged, and that in such sort, that the soul will spend itself to nothing, as it were, rather than it go without that good desired, even communion and solace with Christ. And hence it is that the saints have spent their strengths, and lost their lives, rather than go without the blessing (Ps. 69:3; 38:9–10; Gen. 32:24–26).

Eternity's Terrace

Thomas Watson

he privilege of life is a believer's; that is, life to a child of God is an advantage for heaven. This life is given to him to make provision for a better life. Life is the porch of eternity; here the believer dresses himself that he may be fit to enter in with the Bridegroom. We cannot say of a wicked man that life is his. Though he lives, yet life is not his; he is dead while he lives. He does not improve the life of nature to get the life of grace; he is like a man that takes the lease of a farm, and makes no benefit of it. He has been so long in the world, as Seneca speaks, but he has not lived. He was born in the reign of such a king, his father left him such an estate, he was of such an age, and then he died; there is an end of him; his life was not worth a prayer, nor his death worth a tear. But life is yours; it is a privilege to a believer; while he has natural life, he lays hold upon eternal life; how does he work out his salvation? What ado is there to get his evidences sealed? What weeping? What wrestling? How does he even take heaven by storm? So that life is yours; it is to a child of God a season of grace, and seed-time of eternity; the longer he lives, the riper he grows for heaven. The life of a believer spends as a lamp, he does good to himself and to others; the life of a sinner runs out as the sand; it does little good. The life of the one is as a figure engraved in marble; the life of the other as letters written in dust.

By humility and the fear of the LORD are riches, and honour, and life.
Proverbs 22:4

> Life is yours; it is to a child of God a season of grace, and seed-time of eternity.

The Foundation

Isaac Ambrose

Be of good courage, and he shall strengthen your heart, all ye that hope in the LORD.
Psalm 31:24

We must hope in Jesus . . . It is not enough to know, and consider, and desire. We must hope and maintain our hope as to our own interest. Now, hope is a passion where we expect probably, or certainly, that some future good will come to us. As the question is, whether that salvation, concerning which the great transaction between God and Christ, belongs to us, and what are the grounds and foundation on which our hope is built? I know some abuse this doctrine, "If God had before all worlds appointed me to salvation, then I may live as I wish; I do not need to hear, pray, confer, or perform any holy duty, for I know I shall be saved." And so they take away all grounds of hope. It is true, God's decrees are unchangeable, but they do not afford any such inferences or deductions as these. You might as well say that the Lord has appointed you to live for such a time, and before that time you cannot die, and therefore you do not need to eat, drink, wear clothes, or any other such thing. This is silly, foolish, devilish arguing! God's decree is for the means as well as the end; those whom God has decreed to save, He has also decreed to call, justify, and sanctify, before He saves. . . . Therefore, look to the grounds on which your hope is built; if the grounds are weak, then your hope is weak, but if those are strong, then your hope is strong and will prove most strong, certain, and prudent.

> God's decree is for the means as well as the end.

Worthy Love

John Rogers

The unregenerate cannot love their neighbors. For a while they are kind to their bodies, yet they have no love for their souls—and is this worthy to be called love? It is as if one's friend or child should have a hurt in the brain, and another in the heel, and he should carefully look to the heel and let the brain suffer. Carnal parents that pamper their children's bodies and store great portions for them but let their souls welter in sin and die and perish for want of instruction, admonition, prayer, and holy example—is this to be called love? The magistrate who is friendly to all the country, and keeps a good house all the year, and yet suffers sin to reign and houses of disorder to abound in his country, the Sabbath to be profaned, and cares for none of those things, call you this love? The negligent minister that gives money to the poor, keeps good hospitalities among his neighbors, and yet suffers their souls to famish for want of breaking to them the Bread of Life . . . this is hatred and not love.

Ye that love the LORD, hate evil: he preserveth the souls of his saints; he delivereth them out of the hand of the wicked.
Psalm 97:10

> Want of instruction, admonition, prayer, and holy example — is this to be called love?

Experience God

Samuel Annesley

Lord, all my desire is
before thee; and my
groaning is not hid
from thee.
Psalm 38:9

Seriously determine to find out experimentally what it is to enjoy God, and to have communion with Him. Long for it, that you shall never lose your longing. Pant after it; God understands the rhetoric of your breathing as well as your cry. "If," says Augustine, "I desire nothing else but thee, I beseech thee Father, let me find thee; if I do desire anything superstitious, do thou thyself cleanse me, and make me fit to see thee." Christians, rouse up your spirits; what is it that makes you so low spirited, as to have the least contentment in the greatest enjoyment this side of heaven? . . . You have a promise that your knowledge shall increase, from the morning of regeneration to the noonday of glory. What hinders you? Is it fears? . . . God the Father bids you to cast your cares on Him; "the earth is the Lord's and the fullness of it" (Ps. 24:1), and He knows what things you need. Christ bids you to bring your doubts to Him. Do you have any doubt that Christ cannot answer? . . . surely He has done and suffered enough to persuade you of His willingness. . . . Be persuaded to walk closely with God. Act in faith, and strengthen it with obedience, that you may be able to say, "Whom have I in heaven but thee, and there is none upon earth that I desire besides thee" (Ps. 73:25).

> **Your knowledge shall increase from the morning of regeneration to the noonday of glory.**

Always Light

Robert Dingley

When Christ the sun of righteousness shines with full face, with perpendicular rays, this drowns the lesser glory of moon and stars; this darkens your outward comforts, which indeed are not worthy of a glance of your eye in respect to Christ. The soul that sees Him is in a continual rapture, and with heart-siftings and leaping, sings, "There is no beloved like this beloved, He is the fairest of ten thousand." And then looking upon other things, it counts all but dross and dung for Christ. We are not much troubled when we see the sun set, because we expect it shall arise the next morning. And the sun cannot be totally eclipsed, as the moon may, because the moon which interposes is far less than the sun. It is so here; let us not be overmuch dismayed when this sun of righteousness sets, "for though sorrow endure for a night, yet joy may return the next morning" (Ps. 30:5). Jesus Christ may be eclipsed, but never totally (as the world's comforts may), for though His face be hidden in great part, yet some crevice of light remains to cheer and sustain the soul, because sin which interposes between Christ and us is far less than Christ; if sin abound, His grace will much more abound, for His mercy is broader than our sin or misery.

But unto you that fear my name shall the Sun of righteousness arise with healing in his wings; and ye shall go forth, and grow up as calves of the stall.

Malachi 4:2

> Jesus Christ may be eclipsed, but never totally.

Deny Presumption

John Collinges

Keep back thy servant also from presumptuous sins; let them not have dominion over me: then shall I be upright, and I shall be innocent from the great transgression.

Psalm 19:13

Presumptuous sins rob God of the glory of His justice; they indeed seem to give God the honor of His goodness and mercy, but they make Him an idol of mercy, and despoil Him of His justice, and purity, and holiness. God indeed is gracious and merciful; but He is also a God of purer eyes than to behold iniquity; a God before whom sinners shall not stand in judgment, a God that cannot clear the guilty. Now that soul that goes on in its sinful courses, and yet hopes to find favor with God, and to go to heaven at last, thinks that God is not so holy and pure a God as indeed He is, or that He is not so just as He is; either that He has not power to be revenged upon sinners, or not so just a will and steady a resolution to be revenged upon such as go on in their courses of ungodliness, as indeed He has. Now consider how great a sin it must be, either to deny the purity and holiness of God, or the power and justice of God.

The presumptuous sinner says, "God is not of so pure eyes, but He can abide iniquity; a sinner may dwell in His sight," whereas God could not be God if He could not be just, or not be holy and pure. Holiness is a piece of God's glory, He is not only glorious in majesty, but He is also glorious in holiness. And as the justice and purity of God is impeached by presumption, so God's truth is also impeached. The presumptuous sinner in effect says, "The Scripture is a lie and a romance"; for the language of his heart is directly contrary to the language of Scripture that says, such and such sinners shall never enter into the kingdom of God, but shall have their portion in the lake which burns with fire and brimstone.

> He is not only glorious in majesty, but He is also glorious in holiness.

Be Mindful

Richard Alleine

hough the gospel may still be received as an un-doubted and unquestionable truth, though the evidence of its truth may be so clear that we can-not contradict or question it, yet the weight of it may not be so much felt upon our hearts; the truths believed may not be so much minded, nor so thoroughly considered as to leave any powerful impressions of them upon our hearts. Those great things, the worth and value of a soul, the dreadfulness of losing a soul, the danger that they are in of losing their souls, the excellency and necessity of Christ, the eternal weight of glory, the everlasting vengeance of God against the unrighteousness of men, though all these things be believed and acknowledged, yet they may not for the time be so duly minded and meditated on; they may be so much out of our eye, out of our thoughts, that the sense of them, and the efficacy of that sense, may seem even to be utterly lost. Friends, it is not the being of these great things, no, nor the bare believing that they are, but the minding and frequent considering of them, the having that height and depth, that life and death in our eye, that will affect and work upon the heart; and Christians, through their own carelessness and heedlessness, may have even lost the sight both of heaven and hell. Things present may have so filled and overpowered their hearts, as to put things to come quite out of mind; the heart may be so bewitched by this present world, so sur-rounded with a crowd of carnal pleasures and delights, so swallowed up of worldly cares and contrivances, so intent upon our worldly business and commodity, that we may hereupon drive so heavily on in the mat-ters of eternity, as if we had forgotten that we had a Christ or a soul to be minded.

Get wisdom, get understanding: forget it not; neither decline from the words of my mouth.
Proverbs 4:5

> It is not the being of these great things, nor the bare believing that they are.

The Devil's Wiles

Edmund Calamy

Be sober, be vigilant; because your adversary the devil, as a roaring lion, walketh about, seeking whom he may devour.
1 Peter 5:8

Sincere love is a grace without which all profession of religion is but gilded hypocrisy. Where love is, God dwells. But where it is not, the devil dwells. The more love, the more like to God we are, but the less of it, the more like the devil we become. Woeful experience shows that those who have great gifts and little or no love show more of the devil's nature than of God's, and act more like the devil than God . . . Love is the sweetest flower in all the garden of God, but it is a flower which the devil cannot endure the smell of because he is not capable of it, and knows that where love dwells he must vanish. Therefore it is the devil's main design to destroy love, if possible, in all sorts and sects, and to root it up and banish it from the hearts of all. The devil is well content that we should pray, preach, read, hear sermons, and make a fair show outwardly, provided that these activities do not spring from love, and tend not to increase love to God or others. But if he sees that love is the root and fruit of our service, then he goes cunningly, and serpent-like, to work, to make breaches in this wall, that he may get in and destroy this flower; he devises ways to divide people's judgments, to the end he may destroy this affection of love out of their hearts. If he does not prevail in this way, he will raise up jealousies to destroy love and charity, yes sometimes render the best of graces, the worst of vices. And in tempting the carnally minded, he sometimes styles lust, love; so in tempting the spiritually minded, he sometimes styles sincere love, lust, and by these wiles makes a breach on charity, to the end that he may get into the garden of God, and root up this sweet grace of love.

> **Love is the sweetest flower in all the garden of God, but the devil cannot endure the smell.**

Golden Words

Thomas Watson

S inners, in their ordinary discourse, bring forth Scripture as the Philistines did Samson, to make sport, as if the Bible were the best minstrel to play with, and a jest were worth nothing unless it were seasoned with the salt of the sanctuary. It is a saying of Luther, "Whom God has a mind to destroy, He lets them play with Scripture." But in this sense the righteous is more excellent. "The tongue of the just is as choice silver" (Prov. 10:20). Gracious words drop as silver from him to the enriching of the souls of others. "The words of a wise man's mouth are gracious" (Eccl. 10:12). In the Hebrew it is, "they are grace." His words are not as vinegar to fret but as salt to season others (Col. 4:6). The roof of the mouth is called heaven. A godly man's mouth is full of heaven. He speaks as if he had already been in heaven. The holy conference of the two disciples going to Emmaus brought Christ into their company. "While they communed together, Jesus Himself drew near and went with them" (Luke 24:15). Such savory speeches drop from holy lips that God has a notebook to write them down. "Then they that feared the Lord spake often one to another, and God hearkened, and a book of remembrance was written" (Mal. 3:16). It is reported of Tamerlain (the Mongol conqueror) that he kept a register of the names and good deeds of his soldiers. God registers the speeches of His people that they may not be lost.

Let the words of my mouth, and the meditation of my heart, be acceptable in thy sight, O LORD, my strength, and my redeemer.
Psalm 19:14

> **A godly man's mouth is full of heaven.**

Living Waters

George Swinnock

The Word of God is a spring of living water, a deep mine of costly treasure, a table furnished with all sorts of food, a garden with a variety of pleasant fruits, and the church's charter, containing all her privileges and deeds, manifesting her title to this possession. This Word contains pious precepts for the Christian's reformation and precious promises for consolation. If the saint is afflicted, it can hold his head above water and keep him from sinking when the billows go over his soul. There are cordials in it rich enough to revive the most fainting spirit. If the saint is assaulted, the Word is armor of proof, with which he may defend himself manfully, and wound his foes mortally. If the soul is unholy, this Word can sanctify it: "Ye are clean through the word which I have spoken to you" (John 15:3). This water can wash out all spots and stains. If the soul is an heir of hell, this Word can save it: "From a child thou hast known the holy Scriptures, which are able to make thee wise to salvation" (2 Tim. 3:15). Other writings may make a man wise to admiration, but this only can make him wise to salvation.

If the saint is assaulted, the Word is armor of proof.

The Father's Love

John Owen

he love of the Father is a love of bounty, a descending love, such a love as carries Him out to do good things to us, great things for us. His love lies at the bottom of all dispensations towards us; and we scarce anywhere find any mention of it, but it is held out as the cause and fountain of some free gift flowing from it. He loves us, and sends His Son to die for us. He loves us, and blesses us with all spiritual blessings. Loving is choosing. He loves us and chastises us. It is a love like that of the heavens to the earth, when, being full of rain, they pour forth showers to make it fruitful; and as the sea communicates its waters to the rivers by the way of bounty, out of its own fullness, they return unto it only what they receive from it. It is the love of a spring, of a fountain, always communicating; it is a love from whence proceeds everything that is lovely in its object. It infuses into, and creates goodness in, the persons beloved. . . . He that loves works out good to those that he loves, as he is able. God's power and will are equal; what He wills He works.

In all their affliction he was afflicted, and the angel of his presence saved them: in his love and in his pity he redeemed them; and he bare them, and carried them all the days of old.

Isaiah 63:9

> Loving is choosing. He loves us and chastises us.

To Know Oneself

Jeremiah Burroughs

We read that God led His people through the wilderness, to humble them, to prove them, and to know what was in their hearts. God knew before, but He would make them and others to know. I read of Nazianzen, walking by the sea shore, seeing how the sea brought in a storm, that it cast up light and empty things, but not things solid and heavy; he applies this to afflictions, and says, that light and empty spirits are tossed up and down by them, and keep not their constancy; but solid spirits are like the rock that stand firm, and abides the same. We do not know our own hearts. We find our hearts otherwise when troubles come, than ever we thought before. We never thought they had so much pride, so much impatience, and so much unbelief. We thought before that we could have submitted to the hand of God, and that we could have borne more than is now upon us. But now we find our hearts to murmur, repine, fret, and vex . . . When a pond is empty, we can see the mud, the filth, and toads in the bottom; so when God empties us, when He takes from us His blessings, then much filth, many crawling lusts appear that did not before. Sometimes more grace appears in affliction than before; some of God's people are low in their own eyes, they suspect and fear themselves, they think their graces will fail them in trouble, that their peace is false, yet when it pleases God to bring them into trouble, they find more peace, more assurance, more strength than ever before, or than they thought they should have done; never such sweet joy, never such full assurance, never such use of faith, and patience, and love, as in the sorest and strongest afflictions. This indeed is very rare; there are few that find more good in their hearts in afflictions, than they thought they had before; but where this is, it may be a sweet seal to the soul of the sincerity of it ever after. When corn stands in the field, we may guess what it may yield, but we cannot know fully, till it come to the harvest. . . . When grapes come to be pressed, then we know what is in them.

Excellency of Grace

Robert Harris

editate seriously upon the excellency of grace, and so set your mouth on watering after more of it. The least saving grace is a pledge of heaven; it is our life, our comfort, our honor. Think this to yourself: "Oh that I had but a little more faith, a little more knowledge, a little more patience, and strength against my corruption. I should pray the better for it as long as I live, be the better for it when I die, yes, a thousand years hence, yes, have the more glory and comfort when I rise again." Thus you should set an edge on your desires after more grace by meditation upon the excellence of grace. Provoke yourselves to a more eager pursuit of things spiritual by observing that insatiable desire that is in worldly-minded men after temporal things. They, if they are never so rich, never so high, never so great, would still be greater; nay, if they had engrossed the whole world, they would yet covet more and be grieved that there were no more worlds left for them to grasp. Thus they enlarge their desires toward hell, as the prophet speaks of gold-thirsty Nebuchadnezzar. Now, do we see men so toil and travail for earthly commodity, rising up early and lying down late for dung, for trash that perishes when used, which they must shortly leave, which will yield them no sound comfort here, and even less hereafter? Oh, then, reflect upon yourselves? Chide and quicken yourselves to a more ready and earnest pursuit of spiritual things, which are so desirable and so durable.

That in the ages to come he might shew the exceeding riches of his grace in his kindness toward us through Christ Jesus.
Ephesians 2:7

> Set an edge on your desires after more grace by meditation upon the excellence of grace.

Life and Power

Christopher Nesse

For bodily exercise profiteth little: but godliness is profitable unto all things, having promise of the life that now is, and of that which is to come.

1 Timothy 4:8

Godliness has life and power in it. There may be many carcasses and forms of religion, but there is but one life, one power; there is a form of knowledge and a form of godliness, yet both may want the power. You may live by a form, but you cannot die by a form. It is the power of godliness that is godliness indeed. Godliness is quasi-Godlikeness; it makes you like God (as ungodliness makes you unlike God) holy as He is holy (1 Pet. 1:15–16). As godliness is the recovery of the image and likeness of God, which man lost by ungodliness (in eating the forbidden fruit), so it is the whole frame of grace spreading (like blessed leaven) over all three measures of the meal (not only the understanding, will, and memory, but also the body, soul, and spirit), through the gracious overshadowing of the Holy Ghost. Godliness is (as it were) God manifest in the flesh, as God was manifest in the flesh of His Son bodily. So God is manifest in the flesh of His saints spiritually, as the Father, Son, and Holy Ghost are all said to take up their abode and to live, to dwell, to tabernacle, and to temple in them. Godliness is a compound of all the graces of the Spirit, as so many ingredients make up this blessed composition; it is the life and exercise of every grace, of faith and love, of joy, peace and praise, of self-denial and devotion, of patience, obedience, hope and perseverance. It contains in it your trusting in God, your worshipping of God, and your obedience to God; yes, your very victory and triumph over all your enemies, the flesh and the devil. Godliness therefore must be the main thing that you must look for and labor after, as it is the main thing that God looks after. God looks down from heaven, what for? Not to see how fair, how strong, how rich, how great, how honorable men are, but how good, how godly, how righteous, and how religious they are.

Scruples

Timothy Cruso

A tender conscience is not a troubling or tormenting ourselves with frivolous or groundless scruples, and so living in melancholy bondage all our days. This may be indeed an indication of grace, but yet it is an infirmity, like the tenderness of Leah's eyes, and makes the soul to refuse that comfort and satisfaction, which it ought to receive. At this rate, conscience must always be removed far from peace, and every trifle, yes every nothing, will give us as much disturbance as the most terrifying reality. Fearing to offend, where no reason to fear is, must needs be accounted rather an instance of weakness than perfection. Peter had a rebuke for calling that unclean, which God had cleansed; and no man is to be commended for the puzzling and perplexing of himself, when the case is so plain, that it is only his own perplexity which obscures it. What is this but to stumble upon hollow ground or choose to walk in pain, like the traveler with a stone in his shoe, when he ought rather to sit down, and endeavor to take it out? God does nowhere put us upon flying from shaken leaves, or turning innocent things into grieving thorns and piercing swords; he that does so embitters his life through his own folly, for a man may spend all his years upon the rack, if he will indulge every dark imagination that rises up in his mind. That rule of the Apostle is of a larger extent than the single case, which it was laid down for: "Whatsoever is sold in the shambles, that eat, asking no question for conscience's sake" (1 Cor. 10:25).

Beware lest any man spoil you through philosophy and vain deceit, after the tradition of men, after the rudiments of the world, and not after Christ.

Colossians 2:8

> A man may spend all his years upon the rack, if he will indulge every dark imagination.

The Spirit's Help

John Bunyan

Likewise the Spirit also helpeth our infirmities: for we know not what we should pray for as we ought: but the Spirit itself maketh intercession for us with groanings which cannot be uttered.
Romans 8:26

The soul that rightly prays, it must be in and with the help and strength of the Spirit; because it is impossible that a man should express himself in prayer without it. When I say, it is impossible for a man to express himself in prayer without it, I mean, that it is impossible that the heart, in a sincere, sensible, and affectionate way, should pour itself out before God, with those groans and sighs that come from a truly praying heart, without the assistance of the Spirit. It is not the mouth that is the main thing to be looked at in prayer, but whether the heart is so full of affection and earnestness in prayer with God, that it is impossible to express their sense and desire; for then a man desires indeed, when his desires are so strong, many, and mighty, that all the words, tears, and groans that can come from the heart, cannot utter them. That is but poor prayer which is only discovered in so many words. A man that truly prays one prayer, shall after that never be able to express with his mouth or pen the unutterable desires, sense, affection, and longing that went to God in that prayer. The best prayers have often more groans than words: and those words that they have are but a lean and shallow representation of the heart, life, and spirit of that prayer. You do not find any words of prayer, that we read of, come out of the mouth of Moses, when he was going out of Egypt, and was followed by Pharaoh, and yet he made heaven ring again with his cry (Exod. 14:15). But it was inexpressible and unsearchable groans and cryings of his soul in and with the Spirit. God is the God of spirits, and His eyes look further than at the outside of any duty whatsoever (Num. 16:22). . . . But prayer, as aforesaid, is not only a duty, but one of the most eminent duties, and therefore so much the more difficult: therefore Paul knew what he said, when he said, "I will pray with the Spirit." He knew well it was not what others wrote or said that could make him a praying person; nothing less than the Spirit could do it.

Consider His Courts

Thomas Manton

f we have a Father in heaven and a Savior at His right hand, to do all things that are needful for us, let us look upon the visible heavens with an eye of sense, with our bodily eyes. It is good to contemplate the glory of the heavenly bodies, or the outside of that court which God has provided for the saints. It is not an idle speculation I press you to; the saints of God have thought it to be worthy of their morning and evening thoughts. It is notable, David does, in two psalms especially, contemplate heaven; one seems to be a nightly, the other a morning, meditation. In the night meditation you have, "When I consider thy heavens, the work of thy fingers, the moon and the stars, which thou hast ordained" (Ps. 8:3). David was abroad in a moon-shining night, looked up, and had his heart affected. But now the nineteenth Psalm seems to be a morning meditation; he speaks of the "sun coming out like a bridegroom from his chamber in the east" (v. 5) and displaying its beams, and heat, and influences to the world; and then he says, "The heavens declare the glory of God" (v. 1). Morning and evening, or whenever you go abroad to see the beauty of the outward heavens, say, I have a Father there, a Christ there; this is the pavement of that palace which God has provided for the saints. Christians, it is a sweet meditation when you can say, He that made all things is there. It will be a delightful, profitable thing sometimes, with an eye of sense, to take a view of our Father's palace, as much as we can see of it here below.

Behold, the heaven and the heaven of heavens is the LORD's thy God, the earth also, with all that therein is.
Deuteronomy 10:14

> Christians, it is a sweet meditation when you can say, He that made all things is there.

Ineffable Glory

Robert Dingley

Our eyes shall see the palace of the great King, the glittering glory of the New Jerusalem; it is at large described by Saint John in Rev. 20—made of crystal, gold, pearl, and several kinds of most precious jewels. We read that the foundations, pavements and gates are made of these treasures. How resplendent then will be the roof? How astonishing the throne? Well, our eyes shall see it, and our fingers shall handle it, and eternity shall be little enough to take the survey of its glory, and to wonder at its splendor. . . . If the world that was made in six days is a fabric so excellent, what will that city be, which has been building and beautifying from eternity? Enter (will Christ say) into the kingdom prepared for you! God is still preparing, furnishing and perfuming heaven for you. What shall I say? "For eye hath not seen, ear hath not heard, nor hath it entered into the heart of man, to conceive the things that God hath provided for them that love Him" (1 Cor. 2:9). That joy cannot enter into us; it is sufficient that we shall enter into it. When we come to see ourselves encompassed with all this glory, we shall say as the Queen of Sheba of Solomon, when she saw the order and splendor of his court: "The one half of his glory was never told us" (1 Kgs. 10:17). And thus you see what it is herewith our eyes shall be feasted; though the manner is ineffable, when we come to our Father's house, we shall reflect upon ourselves and see our own glory. Then we shall view the enameled bodies of the saints, surrounding the body of Christ, to which the sun is but a globe of darkness, and finally survey the splendor of the New Jerusalem; and all this eternally, without astonishment, trembling or weariness. . . . there is a glory, a glory surpassing our imagination, that would not only busy and employ, but puzzle and dazzle and extinguish our eyes to look upon it, were they not supported by the infinite power and wisdom of God; for otherwise they would crush and destroy us.

Worst of Times

Thomas Watson

Desertion is the saddest condition that can befall God's children in this life. God now rains hell out of heaven (to use Salvian's expression). "The arrows of the almighty are within me, the poison whereof drinketh up my spirits" (Job 6:4). This is the poisoned arrow that wounds to the heart. Desertion is a taste of the torments of the damned. God says, "In a little wrath I hid my face from thee" (Isa. 54:8). I may here gloss with Bernard, "Lord, doest Thou call that a little wrath when Thou hidest Thy face?" God is in Scripture called a light, and a fire; the deserted soul feels the fire, but does not see the light. But yet you who are adopted may spell love in all this. They say of Hercules' club, that it was made of the wood of olive; the olive is an emblem of peace. So God's club, whereby He beats down the soul in desertion, has something of the olive. There is peace and mercy in it. . . . In time of desertion God leaves a seed of comfort in the soul. "His seed remaineth in Him" (1 John 3:9). This seed of God is a seed of comfort. Though God's children in desertion want the seal of the Spirit, yet they have the unction of the Spirit; though they want the sun, yet they have a day star in their hearts. As the tree in winter, though it has lost its leaves and fruit, yet there is sap in the root, so in the winter of desertion there is the sap of grace in the root of the heart. As it is with the sun masking itself with a cloud, when it denies light to the earth, yet it gives forth its influence. So, though God's dear adopted ones may lose the light of His countenance, yet they have the influence of His grace.

In a little wrath I hid my face from thee for a moment; but with everlasting kindness will I have mercy on thee, saith the LORD thy Redeemer.

Isaiah 54:8

> In the winter of desertion there is the sap of grace in the root of the heart.

Sacred Submission

William Bates

Consider what a reproach is cast upon Christianity, that so many virtuous heathens in great afflictions, were in some measure supported by the precepts of human wisdom; and that Christians, to whom there is revealed from heaven, that an eternal state of glory and joy shall be the reward of their patient sufferings, remain utterly disconsolate. I will single out one example. Stilpon the philosopher, when his city was destroyed, with his wife and children, and he escaped alone from the fire, being asked whether he had lost any thing, replied, "All my treasures are with me—justice, virtue, temperance, prudence, and this inviolable principle, not to esteem any thing as my proper good, that can be ravished from me." His mind was erect and steadfast under the ruins of his country. And others upon lower and less generous considerations have borne up in their sufferings. How do such examples upbraid us, that their twilight excels our noonday brightness? If common cordials raised such courageous spirits in them, shall not the waters of life, the divine strong comforts of the gospel, fortify us to bear all sufferings with a valiant resignation to the good will of God? Can the spirit of a man, by rational principles sustain his infirmities, and cannot the spirit of God, the great comforter, support us under all troubles?

> Shall not the waters of life, the divine strong comforts of the gospel, fortify us to bear all sufferings.

Life's Rudder

Robert Dingley

Be advised carefully to watch over the heart. Keep the fountain clean, and the streams will run pure. Let not the main fort be taken, and the out-works will be regained. In keeping the heart, the eye is preserved. "Keep thy heart with all diligence (or above all keeping), for out of it are the issues of death; Let thine eyes look right on, and thine eyelids straight before thee" (Prov. 4:23, 25). And again, "My son give me thine heart, and let thine eyes observe my ways" (Prov. 23:26). Junius and Tremellius do thus expound our text: "Turn away mine eyes, that is to say, my thoughts and studies from vanity." Which way the thoughts and desires of your hearts go, that way goes the eye. Our blessed Savior expresses that "from within, out of the heart proceeds an evil eye" (Mark 7:21–22). If there is not an evil heart, there cannot be an evil eye, I mean, habitually evil. The eye, ear, tongue, and all the members are led and acted by the heart. Get then a humble, honest, and clean heart; watch over it, it is very slippery, a gulf of deceitfulness. Get the law of God written on your heart in golden characters of the Spirit; this being done, your heart will give laws to the senses, it will hold the reins of the eyes.

Keep thy heart with all diligence; for out of it are the issues of life.
Proverbs 4:23

> The eye, ear, tongue, and all the members are led and acted by the heart.

Redemption's Taste

John Flavel

Glory ye in his holy name: let the heart of them rejoice that seek the LORD.

Psalm 105:3

Be thankful, as well as content, in every state. "Blessed be the God and Father of our Lord Jesus Christ, who hath blessed us with all spiritual blessings in heavenly places in Christ" (Eph. 1:3). O think what are men to angels, that Christ should pass by them to become a Savior to men? And what are you among men that you should be taken, and others left! And among all the mercies of God, what mercies are comparable to these conferred upon you? Bless God in the lowest ebb of outward comforts, for such privileges as these. And yet you will not come up to your duty in all this, except you are joyful in the Lord, and rejoice evermore after the receipt of such mercies as these, "Rejoice in the Lord ye righteous, and again I say rejoice" (Phil. 4:4). For has not the poor captive reason to rejoice, when he has recovered his liberty? Or the debtor to rejoice when all scores are cleared and he owes nothing? Or the weary traveler to rejoice, though he is not owner of a shilling, when he has come almost home, where all his wants shall be supplied? Why this is our case, when Christ once becomes yours: you are the Lord's freeman, your debts to justice are all satisfied by Christ; and you are within a little of complete redemption from all the troubles and inconveniences of your present state.

> **You are the Lord's freeman. Your debts to justice are all satisfied by Christ.**

The Saint's Beauty

William Dyer

What is the reason that the saints are excellent above all others? Is it for their birth, breeding, learning, riches, greatness or honor? No, no, it is for none of these; but if you will know the reason, it is because Christ is formed in them, and married to them; they have the new name, the new nature, the new heart, and the new spirit. This is the reason, if there were any thing besides Christ that could make any nation, or family, or person, truly desirable, it must be either birth, or greatness, or learning, or riches, beauty, or wisdom, or strength; now all these do not make anyone desirable, for if they did, then those that sit upon the nations would be the most desirable persons under heaven, because they have most of these. But for this, see Dan. 4:17, "And setteth up over it, the basest of men." So that none of these can then do it, but Christ only (Rev. 5:10). He has made us unto our God, kings and priests; Christ has made every believer a king; it is Christ's beauty that makes us beautiful; it is His riches that make us rich; it is His righteousness that makes us righteous; He only makes us truly honorable and desirable; well may Christ be called the desire of all nations, for it is He that makes a nation desirable.

Now therefore ye are no more strangers and foreigners, but fellow citizens with the saints, and of the household of God.
Ephesians 2:19

> It is Christ's beauty that makes us beautiful; it is His riches that make us rich.

Heaven to Earth

John Durant

And no man hath as-cended up to heaven, but he that came down from heaven, even the Son of man which is in heaven.

John 3:13

Consider from whence Christ came. He was in the bosom of the Father, where He lay, and lived in His Father's love; hence He came to declare love to believers. John tells us, "He came down from heaven" (John 6:38). Jesus Christ from all eternity was in heaven. There He had His Father's company; there He enjoyed His Father's love; there He was blessed in His Father's bosom (for so the Scripture says); He was living in the light of the Father's love (John 1:18). And being with God, He solaced Himself in God. In that very light and glory in which God was, in that same light and glory did Christ triumph. And yet from this, from this He came for believers' sakes. He forgot (as it were) His kindred, and Father's house, to be born for believers. To undertake a long journey, and from a rare place, for any, declares much love to them. O how long a journey did Christ undertake and from what a paradise of pleasure did He come to believers when He was born? Surely great was His affection, transcendent in His love, who came (at least for a time) from the house of love (His Father's bosom) to open to believers the fountain of love (His own bosom).

He forgot, as it were, His kindred and Father's house to be born for believers.

Lasting Monument

William Fenner

Where was the thief pardoned? Was it not in Golgotha, where Christ was crucified, the place where Christ did triumph, where He was crowned, where He forgave transgressions and sins? There it was where Christ pardoned him. Now as it is with a captain, when he has his victory, he will set up some monument at the place, that it may be a token thereof, so Christ, having wrought the salvation of the world, set up a monument there where He wrought it, whereof none greater than this could be, not the rending of the rocks, nor the earthquake, nor any of the wonders besides did so honor the depth of Christ, as the conversion of this thief, who like a physician having made an excellent medicine, and desirous to try it, will do that for nothing, which he will not do again for much. So Christ having made an admirable sovereign plaster for the salvation of mankind, so soon as ever He had made it, He makes an experiment thereof on this thief, as if He should have said, "Now you shall see what my death can do." So then, you see that the conversion of this thief was no ordinary, but an extraordinary wonder.

And Jesus said unto him, Verily I say unto thee, Today shalt thou be with me in paradise.
Luke 23:43

> **Now you shall see what my death can do.**

Assurance

John Owen

Evangelical assurance is not a thing that consists in any point, and so incapable of variation. It may be higher or lower, greater or less, obscure or attended with more evidence. It is not quite lost when it is not quite at its highest. God sometimes marvelously raises the souls of His saints with some close and near approaches to them; He gives them a sense of His eternal love, a taste of the embraces of His Son and the inhabitation of the Spirit, without the least intervening disturbance; then this is their assurance. But this life is not a season to be always taking wages in; our work is not yet done; we are not always to abide in this mount. We must go down again into the battle, fight again, cry again, complain again. Shall the soul be thought now to have lost its assurance? Not at all. It had before assurance with joy, triumph, and exultation; it has it now, or may have, with wrestling, cries, tears, and supplications. And a man's assurance may be as good, as true, when he lies on the earth with a sense of sin, as when he is carried up to the third heaven with a sense of love and foretaste of glory.

Shall the soul be thought now to have lost its assurance? Not at all.

Delights

Edmund Calamy

A godly man delights more in God and His Word than in any worldly thing whatsoever. "Lord, lift thou up the light of thy countenance upon us; thou hast put gladness in my heart, more than in the time that their corn and their wine increased" (Ps. 4:6–7). The delight of a saint in God's Word, overtops all his creaturely delights and enjoyments, and for the joy he finds in it, "he will sell all that he hath to purchase it" (Matt. 13:44). But the joy of the wicked rejoices more in corn, wine and oil. When it comes into competition, he will leave his spiritual and heavenly, rather than lose his creaturely and carnal pleasures. Thus Herod rejoiced in the word that John the Baptist preached, but he rejoiced more in his Herodias; and when it came to the trial he chose to behead John the Baptist, rather than to part with Herodias. The stony ground when persecution arose parted with all its joy and earth, rather than lose its estate or life (Mark 4:16–17). As a godly man rejoices in worldly things, as if he rejoiced not (1 Cor. 7:30), so a wicked man rejoices in spiritual things as though he rejoiced not. In the Old Law those fowls that did both fly and swim, were unclean. A wicked man would at times fly aloft in spiritual delights, but he would also bathe himself and swim in carnal pleasures, and his heart is more affected with worldly advancement and bodily recreations than with heavenly; and this is a sign that he is an unclean Christian, and that his delights in God and His Word are not right, because they are not overtopping and superlative.

I will worship toward thy holy temple, and praise thy name for thy lovingkindness and for thy truth: for thou hast magnified thy word above all thy name.
Psalm 138:2

> A godly man rejoices in worldly things, as if he rejoiced not.

183

Sharp and Gentle

Timothy Cruso

That ye may be blame-less and harmless, the sons of God, without rebuke, in the midst of a crooked and perverse nation, among whom ye shine as lights in the world.
Philippians 2:15

God knows that there is a necessity sometimes of using sharpness with His own, to bring them to their right mind, and keep them in it. Though there is a great unlikeness between the case of good and bad men in this particular, as there are very manifest degrees of hardness in natural things, and as short slumbers do differ from the spirit of a deep sleep. Bad men are scarcely awakened but by some amazing stroke, or by the thunder of God's power, as men in a lethargy are not roused without some more than ordinary noise, whereas good men are wrought upon by more gentle means. It must be the tormenting sting of some deadly scorpion which recovers any sense in the one, but the smart of a rod will be sufficient, through grace, to the other. And so much we find by many instances, is both proper and needful. For God beats with few or with many stripes, as He sees occasion; He throws us into a hotter or cooler furnace, according as we have more or less need of melting. He does not delight in causing His children (as some barbarous idolaters did theirs) to pass through the fire, but when the case requires it He performs His work upon them by it.

Good men are wrought upon by more gentle means.

Better to Depart

John Shower

From what our Savior said to the penitent thief on the cross, and from what we may gather from the parable concerning Lazarus, the immediate happiness of the souls of Christians in another state is affirmed, that they are not to tarry for their felicity till the resurrection. So when the body of Stephen fell asleep, the Lord Jesus received his spirit. And the apostle desires to be unclothed of this earthly tabernacle that his soul might enter into the house not made with hands, that he might be present with the Lord. He desired to be dissolved, that he might be with Christ, as what was far better (much better). And the same phrase, "being with Christ," or being "present with Him," is used for the happiness of the saints after the resurrection, intimating that it is the same sort of happiness, and is so much preferable to any present enjoyment of God in this world, that is called an "absence from Him." We likewise read of the souls of the martyrs, who came out of great tribulation, and had washed their robes, and made them white in the blood of the Lamb, "That they are before the throne of God, serving Him in His temple" (Rev. 6:14). And that is interpreted of His immediate presence in another place, for the Lord God Almighty, and the Lamb are said to be the Temple (Rev. 21:22).

For I am in a strait betwixt two, having a desire to depart, and to be with Christ; which is far better.
Philippians 1:23

The apostle desires that his soul might enter into the house not made with hands.

True Pleasures

Jeremiah Burroughs

For whosoever will save his life shall lose it: and whosoever will lose his life for my sake shall find it. For what is a man profited, if he shall gain the whole world, and lose his own soul? or what shall a man give in exchange for his soul?

Matthew 16:25–26

Oh, that you would test the ways of God, tasting to see that He is good! If your hearts were such that you would be satisfied without earthly pleasures, it would make the moderation of them more pleasant than the excess. You would find more pleasure in the very act of self-denial than in all the pleasure of your lives, and if there is so much enjoyment in denying false pleasure, what joy is there in enjoying true pleasure? Surely God has pleasure enough for you, if you had a heart to trust Him with your pleasure; you shall only lose your sin, not your pleasure. Bernard has a notable expression: "If you are willing to sacrifice your Isaac (which signifies laughter), your Isaac, which is your pleasure, shall not die." It is the ram, that is, your stoutness of spirit, your selfishness, that shall die. Isaac shall live, and you shall have pleasure still. Do not harbor ill thoughts of God, to think that He is an enemy to your pleasure and delight. He does not delight to grieve your spirit. If you would trust Him with your pleasure, you would have pleasure. . . . You must trust God with your soul's eternal condition; will you not trust Him with your pleasures? Do you think Christ came to die and shed His precious blood to bring you into a worse condition than before? Oh no, certainly Christ did not come to take away any pleasure from His people, but to bring them the pleasures of heaven, and of earth too, as far as they are needful. Is it not true that you should have pleasure when you are reconciled to God, and not when you are an enemy?

> You must trust God with your soul's eternal condition; will you not trust Him with your pleasures?

Serious Questions

Richard Alleine

o we live as people that do verily believe we must shortly be in another world, where we must eternally reap the fruit of our doings here? Do we live as men that have that eternity in our eye, and the lively sense upon our hearts of that death and judgment, that glorious reward and eternal punishment that is before us? Surely we do not—O how few of us do thus live! Do we pray, and hear, and buy, and sell, and converse in the world, as men and women that see and look for so great a change? Was there never a time when we felt more of the eternal things upon our hearts than now? Was there never a time when we were more serious, and in good earnest in our religion; when we were more deeply engaged in laying up treasure in heaven, and making an escape from the wrath to come? Was there never a time, when such serious questions should be pondered: What must I do to be saved? What if I should be damned and shut out of the everlasting kingdom, shut up in everlasting darkness? What may I do to please God, and to walk worthy of His holy calling, and to make sure of a part in Christ? Was there never a time when such questions were more ordinarily put than now and when we should be more solicitous about having them answered?

And thou shalt make a plate of pure gold, and grave upon it, like the engravings of a signet, HOLINESS TO THE LORD.
Exodus 28:36

> Was there never a time when we felt more of the eternal things upon our hearts than now?

Prayer's Essence

Henry Scudder

For ye are bought with a price: therefore glorify God in your body, and in your spirit, which are God's.

1 Corinthians 6:20

When there is cause, we may use long prayers or repetitions, and therefore many words in some prayers, namely, when the matter of our prayer is large, and when in repetition of the same things we renew and double our desires, and express a further degree of seriousness and earnestness of our heart in putting up the said desires. The examples of the prayers of David, of Solomon, of Daniel, and of our blessed Savior Christ Jesus, who spent whole nights in prayer, and therefore must have used many words, give us a sufficient warrant. But in numerous cases many words in prayer are unlawful, such as words in prayer without matter, many words and repetitions without understanding and new affections, when men think they shall rather be heard for their oratory or much speaking, when men make long prayers that they may be thought to have a large gift in prayer, or when they do it under a pretense to serve their base ends. Consideration of the infinite heavenly majesty and goodness of our God and Father teaches us that when we pray unto Him we must perform it with holy adoration and devotion. We must have a holy reverence inwardly in our hearts as well as outwardly (when time, place, and ability allow), with reverent and appropriate gestures of the body. For Christ hath redeemed both our souls and bodies; therefore we must serve Him and glorify Him in and with our body and spirit, which are God's. Though the essence of prayer consists of the desire and lifting up of the heart, and though God is a Spirit who is not moved with mere bodily gestures, yet fitting gestures are of special use in prayer. They are partly to help the inward man, making the spirit more apt and lively and the mind to be more attentive to what we are doing, and partly to express the inward devotion and affection of our heart.

Stages in Grace

Richard Alleine

Among the saints, some have more religion in them, abound in the grace of God, and in the work of grace. Others of them have something, but it is but little of religion they have; they are but of little faith (Matt. 6:30), and have but little strength. Some good thing is found in them towards the God of Israel, yet it is but a day of small things. Of these that have but little, some never had much. We read of babes in Christ (1 Pet. 3:1), of children in understanding; and of these, some are but new born babes, beginners in religion; others, as Heb. 5:12 describes, for their time might have been grown up to be men, to be strong in the Lord; yet after a long time of profession of Christianity, they have not had one cubit added to their stature in the grace of God. Though they have been Christians of long standing, yet their souls are as Zacchæus's body, of little stature. Of those that have but little grace, some never had more; it has been ever but low with them from the beginning. Others once had more grace, but they are fallen, and sunk in their estates; like Naomi, the time was when they went out full, but they have returned empty. They have wasted their talents, and are consumed in their strength; their light burns dim, their flaming lamp has become but like smoking flax, they have little more than the snuff of religion left them. Now there is need of stirring up themselves in religion in all these sorts. Those that have the most of grace, had need bestir themselves to get more: those that (live) most in the diligent exercise of grace, that live most spiritually, most circumspectly, had need be giving more diligence daily; you that are highest, you are not yet come to your full growth, there is still more to be gotten, and more to be done for God and your souls.

I write unto you, fathers, because ye have known him that is from the beginning. I write unto you, young men, because ye have overcome the wicked one. I write unto you, little children, because ye have known the Father.
1 John 2:13

> Those that have the most of grace had need bestir themselves to get more.

Gratitude

Thomas Manton

Enter into his gates with thanksgiving, and into his courts with praise: be thankful unto him, and bless his name.
Psalm 100:4

When we come to pray, we must remember not only what we want, but what we have received, acknowledging that we have all from God. He is our Father: "Do ye thus requite the Lord, O foolish people, and unwise? Is not He thy father that hath bought thee? Hath He not made thee and established thee?" (Deut. 32:6). We must acknowledge the good we have, as well as that which we expect to come from Him. Therefore, if we would have a praying frame, and be eased of our solicitude, and that anxious care which is a disparagement to providence, it is good to take up God under the notion of a Father, which makes us rest upon Him for all things: "Take no thought for your life, what ye shall eat, or what ye shall drink; nor yet for your body, what ye shall put on" (Matt. 6:25). Why? "For your heavenly Father knoweth that you have need of all these things" (v. 32). You that are able fathers would think yourselves disparaged if that your children should filch and steal for their living, and beg and be solicitous, and go up and down from door to door for their maintenance and support, and not trust to your care and provision. A believer which knoweth he has a heavenly Father will not be negligent in his calling, but be active and industrious in his way, and use those lawful means which, by the providence of God, he has been brought up in; and then, "be careful for nothing," as the apostle's advice is (Phil. 4:6), and "in everything, by prayer and supplication, make your request known unto God." Oh, could we turn carking into prayer, and run to our Father, it would be happy for us. Care, and diligence, and necessary provision: that is our work and labor; but for the success and event of things, leave it to God. When we are carking in the world with such anxiousness, and troubled with restless thoughts, how we should be provided for in old age, and what will become of us and ours, we take God's work out of His hands. This is a disparagement to our heavenly Father, and a reproach to His providence and fatherly care.

The Divine Life

William Bates

And Enoch walked with God.
Genesis 5:24a

After a principle of life and holiness is planted in us, we are, by a continual supply of strength from Christ, assisted to exercise it in all the acts that are proper to the divine life. There is a resemblance between the fruits of the earth, and the graces of a Christian: seed must be first sown in the earth, before it springs out of it; and when it is sown, the natural qualities of the earth, coldness and dryness, are so contrary to fructifying, that without the influences of the heavens, the heat of the sun, and showers of rain, the seed would be lost in it. Grace is drawn forth into flourishing and fruitfulness by the irradiating and warm influx of the Spirit. But we are subordinate agents in carrying on the work of grace to perfection. The apostle exhorts us to work out our own salvation with fear and trembling; for it is God who works in us to will and to do. Carnal men abuse the freeness of grace to looseness and security, and the power of grace to negligence and laziness. Our dependence on God infers the use of means to save our souls. Our Savior commands us to "watch and pray, that we may not enter into temptation" (Matt. 26:41). To watch without prayer is to presume upon our own strength: to pray without watching is to presume upon the grace of God. The Lord's Prayer is the rule of our duty and desires: we are engaged by every petition to cooperate and concur with divine grace to obtain what we pray for. Naaman presumed that he should be immediately cleansed from his leprosy by the prayer of Elisha; but he was commanded to go and wash himself in Jordan seven times for his purification. A stream preserves its crystal clearness by continual running; if its course be stopped, it will stagnate and putrefy. The purity of the soul is preserved by the constant exercise of habitual grace.

Thanksgiving

George Swinnock

Every good gift and every perfect gift is from above, and cometh down from the Father of lights, with whom is no variableness, neither shadow of turning.

James 1:17

Consider what a distinguishing mercy and precious treasure the Word of God is, how without it you would have forever been both unholy and unhappy, and how by it you may eternally be both gracious and glorious. Without question you will find cause to bless the Giver for such a rare and profitable gift. The apostle ranks this favor among the blessings of the highest form: "What advantage hath the Jew? Or what profit is there of circumcision?" (Rom. 3:1). The answer is chiefly, that unto them were committed the oracles of God. The psalmist, mentioning this mercy, concludes with "Praise ye the Lord" (Ps. 147:19–20). The light of the sun, moon, and stars is of such concern to men, that without them the beauty of the old creation would be buried in darkness, and therefore the children of God have given the Most High the credit of those greater and lesser candles (Ps. 136:7–9). . . . The light of God's law and Word is of infinitely more worth, for by it the glory and beauty of the new creation, and that curious piece of man's redemption, is seen and known. What honor God deserves for this favor!

> The light of God's law and Word is of infinite worth.

Seize the Day

Robert Harris

Ask and consider, "What mercy have I shown to the miserable? How often have I prayed for them, mourned with them, put myself out to minister to their necessities?" And if you find the reckoning to rise but slowly and poorly, be ashamed for it; bewail it. And in the future, never be afraid to show mercy, as if God, in calling us thereunto, meant us any harm. But seize all opportunities and thankfully embrace them, taking occasion to bless God that He has furnished us with any ability and opportunity to be helpful, serviceable, comforting to any sad heart or ruinous estate. You can easily be persuaded that it is a blessed thing to receive help, comfort, ease, and relief when you are in distress. Then take Christ's word once uttered by Saint Paul in Acts 20:35, it being a proverb much used by our Savior, namely, "It is a more blessed thing to give than to receive," in good things. It is better to be an agent than a patient, as on the contrary in evil things. Would you then be thankful for receiving good at the hands of others? Be more thankful if God has given you ability and opportunity, and (which is the greatest of all) a heart to do good to others.

As we have therefore opportunity, let us do good unto all men, especially unto them who are of the household of faith.
Galatians 6:10

It is a blessed thing to receive help, comfort, ease, and relief when you are in distress.

Prayer's Might

Christopher Nesse

And he said, Let me go, for the day breaketh. And he said, I will not let thee go, except thou bless me.

Genesis 32:26

There is a kind of omnipotency ascribed to prayer (as Luther said) when it is the prayer of faith, and so acted by that best of graces. You may stand and wonder what the Scripture attributes to faith and prayer, or the prayer of faith. It can do more than all the witches in the world can do, for it can set God at work, whereas they can but set the devil at work. None know what prayer can do but those that know what God can do. In this sense prayer is said to be omnipotent as it sets omnipotency at work; it has had command over all the four elements, as over the air in Elijah (Jas. 5:17), to whom God gave this key to open and shut up heaven at His pleasure, and over the fire which the same Elijah fetched down at pleasure by his prayer one time in a way of wrath (2 Kgs. 1:16), and another time in way of mercy and merciful acceptance (1 Kgs. 18:37–38). Prayer had power over the water in Moses (Exod. 14:15–16), and over the earth in the same man of God, who by His powerful prayer first cleaved the sea asunder to save Israel, and then the earth asunder to destroy the accomplices of Korah (Num. 16:29). As those two great comforts of Christ on Mount Tabor (Moses and Elijah) had command over the four elements, so Joshua over the sun itself (Josh. 10:12), and by Moses' prayer, he had command over Amalek before (Exod. 17:11–12). Yet higher, Elisha by prayer had command over the angels, fetching them out of heaven, for his protection and comfort (2 Kgs. 6:17), but yet higher than that over the God-man, the angel of the covenant, the Lord of Angels in Jacob, who wept and supplicated Jacob, saying, "Let me go for the day dawns" (Gen. 32:26).

> **Prayer is said to be omnipotent as it sets omnipotency at work.**

King of Kings

William Dyer

Christ is King over His enemies; He is King above all kings, and over all things, and therefore Scripture calls Him "King of kings," as you have it in 1 Tim. 6:15. Christ is a King above all kings; for if He were not a King above all kings, He could not be a King over all things. Now that He is a King above all kings, two Scriptures prove it. In Ps. 89:27, God says, "I will make my first-born higher than the kings of the earth." Now who is the first-born? It is Jesus Christ, as He is elsewhere called, the first-born of every creature. Now, says God, I will make my first-born higher than the kings of the earth, higher in glory, higher in power and higher in majesty. So in Rev. 1:5, Christ is called "the Prince of the earth." Alas, alas, what are all the mighty men, the great men, the honorable men of the earth to Jesus Christ? They are but a little bubble in the water. For if all the nations, in comparison to God, are but as the drop of a bucket, or as the dust of the balance, as the prophet speaks in Isa. 40, O how little then are the kings of the earth. Nay, beloved, Christ Jesus is not only above the kings of the earth, and higher than the kings, but He is higher than the angels, yes, He is the head of angels (Col. 2:10); "He is the head of all principalities and powers," which includes the angels. And in Heb. 1:6, "Let all the angels of God worship Him." God will have the angels worship Christ as well as men. Christ is a King, before whom the angels veil their face, and the kings of the earth do cast down their crowns.

And he hath on his vesture and on his thigh a name written, KING OF KINGS, AND LORD OF LORDS.
Revelation 19:16

> O how little then are the kings of the earth.

Future Redemption

John Bunyan

Who shall change our vile body, that it may be fashioned like unto his glorious body, according to the working whereby he is able even to subdue all things unto himself.
Philippians 3:21

There is yet a redemption to come, which is called the redemption of our body (Rom. 8:23). Of this redemption we have both the deposit and the seal, to wit, the Spirit of God (Eph. 1:14, 4:30). And because the time to it is long, therefore we are to wait for it; and because it will be that upon which all our blessedness will be let out to us, and we also let into it, therefore we should be comforted at all the signs of the near approach thereof; "then," says Christ, "look up and lift up your heads" (Luke 21:28). The bodies of saints are called the purchased possession; possession, because the whole of all that shall be saved shall be for a temple or house for God to dwell in, in the heavens. A purchased possession, because the body, as well as the soul, is bought with the price of blood (1 Cor. 6:14–20). But what then does He mean by the redemption of this purchased possession? I answer, He means the raising it up from the dead; "I will ransom them from the power of the grave, I will redeem them from death" (Hos. 13:14). And then shall be brought to pass the saying that is written, "Death is swallowed up in victory. This saying and that in Isaiah speak both the selfsame thing (1 Cor. 15; Isa. 25:8). And this was signified by Moses, where he speaks of the year of jubilee, and of the redemption of the house that was sold in Israel, how of that year it should return to the owner (Lev. 25). Our bodies of right are God's, but sin still dwells in them; we have also sold and forfeited them to death and the grave, and so they will abide; but at the judgment day, that blessed jubilee, God will take our body, which originally was His, and will deliver it from the bondage of corruption, unto which, by our souls, through sin, it has been subjected; He will take it, I say, because it is His, both by creation and redemption, and will bring it to that perfect freedom that is only to be found in immortality and eternal life. And for this should Israel hope!

Holy Resolution

Thomas Watson

Gregory Nazianzen said of Athanasius that he was both a lodestone and an adamant: a lodestone for the sweetness of his disposition, and an adamant for the invincibleness of his resolution. When the emperor Valens promised Basil great preference if he would subscribe to the Arian heresy, Basil responded, "Sir, these speeches are fit to catch little children, but we who are taught by the Spirit are ready to endure a thousand deaths rather than suffer one syllable of Scripture to be altered." A righteous man is willing to take the cross for his jointure and, with Ignatius, wear Christ's sufferings as a collar of pearl. "We glory in tribulation" (Rom. 5:3). St. Paul rattled his chain and gloried in it as a woman who is proud of her jewels, said Chrysostom. "It is to my loss," said Gordius the martyr, "if you abate me anything of my sufferings." Of what heroic undaunted spirits were the primitive Christians who could scorn preferments, laugh at imprisonments, snatch up torments as crowns, and whose love to Christ burned hotter than the fire insomuch that the heathens cried out, "Great is the God of the Christians!"

I have set the LORD always before me: because he is at my right hand, I shall not be moved.
Psalm 16:8

> With Ignatius, wear Christ's sufferings as a collar of pearl.

Behold Love

John Owen

For mine eyes have seen the King, the LORD of hosts.
Isaiah 6:5b

Eye the Father as love. Do not look on Him as a Father always disappointed, but as one most kind and tender. Let us look on Him by faith, as one that has had thoughts of kindness towards us from everlasting. It is a misapprehension of God that makes any, who has the least breathing wrought in them after Him, run from Him. "They that know thee will put their trust in thee" (Ps. 9:10). Men cannot abide with God in spiritual meditations. He loses their soul's company by their want of this insight into His love. They fix their thoughts only on His terrible majesty, severity, and greatness; and so their spirits are not endeared. Would a soul continually eye His everlasting tenderness and compassion, His thoughts of kindness that have been from of old, His present gracious acceptance, it could not bear an hour's absence from Him; whereas now, perhaps, it cannot watch with Him one hour. Let, then, the saints' first notion of the Father be full of eternal, free love towards them; let their hearts and thoughts be filled with breaking through all discouragements that lie in the way. Consider . . . whose love it is. It is the love of Him who is in Himself all sufficient, infinitely satiated with Himself and His own glorious excellencies and perfections; who has no need to go forth with His love unto others, nor to seek an object of it without Himself. There might be rest with delight and complacency to eternity. He is sufficient unto His own love. He has His Son, also, His eternal Wisdom, to rejoice and delight in from all eternity (Prov. 8:30). This might take up and satiate the whole delight of the Father; but He will love His saints also. And it is such a love, as wherein He seeks not His own satisfaction only, but our good therein also; the love of a God, the love of a Father, whose proper outgoings are kindness and bounty.

Mercy with God

John Shower

et the wicked and unrighteous forsake the evil of his heart and ways, and turn to the Lord, and he shall find mercy. Observe that the vilest and most heinous transgressors (let their sins be what they will) if they penitently return to God, they may be assured of pardon. Whatever wickedness against God, or unrighteousness against men, whatever iniquity or sin, in heart or life, open or secret, they are charged with, yet there is mercy with God upon true repentance. The Holy Scriptures are full of this doctrine. How large and general are the invitations and calls of God to all sorts of sinners? How express and positive are the declarations of His Word? That even the scarlet and crimson sins shall be as snow and wool; that all sin and blasphemy shall be forgiven, except that sin against the Holy Ghost, which is joined with obstinate impenitence, that our Lord Jesus Christ came to save the chiefest of sinners, and that His blood cleanses from all sin. What a large and black catalogue is there, of such as shall not enter into the kingdom of God, fornicators, adulterers, revilers and extortioners, and yet it is added, "such were some of you, but ye are washed" (2 Cor. 6:9–11). How affectionately does God expostulate with sinners? Even the vilest of them, and urge them to cast away their transgressions, and assure them that He has no pleasure in their ruin? How earnestly does He beseech them to be reconciled, and hearken to the voice of His mercy? With what variety of arguments does He plead with them? From the freeness and riches of His grace, from the absolute necessity of it? . . . The aggravations of your guilt can never be such as to condemn you, but the virtue of the blood of Christ is greater to pardon you, if you return to God by Jesus Christ. As far as heaven is above earth, God's thoughts are above ours in this matter.

But there is forgiveness with thee, that thou mayest be feared.
Psalm 130:4

> How affectionately does God expostulate with sinners.

Royal Guest

Richard Alleine

For God is the King of all the earth. Sing ye praises with understanding.
Psalm 47:7

If you had a great friend, a lord or a knight, who would come to lodge a night in your house, what would you do? How would you prepare your house to entertain such a friend? What sweeping, washing, rubbing, scourging, and adorning would there be? Every vessel would be brightened, every room would be beautified! Would you let it lie all dirty and dusty, with hanging cobwebs and spiders? Would you let it lie nasty and filthy, everything out of place and order? Surely you would not! And when he had come in, would you open your doors to let in a rabble of sordid beggars, or common rogues or drunkards, to come and drink and roar, and spit in the very room where your friend was being entertained? No, you would sweep all within, and set a porter at your doors to keep the unclean rabble out. Oh, what is the greatest friend in the world to the great and holy God? Prepare Him a holy habitation; open the doors and let the King of glory come in. Then shut the door, and let no unclean thing enter to offend and displease Him, so that the Lord may take pleasure in you, and delight in you, and may say concerning you, "This heart is My rest; here will I dwell forever."

> **Then shut the door, and let no unclean thing enter to offend and displease Him.**

The Armor of God

Nathaniel Vincent

he apostle, looking upon the Ephesians as militant saints and fighting not against flesh and blood, but against principalities and powers of darkness, instructs them how they might become more than conquerors. To this end he tells them first of all where their strength lies; they must "be strong in the Lord, and in the power of His might" (Eph. 6:10), and then he gives them a complete armor. . . . They must be girded about with the girdle of truth. . . . A judgment rightly informed and well settled, that buys the truth and will by no means sell it, has a great influence to a Christian's steadfastness and growth in grace. They must have on the breastplate of righteousness. . . . Satan cannot so easily disquiet them that are sincere, neither is he able to corrupt them. . . . Their feet must be shod with the preparation of the gospel of peace. They must be encouraged by that peace which the gospel publishes, to run in the way of God's commandments; and that through those wars which are never so difficult and unpleasant to flesh and blood, they must hold fast the profession of their faith, and depart from evil, and go in the path that is called holy; though by thus doing, they never so much expose, and make themselves a prey. Above all, they must take the shield of faith, whereby they may quench the fiery darts of the wicked. Satan's temptations are darts. . . . But faith is a shield to repel and beat them back; faith makes application of the righteousness and strength of Christ, and by this means not only former wounds are assuaged and healed, but the soul is more secure for the future. The helmet of salvation must cover their heads in this day of battle with evil angels. A lively hope of salvation is very encouraging both to patient continuance in well-doing, and also unto suffering for the sake of righteousness. The apostle tells them that the sword of the Spirit, which is the Word of God, must be made use of. If this Word is understood, believed, thought on, loved, stood in awe of; if it thus abide in us, we shall be strong, and overcome the evil one.

Put on the whole armor of God, that ye may be able to stand against the wiles of the devil.
Ephesians 6:11

Common Mercies

Samuel Lee

For thou preventest him with the blessings of goodness: thou settest a crown of pure gold on his head.

Psalm 21:3

The infinite goodness of God bestows more mercies upon us in the method of prevention, than of answer to particular prayers. We enjoy most things before we ask, and often more excellent in kind, and more abundant in measure than we ask. . . . He makes His sun to rise every morning upon the unjust, and His moon to fill her orb with light upon the ungodly crescent. His paths in the clouds drop fatness upon the fields of bloody tyrants, and His ocean is open, and sweet western gales often swell the sails of rambling and roving pirates. The earth is full of His goodness. He spread and filled the tables of Heliogabalus with His hidden treasures. There is no inhabitant but is laden with His benefits, however abused to their luxury, pride, and wantonness. His mercies are over all His works; He makes the out-goings of the morning and evening to sing. He preserves the goings out and the comings in of all the children of Adam.

There is no inhabitant but is laden with His benefits.

Be Not Silent

Thomas Watson

childlike heart is a zealous heart. It is impatient of God's dishonor. Moses was cool in his own cause, but hot in God's. When the people of Israel had wrought folly in the golden calf, he broke the tables. As we shall answer for idle words, so we shall answer for sinful silence. It is dangerous in this sense to be possessed with a dumb devil. David says that the zeal of God's house had eaten him up (Ps. 69:9). Many Christians, whose zeal once had almost eaten them up, now they have eaten up their zeal. Let some talk of bitterness, but I can never believe that he has the heart of a child in him, that can be patient when God's glory suffers. Can an ingenious child endure to hear his father reproached? Though we should be silent under God's displeasure, we must not be silent under His dishonor. When there is a fire of zeal kindled in the heart, it will break forth at the lips. Zeal tempered with holiness, this white and sanguine is the best complexion of the soul. . . .
It is reported of Chrysostom, that he reproved any sin against God, as if he himself had received a personal wrong.

For the zeal of thine house hath eaten me up; and the reproaches of them that reproached thee are fallen upon me.
Psalm 69:9

> Though we should be silent under God's displeasure, we must not be silent under His dishonor.

Tears Overcome

Robert Dingley

Therefore also now,
saith the LORD,
turn ye even to me
with all your heart,
and with fasting, and
with weeping, and
with mourning.
Joel 2:12

A true penitent wishes that his head were a fountain, and his eyes spouts or rivers of tears, that he might weep day and night for his sins. The eyes of David gushed out with tears for the sins of others, and he "watered his couch with his tears" for personal failings (Ps. 6:6). Peter wept bitterly for denying Christ three times. Mary Magdalene, that had abused her eyes by lascivious glances, her hair by wanton curling, and her lips by unchaste kisses, did upon repentance otherwise employ them. For she washed the feet of Christ with her tears, kissed them with her lips, and wiped them with the hair of her head. So then, the eye that has looked wantonly must weep penitently. Tears do rebaptize us. The rarest music is heard upon the water, and our prayers to make best melody over a flood of tears. "Prayers entreat, and tears overcome," says Jerome. "I have heard thy prayers, and seen thy tears," said God to Hezekiah (2 Kgs. 20:5). Then our prayers do pierce the clouds, when they are pointed with tears. He that can weep for worldly losses, and not spiritual failings, has in him nothing but nature. Augustine says that he did wonderfully weep in reading the fourth book of Virgil, when Dido was killed; "Oh," says he, "what a wretched soul had I, that could weep for her misery and not for my own!" "Tears," says Bernard, "are the wine of angels, who rejoice over a sinner's compunction." The hammer of the law may break an icy heart, but the sunshine of the gospel dissolves it into tears. You know Peter was melted by a love-glance of Christ. . . . "After a wet seed-time follows often a glorious harvest, and after a shower of tears, the sunshine of joy," says Chrysostom. Though tears are not meritorious, yet they may be evident of our interest in Christ. . . . The sense of unkindness offered to Christ sets a broach the sorrow of His heart at His eye. Revenge is one fruit of repentance, and the true penitent observing the past failings of his eye studies a holy revenge upon himself; and those eyes that have been the inlets of vanity shall be the outlets of sorrow.

The Habit of Grace

Edmund Calamy

aith is permanent and persevering, it holds out unto the death; it is never totally lost. True believers, as they live in the faith, so they die in the faith. The apostle, speaking of true believers, says, "These all died in the faith" (Heb. 11:13). And true it is that a true believer always dies in the faith, in the faith of adherence, if not of evidence. This is vigor fit to the name of a true believer: "We are made partakers of the Holy Ghost, if we hold the beginning of our confidence steadfast unto the end" (Heb. 3:14). These words plainly evidence that justifying faith is persevering faith; it holds out unto the death and ends in fruition. It can never totally nor finally be lost, and this indeed is its distinguishing property and the property of every renewing grace. Every renewing grace holds out unto the end; that grace which wears the crown of glory is persevering (Rev. 2:10). It is not always so in appearance, but in truth. True believers may at times, and in some cases, seem to themselves and to others to have lost their faith, and other graces, as many examples in Scripture show but yet as Job speaks, "The root of the matter is with me" (Job 19:28), truth of grace in the inward parts, and it abides there. However true believers may and sometimes do, for a time, lose the comfort of grace and the sight of grace . . . yet they never totally lose the habit of any renewing grace; these gifts of God are given without repentance.

But I have prayed for thee, that thy faith fail not.
Luke 22:32a

> **Justifying faith is persevering faith; it holds out unto the death and ends in fruition.**

Daily Provisions

William Spurstowe

If then God so clothe the grass, which is to day in the field, and to morrow is cast into the oven; how much more will he clothe you, O ye of little faith?

Luke 12:28

Faith exercised on the temporal promises, will much help to strengthen our adherence to the promises of a better life, and cause us to trust more perfectly in God for the salvation of our souls. Our Savior tells His disciples that if God fed the fowls and clothed the lilies, He will much more provide for them which are better than they. And so may a believer argue that if God has made so many rich promises of provision for the body, He will not be wanting to the happiness of the soul. If He is so careful of the casket, He will not be unmindful of the jewel. If He gives daily bread to the one, He will surely give manna to the other. If He makes our pilgrimage delightful, and makes the paths of our feet to drop fatness, He will make our rest and habitation with Himself to be glorious. If the feet tread on roses here, and on the moon and stars hereafter, how right and beautiful will be that crown of life that shall be set upon our heads?

Such kind of argumentations are very helpful to a believer, who owns all the outward comforts that arise from God's faithfulness to His promises, though in the mere and naked having of them no one can know love or hatred (Eccl. 9:1).

If God has made so many rich promises for the body, He will not be wanting to the happiness of the soul.

Christ's Love

Samuel Bolton

hrist exceedingly loves His church; we are said to be the dearly beloved of His soul (Jer. 12:7) . . . so Christ loves us beyond all conceptions (Eph. 3:19); it is a love which passes knowledge . . . the apostle went about to measure this love, height, depth, breadth, length, but he found his line too short, his measure would not reach, and therefore he concludes it a love beyond all knowledge. A man may express much love, but he may conceive of more than he can express. Why, this love of Christ is above all we can conceive, above knowledge. It is an infinite love. It is, I say, an infinite love, which is more than if I should lay all the hearts of the creatures together. His love is greater than all. Witness what He has done, what He has suffered, and yet He loves above all. And therefore Christ's heart is exceedingly taken with His church and people . . . we are His riches, His treasures . . . His precious ones, His people, His spouse, and therefore, He rejoices over us: "Thou shalt be called Hephzibah, for the Lord delighteth in thee" (Isa. 62:4–5); yes, as the bridegroom rejoices over the bride, so shall your God rejoice over you: "The Lord will rejoice over thee with joy, He will rest in His love, He will joy over thee with singing" (Zeph. 3:17). And therefore, seeing that Christ does rejoice, His heart must be exceedingly taken with us.

Behold, what manner of love the Father hath bestowed upon us, that we should be called the sons of God: therefore the world knoweth us not, because it knew him not.

1 John 3:1

A man may express much love, but he may conceive of more than he can express.

To Be with God

Jeremiah Burroughs

Surely the righteous shall give thanks unto thy name: the upright shall dwell in thy presence.
Psalm 140:13

The glorious presence of God that the saints shall have of God in heaven is a great part of their happiness. Heaven would not be heaven without the presence of God. The presence of God in the most miserable place possible would be a greater happiness than the absence of God in the most glorious place possible. David would not be afraid though he walked in the valley of the shadow of death, because God was with him (Ps. 23:4). Luther would rather be in hell with God's presence, than in heaven, God being absent. If the presence of God takes away the dread of the shadow of the valley of death and makes hell to be more desired than heaven, what will the presence of God make heaven to be? The three children in the fiery furnace with God's presence were happy; how happy then are the saints with God's presence in heaven? The saints desire God's presence even when He is angry; they hate to be out of His presence. In Ps. 51:9

> **The saints desire God's presence even when He is angry; they hate to be out of His presence.**

David cried to God to hide His face from his sins, for God's face was then an angry face against him. Yet in v. 11 he cried out again, "Cast me not away from thy presence." He was not willing to be out of God's presence. Saint Augustine has this expression: "Whose face he fears, even his face he invocates." God made rich promises to Moses, yet Moses could not be satisfied without the presence of God. "If thy presence be not with us, bring us not hence" (Exod. 33:15). The apostle, when describing the misery of those that are damned, in 2 Thess. 1:9 says, "Who shall be punished with everlasting destruction from the presence of the Lord, and from the glory of His power." The presence of God needs to be the happiness of the saints.

Built on a Rock

John Arrowsmith

s when Peter went walking upon the waves, and perceiving how boisterous the winds were, began to sink, Jesus immediately stretched forth His hand and caught him. So when the psalmist's flesh and heart failed, God even then was the strength of his heart; according to the original, "the rock" of it. Rocks are not more fortifying to cities and castles built upon them, than God is to His people's hearts. A sincere believer's soul is therefore likened by our Savior to a house founded upon a rock, which was every way assaulted, in the roof by rain descending upon it, in the foundation by floods washing upon it, in the walls by winds blustering against them; and yet stood because it was strong, was strong because founded on a rock. Such a rock is our God, and that even in such a case as has been described. Hezekiah, whom God had chosen to life, was sick unto death. Lazarus, whom Jesus loved, sickened and died. Timothy had his frequent infirmities. The psalmist's flesh failed him, or, to speak in Paul's phrase, his outward man perished, yet God meanwhile was the rock and strength of His sick servant's heart.

There is none holy as the LORD: for there is none beside thee: neither is there any rock like our God.

1 Samuel 2:2

> Rocks are not more fortifying to cities and castles built upon them than God is to His people's hearts.

The Shepherd's Voice

Obadiah Sedgwick

He shall feed his flock like a shepherd: he shall gather the lambs with his arm, and carry them in his bosom, and shall gently lead those that are with young.
Isaiah 40:11

Carefully regard your Shepherd's voice. You cannot make the least stray but His whistle is at your ears, and His Word and Spirit beat at your consciences. Now hear His voice, feed only in His pastures, wander not after any pastures besides, though they seem more plentiful or more delightful. My meaning is, keep only in His ways, according to His directions, and do not be withdrawn or wander, through any enticements of sin or the world. Though other pastures seem more pleasant, yet they are full of thorny bushes. You cannot feed long on them, but you are caught and scratched, and shall hardly escape without much loss of your fleece. You may delight for a while in a sinful way, but your consciences will pay for it, and your graces. You cannot return without a great diminution of the one, and a strange vexation of the other; he, who will wander to get some pleasant evil, must necessarily be less good and more troubled. And what defense do you have when you do not hearken to your Shepherd? You are then as the silly sheep alone upon the mountains of Gilead.

> He who will wander to get some pleasant evil must necessarily be less good and more troubled.

Soundness of Heart

William Greenhill

The devil seldom prevails where there is soundness of heart. Job was a man that feared God, and eschewed evil, a perfect man . . . and could the devil prevail with him? God lets loose the devil, and gives him more power over Job, than ever we read he had over any other man, and could the devil prevail against Job? No, he was a sound hearted man, and he could not prevail. Job wearied out the devil; he did strike him in his servants, and cattle, and children, in his body, by his friends, and by his wife he tempts him, yet nothing could so; why here was a sound hearted man, and when a man is sound hearted, he will not stand parleying with the devil, but will resist the devil. He shuts the door presently and turns his back upon the devil; he brings forth the shield of faith, and quenches his fiery darts; he brings forth the Scripture, "It is written." He resists the devil, and he flees. But if you are sickly, or faint hearted, the devil will make you fly or fall; but a sound hearted man resists the devil, and makes him flee, and so the devil is discouraged and disappointed.

So went Satan forth from the presence of the LORD, and smote Job.
Job 2:7a

> When a man is sound hearted, he will not stand parleying with the devil, but will resist the devil.

Complete Armor

Paul Baynes

Put on the whole armour of God.
Ephesians 6:11a

A Christian is born with his armor on his back, so that he can as well cease to be a Christian as cease to be armed. That which is fabulously spoken of the race of giants is truly spoken of us—we are no sooner born than we have our swords girded to us, and our shields on our arms. For the Word begets us, and faith is the first thing formed in us. Now that we must have complete armor, it is hence manifest because it were in vain to have some parts covered, and others open to mortal wounds. The devil is like those champions, who if they cannot wound the head or the heart, will prick any part rather than fail. Christians must then have their complete harness covering them from top to toe, which shows how unchristian many are, who do not know there is any such armor; they are like Israel when there was not a blacksmith, nor a weapon to be found . . . If you do not have this armor, know the devil has surprised you, and holds you as a slave to him. Again, many forget that they must have complete armor; such as must cover them all over, and therefore in some things they seem covered, yet in others they are without defense.

> Christians must then have their complete harness covering them from top to toe.

The Smallest Sins

Timothy Cruso

We must impartially shun the smallest sins. These are accustomed to be overlooked, and left alone, by the most of the world, while greater wickedness is severely condemned. But indeed, as breaking with God for a little, does endanger His delivering us to the worse and more heinous crimes, so it argues a vile and wretched contempt of God, and unfaithfulness to Him. "He that is unjust in the least, is unjust also in much" (Luke 16:10). We ought always to consider the greatness of the person forbidding, more than the aggravations of the thing forbidden, as for example, who it is that says, "Thou shalt not steal," rather than what, or how much it is, which we are tempted to the stealing of. And if our hearts are endued with that tenderness which becomes them, we shall do so. . . . Even little sins are great ones in the eye of such persons; they do not say, as Jonathan did, "I have but tasted a little honey with the end of the rod that was in my hand, and lo I must die" (1 Sam. 14:43), but heartily consent and agree to this, that their damnation is justly inflicted, by whom the least iniquity is knowingly allowed. We find that Abraham would not take from a thread to a shoe latchet of any thing that belonged to the king of Sodom. And, when Pharaoh yielded, that the people of Israel and their little ones should go and sacrifice to God, only their flocks should be stayed, Moses told him, that their cattle also should attend, and not a hoof be left behind. So far were the churches planted by the apostles from keeping the whole of the abolished Jewish festivals, that Paul tells the Colossians that no man should judge them. One of the ancient church historians tells us of Marcus, Bishop of Arethusa, who having destroyed an idolatrous grove in Constantine's time, and afterwards in Julian's reign, being persecuted for it . . . at length proposed to him to repair what he had destroyed, or to furnish, at least, one half of the sum, or some small portion, but he refused and told them that it would be as wicked to give one half-penny for such a purpose as to give all that it required.

Let no man therefore judge you in meat, or in drink, or in respect of an holyday, or of the new moon, or of the sabbath days. Which are a shadow of things to come; but the body is of Christ.
Colossians
2:16–17

A Sound Judgment

Henry Scudder

For God hath not given us the spirit of fear; but of power, and of love, and of a sound mind.
2 Timothy 1:7

Let a sound and clear judgment discern what is good and what is bad. Also what is best and what is least, preferring things spiritual, heavenly, and eternal, incomparably before those which are earthly and temporal. Make those best things your treasure (Matt. 6:21). Then your heart will be chiefly set, and your thoughts will chiefly run on them, and you will be moderate in thinking of those things which are less needful. Do as a wise counselor at law, or as a master of request, who must hear many clients, and receive and answer many petitions. Consider whose turn it is and what is the most important suit, and dispatch them first. Let thoughts of worldly business be shut out, and made to stand at the door, till their turn come to be thought upon, and let the more excellent, and more needful be dispatched first. If thoughts of the world will imprudently intrude themselves, and will not be kept out, rebuke them sharply. Do not give them a hearing, but dishearten them and rebuke the porter and keeper of the door of your heart; that is, smite, wound, and check your conscience.

> Let thoughts of worldly business be shut out, and made to stand at the door, till their turn come to be thought upon.

Woeful Ignorance

James Janeway

Lack of knowledge of God and acquaintance with God is the necessary cause of sin. There is no greater evil on this side of hell than that of a necessity of sinning (2 Pet. 2:14). Those of which it is said that they cannot cease from sinning are called cursed children. One that chooses any sin rather than affliction does it through the blindness of his mind. This is laid as a heavy accusation in Job 36:21: "For this hast thou chosen rather than affliction." To choose iniquity rather than affliction is the greatest folly imaginable. It is one great part of the misery of hell that they never cease from sinning, and this is the greatest misery on earth, our being so much under the power of sin. I appeal to any gracious soul that has the feeling of the burden of sin: what is its great trouble and sorrow? Is it not because of sin? What are his secret moans to God? Is it not the sense of corruption? "Oh wretched man that I am! who shall deliver me from the body of this death," says Paul (Rom. 7:24). He had been complaining of the mass of corruption that did still press hard upon him, and in the strong workings of his spirit against it, he calls it the body of death. It was as grievous to him as if he had been bound to a stinking rotten carcass. How wretched then is the state of every soul unacquainted with God! It can do nothing but sin, because it lacks the right rule of action, a right pattern of imitation, a right principle for action, a right object for action, a right end for action, and the only assistance of action. It concerns us then as we discern between good and evil, if we have any respect unto holiness and purity before sin and iniquity, to see to get acquaintance with God, because without acquaintance with God, we are in a woeful necessity of sinning.

Though a sinner do evil an hundred times, and his days be prolonged, yet surely I know that it shall be well with them that fear God, which fear before him: But it shall not be well with the wicked, neither shall he prolong his days, which are as a shadow; because he feareth not before God.

Ecclesiastes 8:12–13

Faith's Necessity

John Collinges

Watch ye, stand fast in the faith, quit you like men, be strong.
1 Corinthians 16:13

When the jailor fell down at the Apostle's feet and said, "What shall I do to be saved?" (Acts 16:30), the Apostle answered, "Believe in the Lord Jesus Christ, and thou shalt be saved." When the ruler feared, Christ said, "Be not afraid, only believe" (Mark 5:36). When the poor man came for mercy for his son (Mark 9:32), Christ told him that if he could believe, all things were possible to him. When we pray, if we can but believe, we shall receive, and we shall surely not fail. Many glorious things are spoken of this mother of graces, which faith seems to be our whole duty. Demosthenes was asked how many things were necessary for an orator; he answered three: first, action; second, action; and third, action, meaning, action was more than all. And when a certain prince asked a great commander, what was necessary for war, he answered him three things, money, money, money, meaning that that is the ligament and nerves of war. And truly, if any should ask me what the one thing necessary for a Christian is, I would say, faith; if I should be asked again, I would say, faith; if the third time, still I should say, belief. To the first, pray for faith; to the second, use faith; to the third, grow and increase in faith. Faith and believing is the whole duty of a Christian, in a safe sense; for it supposes humiliation and it commands newness of life.

> **Faith and believing is the whole duty of a Christian.**

Two Destinies

John Shower

et us consider that both states of happiness and misery are unchangeable and everlasting. The state of Lazarus in blessedness, and of the rich man in torment, was neither of them to be altered. There is an impassable gulf fixed by the eternal counsel and irrevocable decree of God that the damned shall never ascend to heaven, nor the blessed ever sink into hell. The calamities of the one and the felicity of the other will never cease! It is everlasting life; it is everlasting destruction. The whole frame of the Christian religion is built upon this truth, that life and immortality are brought to light by the gospel, as to the blessedness or misery after death. We must renounce our Christianity, throw away our Bibles, condemn the Son of God for an imposter, the Holy Scriptures for a fable, and all the wisest men that have ever been in the world, as fools, for believing the gospel of Christ, if there are not two eternal states of blessedness or misery after death. Our Lord's account of the proceedings of the last day, and the issue of the final judgment is expressed in this matter. And it is called "eternal judgment" (Heb. 6:2), not for the continuance of its administration, but in regard of the effects and consequences of it. Though we do not know how long the day of judgment will last, yet the execution is to follow, of eternal rewards, and punishments.

And he cried and said, Father Abraham, have mercy on me, and send Lazarus, that he may dip the tip of his finger in water, and cool my tongue; for I am tormented in this flame.
Luke 16:24

Life and immortality are brought to light by the gospel.

The Sure Word

Edmund Calamy

Let us bless God, not only for revealing His will in His Word, but for revealing it by writing. Before the time of Moses, God disclosed His will by immediate revelations from heaven. But we have a surer word of prophecy (2 Pet. 1:19). Surer than a voice from heaven, for the devil (says the apostle) transforms himself into an angel of light. He has his apparitions and revelations, he is God's ape, and in imitation of God, he appears to his disciples and makes them believe that it is God that appears, and not the devil. Thus he appeared to Saul, in the likeness of Samuel. And if God should now at this day disclose His way of worship and His divine will by revelations, how easily would men be deceived and mistake diabolical delusions for divine revelations. Therefore let us bless God for the written Word, which is surer and safer than an immediate revelation. There are some that are apt to think that if an angel should come from heaven and reveal God's will to them, it would work more upon them than the written Word, but I would have these men to study the conference between Abraham and Dives (Luke 16:27–31). "They have Moses and the prophets"; if they will not profit by them, neither would they profit by any that should come out of hell or down from heaven to them, for it is the same God that speaks by His written Word, and by a voice from heaven. The difference is only in the outward clothing; and therefore if God's speaking by writing will not amend us, no more will God's speaking by a voice. O bless God exceedingly for the written Word! Let us cleave close to it and not expect any revelations from heaven of new truths, but say with the apostle (Gal. 1:8–9): "But though we, or an angel from heaven, preach any other gospel unto you than that which we have preached unto you, let him be accursed."

> **If God's speaking by writing will not amend us, no more will God's speaking by a voice.**

Thoughts of Heaven

Henry Scudder

I n heaven there is perfect obedience. There is no failing, not in the least circumstance. "Now I know in part," said the apostle, "but then (that is, when he should come to heaven) shall I know even as also I am known" (1 Cor. 13:12). Peter when speaking of the new heavens said, "therein dwelleth righteousness" (2 Pet. 3:13). For heaven is the holy place into which no unrighteous person can enter; for when there were disobedient persons in heaven, namely the devil and his angels, which kept not their first estate, heaven did vomit them forth, never to be burdened with them or the like again. In heaven there are no tempters; there are none but God, angels, and the spirits of just men made perfect. Therefore also there are no temptations to sin. The thoughts of this will moderate grief when we have friends which die in the Lord. For the place where death has made a passage for them is heaven. This does secure us, that they are there where they are made perfect, where they shall neither offend nor be offended. Does not this meditation work in God's children not only contentment, but a longing to lay down this tabernacle, to be translated when the Lord shall please, since the exchange will be so happy? It is but a parting with a sinful miserable earth, for this heaven, wherein dwells perfect righteousness. It is leaving mortality for life, sin for grace, and misery for glory. In that place they shall neither be actors nor beholders of sin. There is no sin there, either to infect or vex them. When we are wearied and almost fainting in our combat against sin and this wicked world, we should only consider that before long if we do hold out manfully awhile, this sin and flesh shall annoy us no more. For when death comes, it is the portal to heaven. Death as certainly separates sin from soul and body for ever as it does the soul from the body for awhile. For our place is this heaven, where are angels, the patterns of our obedience. When we come there, we shall be as the angels (Luke 20:36), and shall ever be with the Lord.

And the city had no need of the sun, neither of the moon, to shine in it: for the glory of God did lighten it, and the Lamb is the light thereof.

Revelation 21:23

Spiritual Life

Isaac Ambrose

If we live in the Spirit, let us also walk in the Spirit.
Galatians 5:25

The Spirit works in us a principle of spiritual life. The Scripture sometimes calls it a seed, sometimes a spring or fountain, and sometimes the life of Christ, because it is conveyed to us by the Spirit of Christ, by means of our inseparable union with Christ. Whatever name we give it, we may not conceive it to be a new faculty added to those which are in us by nature, but an improvement of those abilities to work spiritually, as they did naturally before regeneration. Hence it is that the regenerate person is said to walk after the Spirit, to be led by the Spirit, or to walk in the Spirit. Now, from this fountain springs all those habits of spiritual grace, which are severally distinguished by the names of faith, hope, and love, although to speak properly, they are but the diversifications of that spiritual principle within us, distinguished by these names. From these habits of grace abiding in us, ordinarily proceed spiritual motions and operations according to those habits. And as it is with natural habits, so it is with spiritual; they are much increased and strengthened in their exercise, and are much weakened by neglect. I deny not, but for all this, there is within us a woeful, sinful nature, cross and contrary to holiness and leading us daily into captivity; yet here is our privilege, even sanctification in part. Surely the Lord has given us another name, and a new nature. There is something else within us, which makes us wrestle against sin and shall in time prevail over all sin.

> **Surely the Lord has given us another name, and a new nature.**

True Penitence

Arthur Hildersam

e that is truly penitent will not hate or storm against the one that shall admonish or reprove him for sin, but love him the better. He that is poor in spirit and mourns for sin will be meek also. . . . He counts it no disgrace, but an ornament and honor to him, to be thus faithfully dealt with. David esteemed better of Nathan after he had so plainly rebuked him than he ever did before; see the reverent respect he showed unto him when he came to speak with him, and had present access to him (Kgs. 1:23), and you shall find that the king was not wont to conceal from him, but to discuss with him all his affairs of greatest moment. So in Acts 2, the same men that had mocked the apostles before, when by their ministry they were plainly rebuked, esteemed reverently of them (Acts 2:37). So did he also of whom we read, "He reported that God was of a truth in that ministry" (1 Cor. 14:25). They did so because they know God is the Author of that reproof that is given them according to His Word, whosoever is the instrument. Though Pharaoh Neco were Josiah's enemy, yet the counsel and reproof he sent him came from the mouth of the Lord, and it was his ruin that he hearkened not to it. He that reproves me for any sin, according to the Word, speaks to me on God's behalf. This is not his word, but God's, and so to be received, not as the word of an inferior, but as the Word of God.

My son, despise not the chastening of the LORD; neither be weary of his correction.
Proverbs 3:11

> He that reproves me for any sin, according to the Word, speaks to me on God's behalf.

Heaven's Taste

Jeremiah Burroughs

Behold, how good and how pleasant it is for brethren to dwell together in unity! It is like the precious ointment upon the head, that ran down upon the beard, even Aaron's beard: that went down to the skirts of his garments.
Psalm 133:1–2

It is a taste of heaven already to join with the people of God in communion. The Scripture calls the church of God and church communion heaven. In Isa. 65:17 we find a promise of God to restore His church and recover it from misery. It says, "For, behold, I create new heavens and a new earth: and the former shall not be remembered, nor come into mind." In Rev. 21 where the vision of the restoring of the Church was shown to John, it was shown also in that way. There was a new heaven, and a new earth. The church of God is heaven. It is not only a company with which we shall live in heaven hereafter, but it is heaven now, and therefore our Savior says that the least in the kingdom of heaven shall be greater than John. . . . The kingdom of heaven is like a man sowing his field with wheat. In other words, the church is a field sown with wheat. After the wheat is sown, the adversary sows tares in it. Chrysostom says in one of his sermons on the Corinthians, "The Church is the place of angels, the palace of heaven, yes heaven itself." If it is that communion with God's people is heaven already, surely it is worth the enduring of much affliction to be with them.

> The church is not only a company with which we shall live in heaven hereafter, but it is heaven now.

Relish Religion

Richard Alleine

O friends, get such a relish of religion, and strive not only to be knowing and understanding Christians, but savory Christians, of a savory spirit: "Those that are after the Spirit do mind (the word signifies 'favor') the things of the Spirit" (Rom. 8:5). Spiritual things are savory things to spiritual men. Get yourself to be so spiritually minded, that you may be spiritually affected; that the knowledge of God, and the thoughts of God, and the worship of God, that communing with God and with your own hearts and one with another about the things of God, may be affecting and pleasant to your souls. Lively affectionate Christians, it is a sign they have drunk in the spirit of religion into their very hearts; and it will be a help to the begetting and warming of affections in others; when once you have experimentally tasted the sweetness, and are thereby deeply affected with religion, then you are likely to hold to it, and prosper in it. This taste and relish of religion is not to be gotten but by our inward and experimental acquaintance with it; whilst it dwells but in the head and upon the tongue, it will be but a dry and insipid thing to you; whilst you dwell upon the surface, and outside, and are but triflers in religion, you may say of all your religion, as it was said of Samaria's idolatry, "It hath no stalk, the bud yields no meal" (Hos. 8:7); or if it has any stalk, or seems to yield any meal, yet neither stalk nor meal has any sweetness in it. Friends, you must go deeper in religion if ever you will taste the sweetness of it. Get your hearts to be so leavened and seasoned with it, get religion to be so naturalized to you, drink in the spirit of religion into you, that you may be metamorphosed and changed into its own image and nature, and then you will find how pleasant it will be to you.

And by knowledge shall the chambers be filled with all precious and pleasant riches.

Proverbs 24:4

> Friends, you must go deeper in religion if ever you will taste the sweetness of it.

Charity

Thomas Watson

And now abideth faith, hope, charity, these three; but the greatest of these is charity.

1 Corinthians 13:13

A righteous man is helpful to the bodies of others. He is a temporal savior. He has one eye shut to wink at the failings of others and another eye open to observe their wants. He is like the heavens diffusing his influence and sending down his silver drops of charity; he is a staff to the lame and bread to the hungry. He puts a golden crutch under others when they are falling. It is reported of young Lord Harrington that he gave a tenth of his yearly revenue to charitable uses. As Mary brought her sweet ointments to anoint Christ's body, so a gracious soul brings his ointments of charity to anoint the saints, who are Christ's living Body. A good man judiciously considers how he himself lives upon contribution: the earth enriches him with veins of silver and crops of corn. One creature brings him wool, another oil, another silk. Observing every creature conspiring for his good, he studies to lay out himself for the good of others. Faith, if it has not works, is dead (Jas. 2:17). Faith sanctifies works and works testify of faith. A believer, with one hand, receives Christ's merits; with the other hand he relieves his fellow members. And he not only gives to the necessities of the poor but gives freely. Charity drops from him as myrrh from the tree. He does not put his alms among his desperate debts; he is thankful that God has made him in the number of givers and not receivers.

> **Faith sanctifies works and works testify of faith.**

Double-Tongued

Thomas Adams

If God has given us one tongue, then why do we act as though we have two? Some are double-tongued because they are double-hearted. But God has given us one tongue, and one heart, that they might indeed be one, as they are in number. It is made simple; let it not be double. God has made us decent, but we make ourselves monsters. He has given us two eyes, two ears, two hands, and two feet. But we act as if we only have one. We have one eye to pry into others' faults, but not another to see our own. We have one ear to hear the plaintiff, but not the other for the defendant. We have a foot swift to tread forbidden paths, but not another to lead us to God's holy place. We have one hand to exhort, and scrape, and wound, but not another to relieve, give alms, and heal the wound. But now where God has given us but one tongue, and one heart, and bidden us to be content with their singularity, we will have two tongues and two hearts; thus we are cross to God, nature, and grace; we have become monstrous, having one eye, one foot, two tongues, and two hearts. The slanderer, the flatterer, the swearer, and the gossiper, are monstrous; they are misshapen, as if they had two tongues and but one eye; two heads and but one foot.

Whoso keepeth his mouth and his tongue keepeth his soul from troubles.
Proverbs 21:23

> **Some are double-tongued because they are double-hearted.**

Spectacles

John Bunyan

Having your conversation honest among the Gentiles: that, whereas they speak against you as evildoers, they may by your good works, which they shall behold, glorify God in the day of visitation.

1 Peter 2:12

The believer is the only person by whom God shows to the world the power of His grace and the operation of His people's faith. The unbelievers read indeed of the power of grace; of the faith, hope, love, joy, peace, and sanctification of the heart of the Christian; but they feel nothing of that sin-killing operation that is in these things; these are to them as a story of Rome or Spain. Wherefore to show them in others, what they find not in themselves, God works faith, hope, and love in a generation that shall serve Him; and by them they shall see what they cannot find in themselves; and by this means they shall be convinced, that though sin, and the pleasures of this life, be sweet to them, yet there is a people otherwise minded; even such a people that do indeed see the glory of that which others read of and from that sight take pleasure in those things which they are most averse unto. To this, I say, are Christians called; herein is God glorified; hereby are sinners convinced; and by this the world condemned.

God works faith, hope, and love in a generation that shall serve Him.

Forgiveness

John Owen

onscience naturally knows nothing of forgiveness; yes, it is against its very trust, work, and office to hear anything of it. If a man of courage and honesty be entrusted to keep a garrison against an enemy, let one come and tell him that there is peace made between those whom he serves and their enemies, so that he may leave his guard, and set open the gates, and cease his watchfulness; how wary will he be, lest under this pretense he be betrayed! "No," says he, "I will keep my hold until I have express orders from my superiors." Conscience is entrusted with the power of God in the soul of a sinner, with command to keep all in subjection with reference unto the judgment to come. It will not betray its trust in believing every report of peace. No; but this it says, and it speaks in the name of God, "Guilt and punishment are inseparable twins; if the soul sin, God will judge. What do you tell me of forgiveness? I know what my commission is, and that I will abide by. You shall not bring in a superior commander, a cross principle, into my trust; for if this be so, it seems I must let go my throne, another lord must come in," not knowing, as yet, how this whole business is compounded in the blood of Christ. Now, whom should a man believe if not his own conscience, which, as it will not flatter him, so it intends not to frighten him, but to speak the truth as the matter requires? . . . It will allow men to talk of forgiveness, to hear it preached, though they abuse it every day; but to receive it in its power, that stands up in direct opposition to its dominion. "In the kingdom," says conscience, "I will be greater than you," and in many, in the most, it keeps its possession, and will not be disposed.

But there is forgiveness with thee, that thou mayest be feared.
Psalm 130:4

> Whom should a man believe if not his own conscience?

227

Restless Prayer

William Fenner

Pray without ceasing.
1 Thessalonians
5:17

What is importunate prayer? I answer, it is a restless prayer, which will take no negative answer, but is in a holy manner impudent until it is answered. . . . If you are importunate, you cannot rest until you have an answer in your suit before God. As the poor woman of Canaan, she sought the Lord God of heaven and earth (she was of the cursed stock of Ham, whom the Lord commanded to destroy; yet she repented and became of the faith of Abraham) to see if the Lord would own her. But the Lord seemed to reject her, and suffered the devil to possess her daughter. Might not this poor woman think she had made a sorry change of religion, seeing that God the author of it would not own her, but suffered the devil to possess her daughter? But see the importunity of this woman. She would not be quiet until she had found Christ (Mark 7:24–25). Christ could not be hid. No? What, could He not hide Himself in some corner? No, no, thinks she, there is a Christ, and if He is to be had under the scope of heaven, I will have Him. Even so it is with the soul that is importunate in prayer; it is restless. What if Christ hid Himself in the world and will not own a poor soul, yet the poor soul knows there is a Christ, and if He is to be found in the whole world, he will have Him?

> So it is with the soul that is importunate in prayer; it is restless.

Light and Dark

Peter Sterry

David says, "The darkness and the light are both alike to thee." O wonderful union of contraries! O unsearchable power; O powerful matter of universal joy! God is the only truth, and the measure of truth; darkness and light are both alike to Him, who is the First and the Last. As light holds from darkness, and makes manifest all excellencies in itself, so darkness holds forth light, and is a manifestation of all glories, an image of all images of beauty and pleasure before God. Light has its own proper appearance, and is seen by God in its own distinct shape, as it is in itself, yet in the seeing of it all things are seen. So does darkness appear before God in its darkest and best form; and all lights of comforts, holiness, and truth appear together with it in the same appearance. Blessed are they that abide in God, or are like to God; for no darkness hides any joy from them, not the darkness of death itself. The grave shines to them, as heaven, and shows the same spirit, life, and glory to their eyes. This is the work of the power of God, which makes light from above, and darkness from below to meet, and kiss; and like the man, and the woman to bear one image, to become one light.

Yea, the darkness hideth not from thee; but the night shineth as the day: the darkness and the light are both alike to thee.
Psalm 139:12

> Darkness and light are both alike to Him, who is the First and the Last.

Revealed Reason

John Arrowsmith

*For with thee is the
fountain of life: in thy
light shall we see
light.*
Psalm 36:9

Religion is a thing which distinguishes men from beasts more than reason itself does. For some brute beasts have the appearances of reason, but none of religion. "Man is a creature addicted to religion," may perhaps be found as true a definition, as that which is commonly received, "Man is a living creature endued with reason." Some kind of deity is acknowledged everywhere throughout the world, and wherever a deity is acknowledged, some kind of worship is observed. Should a synod of mere philosophers be convened to consult about the matters of God, I make no question but in the issue of their debates they would pronounce one anathema against atheism, and another against irreligion. Among the Romans to worship sparingly was accounted the next door to being an atheist. None but the true God can disclose what the true worship of God is. As that glorious eye of heaven is not seen but by its own proper light; a million torches cannot show us the sun, so all the natural reason in the world can neither discover what God is nor what worship He expects, without divine and supernatural revelation from Himself.

> All the natural reason in the world can neither discover what God is nor what worship He expects.

Heart Religion

William Dyer

et it be your art in duty to give God your heart in duty: "My son, give me thy heart" (Prov. 23:26). You see God calls for the heart; the heart is that field from which God expects the utmost plentiful crop of glory. God bears a greater respect to your hearts than He does to your works. God looks most where man looks least. If the heart is for God, then all is for God—our affections, our wills, our desires, our designs, our time, our strength, our tears, our alms, our prayers, our estates, our bodies, our souls—for the heart is the fort-royal that commands all the rest; the eye, the ear, the hand, the tongue, the head, the foot—the heart commands all these. Now if God has the heart, He has all. If He has not the heart, He has none. The heart of obedience is the obedience of the heart. As the body is at the command of the soul that rules it, so should the soul be at the command of God that gave it. "Ye are bought with a price," says the apostle, "therefore glorify God in your bodies, and in your spirits" (1 Cor. 6:20). He that is all in all for us would have that which is all in all in us. The heart is the presence-chamber, where the King of glory takes up His lodging. That which is most worthy in us should be given to Him who is most worthy of us. The body is but the cabinet, the soul is the jewel; the body is but the shell, the soul is the kernel. The soul is the breath of God, the beauty of man, the wonder of angels, and the envy of devils.

O that there were such a heart in them, that they would fear me, and keep all my commandments always, that it might be well with them, and with their children for ever!
Deuteronomy 5:29

> He that is all in all for us would have that which is all in all in us.

Glorify God

Thomas Manton

Our chiefest care and affection should be carried out to the glory of God when we pray. We should rather forget ourselves than forget God. God must be remembered in the first place. There is nothing more precious than God Himself; therefore nothing should be dearer to us than His glory. This is the great difference between the upright and the hypocrite: the hypocrite never seeks God but when his necessities do require it, not in and for God himself; but when the upright come to seek God, it is for God in the first place; their main care is about God's concerns rather than their own. Though they seek their own happiness in Him, and they are allowed so to do; yet it is mainly God's glory which they seek, not their own interests and concernments. See Ps. 115:1, "Not unto us, not unto us, O Lord, but unto thy name give glory, for thy mercy, and for thy truth's sake." It is not a doxology, or form of thanksgiving, but a prayer; not for our safety and welfare, so much as God's glory; not to wreak and satisfy our revenge upon our adversaries; not for the establishment of our interest; but for the glory of God's grace and truth, that He may be known to be a God who keeps His covenant; for mercy and truth are the two pillars of the covenant. It is a great dishonoring of God when anything is sought from Him more than Himself, or not for Himself. Augustine says that it is but a carnal affection in prayer when men seek self more than God. Self and God are the two things that come in competition. Now there are several sorts of self; there is carnal self, natural self, spiritual self, and glorified self. Above all these God must have the pre-eminence.

> **Mercy and truth are the two pillars of the covenant.**

Strive for Perfection

Henry Scudder

et it be our prayer and endeavor to do good things well, and to fulfill God's will. And though there are failings in the matter of what is done (which also is not to be allowed), yet if the heart is upright in the manner, God bears with much weakness, and accepts truth and uprightness. Christians must aim at perfection. They must always press hard forward to attain it. Now may the God of peace make you perfect, to do His will, said the apostle in Heb. 13:20–21. . . . It may justly be doubted that someone is truly a Christian, if he has not a desire and longing after perfection of Christianity. This casts blame on all that think they know enough and have made progress far enough in the race of Christianity. What says the apostle? Not all that run, receive the prize. If men fall back, or stand still, they can never finish their course. Wherefore He would have others do as He did: so run that they might obtain, and so fight that they might get the mastery, and win the crown. He that puts his hand to the plow, and looks back is not fit for the kingdom of God (Luke 9:62). The thoughts of heaven, the patterns for imitation which are in heaven, and the state of perfection in which we shall be when we come to heaven should be lodestones to draw us heavenward, and to perfection. Be perfect, says Christ, as your heavenly Father is perfect (Matt. 5:48); in every thing, and in every way, be perfect. The way to attain this is first to convince the heart that we ought to be perfect. Then we must see with the apostle that we are not already perfect. Thirdly, let us not look on what we have done, and what is behind, but on that which is before us to be done. Fourthly, we must be daily purging ourselves from filthiness of flesh and spirit, and so perfect holiness. Fifthly, that we may do all these, we must daily be reading, hearing, and meditating on the Holy Scriptures; for their end is to make the man of God perfect. Lastly, give all diligence, and press forward, as the apostle did, toward the mark and prize of the high calling of God in Christ. Do these things because those that do not aim at perfection do not have the perfection of truth.

I press toward the mark for the prize of the high calling of God in Christ Jesus.
Philippians 3:14

Perpetual Streams

William Spurstowe

There is a river, the streams whereof shall make glad the city of God, the holy place of the tabernacles of the most High.
Psalm 46:4

The comforts of the promises of God are abiding and sure mercies (Acts 13:34); such which are the crystal streams of a living fountain, and not the impure overflowing of an unruly torrent, which sometimes with its swellings puts the traveler in fear of his or her life, and at other times shames the expectation of being refreshed by it. Geographers in their description of America report that in Peru there is a river called Diurnal, or day river, because it runs with a great current in the day but is wholly dry at night; which is occasioned, as they say, by the heat of the sun, that in the day-time melts the snow that lies on the mountains thereabouts. But when the sun goes down, and the cold night approaches, the snow congeals, which only fed it, and the channel is quite dried up. Not much unlike this river are all worldly contentments, which are only day-comforts, but not night-comforts. In the sunshine of peace and prosperity, they flow with some pleasing streams, but in the night season of affliction they vanish and come to nothing. Then the rich man, as Cyprian says, lies restless upon a bed of down, and fetches deep groans though he drink pearls and sapphires. But it is far otherwise with the promises of God, whose streams of comfort in the time of trouble do usually run most plentifully, and refresh most powerfully the weary and afflicted soul.

> **All worldly contentments are only day-comforts, but not night-comforts.**

Pilgrims

Richard Alleine

Who shall lead me through the wilderness? There are many ways, many false ways, many cross ways, and but one that is the right way: How shall I hit my way to heaven, the right way that leads thither-wards? And who will show me and lead me in this way? Here Trust answers, Christ will do it; I lean upon Him to be my Moses to lead me in the way that I should go: "Thou wilt guide me with thy counsel," (Ps. 73:24). Christ has gone the way before His saints, and He will show them His steps to direct them. Therefore the apostle exhorts, "Run the race—looking to Jesus" (Heb. 12:2), as for encouragement, so for direction; follow not the footsteps of the sheep only, but follow the footsteps of the Shepherd, and walk on as He walked before you. But how shall I find the way, or the steps wherein Christ walked? "It is not in man that walketh, to direct his steps" (Jer. 10:23). "How can a man understand his own ways?" (Prov. 20:24). There are many hard and intricate cases, where I may be at a stand, and not know which way to take: their answer is, as Ps. 143:8, "In thee do I trust; cause me to know the way wherein I should walk, for I lift up my soul to thee," and v. 10: "Thy Spirit is good, lead me into the land of uprightness"; I trust that "thou wilt guide me by thy counsel, and bring me to glory" (Ps. 73:24).

He clave the rocks in the wilderness, and gave them drink as out of the great depths.
Psalm 78:15

> Follow not the footsteps of the sheep only, but follow the footsteps of the Shepherd.

Sick with Love

John Owen

I charge you, O daughters of Jerusalem, if ye find my beloved, that ye tell him, that I am sick of love.
Song of Solomon 5:8

The spouse is quite ravished with the sweetness of Christ's entertainment, finding love, care, and kindness, bestowed by Him in the assemblies of the saints. Hence she cries out, "Stay me with flagons, comfort me with apples; for I am sick of love" (Song 2:5). Upon the discovery of the excellency and sweetness of Christ in the banqueting-house, the soul is instantly overpowered, and cries out to be made partaker of the fullness of it. She is "sick of love," not (as some suppose) fainting for want of a sense of love, under the apprehension of wrath; but made sick and faint, even overcome, with the mighty acting of that divine affection, after she had once tasted of the sweetness of Christ in the banqueting-house. Her desire deferred makes her heart sick; therefore she cries: "Stay me; I have seen a glimpse of the King in His beauty, tasted of the fruit of His righteousness; my soul melts in longing after Him. Oh! support and sustain my spirit with His presence in His ordinances, those 'flagons and apples of His banqueting-house,' or I shall quite sink and faint! Oh, what hast Thou done, blessed Jesus! I have seen Thee, and my soul is become as the chariots of Amminadib. Let me have something from thee to support me, or I die." When a person is fainting on any occasion, these two things are to be done: strength is to be used to support him that he sinks not to the ground; and comfortable things are to be applied, to refresh his spirits. These two the soul overpowered and fainting with the force of its own love (raised by a sense of Christ's), prays for. It would have strengthening grace to support it in that condition, that it may be able to attend its duty; and consolations of the Holy Ghost, to content, revive, and satiate it, until it come to a full enjoyment of Christ.

> Upon the discovery of the excellency and sweetness of Christ the soul is instantly overpowered.

The Perfect Heart

Robert Harris

An upright heart is first a perfect heart, as the Scripture terms it. It is an entirely whole heart, which is when all the powers go one and the same way, when the whole soul is bent after God and is driven only to seek and honor Him. You may best know it by the contrary; the hypocrite's heart is a divided heart. He looks two ways at once, as one power and faculty of the soul is against another. There is ('tis true) a fight within the best people, but then it is between grace and flesh, between a man and his enemy. But in the hypocrite, one faculty takes part against the other. Here is reason and conscience against affection, and one affection against another. There is a wise difference between civil war, where one neighbor is against another, and a national war, where they all join together against a common enemy. The Christian man's fight is of the whole regenerated part against corruption; but in the hypocrite's heart there is civil war. The powers are altogether at odds with themselves, as if one member in the body should fight against the other or one subject in a kingdom against another. Passion commends a thing, reason condemns it; lust affects a thing, conscience refuses it; one part would have one thing, and another part another. In the upright man it is far otherwise; his heart is entire, and goes all one way; he desires in all things to please God and fight against sin.

And the LORD said unto Satan, Hast thou considered my servant Job, that there is none like him in the earth, a perfect and an upright man, one that feareth God, and escheweth evil? and still he holdeth fast his integrity, although thou movedst me against him, to destroy him without cause.
Job 2:3

> There is, 'tis true, a fight within the best people, but then it is between grace and flesh.

Persecution's Pearls

Jeremiah Burroughs

And when they had called the apostles, and beaten them, they commanded that they should not speak in the name of Jesus, and let them go. And they departed from the presence of the council, rejoicing that they were counted worthy to suffer shame for his name.
Acts 5:40–41

God's people are here afflicted, that Christ in them, and they in Christ, may in the conclusion of all be more glorified. This occurs first, in the overcoming of all evils and the final destruction of all their enemies. Secondly, we see it in their happiness after so many evils endured; the bitterness of foregoing grief commends the sweetness of following joys. Thirdly, their afflictions work to the increase of their glory. Second Corinthians 4:18 says, "Our light afflictions work for us an exceeding weight of glory." Gordius, a blessed martyr (whom Basil so much commends in an oration of his), accounted it a loss to him not to suffer many kinds of tortures. He said that tortures were but trading with God for glory. Tertullian has an expression to that effect: the greater the combats, the greater are the following rewards. Bernard says of persecutors that they are but His Father's goldsmiths, who are working to add pearls to the crowns of the saints. The seeds of happiness are sown in the deep furrows of affliction, and the deeper the furrows are, the more precious are the seeds that are there sown, and the more glorious and plentiful the harvest will be. When a curious glorious picture is to be drawn, the grounds used are to be laid in black, but not in dirt. So our grounds may be laid here in afflictions, but let them not be laid in sin. Here then we see, that although afflictions are a bitter root, yet spring from them fair flowers, and pleasant fruit. It is no marvel then that though God orders all things, yet His people are in such an afflicted condition. From God's determining things to be thus, let us learn.

> **Although afflictions are a bitter root, yet spring from them fair flowers and pleasant fruit.**

Vanishing Pleasures

Robert Dingley

We must at last vanish from this-worldly glory; as the ship under sail, we are in constant motion, and shall suddenly reach the coast of eternity. Although the glory of the world should be true to us, and attend us to the grave, yet it cannot go with us a step farther. Hadrian the Emperor, that had lived so gloriously, died as despairingly. It was a divine speech of Cicero, "Death must be frightful to them, whose happiness ends with their life." And Seneca says: "Your last day will resolve you whether indeed you are happy." At the hour of our death, the world will appear in its vanity; for naked we must return to the earth, our common mother. See then the folly and madness of our spirits in doing and fastening our eyes and hearts upon outward and transitory things, "in lifting up the soul to vanity," as the psalmist expresses it (24:4)... . How are the hearts of many (who yet profess Christ) riveted and glued to the world, the follies and advantages of it, saying with Peter, "Lord, it is good for us to be here" (Matt. 17:4). But let the mammonists and mere earth-worms (especially) consider their estate. If the world cannot represent earth's vanity to you, death will. Offer a man that is struggling for breath, embroidered apparel, coffers of gold, titles of honor, the most exquisite music, or the most sumptuous buildings; he will disregard your offers, and tell you, "Now I see all this is vanity." Dreadful to worldlings will be the hour of their death; when their friends shall bemoan them, physicians forsake them, God frown upon them, senses fail them, earth leave them, heaven refuse them, and Tophet challenge them; then assuredly the note will be changed. No more, "Vanity of vanities, all is vanity," but now, "Misery of miseries, all is misery!" This will be an everlasting sting in their hearts, to ponder how much they have lost for how little; that they have lost glory for vanity, happiness for vexation, Christ for a crust, and immortal life for the dream of a shadow; like them that sold the righteous for a pair of shoes. Millions do lose endless pleasures for things that perish in the using.

For all flesh is as grass, and all the glory of man as the flower of grass.
1 Peter 1:24a

Hearing the Word

Christopher Nesse

I rejoice at thy word, as one that findeth great spoil.
Psalm 119:162

That you have the Word of God to read and hear, you must prize as a precious privilege, and praise the Lord for it with your heart, lips, and life. God has deposited a rich treasure with you in lending you His Word and gospel. You might have been begging drops of mercy in hell at this time, when behold God offers you oceans of grace on earth in His Word and gospel. O what would the damned give (even ten thousand worlds if they had them) to enjoy such means of grace (yes but one day thereof) and such days of salvation as are bestowed upon you; God has not dealt so with many nations, nor with many persons, as He has dealt with you in the land of your nativity (Ps. 147:19–20). It was a special favor and vouchsafement to Israel, that God committed to them the lively (and life-giving) oracles (Rom. 3:2). It is truly a choice talent, a matter of great trust, to know your Master's will. There is much in that of Luke 12:48; "Unto whomsoever much is given, of him shall much be required." The poor pagan world lay under a long night of darkness (having only the twinkling starlight of the fallen nature) wherein they wander woefully, yet not so wide as to miss of hell. Their starlight indeed leaves them inexcusable (Rom. 1:20), but cannot lead them to the star of Jacob, the bright Morning Star, nor to life and salvation (Acts 4:12).

> Their starlight indeed leaves them inexcusable but cannot lead them to the star of Jacob.

God's Mercy

John Shower

o and proclaim these words toward the north, and say, Return, thou backsliding Israel, saith the LORD; and I will not cause mine anger to fall upon you: for I am merciful, saith the LORD, and I will not keep anger for ever. Only acknowledge thine iniquity, that thou hast transgressed against the LORD thy God" (Jer. 3:12–13), that is, "Let them not cherish any such hard thoughts of Me, as if there were no forgiveness; let them not despair of My mercy, as if I would not receive them, when they return." This gives the greatest encouragement to convinced sinners, that here is a plank to save them from shipwreck, a remedy against despair; here is a ground for them to return to God with hope. Here is a motive to seek mercy, that God has proclaimed His readiness to forgive, and abundantly to pardon. And it is very plain that the doctrine of repentance would never have been preached, if there were no hope of forgiveness. The fallen angels, having no mercy offered, were never called to repent; for let there be never so deep conviction of sin, and sorrow for it, there could be no repenting and returning to God, without believing that mercy might be had. All would end in death and desperation. Repentance would never be commanded as a duty, nor urged upon sinners as a duty, were it not for this truth, that if the wicked forsake his way, God will have mercy.

O give thanks unto the LORD; for he is good; for his mercy endureth for ever.
1 Chronicles 16:34

> The doctrine of repentance would never have been preached if there were no hope of forgiveness.

To Know God

Richard Stock

Without the knowledge of God, a man cannot know himself. The knowledge of a man in things natural is an excellent knowledge, yet it is nothing without the knowledge of self, as Saint Augustine says. Though a man knows all mysteries, to the breadth of the earth, and the depth of the sea, but does not know himself, he is like to a man that makes a building without a foundation. Without the knowledge of God, no man can know himself, because of that wicked pride that is naturally in man, that when he looks upon himself, he thinks he is so holy, just, and pure, that he perceives injustice to be justice, impurity to be purity; but if once he comes to see the face of God, then he sees his own justice to be injustice, and his own purity to be impurity, and his own righteousness to be folly; therefore it is the principal thing for a man to know God. Without this a man cannot worship God rightly, which is the end of his creation, and to this purpose there are many places of Scripture, "Come, let us worship the Lord, for He hath made us" (Prov. 12:13). The worship of God is commanded in the first table, and the principal thing in the first table is the knowledge of God; thus, there is no worship of God where there is no knowledge of God. Therefore, that man might know how to worship Him, He first declares Himself, "I am the Lord thy God, which brought thee out of the land of Egypt, out of the house of bondage" (Exod. 20:2); and this is the method which David lays down to Solomon, "Know thou the God of thy father," and then, "serve Him with a perfect heart, and with a willing mind" (1 Chr. 28:9).

> **Without the knowledge of God no man can know himself.**

242

Heaven's Diamond

Thomas Watson

ob says, "In my flesh shall I see God" (Job 19:26). The sight of Jesus Christ will be the most sublime and ravishing object to a glorified saint. When Christ was upon earth, His beauty was hidden. "He hath no form or comeliness" (Isa. 53:2). The light of the divine nature was hidden in the dark lantern of the human; it was hidden under reproaches and sufferings; yet even at that time, there was enough beauty in Christ to delight the heart of God. "My elect in whom my soul delighteth" (Isa. 42:1). His veil was then upon His face, but what will it be when the veil shall be taken off, and He shall appear in all His embroidery? "In Him dwells the fullness of the Godhead bodily" (Col. 2:9), an expression which we shall better understand when we are in heaven. Such glittering beams shall sparkle forth from Christ at that day as will infinitely amaze and ravish the eyes of the beholders. Imagine what a blessed sight it will be to see Christ wearing the robe of our human nature, and to see that nature sitting in glory above the angels. It is heaven enough to see Christ. "Whom have I in heaven but thee?" (Ps. 73:25). There are, says Musculus, angels and archangels; but they do not make heaven. Christ is the most sparkling diamond in the ring of glory. Therefore the apostle does not say, I desire to be dissolved and to be in heaven, but to be with Christ, because His presence is the heaven of heavens.

His cheeks are as a bed of spices, as sweet flowers: his lips like lilies, dropping sweet smelling myrrh.
Song of Solomon 5:13

> What a blessed sight to see Christ wearing the robe of our human nature, sitting in glory above the angels.

Better in God

William Whittaker

Then said Elkanah her husband to her, Hannah, why weepest thou? and why eatest thou not? and why is thy heart grieved? am not I better to thee than ten sons?
1 Samuel 1:8

Look upon God not only as the fountain of all good, but as the sum and quintessence of all good. This must be comfortable to His people, for whatever is of comfort in any creature must be much more comfortable in God, for God that makes any creature comfortable to us, can in the absence of that creature communicate the same comfort to us from Himself. Observe it according to that old rule, "That which makes anything such, must itself be much more." The schoolmen speak of three ways by which we may come to the knowledge of God. The first is by way of causality, when we take notice of those various excellencies that are scattered up and down in the creatures, and all these meet in God; yes, and meet in Him without the least mixture of those imperfections wherewith they are clogged in the creature. But that is not all. Secondly, they are all in God by way of infiniteness. Is a friend comfortable? God is a friend beyond all friends. Is a faithful counselor of great help? What help can you liken to God? In respect of His being, "To whom will you liken me?" (Isa. 40:18). Where is the person, or that friend who can do that for you, which I have done, and am still ready to do? Do you look upon ease as a great privilege? There is no ease as that which God gives; He gives ease to troubled minds, and peace to wounded consciences. Nay, is life itself desirable? You read in Ps. 63:3 that God is much more desirable; in life and death God is desirable. "Thy loving-kindness," says he, "is better than life." He had rather die in the favor of God, than live in a condition of estrangement from God. Alas! What is the light of a candle to the light of the sun? God is not only as good as earthly comforts would be, but He is much better, as Elkanah said to Hannah, "Am I not better to thee than ten sons?" (1 Sam. 1:8).

> He had rather die in the favor of God, than live in a condition of estrangement from God.

Rusting Graces

Thomas Taylor

ire is quenched when it is suffered to die of itself; so is the fire of grace quenched, when we use not our graces, but let them be idle, neither by them procuring glory to God, nor good to others. As iron, let it be as bright as crystal, but if it is cast in a corner and not used, it will grow rusty and unprofitable; even so will grace. And the drowsy Christian, though endued with good graces, if he wax idle, his heart shall be like Solomon's field of the sluggard, all overgrown with moss and weeds, which choke the good seed. The health of the body is preserved by exercise; so is the health of the soul, by the exercise of grace. The moth frets the finest garment, when it is not worn, and standing water is sooner frozen than the running stream. As fire dies of itself, when we prepare not or add not fit matter for the fuel, so we suffer our graces to decay, when we neglect the means that God has set apart for the strengthening and confirming of grace. . . . If a man forbear his ordinary meals, the natural heat will decay, and vigor, and health, and life, and all; so will the Christian, if he neglects the Word, the sacraments, meditation, prayer, watchfulness, and the like.

I know thy works, that thou art neither cold nor hot: I would thou wert cold or hot.

Revelation 3:15

Standing water is sooner frozen than the running stream.

On a Lie

Richard Capel

A lie (to speak properly) is a signification of that which is false with a will to deceive the ears of the hearer with that which is not true. So that ironical speeches and some hyperbolical phrases are not truly lies. Feigning or simulation is not lying, when it is only unlike the truth, and not contrary to the truth. So parents are not thought to lie when they frighten children on just occasions. . . . In setting down the definition of a lie, the word properly must not be taken strictly; for it may be, and is, a lie when we speak that which is false, however we take it to be true. Aquinas calls it a formal lie when it is false and we that say it do know or think it to be false. A material lie is when the matter we utter is false, but we think it to be true. . . . For the word "lie" is usually taken among us in the more odious signification, but if we look to the true, and full nature of a lie, it is certain that in case the thing we speak is false, we do lie, though we think it be never so true. So says the Scripture, "If we say that we have fellowship with Him, and walk in darkness, we lie" (1 John 1:6). But how many are there that walk in darkness, and do not only profess, but think themselves to be Christians? Yet John says of all such that they are liars. Whether we think so, or do not think so, it is still a lie.

> It may be, and is, a lie when we speak that which is false, however we take it to be true.

246

Our Elder Brother

Matthew Lawrence

aith argues from the present possession of heaven by our elder brother (John 14:1–2). The elder brother sometimes takes possession of the whole estate, in the right of all the family, though the rest do not come to possess their part until a long while after. And this act is an assurance to them all, as if they had their estate present. Thus is a believer ascertained by Christ's possessing heaven, so that, as we are said to be risen again with Christ (Col. 3:1), so may we be said to be (in a manner) ascended with Christ. The Apostle speaks as if believers were in heaven already, because Christ has taken possession of heaven in their behalf. And thereby offers strong assurance, that they also shall possess it in due time. Hence also is Christ called our forerunner (Heb. 6:20). All true Christians are compared to seafaring men, and Christ comes first to haven, to take possession for all the rest. So that, the world is as the sea, the church as a ship (out of which there is no safety), Christ as the Pilot. All true believers are passengers that have a common adventure. The land it is bound for is the kingdom of heaven; the card or compass is the word of God; the wind that drives it along is the Spirit of God. For the materials, the bottom and ballast of this ship are made of humility; the top, of open simplicity; the sides, of patience; the sails and banner, of love; the cords, of charity; the rudder, of faith; and the anchor, of hope. This anchor is described (Heb. 6:19) to be sure, and steadfast; such an anchor will hold, till the storm be over, and till we come at heaven.

In my Father's house are many mansions: if it were not so, I would have told you. I go to prepare a place for you.
John 14:2

> All true believers are passengers that have a common adventure.

The Morning Star

William Greenhill

I am the root and the offspring of David, and the bright and morning star.
Revelation 16:22b

Christ is a bright and morning star especially in that the morning star brings notice of good tidings that the day is at hand. When the morning star is up, then the day is near. So Christ has brought good tidings that the day is at hand and that the night is past. In Luke 2:10–11, at the incarnation of Christ, the angel said, "Fear not, for behold, I bring you good tidings of great joy which shall be to all people, for unto you is born this day in the city of David a Savior, which is Christ the Lord." And what then? "Glory to God in the highest, and on earth peace, good will toward men." The night of God's anger had passed and the day of God's favor was coming. Christ brought back the sun of God's favor and fatherly goodness and love to us, "salvation unto His people by the remission of their sins, through the tender mercy of our God; whereby the dayspring from on high hath visited us, to give light unto them that sit in darkness and in the shadow of death, to guide our feet in the way of peace" (Luke 1:77–78). So here good tidings have come. The day is now at hand, and Christ has brought immortality and life again into the world, which are now made manifest by the appearing of our Lord and Savior Jesus Christ, who has abolished death and has brought life and immortality to light through the gospel.

> The night of God's anger had passed and the day of God's favor was coming.

Sweet Providences

Samuel Lee

The stupendous mercies, which the ungrateful world calls hap and fortune, are the sudden and sweet dispensations of God's heavenly and holy providence. He is pleased out of His munificent bounty to procure our expectations with sudden and surprising benefits to amuse, yes amaze, us under the sense of divine goodness, and to draw our hearts with the silken cords of love. It is His favor that drops the inclinations of affection into the hearts and tempers, the reciprocal tides in the breasts of such whom He ordains for marital relation. His eye guided outcast Hagar to a shrub in Paran, and so that her son would not perish for thirst, an angel pointed out a well to soften her sorrow. Wonderful are the instances both in sacred and civil history of discovery of means, ordering of method, and guiding of accidents to the prevention of dangers, preservation of life, and the sudden issuing of sudden distresses. No less admirable are many quick and stupendous deliverances out of dungeons and prisons to great and famous advancements; and by providences to us occasional and accidental, flow high and exalted manifestations of God to His church and people.

And said, Naked came I out of my mother's womb, and naked shall I return thither: the LORD gave, and the LORD hath taken away; blessed be the name of the LORD.
Job 1:21

> Wonderful are the instances both in sacred and civil history of discovery of means.

Faith Goes Before

John Rogers

Get knowledge and understanding, search the Scriptures, make use of such good helps as the time affords. . . . Say not, "I am dull, I have a bad memory." God has taken away these pretenses; therefore they will not go for payment at the last day. Next, observe that faith and love are joined together as two inseparable companions. Wherever one is, there is the other also, and if you miss the one, you miss both. Those that have faith must have love, for faith works by love (Gal. 5:6). Faith assures us of God's love to us, makes us love God again, and our neighbor for His sake. . . . And wherever true love is, there certainly faith has gone before. These can be no more severed than the sun and light, or a good tree and its fruit.

> Faith assures us of God's love to us, makes us love God again, and our neighbor for His sake.

Fervent Love

John Rogers

Our love must be fervent. We must love as earnestly and as hotly as we can. And secondly, constantly; for in these two things stands fervency. First, let us consider the earnestness of our love. As we must stretch it to as many persons, and in as many duties as we can to soul, to body, in giving, forgiving, and so on . . . we must not be sparing, but in giving, liberal, for "he that sows sparingly shall reap sparingly" (2 Cor. 9:6). So in forgiving we must be plenteous, to seventy times, for thus is God to us, in giving soul, body, goods, and name to ourselves and ours, day and night, never wearying in doing us good, and never upbraiding us. In forgiving, how merciful God has been in passing by our manifold offenses, and that daily . . . therefore we must so love . . . that we suffer our love not to be extinguished. And we must love fervently, not delaying these duties . . . but we must forget our pleasure, profit, and ease, to do our neighbor good. Love seeks not her own things. It is laborious (1 Cor. 13), as in the Samaritan who set the wounded man upon his horse and went on foot himself and left all the money in his purse for his charges and promised to send more, as he that rose out of his warm bed to lend his neighbor loaves, and as they that gave out of their main stock or sold their land to relieve the necessities of the church (Acts 2:44). Above and beyond all comparison ten thousand times, was the fervency of the love of God the Father, when He parted with His own and only Son, out of His bosom, for our redemption, and of our Lord Jesus Christ, who forsook the glory of heaven, and laid down His life here upon earth, to save us miserable sinners, His utter enemies. Oh, how does this condemn the cold, yes, frozen love of the world! And where there is a spark, yet it is so weak, as the least drop of water will quench it!

And above all things have fervent charity among yourselves: for charity shall cover the multitude of sins.
1 Peter 4:8

> In forgiving we must be plenteous, to seventy times, for thus is God to us.

Prizing Christ

Edmund Calamy

Who, when he had found one pearl of great price, went and sold all that he had, and bought it.
Matthew 13:46

True faith is a Christ-receiving faith; it receives and embraces the whole Christ, Christ as a Savior and Christ as a Lord in all His offices, Prophet, Priest, and King. It causes those that have it to give up themselves wholly to Christ, to be ruled by Him in all things, according to His Word. Thus the gospel tenders Christ, and thus a true believer receives Christ. "My Lord and my God," says believing Thomas of Christ (John 20:28), and it is the property of justifying faith thus to embrace Christ. "They gave themselves unto the Lord," says the apostle of some true believers (2 Cor. 8:5). And this is universally true of all that are true believers; they give themselves unto the Lord, and that freely and voluntarily. This faith also puts a price upon Christ above all things, and cleaves to the mercy of God in Christ as better than life, both positively and comparatively. "To you which believe He is precious" (1 Pet. 2:7); "He is the chiefest of ten thousand" (Song 5:10); "fairer than all the children of men" (Ps. 45:2); "He is altogether lovely" (Song 5:16); "as the apple tree amongst the trees of the forest, so is my beloved among the sons" (Song 2:3); "His mouth is most sweet" (Song 5:16); "His love is better than wine" (Song 1:2). . . . By all these places it is evident that it is the property of true faith highly to prize Christ in all things, places, persons, and conditions, above all things, and beyond all time.

This faith also puts a price upon Christ above all things.

Changeless Love

Isaac Ambrose

Sometimes we think that the Lord does not love us because we do not feel or know His love. But do we not love our children even when they are young and do not know us? . . . We may think that because we have so many sins, or so many afflictions, that therefore the Lord does not love us, but do we judge righteously? Have our children no love from us when they are sick? God knows our mold that we are but dust. He has freely chosen us to be His children, and therefore (notwithstanding all our sins and sufferings) He loves us still. If He sees Ephraim bemoaning his stubbornness, as well as sickness, the Lord cries out, and cannot refrain: "Is Ephraim my dear son? Is he a pleasant child? For since I spake against him, I do earnestly remember him still: therefore my bowels are troubled for him; I will surely have mercy upon him, saith the LORD" (Jer. 31:20).

I have loved thee with an everlasting love.
Jeremiah 31:3b

> Do we not love our children even when they are young and do not know us?

One Thing

Nathaniel Vincent

But one thing is needful.
Luke 10:42a

What tongue can name the thing that is of greater, or of so great necessity, as conversion? This has been necessary in all ages, ever since the fall of man, and it will be necessary to the world's end. This is necessary for all sorts of persons, Jews and Gentiles, high and low, rich and poor, young and old, male and female, bond and free. All must perish, and that forever, without it. None but converts will live to God in this world, and none but converts shall live with Him in the world to come. We call food to eat, and clothing to put on, and air to breathe, necessities. And so in a sense they are, because frail nature cannot live without them. But how much more necessary is conversion, without which the precious soul will be lost; and there is no escaping eternal death and condemnation.

> How much more necessary is conversion, without which the precious soul will be lost.

Loving Christ

Thomas Vincent

The love of Christians to Christ is a grace wrought in their hearts by the Spirit. It is a flower most sweet and fragrant, but there is no seed of it in the nature of anyone since the fall. It is planted in the soul by the Spirit of God. Love to Christ is a divine spark that comes down from above; it is a fire that is kindled by the breath of the Lord, whose essence is Love. The ground of this love to Christ is the discovery and believing apprehensions of Christ's loveliness and love. There must be first a discovery of Christ as a suitable object for love, and not a bare notion of this, but believing apprehensions of it, that Christ is infinitely lovely, superlatively excellent, and that His love is matchless and transcendent towards the children of men; that there is a treasury in Him, and a storehouse of all graces, and the most needful and rich supplies; otherwise there will be no going forth of the heart in love unto Him. The acting of Christians' love to Christ is in their desires after union unto, and communion with Christ. It is the nature of love to desire union to the object beloved; especially of this love to Christ, and this union being attained, the desires are after communion with Christ, conversation and fellowship with Him. No conversation is as desirable as with the persons whom we most dearly love. And this communion being attained, there is chief complacency therein; the soul sweetly rests and reposes itself in Christ, and rejoices in His presence and love. . . . Lovers do give themselves unto those whom they love; this accompanies the marriage union, and such as love Christ, they are espoused and joined unto Him, and they give themselves unto Him, to be His, and wholly for His use.

Let him kiss me with the kisses of his mouth: for thy love is better than wine.
Song of Solomon 1:2

> No conversation is as desirable as with the persons whom we most dearly love.

Beware of Pride

James Janeway

An high look, and a proud heart, and the plowing of the wicked, is sin.
Proverbs 21:4

Some see pride as only that which manifests itself in costly apparel and bodily ornaments, beyond the degree and rank of the person. Some look no further than the treatment of one man towards another. Now consider with me that the greatest pride in the world is man's undue esteem of himself toward God, and this is in the heart of everyone by nature. Everyone by nature lifts up himself against God, goes about to dethrone God, and to crown himself. Everyone takes counsel in his heart against the Lord, saying, "Let us break His bands asunder, and cast His cords from us" (Ps. 2:3). This is the voice of everyone that dares willfully to sin. This is the working of the pride of a man against God, to thrust God out of the throne of His majesty, and to set himself in. For what is God's glory and respect among His creatures? Is it not that He, being the beginning and Author of all, should be likewise the end of all? This is the very purpose for which God made man, that having received himself from God, he should have what he might freely give up to God. All man is, and all that he has, is to be offered to God, as the end and center of all. But a sinning creature brings God under to serve him, to provide for him. And though this pride of man against God is not always so easily noticed, it is the very daring sin of the world. . . . Consider how far man's pride is from his true excellency in his union with God. We must therefore distinguish between the high esteem that man is to have of himself, and pride. For man to look on himself as a noble being, of rank above all the natural world, is not pride, for in this way he is (being a spiritual understanding agent) in a capacity of being acquainted with God and of being united to God.

> Consider how far man's pride is from his true excellency in his union with God.

Keep Close to God

Richard Alleine

hrist is to be trusted not only for the world to come, to give us entrance into heaven, but for this world also, to lead and help us on, to be with us in all our way from first to last. Our great difficulty, and our great danger of miscarrying, is not so much in our end, as in our way to it: As hard as it is to die well, it is harder to live well: though the last enemy, death, looks with a more frightful face, yet our enemies that we meet with all along our lives, sin, and lust, and temptation, do us the most deadly mischief. He that has conquered sin need not fear to encounter death; do but live a holy life, and then be nothing careful how ye shall die. Of those saints in Heb. 11, Abel, Abraham, Sarah, and the rest of them, it is recorded that they lived by faith; it is said of them, "They all died by faith" (v. 13); not one among them miscarried in death, who by faith kept close to God in their lives.

The LORD recompense thy work, and a full reward be given thee of the LORD God of Israel, under whose wings thou art come to trust.
Ruth 2:12

As hard as it is to die well, it is harder to live well.

The Last Triumph

Thomas Watson

O death, where is thy sting? O grave, where is thy victory?
1 Corinthians 15:55

What man is he that liveth and shall not see death?" (Ps. 89:48). Grace itself gives no charter of exemption from it. An earthen pot, though full of gold, may break. The righteous, who are earthen vessels, though they are filled with the golden graces, are not freed from breaking by death. But their death is precious. Wicked men, like hawks, are set high upon a perch, decked with jingling bells, but then comes their passing bell and calls them away; and, when they die, there is no missing them. Their life was scarcely worth a prayer, nor their death worth a tear. The wicked die in their sins (John 8:24). Death to them is but a trap door to let them into hell. But when a righteous man dies, his sins die with him. The pale face of death looks ruddy, being sprinkled with the blood of the Lamb. When a believer has death in his body, he has Christ in his soul. The day of his death is his ascension day to heaven. The death of a saint is precious to God; the righteous are said to be gathered. A sinner is carried away in a storm, whereas the righteous are gathered like we gather precious fruit and candy it. So greatly does God value the death of a saint that He makes inquisition for every drop of his blood. His death is precious to the saints who survive him. . . . The saints living are affected with the loss of the godly, and carry them to their grave with a shower of tears. When the bodies of the wicked are laid in the grave, there lies a heap of dust to be tumbled into hell. But the dust of a righteous man is part of Christ's mystical Body. The dust of a saint is united to Christ while it is in the grave, and as the dust of believers is now excellent, so it will appear shortly in the sight of men and angels. Emperor Trajan's ashes were honored at Rome, so the ashes of the saints at the resurrection shall be honored when they shall be made like Christ's glorious body in its beauty, strength, agility, and immortality.

We Shall Reign

William Dyer

rue believers do reign now over the creatures, over the pomp and pride of the world, over all spirits, over sin, over the consciences of wicked men, and over sufferings; but besides all this, they shall reign with Christ, and over those that now reign over them. "And we shall reign on the earth" (Rev. 5:10); "and they lived and reigned with Christ a thousand years" (Rev. 20:4). The Lord promises that the meek shall inherit the earth. Does not the Scripture say that in the last days the mountain of the Lord's house shall be lifted up above the hills, and shall be established in the top of the mountains (Isa. 2:2)? And that the kingdoms of this world must become the kingdoms of our Lord Jesus (Rev. 11:15)? And He that loves to see the face of His church beautiful will before long wipe away those bloody tears; it is not long before you will triumph and say, "Lo, the winter is past, the rain is over and gone, the flowers appear on the earth, the time of singing of birds is come" (Song 2:11–12).

And ye shall tread down the wicked; for they shall be ashes under the soles of your feet in the day that I shall do this, saith the LORD of hosts.
Malachi 4:3

The Lord promises that the meek shall inherit the earth.

Search Scriptures

William Gouge

And the brethren immediately sent away Paul and Silas by night unto Berea: who coming thither went into the synagogue of the Jews. These were more noble than those in Thessalonica, in that they received the word with all readiness of mind, and searched the scriptures daily, whether those things were so.

Acts 17:10–11

We ought to search the Scriptures that we may know the will of God. For in them is the will of God contained. This is that searching, to which knowledge and understanding is promised. And for our better help herein, we ought diligently to frequent the ministry of God's Word. As it is noted of the converted Jews, that they continued steadfastly in the apostles' doctrine, whereby is declared that they were diligent and constant hearers of the apostles, and also faithful professors and practitioners of their doctrine. The former was the cause of the latter. The preaching of the word is a great help to bring us to do the will of God. And that is in a double respect. First, because the will of God is thereby the more clearly, distinctly, and fully opened to us. Secondly, because it is a means sanctified of God to breed credence to the truth of that which is revealed, and affiance therein; yes, and to bow our will, heart, and affections to yield thereto, and to be settled thereon. In this respect says the wisdom of God, which is especially set forth in the preaching of His Word, "Blessed is the man that heareth me; watching daily as my gates, waiting as the posts of my doors" (Prov. 8:34).

> The preaching of the word is a great help to bring us to do the will of God.

Singing

Christopher Nesse

avid did not only raise himself up from his indisposing drowsiness (going out with Samson to shake it off from him [Judg. 16:20]) but he reckoned God's statutes, which he made his songs in the house of his pilgrimage, to be better to him than ten thousands of gold and silver. They were the rejoicing of his heart, as his best inheritance. "Let the word of Christ dwell in you richly" (Col. 3:16). Indwell in you: it must be in you and in you again, well digested and turned into juice and blood, and this cannot be so well effected by a brief and cursory reading of the Word, as it may by the singing of it. Wherein there is a distinct and fixed meditation upon it, and upon every syllable of it while it is leisurely sounded out by the voice; the longer that you ponder it in your mind, the more likely may it have a strong influence on your affections; this pausing and pondering does chase, supple and work the Word into your spirit, and so makes it both a refreshing and a ravishing ordinance to you, having a more intense violence upon your heart than bare reading; for hereby God's Word takes a deeper impression upon you, and those things that you did know before, come to be better known and more graciously understood, the Spirit of God sealing them upon your soul. Then does the Word of Christ dwell in your richly, and you give rich and liberal entertainment to it, and you will account all other but trivial trash to this true treasure.

Sing unto the LORD, all the earth; shew forth from day to day his salvation.
1 Chronicles 16:23

He made his songs in the house of his pilgrimage to be better than gold and silver.

Better to Obey

Thomas Manton

As ye have therefore received Christ Jesus the Lord, so walk ye in him.

Colossians 2:6

Christ is not received and entertained as Lord and King, but where His laws are obeyed. If you receive Him as Lord and King, so also obey Him. In the Lord's Prayer, first, we say, "Thy kingdom come," then we add, "Thy will be done." We do but prattle on the Lord's Prayer, and say it with our lips only, until we are resolved to do what God would have us to do—to love and hate, fear and rejoice, as God directs. Until we are brought to this frame, we do not in good earnest say, "Thy kingdom come." An earthly king will do according to his will. So Christ stands upon His will in His law. If you have taken God for your God, and Jesus Christ for your King, then say, with David, "Teach me to do thy will, for thou art my God" (Ps. 143:10). It is a universal maxim, "His servants you are whom you do obey." Where is your obedience? If you are subjects of grace, then every thought will be brought into subjection (2 Cor. 10:5). You will watch not only against your irregular actions, but every thought which lifts up itself against the obedience of Christ. There will be a greater tenderness upon us not to break any of the holy laws which belong to Christ's government. Hereby you may know whether you come under another king. Do you fear a commandment? . . . It is not he that feareth a punishment, but he that feareth a commandment, when the heart is brought under an awe of Christ's laws; so that when a man is tempted to sin, "Oh, I dare not; the Lord has commanded me the contrary." This is more than if a flaming sword stood in his way. If we have such workings of heart when we are tempted to this and that sin, so when we are doing any duty, though irksome to flesh and blood, yet it is the will of my Lord, to whom I have entirely given up myself in a way of subjection; this is a sign that you are brought under His government.

Follow Humility

Robert Harris

There must be humility if we mean to be at peace; for it is only by pride that men make contention, but humility pulls down the heart and makes it pliant and easy to be dealt with. But where wrongs lie heavy, sin lies light; where those seem great, this seems little, which humility would easily remedy. For humility makes a man nothing in himself and despised in his own eyes; and if he is so, he will not make a great matter of a small one, or stand upon his terms of reputation. And thus the mind must be purified and qualified if you would have peace. Furnish the will with love and charity towards God and men. For when we think, "God loves me, bears with my infirmities, forgives me my offenses and trespasses," this will cause us, out of love and thankfulness to God, to count it a very small matter to pass by and forgive the weaknesses of our brethren. Besides, love is sociable. A good interpreter takes everything in the best way. It "suffereth long, is kind, is not easily provoked, thinketh no evil, beareth all things, seeketh not her own" (1 Cor. 13:4–7). Love puts aside all private claims, and shares all in common. It is not selfish, looking not on its own things, but on the things of others also, prizing their well-being even as its own.

By humility and the fear of the LORD are riches, and honour, and life.
Proverbs 22:4

> **Love puts aside all private claims and shares all in common.**

Reliability

Timothy Cruso

For that ye ought to say, If the Lord will, we shall live, and do this, or that.
James 4:15

It was one branch of an admirable character given to Richard Fairclough (now with God) that he was of such punctual fidelity, that his numerous appointments, even in the smallest matters were so sure, that anyone might as certainly depend on them, as the constant returns of day and night, unless some extraordinary providence did intervene. It is good not to be too positive and preemptory, in saying, "We will do this or that," without expressing a due reservation upon the account of God's secret pleasure, "if the Lord will." The Apostle Paul does so frequently; and the Apostle James enjoins us to do so. But when there is plain insincerity in the case, that is far worse than an unthought-of hindrance, and upon that score, we see lavish professions of the greatest kindness too often expiring in ungenerous accomplishments. Men, who take it ill to be distrusted in what they say, take leave to confute themselves. Now a tender heart will not suffer a man to change or go back, though he has sworn never so much to his own hurt.

> **When there is plain insincerity in the case, that is far worse than an unthought-of hindrance.**

Another Paradise

Jeremiah Burroughs

God, says Bernard, has not cast us out of paradise to seek another paradise in this world. No, we are born to labor. Why do you seek the living among the dead? Why do you seek for living comforts, when you must expect to die daily? It is only heaven that is above all winds, storms, and tempests; rest must be after labor. Our rest is the crown of our labor; to seek it here is to seek it preposterously. Why do you require that in one place (says Ambrose) which is due in another? Why would you preposterously have the crown before you have overcome? Imagine the most settled condition you can in this world, and even if you had it, yet it would be but vanity. So says the psalmist in Ps. 39:5; "Man in his best estate is vanity." The original is, "In his settled estate he is vanity"; not only vain, but vanity itself. It was a heavy charge that Saint James laid upon some in Jas. 5, that they lived in pleasure upon earth. It is as if he said that earth is not the place for pleasure; this is the place of sorrow, of trouble, mourning, and affliction. Thus Abraham charged Dives; in your lifetime, says he, you had your pleasure. The emphasis lies there, in your lifetime. That should not have been the time. Let us take heed that we be not too hasty in seeking our rest, pleasure and delight; we may perhaps have a little for a while to the flesh, and because we will not be content with that condition that God hath appointed for His people, here we may lose our part in that glorious eternal rest which God has prepared for His people hereafter. Seek for that which you do, namely for rest, but do not seek for it where you do; if we seek our rest in this world even though we meet with so many troubles in it, what would we do if the Lord should let us prosper? Behold (saith an ancient), the world is troublesome, and yet it is loved; what would it be if it were peaceable? You embrace it though it is filthy; what would you do if it were beautiful? You cannot keep your hands from the thorns, how earnest would you be in gathering the flowers?

And be not conformed to this world: but be ye transformed by the renewing of your mind, that ye may prove what is that good, and acceptable, and perfect, will of God.
Romans 12:2

Suitable Fear

Thomas Adams

Come, ye children, hearken unto me: I will teach you the fear of the LORD.
Psalm 34:11

We must love our good God; we must fear our great Lord. It is objected to this, that "perfect love casteth out fear" (1 John 4:18). It is answered that fear brings in perfect love, as the needle draws in the thread. And it is not possible that true love should be without good fear; that is, a filial reverence. For slavish fear, be it as far from your hearts, as it shall be from my discourse. Now this fear is a most due and proper affection, and (I may say) the fittest of all to be towards God. Indeed God requires our love. But we must think that then God stoops low, and bows down to be loved of us. For there is such an infinite inequality between God and us, that without His sweet descending to us, there could be no fitness of this affection. But if we look up to that infinite glory of our great Lord, and we look down on the vileness of ourselves, sinful dust, and we will say that by reason of the disproportion between us, there is nothing so suitable to give so high a God, as fear.

Without His sweet descending to us there could be no fitness of this affection.

Tender Love

John Durant

C hrist discovers a sweet carriage not only in preserving the weak beginnings of grace, in the hearts of believers, but also in strengthening their weakness every day. It is noteworthy that Christ not only does not break the bruised reed, nor quench the smoking flax, that is, cherish the faint graces which are in feeble saints, but He strengthens and increases them. He makes an augmentation, brings forth judgment unto truth (Isa. 42:3). The meaning is, as Dr. Sibbes says sweetly, "That the gracious frame of holiness, set up in our hearts by the Spirit of Christ, shall get forward, or increase, till all contrary power be brought down." My feet, says the poor soul, are so feeble that I am ready to stumble at every straw. Sure, I shall never be able to stride over a log, to go over a mountain. Doubt not, O you of little faith. Christ will carry himself tender towards you; and though your feet are now weak as lambs' feet, that you are scarce able to go over a mole-hill, without sliding, He will make them strong as hinds' feet, that you shall be able, before long, to leap over a mountain. "He maketh my feet like hinds' feet," says David (Ps. 18:33). Christ is very careful to carry on the soul from strength to strength (Ps. 84:7). He therefore gave some to the apostles, some to the prophets, that they might be for the perfecting of the saints; that weak believers who are but infants, may grow stronger and stronger, till they come to adult age, as it is in Eph. 4:13. . . . "The path of the righteous is as the shining light, and shineth more and more to the perfect day" (Prov. 4:18). Christ will make it day, and a perfect day in your heart; though it is morning now, and but even sun rising; oh, how sweet is Christ's carriage to His weak members that thus He strengthens their weak graces every day. He will cherish you, O believing babe, till you grow bigger, in His bosom.

How excellent is thy lovingkindness, O God! therefore the children of men put their trust under the shadow of thy wings.
Psalm 36:7

> **Christ will make it day, and a perfect day in your heart.**

No Other Gods

John Dod and Robert Cleaver

Thou shalt have no other gods before me.
Exodus 20:3

The drift of the first commandment is that we should sanctify God in our hearts, and give Him all things that are proper and peculiar to His majesty. . . . To have no other gods is to have nothing where we set our delight, or which we esteem more than God. The doctrine from hence is that we must suffer nothing to withdraw our souls, or anything in us, from God. For that is our god, which is most set upon. Whatever our mind is more carried after than the glory and service of God is another god to us. As for matter of commodity, if we set our hope, and our trust, and our heart upon wealth, this is idolatry. So the rich man in the gospel made his wealth his god, because he trusted in it and did worship it; for here he speaks of the inward worship of God in the soul. If we rely on wealth, and think that we are safe when we have it, when it is removed from us we are undone. . . . So covetousness is called idolatry . . . where our souls and affections, our wit, memory, understanding, and all our faculties stoop to that when we should only stoop to God.

To have no other gods is to have nothing where we set our delight, or which we esteem more, than God.

Beware of Dreams

Robert Dingley

Let me say something about revelations and visions in the dreams of the night, where poor seekers and seduced ones are ensnared by the devil. Familists [members of an antinomian sect originating in Holland] gape for visions and revelations, calling such as have their eyes open and on the Scriptures, literalists. They call the written Word a low and inky divinity. The Anabaptists in Munster were much led by dreams and inspirations, and were a vile crew of monsters in the doublets of men. Violent impulses, moving to break Scriptural bounds, drop from one that can transform himself into an angel of light. Tertullian was sadly deluded by admiring of Montanus and Priscilla as prophets, condemning all others as people in the dark. . . . Of old indeed God did immediately reveal His will in dreams, but now by His Word, to which nothing is to be added to the world's end (Rev. 22:18). Irenaeus tells of some that call themselves Apostle-menders. Muhammad says he discoursed with the angel Gabriel, whose dictates are recorded in the Koran. The Helcesaits, says Bullinger, affirmed that they had a book sent from heaven, in which all divine mysteries were revealed. We read of John of Leiden's deep sleep and dream for three days in a row; at last awaking and feigning himself speechless, he wrote down twelve poor men to be governors of Munster; adding, that a man was not tied to one wife. Now this is what heretics do, for the amazement and amusement of the laity, and to secure their corrupt tenets from the hazard of disputation. Jude calls them filthy dreamers.

For thus saith the LORD of hosts, the God of Israel; Let not your prophets and your diviners, that be in the midst of you, deceive you, neither hearken to your dreams which ye cause to be dreamed.
Jeremiah 29:8

> Of old indeed God did immediately reveal His will in dreams, but now by His Word.

Eternal Inheritance

John Shower

His seed shall endure forever, and his throne as the sun before me.
Psalm 89:36

After millions of years and ages, the felicity of the saints shall be as far from ending, as when their souls were first received into paradise. The infinite love of God, the everlasting merit of Christ, and the unchangeableness of the covenant of grace, assures us they shall be happy forever. They shall eat of the tree of life, in the midst of the paradise of God; and be pillars in the divine temple, and go out no more. To live forever in the light, and love, and joy of heaven; oh! what a thought is that! How may it swallow up all our other thoughts! If one day's communion with God on earth is better than a thousand elsewhere, what shall we think of immediate, everlasting communion with God in heaven? We shall see Him as He is, and love Him more than we can now think; and that not for a day or a week, but for thousands of millions of years, yes for a long blessed eternity, that will never be over. For it is an immortal inheritance, it is an everlasting kingdom. We shall reign with God and with the Lamb forever. We shall see Him, love Him, praise Him, and enjoy Him forevermore. What we shall see and know will never lessen in our eye and esteem; what we shall love will never cease to be lovely. What we shall praise, will always deserve our praise, and what we shall enjoy, we shall never be weary of enjoying.

> **What we shall praise will always deserve our praise.**

Relish Goodness

Richard Alleine

Do you desire God? Do you desire grace? Stir up and enlarge your desires; let those narrow hearts open their mouths wide. Be covetous Christians; covet much, and covet earnestly these best gifts. Say with the psalmist, "This one thing I desire; nothing but God, nothing but grace. Take corn and wine who will, take the gold and the silver who will, let the Lord God be mine, and that shall suffice me." Desire God only, and follow after God fully. Psalm 63:8: "My soul followeth hard after thee." Friends, you have some wishes and some weaker desires after the Lord. Oh, quicken up these faint hearts. Look often at how worthy the Lord is of all your desires. What a jewel, what a treasure the grace of God is! Look often heavenward; get a sight of God and His glorious treasures; live more in the contemplation of His glory and goodness. It is the sight of the object that must kindle and quicken desire. You who have cold hearts heavenward, it is a sign that your eye is little on heaven. Believe it, some clearer views of the love, the goodness, the holiness, the kindness, and the glory of the Lord would whet your appetite, would put life into those dull desires, would make you hungry souls, and thirsty souls, and longing souls. Oh, look often upward; dwell in the mountain of spices; get some taste and relish of the goodness of God by being more constantly conversant with Him, and this will pierce all your vessels. Your souls would stream forth in the words and sighs of the psalmist in Ps. 42:1–2: "As the hart panteth after the water brooks, so panteth my soul after thee, O God. My soul thirsteth for God, for the living God."

LORD, thou hast heard the desire of the humble: thou wilt prepare their heart, thou wilt cause thine ear to hear.

Psalm 10:17

> Get some taste and relish of the goodness of God by being more constantly conversant with Him.

Beware of the Devil

Thomas Manton

Neither give place to the devil.
Ephesians 4:27

Beg for wisdom that you may discern the wiles of Satan, and may not be caught unawares, for he is "transformed into an angel of light" (2 Cor. 11:14). Mark how the devil does not care so much to ride his own horses, as to act and draw the wicked to evil; he has them sure enough, but he labors to employ the saints in his work, if he can, to get one which belongs to God to do his business. Therefore he changes himself into an angel of light. The temptation is disguised with very plausible pretenses; then a child of God may be a factor for Satan, and an instrument of the devil. For instance, would Peter have ever made a motion for Satan if he had seen his hand? Oh, no; the temptation was disguised to him when he persuaded his Master from suffering. He covered his foul designs with plausible pretenses. Carnal counsel shall be pity and natural affection: "Let not these things be; be it far from thee, Lord: this shall not be unto thee. He said unto Peter, Get thee behind me, Satan; thou art an offense unto me" (Matt. 16:22–23). At another time, the disciples, when their Master was slighted and condemned, thought certainly that they should do as Elijah did, call for fire from heaven to consume them (Luke 9:54). Revenge will often go for zeal for God. Revenge, or storming at personal affronts or injuries done to ourselves, is looked upon as zeal; then the disciples may not know what spirit they are of. Many times we are acted by the devil when we think we are acted by the Spirit of God, and that which seems to be zeal is nothing but revenge. Therefore we had need go to God: Lord, deliver us from evil; we are poor unwary creatures; that we may not be ensnared by the devil's fair pretenses and surprised by his enterprises.

> **We had need go to God: "Lord, deliver us from evil."**

272

Unsearchable Depths

John Shower

There are depths and mysteries in divine providence that we must acknowledge to be unsearchable. Let us not then censure what we cannot understand, what we cannot fathom. Is it strange that incomprehensible wisdom should do incomprehensible things? We should not therefore inquire too curiously into the secrets of His providence, nor determine anything, rashly concerning it, which is not revealed to us. We are well assured that He made the world; and yet there are many questions about the works of creation that may puzzle the wisest and most diligent enquirer. So in the government of the world, there are many things above our reach, and yet we may be assured that an unerring wisdom governs all. We are so ignorant and shortsighted, and the designs of God are so far beyond us, and the means He uses are often so various and their connection with His design so much concealed from our weak eyes, that no wonder if we are often at a loss; especially when all the particulars of His works of providence that make up the beauty of the whole are wonderfully interwoven together, so that it is not strange if we comprehend not the reasons of all events and discern not that wisdom and righteousness of God as to many particulars, while yet we believe Him to be wise, and holy in all His ways, and righteous in all His works.

The secret things belong unto the LORD our God: but those things which are revealed belong unto us and to our children for ever, that we may do all the words of this law.
Deuteronomy 29:29

It is not strange if we comprehend not the reasons of all events.

Keep the Way

Henry Smith

*Good and upright is
the LORD: therefore
will he teach sinners
in the way.*
Psalm 25:8

As God taught the Israelites the way to Canaan, sending a fiery pillar before them, which they did follow wherever it went, so, when He ordained a heaven for men, He appointed a way to come unto it, which way He that misses shall never come to the end. As Herod sought Christ over all Jewry, but none found Him but those which followed the star, so there is something still that leads men to Christ, which we must follow, or else we cannot come where He is. There are many wrong ways, as there are many errors; there is but one right way, as there is but one truth. And, therefore, Jacob did not see many, but one ladder, which reached to heaven. And John the Baptist is said not to "prepare the ways of the Lord," but "the way," showing that there is but one right way in this life. Solomon understands the way for the mean, and therefore he said, "Turn not to the right hand or to the left," implying that we may err as well of the right hand as of the left. As if he should say, "Some are too hot, as others are too cold; some are too superstitious, as others are too careless; some are too fearful, as others are too confident." There is a zeal without knowledge, a love without singleness, a prayer without faith, and a faith without fruits. Therefore the apostle warns us to "examine whether we be in the faith" (2 Cor 13:5); not whether we have a kind of faith, but whether we are in the faith, i.e., the true faith.

> When He ordained a heaven for men, He appointed a way to come unto it.

Consider This Love

John Durant

Tremble to think that you should ever sin against Christ, who loves you so much. View your sins in the light of your Savior's love; and when you see the transcendency of that love which is in His bosom towards you, then sit down and bleed to behold your great sinning against Him. Then indeed has transcendent love a sweet working upon your spirit, when the thoughts of it can make you mourn for your sins. How sweetly did love work upon that woman (who was a sinner) when she tasted the transcendent love of her Savior? The sight of the great love which was in His bosom towards her made her sit at His feet, and weep bitterly at the thoughts of her sins. . . . And though nothing in the world can melt the heart for sin, yet the thoughts of the love of Christ will. Well, believers, let it then have such a working in your bosoms. O let His transcendent love (which you may read written with the blood of His heart) dissolve your adamantine heart. And let it make you mourn for your sins greatly. "They shall see Him whom they have pierced and mourn" (Zech. 12:10). Why (believers) do you see Him whom you have pierced with your sins? Do you not mourn, especially when you see Him in the light of love? I say no more but this, either you have not tasted this transcendent love of Christ, or else your spirits are very much hardened, if the sense and thoughts of these do not cause you to mourn for sin. Therefore let this word of exhortation sink deeply into your hearts; weep, and weep tears of blood, to think that ever you should sin against Jesus Christ, who has written by His own blood this truth, that He loves you with a love passing knowledge.

I am distressed for thee, my brother Jonathan: very pleasant hast thou been unto me: thy love to me was wonderful, passing the love of women.
2 Samuel 1:26

Either you have not tasted this transcendent love of Christ or else your spirits are very much hardened.

Evangelical Sorrow

Edmund Calamy

A broken and a con-
trite heart, O God,
thou wilt not despise.
Psalm 51:17b

If we sorrow for sin and rest not on Christ for the pardon of sins, our sorrow is legal and not evangelical, desperation and not contrition. Evangelical sorrow is mixed with hope. The evangelical mourners mourn not without hope. They have hope of obtaining mercy, even in the deepest of their sorrow, as appears by their carriage in mourning. They do not despair, but implore God for mercy. Their sorrow drives them to God, and not from Him, as is evident by the example of the prodigal, who in his deepest distress did not despair but went to his father for mercy. If he did not have hope of obtaining mercy he never would have gone to his father to seek it. Evangelical sorrow is mixed with joy, being mixed with faith and hope. The evangelical mourner looks upon his sorrow as a sacrifice, with which God is well pleased, and therefore he joys that he can sorrow and offer this sacrifice to God. "The sacrifices of God are a broken and contrite heart, and spirit," says the Scripture (Ps. 51:17). This the contrite heart believes and therefore joys when it can sorrow.

The evangelical mourner looks upon his sorrow as a sacrifice, with which God is well pleased.

Turn From Evil

Nathaniel Vincent

God's eye is a most piercing eye, and looks into all, even the darkest places. He sees the wickedness that is concealed from others, and not in the least suspected by them. He looks into the very heart, and takes notice of all the imaginations, desires, affections, and projects that are evil. And as the eye of God is piercing, so it is most pure. God sees all iniquity, but does not behold so as to approve of any. The wicked are apt to think that God is like them, and because they like their own evil ways, they cannot imagine that He does so much dislike them. But the wicked, as they are called fools, never show themselves so much as fools as when they conclude God is not angry at their sin. This unbelief, this security, this most unworthy apprehension of God, stirs up the greater indignation against Him. If God is glorious in holiness, if His wrath is revealed against all unrighteousness, it undeniably follows that turning from wickedness is of absolute necessity.

Let the wicked forsake his way, and the unrighteous man his thoughts: and let him return unto the LORD, and he will have mercy upon him; and to our God, for he will abundantly pardon.
Isaiah 55:7

> As the eye of God is piercing, so it is most pure.

The Lord Avenges

Thomas Watson

O LORD God, to
whom vengeance
belongeth; O God, to
whom vengeance
belongeth, shew
thyself.
Psalm 94:1

If the righteous are more excellent than others, then
how severe will God be against those who wrong
them? The wicked are thorns in the sides of the godly.
Saint Paul was scourged by cruel hands. "Thrice was I
beaten with rods" (2 Cor. 11:25), as if you should see a
slave whip the king's son; but shall not God avenge His
elect? Surely He will. "The sword of the Lord is filled
with blood . . . for it is the day of the Lord's vengeance,
and the year of recompenses for the controversy of Zion"
(Isa. 34:6–8). It is as if the prophet had said, "The time appointed has now come for God to avenge Zion for the
wrongs done to her." Jer. 50:10–11 says, "Chaldea shall be
a spoil, saith the Lord, because ye were glad, because ye
rejoiced, O ye destroyers of Mine heritage." And Jer.
30:16, "All that prey upon thee, will I give for a prey." The
saints are persons of honor; they are God's first-born.
Oh, how enraged will the Lord be against such as offer injury to them! They trample God's pearls in the dust. They
strike at the apple of His eye. The righteous are God's dia-
dem. Will a king endure to have His robes spit upon and
His crown thrown in the dirt? What is done to the righteous is done to God Himself. When the king's favorite is
struck at, the king himself is struck at. "I know thy rage
against me" (2 Kgs. 19:27). The rage of Sennacherib was
against the person of Hezekiah, but, there being a league
between God and His people, the Lord took it as done to
Himself. "I know Thy rage against me: certainly it shall
not go unpunished." He reproved kings for their sakes.
What became of (the pagan Emperors) Julian, Nero, and
Diocletian? One of them had his death wound from
heaven. Others had their bowels come out and died rav-
ing. Charles the ninth of France, who had glutted himself
with the blood of so many Christians in the massacre at
Paris, was in such inward horror that he never dared be
waked without music, and at length blood issued out of
so many parts of his body that he died bleeding. These
were set up as public monuments of God's vengeance.

Heart Judgment

Jeremiah Burroughs

God does not judge in regards to outward appearance; what is this before the Lord? What is it to have gold and fine clothes before God? The things that are grand in the world and attract the eyes—what are these to God? God does not esteem men at all for these things. Neither does He disesteem them for the lack of them. Lack of clothes, money, and worldly riches—what is this to God? Does God look at any man worse for not having these things? God is no respecter of persons; if He looks at any with high esteem it is the poor, humble, and contrite. God delights to look down into the world upon those that are poor. He reserves a poor people that shall trust in His name (Zeph. 3:12). The Lord passes by the great things of the world. He brings down the mighty, and regards the low estate of His handmaid, the low estate of His people. It is a poor and contrite spirit that He looks at from on high; the prayer of the destitute He regards (Ps. 102:17). The word in the original refers to a poor shrub, or that which is in the wilderness that the beasts tread upon, that no man regards, seemingly worthless. It may be that one comes with brave words and mighty expressions and God throws them as dirt in his face. There comes another that can hardly groan out his meaning, and yet with grace, God regards him. If a proud, scornful spirit would hear a poor gracious heart groaning out his complaints to God, he would think it nonsense, but God, knowing the meaning of His Spirit, and seeing His grace, has respect to him.

Every one that exalteth himself shall be abased; and he that humbleth himself shall be exalted.

Luke 18:14

> There comes another that can hardly groan out his meaning, and yet with grace, God regards him.

To Judge Ourselves

Thomas Gouge

Judge me, O LORD my God, according to thy righteousness.
Psalm 35:24a

There is no sin so secretly and closely committed, but that shall be discovered to the view of all. There is scarce a wicked person in the world, though never so formal, but has at some time or other committed some such sin in secret, which he or she would not have others to know for all the world. But know for certain that at the day of judgment, all the world shall hear of it. For then all your secret sins and close villainies shall be discovered, and laid open before the angels, men, and devils . . . yes, not only your words and actions, but also your secret thoughts and imaginations, how vain and wanton, how filthy and abominable they have been, shall appear to the view of all. Never therefore adventure upon the committing of a sin in the hope of secrecy, because you seem safe from the eyes of others. For suppose your sin lie undiscovered to the last and great day, yet then shall it come out with a witness, and be made manifest to the view of all. Now I know no better way to prevent the discovery of your sins at the great day, than here in this time and day of grace to call yourselves to an account, to search and examine your own hearts and lives, and then to judge and condemn yourselves for your manifold sins and transgressions, for as the apostle speaks, "If we judge ourselves, we shall not be condemned of the Lord" (1 Cor. 11:31). Oh therefore, let us here often keep a day of judgment in our own souls and consciences, by a serious examining of ourselves concerning our sins, and judging and condemning ourselves for the sin, and then let us in all humility prostrate ourselves at the throne of grace, pleading the mercy of God and the merits of Christ for the pardon and forgiveness of them all; giving no rest to our souls, till we have some comfortable evidence and assurance, which will cause us to lift up our heads with joy at the great day of account.

Sweeter

Jeremiah Burroughs

Though God's people are afflicted, and the wicked have pleasure, yet afflicted godliness is better than delightful wickedness. It is better to join with God's people in a way of godliness, in all afflictions, than to enjoy all the pleasure that any man in the world can possibly have in any way of sin. The tears of the godly are better than all the merriments of the wicked. It is an expression of an ancient that the very tears of those that seek God are sweeter than the joys that any have in the world. The worst part of godliness is better than the best part of any way of sin. Though Christ is a crucified Christ, and brings sore afflictions to His people, yet He is more delightful to them than all the pleasures that are in the earth. He is delightful in another way. It is a notable speech Luther has: "I had rather fall with Christ, than stand with Caesar; rather suffer anything in the world with Christ, than stand and enjoy all the pleasure of Caesar's court." Thus a godly man, a gracious heart which considers things, would rather have affliction with the people of God than enjoy all the pleasures of the world for a season.

For a day in thy courts is better than a thousand. I had rather be a doorkeeper in the house of my God, than to dwell in the tents of wickedness.
Psalm 84:10

> Though Christ is a crucified Christ, He is more delightful than all the pleasures that are in the earth.

Cling to Christ

Richard Alleine

Holding forth the word of life; that I may rejoice in the day of Christ, that I have not run in vain, neither laboured in vain.

Philippians 2:16

Stick close to Christ, or else you will never be likely to stick fast. By how much the closer our adherence to Christ is, by so much the firmer is our standing, and the less danger of falling off. The root of a tree, if it be loosened from the earth, is more easily plucked up; some small strings there may be that keep their hold, which maintain it in life; but if the main root be loosened, it is the more in danger of being blown down. The cleaving of the soul to Christ is set forth by the cleaving together of husband and wife: "for this cause, shall a man leave father and mother, and shall be joined to his wife" (Eph. 5:31). The word in the original signifies, shall be glued to his wife. What is glued together, if it shrinks or gapes, loses its hold. Take heed of warping and shrinking from Christ; the glue will give off if you do; and when you have once lost your hold, you know not whither you may be blown. O take heed of growing to a distance, of wandering from Christ, keep you near Him if you would stand firm.

Take heed of warping and shrinking from Christ; the glue will give off if you do.

Divine Contentment

Thomas Watson

ontentment is a divine thing; it becomes ours, not by acquisition, but infusion; it is a slip taken off from the tree of life, and planted by the Spirit of God in the soul; it is a fruit that grows not in the garden of philosophy, but is of a heavenly birth; it is therefore very observable that contentment is joined with godliness, and goes in equipage; "godliness with contentment is great gain" (1 Tim. 6:6). Contentment being a consequent of godliness, or concomitant, or both, I call it divine, to contradistinguish it to that contentment which a moral man may arrive at. Heathens have seemed to have this contentment, but it was only the shadow and picture of it—the beryl, not the true diamond: theirs was but civil, this is sacred; theirs was only from principles of reason, this of religion; theirs was only lighted at nature's torch, this at the lamp of Scripture. Reason may a little teach contentment, as thus: whatever my condition is, this is that I am born to; and if I meet with crosses, it is but catholic misery: all have their share, why therefore should I be troubled? Reason may suggest this; and indeed, this may be rather constraint; but to live securely and cheerfully upon God in the abatement of creaturely supplies, only religion can bring this into the soul's exchequer.

Let your conversation be without covetousness; and be content with such things as ye have: for he hath said, I will never leave thee, nor forsake thee.
Hebrews 13:5

> Heathens have seemed to have this contentment, but it was only the shadow and picture of it.

Insufficient Letter

Robert Bolton

For the law made nothing perfect, but the bringing in of a better hope did; by the which we draw nigh unto God.

Hebrews 7:19

The Word of God in the letter, without the spiritual meaning (and the finger of God's Spirit to apply it powerfully to our souls and consciences) is not a sufficient rule of life, nor is it able to bring us into the light of grace. This appears in Nicodemus, who was a great doctor in the law and the prophets, a chief master and teacher in Israel; yet he was an infant in the power of grace and the mystery of godliness. For all his learning of the letter of the law he had not yet made one step towards heaven. He was not only ignorant of the law, but he had a false idea of the new birth, which is the very first entrance into the kingdom of grace. For when Christ told him that he could not be saved, except he were new born, he strangely replies, "How can a man be born, which is old? How can he enter into his mother's womb again, and be born?" (John 3:4). Thus you see, there can be no other means to be named, or thought upon; not all human knowledge, nor worldly wisdom, not good meanings, nor will-worship, not the Word itself in the letter, which can lead us into the ways of righteousness, or bring us unto heaven, but only the light of God's holy Word, laid out to us by a profitable ministry, and the power of the Spirit.

> For all his learning of the letter of the law he had not yet made one step towards heaven.

Valiant in Battle

Christopher Nesse

All you that are baptized must know that therein you have avouched the Lord to be your God (to walk in His ways and to keep His commandments) and the Lord has avouched you in that day to be His peculiar people. The most excellent and honorable name of Christ is then put upon you; O walk worthy of that worthy name, that the name of our Lord Jesus Christ may be glorified in you and you in Him. This is your engagement and that by the most solemn vow that ever was made or taken. The covenant of your God is upon you, the bond of the covenant should bind you fast (as the word "religion" signifies) unto God and godliness. O break not those bands, nor cast away those cords from you, for then you are sure to be broken as a potter's vessel that cannot be patched up again. O be not among that black bed-roll. Much less he that breaks His covenant with the great God who will assuredly avenge the quarrel of His covenant. O keep yourselves in the love of God and continue in Christ's love, which constrains you to obedience and holiness. You are soldiers of Jesus Christ. O do valiantly and (as good soldiers) fight the good fight of faith against those adversaries that war against your souls. The Romans of old had their oath of service in war, to bind them sufficiently to their military service. And such as run away from their general were to be hanged. Thus you have taken God's oath and the gospel oath is upon you, you have enrolled in Christ's muster book; of how much sorer punishment shall you be thought worthy (to wit, to be hanged up in hell) if you forsake the camp without the leave of your general? Yea, if you revolt and run to the enemy as apostates do; or if you stay in the camp, yet hold private correspondence with the adversary; or if you do neither of these, yet out of cowardice and contempt never strike a blow, or perform a duty. It is worst of all to be in God's camp, and yet fight the devil's battles, and not God's. This contracts more guilt than if you had never contracted with God to serve Him at all.

Through God we shall do valiantly: for he it is that shall tread down our enemies.
Psalm 108:13

God's Name

John Owen

The name of the LORD is a strong tower: the righteous runneth into it, and is safe.

Proverbs 18:10

The name of God is that whereby He reveals Himself unto us, whereby He would have us know Him and own Him. It is something expressive of His nature or properties which He hath appropriated unto himself. Whatever, therefore, any name of God expresses Him to be, that He is, that we may expect to find Him; for He will not deceive us by giving Himself a wrong or a false name. And on this account He requires us to trust in His name, because He will assuredly be found unto us what His name imports. Resting on His name, flying unto His name, calling upon His name, praising His name, things so often mentioned in the Scripture, confirm the same unto us. These things could not be our duty if we might be deceived in so doing. God is, then, and will be, to us what His name declares.

> He will not deceive us by giving Himself a wrong or a false name.

God's Eyes

Robert Dingley

Consider that God's eyes are upon us, to observe all our motions, glances, and deportment. He sees every idle glance of the eye, and reads our thoughts afar off. "He that made the eye shall not he see?" (Isa. 32:1). His eyes run to and fro throughout the earth. Hear Isaiah, great in counsel, and mighty in work, for thine eyes are upon all the ways of the sons of men, to give every one the fruit of His doings. Solomon says, "The eyes of the Lord are in every place, beholding the evil and the good" (Prov. 15:3). Gyges' ring could not make him invisible as to God. There is a vast difference between God's eye and ours. . . . Our eye is but a means or instrument of knowledge, but God's eye is His knowledge. Our eye must have a twofold light to see by, an inward light in the organ, an outward light in the medium, but God sees in the night: "The darkness and light are both alike to Him" (Job 34:22). We see one thing after another, but God sees all things at once. Our eye sees but at a certain distance, but God is omnipresent, and nothing is far from Him. Our eye sees the outside of things, but the Lord is the discerner of the heart, and nothing is hid from Him. Our eye may be deluded and deceived, but God's cannot. Our eye is but of yesterday, but God's eye is from everlasting. . . . Our eye is not always open, or awake, but the Lord's eyes never slumber nor sleep. Our eye may be darkened by dimness, disease, or bribes, but God's cannot. And lastly, our eye may see and observe what is amiss, but is not able to punish it, but God's is notable, for the eye of Jehovah can look us into hell; He can nod us to destruction. O, therefore, stand in awe of God and His eye, which is ever upon you! For if you do but look awry, or think awry, God sees it. He is all eye, that looks upon you, and He cannot abide to behold iniquity in the eye, in the heart. Go which way you will; God sees you, as the eye of a well-drawn picture, which views all that is in the room. Thales Milesius, being asked if God saw our evil actions, said, "Yes, if we do but think amiss."

Doth not he see my ways, and count all my steps?
Job 31:4

Things Above

Thomas Watson

*Set your affection on
things above, not on
things on the earth.*
Colossians 3:2

An earthly saint is a contradiction. The Greek word for saint signifies a person refined and separated from the earth. If an astronomer, instead of observing the planets, and the motions of the heavens, should take a reed in his hand and fall to measuring the earth, would not this be counted a blunder? And is it not as great a blunder in religion when those that pretend to have Christ and heaven in their eye do mind earthly things? Our souls should be like a ship, which is made little and narrow downwards, but more wide and broad upwards. So our affections should be very narrow downwards to the earth, but wide and large upwards towards heavenly things. Thus we see that death is a privilege to believers; death is yours; the heir while he is under age, is capable of the land he is born to, but he has not the use of the benefit of it, till he comes of age. Be as old as you will, you are never of age until you die. Death brings us of age, and then the possession comes into our hands.

> Be as old as you
> will, you are
> never of age
> until you die.

Increase of God

Richard Stock

veryone should labor for the Spirit of God that he or she might be able to profit by the Word preached or read. Without Him a man may have knowledge, but not a saving knowledge. It is an excellent benefit for a man to have good teachers, but it is no benefit in comparison of this, that the Spirit becomes our teacher, for, "who teacheth like Him?" (Job 36:22). Therefore labor for this Teacher. Saint Augustine says, the teachers are without, but He sits in heaven that must teach the heart, and therefore look to Him. We can but make a noise in your ears by our most earnest expressions and vehement cries, but it must be the Spirit that makes all effectual. I pray you tell me, says Augustine, what does the husbandman do? Can he do anything but the outward work? Does he do anything inwardly? Can he make an apple, or a leaf? He cannot; it is God that does that. Ask the Apostle Paul and he will tell you, "It is Paul that plants, and Apollos that waters, but it is God that gives the increase" (1 Cor. 3:6). Therefore, labor that you have that anointing.

Thou visitest the earth, and waterest it: thou greatly enrichest it with the river of God, which is full of water: thou preparest them corn, when thou hast so provided for it.
Psalm 65:9

> He sits in heaven that must teach the heart, and therefore look to Him.

The Picture of God

Richard Bernard

In the beginning God created the heaven and the earth.
Genesis 1:1

God is by definition good, the prime cause of all His creatures; only one, and one alone. Incomprehensible, infinite, invisible, He is a substance without composition, action without motion, a being spiritual, eternal, before time, in time, and beyond all time. He is without beginning, without ending, the Alpha of every thing, and the Omega of all things. He is the first and the last; without measure of time. He is that kingly regency, that lordly sovereignty. He gives to all life, motion, and action; He bestows the quality and increases the quantity; yet He is good without quality, and great without quantity. He is the being and beauty of His creature. He made everything good and still from Him flows goodness. . . . He is eminent above all, superexcellent beyond all, abundant in love to all, and absolutely perfect happiness without all. He is the highest in majesty, the greatest in glory, the largest in magnificence, the most powerful in omnipotence, and the ever only best in unspeakable bounty. Without Him nothing is available, but with Him all things are possible. . . . He can span heaven with His hand, sound the depth of the ocean seas; He can make the earth tremble at His presence. . . . He is in Himself holiness, the very fountain of all goodness; nothing evil can come from Him, and nothing evil by Him. . . . He is majesty, He is mercy, He is excellency, He is glory, He is power, He is principality, He is grace and goodness, life and happiness. . . . To Him be praise perpetually.

> He is the first and the last without measure of time.

A Good Use

Ralph Venning

Everyone should endeavor to make the best use of what they hear and read. All Scripture is profitable, and is written for everyone's learning. Are fathers spoken to? It is for the use of the younger sort, to provoke them to aspire and endeavor after such attainments and experiences. Therefore the apostle resolved to go on and to treat of perfection (strong meat and doctrine) though his hearers were but babes (Heb. 6:1). Are the younger sort spoken to? It is of use to fathers, to call to remembrance what once they were, for such were some of you; and also to stir them up to thankfulness, that God has advanced them to a state of which it may be said, "such honor have not all the saints." And to say as David did, "Who am I, O Lord God, and what is my house, that thou hast brought me hitherto?" (2 Sam. 7:18). I have heard of an eminent person, who had been with others at a sermon, and when some complained and seemed to be offended, because the preacher was a Boanerges, and threatened wrath and the flashes of hell fire to sinners, he told them that it was one of the sweetest and most comfortable sermons that he had heard in a long time, for said he, "I bless God I am delivered from it all." This is to make a good use of a sermon. Do you that are saints hear sermons preached to sinners, to show the misery of their condition? Then bless God that He has converted you. Do you that are sinners hear sermons preached to saints, to show their privileges and happiness? Then pray to God to make you saints also. Thus all and everyone may make a good use of every sermon they hear.

If any man have an ear, let him hear.
Revelation 13:9

Bless God that He has converted you.

Like a God

John Shower

Consider how high the heavens are above the earth, and (which is more) the difference between the creature and the Creator, that His thoughts are not as ours; not like our misgiving, despairing thoughts. He does and will pardon like Himself, like a God; not after the measures of a finite, passionate, weak man. All that you have said, or can say, shall be no impediment, if you return to God, and seek Him in Christ for forgiveness. He will abundantly pardon, beyond what you are able to think, or suppose in the like case. God complains of Israel, as prone and inclined to backslide, yet He cannot find in His heart to destroy them, but expresses a kind of conflict between justice and mercy; and at last resolves, "I am God, and not man," therefore I will not execute the fierceness of Mine anger, but I will cause them to walk after the Lord (Hos. 11:7, 10). He does all things like Himself. If He builds, He makes a world; if He is angry with the world, He sends a flood over the face of all the earth. If He goes out with the armies of His people, He makes the sun stand still, the stars to fight, the seas to swallow up the most dreadful armies. If He loves, the precious heart's blood of His beloved Son is not too dear; if any becomes His friend and favorite through the mediation of Christ, He will make Him a king, give Him a paradise, and set a crown of eternal glory on His head. Let us not consider so much what is fit or likely for us to receive, as for so great a God to give and bestow. If we are contrite, humble, penitent, and fly to Jesus Christ as our refuge of hope, He will think all the meritorious sufferings of His Son, all the promises of His book, all the comforts of His Holy Spirit, all the pleasures and blessedness of His kingdom, little enough for us.

> **Let us not consider so much what is fit or likely for us to receive, as for so great a God to give and bestow.**

Divine Goodness

John Arrowsmith

oses was skilled in all the learning of the Egyptians; yet as not content herewith, he became a humble suitor to God for some further and better knowledge. "I beseech thee," he says, "shew me thy glory" (Exod. 33:18). Other notions may fill the head of a moral man, but nothing short of the knowledge of God can satisfy the heart of a saint. Wherefore in answer to this request, the Lord makes him a promise, saying, "I will make all my goodness pass before thee" (v. 19). The thing desired was a sight of His glory; the thing promised was a view of His goodness, which intimates that however all the attributes of God are glorious, yet God glories most in the manifestation of His goodness, and nothing brings Him so much glory from the creatures that are accustomed to magnify this most. So the church says in Isaiah: "I will mention the loving-kindnesses of the LORD, and the praises of the LORD, according to all that the LORD hath bestowed on us, and the great goodness toward the house of Israel, which He hath bestowed on them according to His mercies, and according to the multitude of His loving-kindnesses" (Isa. 63:7).

Surely goodness and mercy shall follow me all the days of my life.
Psalm 23:6a

> Nothing short of the knowledge of God can satisfy the heart of a saint.

Secret Prayer

Samuel Slater

Closet, or secret prayer, is an excellent and advantageous duty, which all the people of God ought to be very much in the performance of. When you are alone, and have nobody with you, then you should be with God. At night, when you are in bed commune with your hearts and be still; turn your eyes inward before sleep closes them; and before you go to bed, spend some time in seeking and communing with your God. Take your leave of friends and relations; or, if you please, go away from them, that you and your God may be together. When upon an express command given him by God Himself, Abraham went to offer up His only and dearly beloved son, Isaac, "he said unto his young man, abide here with the ass, and I and the lad will go yonder and worship, and come again to you" (Gen. 22:5). He feared that if they went with him, they would be a hindrance to him, and therefore would not admit of their company.

So let worldly business be laid aside, and acquaintance set at a distance, while you go by yourself to perform acts of worship, and to pour out your requests into the bosom of your Heavenly Father. Secret prayer is a choice part of your work . . . be not wanting in it.

> When you are alone, and have nobody with you, then you should be with God.

Better than the Best

Ralph Venning

There is a vast difference between the least or lowest of saints, and the highest of men, that are but mere men and unconverted, between the worst of saints (viz. babes) and the best of men, viz. philosophers and moral men. Socrates and Seneca are great instances of how far men may go by nature's help; and Paul (who was called Saul) before his conversion, how far a man may go by the help of the law (Phil. 3:6). And yet the least saint, in the school of Christ, outgoes and surpasses all these. For he is taught of God, and though he is but a babe, yet he is in Christ, and though as carnal, yet not a carnal man as all are that are not in Christ Jesus, and so new creatures. Gold though but in the ore excels the best of clay and earth; so a babe saint, which is but gold in the ore, does yet exceed and excel all other men, which are but clay and of the earth, earthly.

But even the very hairs of your head are all numbered. Fear not therefore: ye are of more value than many sparrows.
Luke 12:7

> Gold though but in the ore excels the best of clay and earth.

Double Beauty

Jeremiah Burroughs

To appoint unto them that mourn in Zion, to give unto them beauty for ashes, the oil of joy for mourning, the garment of praise for the spirit of heaviness; that they might be called trees of righteousness, the planting of the LORD, that he might be glorified.

Isaiah 61:3

Let all be drawn to love the ways of godliness. . . . Fear not pleasure, but trust God with it; you will find enough. Would you never be sad? "Live well," says Bernard. Tell me, would you embrace the ways of religion, if you were sure of pleasure? I call heaven and earth to record this day that that which I have spoken of the ways of wisdom are truths of God; they are not notions or conceits, but certain realities. God has engaged Himself to make these ways abundantly good. Oh, come and taste how sweet the Lord is! Do not stand aloof; His ways may seem to be unpleasant a great way off, but when you come near, you will see delight. Therefore all of you that have been acquainted with the ways of wisdom, manifest this: that God has brought you into blessed paths and that these things are true. Religion suffers mightily by those who profess it, when those that look on see no such things manifested. It is our duty to rejoice in the Lord, and to walk in the ways of wisdom, so it may appear that they are ways of pleasantness. We must carry ourselves delightfully in these delightful ways. Delightfulness in the ways of godliness gives a beauty. Chrysostom has an excellent comparison to express this: "A beautiful face is always pleasing to the eye, but especially when there is joy manifested in the countenance. Joy in the face gives a new beauty, and makes that which before was beautiful to be exceedingly beautiful. It puts a luster upon beauty." So, though the ways of religion are in themselves beautiful, yet when there is spiritual joy added, they then appear beautiful with a double beauty. We have a sweet promise in Isa. 65:18; oh that we could see it fulfilled! "But be ye glad and rejoice for ever in that which I create: for, behold, I create Jerusalem a rejoicing, and her people a joy." This is a joy even in the abstract, not only joyful, but a joy. God will create this; it must be His work. Though from an earthly perspective there is not a cause for joy, yet God will create a joy for His people. You know what value the prophet lays upon joy and what a comely thing it is; see that you rejoice in all things.

Gracious Words

Robert Harris

You must rule the tongue. "A soft answer pacifies wrath" (Prov. 15:1). If you aim at peace, you must, in case of a controversy with another, apply yourself to using calm language; speak softly, speak wisely, speak silently, and in secret. This will cool the great heat of another, and disarm him of his excessive indignation. Hard words to a hard heart will never yield; if you use hard words on a soft heart, you may break even a flint upon a bed or cushion, which cannot be done by laying one flint upon another. So let a man's heart be never so hard and obdurate, if we use soft words to him, and give him mild speeches, he cannot but be calmed and melted towards us. In so doing, "you shall heap coals of fire on his head" (Prov. 25:22), which shall melt and soften him. Therefore if you would be at peace, take unto yourselves gentle speeches, soft answers. Let your arguments be as hard as you can to convince them of their failings, but let your words be soft; clothe them in as good terms as you can. And so, when you take upon yourself to speak of others, take heed that you never speak of their faults and infirmities but in an ordinance, that is, either to pity them or to pray for them, or else to admonish them for their improvement.

And all bare him witness, and wondered at the gracious words which proceeded out of his mouth. And they said, Is not this Joseph's son?
Luke 4:22

If you would be at peace, take unto yourselves gentle speeches, soft answers.

Evil Appearances

Timothy Cruso

Abstain from all appearance of evil.
1 Thessalonians
5:22

We must abstain from the very appearance of evil. This is an apostolical injunction to be kept always in our eye. So Moses tied up the Israelites to the most critical measures of truth: "Keep thee far from a false matter" (Exod. 23:7). Have nothing to do with that which looks like dissimulation. The stream of our honest intentions should run so clear, that there may be no filth at the bottom, which we are unwilling to have seen at the top. The rich Israelite was forbidden to be a usurer to his poor neighbor, to be guilty of no act that carries in it so much as the resemblance of biting extortion. The Apostle Paul commands his son Timothy to rebuke the younger women with all purity; implying, that in his whole discourse and carriage there should not be the least shadow of levity or wantonness. And therefore (as one observes very well) Titus is directed to put the aged women upon teaching the young. As if it was less advisable to do it himself, not only because of the hazard, but scandal, of overmuch familiarity with a different sex. We know that Haman's falling on the bed where Esther was, was interpreted by the king as if he would force her. It had such an aspect, though there be little ground to imagine that it was his design at the time. A tender heart will be accompanied with the plainest impressions of holiness, without so much as the obscurest show of wickedness.

> In his whole discourse and carriage there should not be the least shadow of levity or wantonness.

Proper Worship

Arthur Hildersam

No man can worship God aright till he knows God to be his Father. The better a man is persuaded and assured of God's fatherly love to him in Christ, the better service he shall do unto Him. Therefore our Savior, teaching us to pray, bids us to say, "Our Father," as if He should say, "Presume not to ask any petition of God, till you can so conceive and be persuaded of Him." And the apostle tells us that it is the spirit of adoption that makes us able to pray, and makes this the voice of the spirit of prayer, crying out, "Abba, Father." Yea, He makes it an impossible thing for any man to pray aright without this assurance: "How shall they call on Him in whom they have not believed?" (Rom. 10:14). The reason of it is first, because until we know God is our Father, and loves us in Christ, we cannot be assured that He will adopt us. When we know He is our Father in Christ, it makes us to go to Him with boldness and confidence. "In Christ we have boldness and access with confidence through faith in Him" (Eph. 3:12). "I will arise and go to my father (says the prodigal), and will say unto Him, Father, I have sinned against heaven, and before thee" (Luke 15:18). Though he had sinned so outrageously, yet the consideration of this that it was his father he was to go to, gave him boldness. It gives us assurance, that notwithstanding our infirmities, He will accept us.

Like as a father pitieth his children, so the LORD pitieth them that fear him.
Psalm 103:13

> Though he had sinned, the consideration that it was his father he was to go to gave him boldness.

Better Joys

Richard Alleine

But as for me, my feet were almost gone; my steps had well nigh slipped. For I was envious at the foolish, when I saw the prosperity of the wicked.

Psalm 73:2–3

Christians, do not envy the world's mirth, nor let your hearts lust after it. You have other joys than their crackling thorns will yield; you have your sorrows while they have their mirth, but you have these advantages over the world. You have joy in your sorrows. As in the midst of laughter the heart is sad, so in the midst of your sorrows your hearts may be joyful. Your sorrows shall end in joy. This shall you have from the hand of your God, you shall lie down in peace. You who sow in tears shall reap in joy (Ps. 126:6), while those who sow in mirth shall reap in tears. You may go on your way weeping while they go on their way laughing, yet mark the end of both. Isaiah 65:13–15 says that however it is now, behold how it shall be hereafter. How shall it be? "My servants shall drink, but ye shall be thirsty: behold, my servants shall rejoice, but ye shall be ashamed: Behold, my servants shall sing for joy of heart, but ye shall cry for sorrow of heart, and shall howl for vexation of spirit. And ye shall leave your name for a curse unto my chosen: for the Lord GOD shall slay thee." Now your enemies eat, and some of you are hungry. But think how it will be in the day when the scales are turned, when the sinner's eating days, drinking days, and jolly, merry days are over, and their hungry days and howling days overtake them. You who now hunger and are sorrowful shall eat and drink and be satisfied with the joy of the Lord.

> As in the midst of laughter the heart is sad, so in the midst of your sorrows your hearts may be joyful.

To Fear Sin

Joseph Mede

I once walked into a garden with a lady to gather some flowers. There was one large bush whose branches were bending under the weight of the most beautiful roses. We both gazed upon it with admiration. There was one flower on it which seemed to outshine all the rest in beauty. This lady pressed forward into the thick bush, and reached far over to pluck it. As she did this, a black snake, which was hid in the bush, wrapped itself around her arm. She was alarmed beyond all description; she ran from the garden, screaming, and almost in convulsions. During all that day she suffered very much with fear; her whole body trembled, and it was a long time before she could be calmed. . . . Such is her hatred now of the whole serpent race, that she has never since been able to look at a snake, even a dead one. No one could ever persuade her to venture again into a cluster of bushes, even to pluck a beautiful rose. Now this is the way the sinner acts who truly repents of his sins. He thinks of sin as the serpent that once coiled itself around him. He hates it. He dreads it. He flees from it. He fears the places where it inhabits. He does not willingly go into the haunts. He will no more play with sin than this lady would afterwards have fondled snakes.

But thou, O man of God, flee these things; and follow after righteousness, godliness, faith, love, patience, meekness.
1 Timothy 6:11

> He thinks of sin as the serpent that once coiled itself around him. He hates it.

Numberless Mercies

Samuel Lee

The glittering stars of heaven, the drops of the briny ocean, and the sands upon the winding shores, the dusts of the earth, and the atoms that swim in the sunbeams, are not so numerous as God's excellent mercies. Archimedes could write *A Treatise of the Sands,* but no person that ever appeared on the stage of being, though he should spend all his time in writing volumes of his own life, could trace the measures of God's mercies, were he never so observant, or did pry never so curiously into the passages of divine providence. Every draught of air into the lungs is attended with mercy. When it carries out the fuliginous vapors of the heart, who can attract it in again for the refrigeration of the blood, and mixing the volatile balsam of the air to circulate that purple liquor in its motions. The pulses of providence are quicker than those of four wrists or temples. "How manifold are His mercies?" (Ps. 139:14). The soul of David knew right well their multiplicity, but could not multiply them aright by any skill in arithmetic. Nay, the very sum or chief heads of divine kindness were innumerable. God's wonderful works and thoughts towards David could not be reckoned up in order by him, they were more than could be numbered.

Every draught of air into the lungs is attended with mercy.

Faithful Friends

David Clarkson

I f you would deal faithfully with those living in sin and your own souls, according to the rule of the gospel, you should seriously admonish them; if admonitions are rejected, or they are not thereby reclaimed, then they are to be avoided (2 Thess. 3:14). Those Athenians are commended, who would not wash in the same bath with the persecutors of Socrates. And it is reported of the Apostle John, that when Cerinthus, a noted heretic in the Apostle's time, came into the bath where John was, he presently left the place, and would not be where Cerinthus was. And Polycarp, the Apostle John's disciple, when Marcion saluted him, and asked if he knew him, said, "Yes, I know you; you are the first-born of the devil." And that was all the countenance he would give that imposter. You know how the Lord resented it, that Jehoshaphat would associate himself with Ahab, and that expostulation which he puts in the mouth of the seer was very pathetic (2 Chr. 19:2). And he is afflicted also for joining with Ahaziah. Why but what danger was there in this familiarity? This, those that knew Jehoshaphat to be a good king, walking in the commandments of the Lord, and seeing him choose Ahab for his friend, might conclude that Ahab's ways are not so abominable, otherwise Jehoshaphat could not be so intimate with him. And thus the bad opinion of Ahab being something taken off, they might be more inclined to comply with him in his ways and worship, and thus Jehoshaphat's familiarity with Ahab would be a snare to others. We judge of a man by his companions, and men are apt to think we approve of those whom we choose for our friends. And so by your company, you may approve of wickedness, and thereby partake of it, though you never act it out.

A man that hath friends must shew himself friendly: and there is a friend that sticketh closer than a brother.
Proverbs 18:24

We judge of a man by his companions.

Godly Examples

William Jenkyn

Brethren, if a man be overtaken in a fault, ye which are spiritual, restore such an one in the spirit of meekness; considering thyself, lest thou also be tempted.
Galatians 6:1

It should be our great desire, by all our own sufferings for sin, to prevent the same sin and sufferings in others. We must not be like those that have the plague, who love to infect others with it. A gracious heart rather desires to hear of converts, won by his falls and woes, than to have companions in either. They who have been by sin examples of imitation, should pray that by their sufferings they may become examples of caution. How rare is this heavenly temper in sufferers! Most Christians, when they are in troubles, only desire the removal of them, and perhaps the sanctifying of them to themselves. But who prays for the sanctifying of them to others? It is ordinary for men under their sufferings to have thoughts of impatience against God, and of revenge against the instrument of their troubles, but unusual for men to have aims at benefiting beholders by their troubles. If the Lord would thoroughly affect us with love of His glory, and hatred of sin, we should be willing to have the house pulled down upon our own heads, so that sin may be destroyed in others. Hereby we may do more good at our death than we have done throughout our whole lives.

> It is ordinary for men under their sufferings to have thoughts of impatience against God.

Addressing God

Henry Scudder

When entering into prayer, God should be represented to the mind, and should be called upon by names, titles, or descriptions that are most apt to kindle the desires and help the faith of them that pray. If many and general requests are raised, then such titles and names must be used that may persuade the hearers that they shall all be heard. If some particular petition is lifted up, then names and descriptions of God are to be used that may help the heart in that particular need. Abraham's servant, praying for success in his master's business, said, "O Jehovah, God of my master Abraham, I pray thee send me good speed this day, and shew kindness unto my master Abraham" (Gen. 24:12). When Peter entreated God to choose an apostle to supply the place of Judas, he said, "Thou, Lord, which knowest the hearts of all men, shew whether of these two thou hast chosen" (Acts 1:24). When David prayed against the enemies of God and His children, he said, "O Lord God to whom vengeance belongeth, O God to whom vengeance belongeth, shew thyself" (Ps. 94:1). When he magnified God's name, and incited all people to pray unto Him, and praise Him, he spoke to God in this description: "O thou that hearest prayer, unto thee shall all flesh come" (Ps. 65:2). A wise choice of apt names and titles with which to represent God shows knowledge of Him, and wisdom is needed to make use of His different attributes. God is pleased and delighted to behold both knowledge and wisdom mixed with faith in His children.

Hearken unto the voice of my cry, my King, and my God: for unto thee will I pray.
Psalm 5:2

> A wise choice of apt names and titles with which to represent God shows knowledge of Him.

Angels about Us

Sir Richard Baker

The angel of the LORD encampeth round about them that fear him, and delivereth them.

Psalm 34:7

We think little that we have a continual guard about us, and think less that we have a whole camp for our guard, but think least of all that it is a camp of angels. Oh how safe should we be if this were so! . . . But how can we think there are angels to guard us when we scarcely think that there are any angels? For if there are, they must be creatures of God, and then certainly creatures of a most excellent nature. . . . But we may think, perhaps, there are none because we can see none, as though we can see a thing that is invisible. Shall we therefore think we have no souls because we cannot see our souls? We live now by faith, and not by sight, and therefore can neither see souls nor angels. We shall then see both, when we shall live by sight, and not by faith. Alas! If we believe no more than we see, we seem not to live by faith either, for faith believes that which it cannot see. Oh, therefore, my soul, in order to make it appear that you live, and that you live by faith, let this be an article of your creed, that the angels encamp and pitch their tents about you . . . But if there are angels to attend the godly, who do they not defend them? Why do they suffer them to be so molested, so afflicted as they are? For who are in such troubles, who groan under such afflictions as the godly? . . . O my soul, you little consider the infinite benefits that the godly receive by the ministry of angels. If perhaps they suffer troubles of the body, do they not escape the far greater troubles of the soul? If they endure perhaps some momentary afflictions, do they not avoid afflictions that would be everlasting? Is there not an army of malignant spirits to assault them, and could they be safe from being torn in pieces if there were not a camp of angels to assist them?

> Consider the infinite benefits that the godly receive by the ministry of angels.

Morning Brightness

Robert Bolton

The wicked in this world do easily run up without rub or interruption, many times with acclaim and applause, with all the golden steps of honors and preferment. But upon the highest stair they find the most slippery standing, and at the top of their earthly felicity is the most immediate and certain descent to their greatest downfall. They are royally mounted here upon earth, and gallop swiftly over the fair and green plains of plenty and pleasure, but at the end of their race they are overturned horse and man, and tumbled headlong into the pit of destruction. They fairly glide over the sea of this world with full sail, with much calmness and serenity, and richly laden, but in the brightest sunshine, and when they least suspect it, they suddenly and without recovery sink into the gulf of darkness and desolation. But it is just otherwise with the children of God, for they many times in their pilgrimage stick fast in the miry clay of poverty and contempt, sometimes they are enclosed even in a horrible pit, as David speaks, of fears and terror of conscience for their sins. They are by the way companions to dragons and ostriches; they walk among rebels, thorns and scorpions and cruel slanders. Neither is the danger in the way all; they have persecutors that are swifter than the eagles of heaven, who pursue and hunt them upon the mountains even like partridges, and lurk for them in the wilderness, as those that lie in wait for blood. Nay, yet besides all these vexations from the world, the immediate malice of hell raises many tempests of temptation against them, and sometimes even all the waves and floods of God Himself go over their heads. This is the way, the race, and the evening of God's children in the world; but joy comes in the morning, their end is peace, their reward is a bright morning star, their haven is endless happiness and life eternal.

He shall deliver thee in six troubles: yes, in seven there shall no evil touch thee.
Job 5:19

> This is the way, the race, and the evening of God's children in the world; but joy comes in the morning.

Heaven's Antonym

Richard Bernard

ell is the place for the impenitent; every such person is the hellish inhabitant. It is the prison for those that separate from God's presence. It is the dread dungeon of utter darkness, the fearful Tophet, and the bottomless pit. It is the lake burning with brimstone, the hollow cause and chaos of confusion. It is terror with lamentation, it is dread with desolation. There is death, there is ever dying, and yet never without beginning. . . . God's justice makes it, His power upholds it, and it is blown with the bellows of His wrath. There is scorching fire unquenchable and freezing cold intolerable. . . . It is the valley of God's utmost vengeance, the fullness of His wrath, and the perfection of His plagues. The Lord's goal is to exile souls . . . Oh what woe is there with wailing from hearts comfortless; what rivers of tears because of torments without remedy. . . . They are in a huge sea of misery, in an ocean of calamity. Fire, flames, and flashing about them, the worm of conscience gnawing within. . . . The revenging hand of God is over them, pouring forth the vials of His wrath.

It is the prison for those that separate from God's presence.

Peace of Mind

Thomas Taylor

If you have obtained peace of conscience, be thankful and bless the God of peace. For since that old serpent had disturbed the peace of heaven, from which he was cast down with his angels, his next work was to dissolve the peace on earth by plucking man from his God. Whereby Satan, the author of all enmity, has corrupted the whole nature of man, and ever since has watered these seeds, and brought them forward. So as all the sons of Adam are children of wrath, turned naked into the fury of God, and lie under the same as vessels of wrath, and the fruits of it, in his soul, mind, conscience, will, and all his motions, being at enmity with God, with his own happy estate, with all the creatures. And this is our estate by nature, till it pleased God by His Son Jesus Christ (called the Lord of peace) to lay the foundation of our peace in his blood, and to bestow the blessed Spirit in the hearts of believers, witnessing peace between God and us; the Spirit by renewing their hearts, they become sons of peace, united again unto God, at agreement in themselves, and in all their faculties; and knit and joined together among themselves in the unity of the Spirit and the bond of peace.

My son, forget not my law; but let thine heart keep my commandments; for length of days, and long life, and peace, shall they add to thee.
Proverbs 3:1–2

The Spirit by renewing their hearts, they become sons of peace, united again unto God.

Union with Christ

John Flavel

I in them, and thou in me, that they may be made perfect in one.
John 17:23

The sympathy that is betwixt Christ and believers proves a union between them. Christ and the saints smile and sigh together. Saint Paul in Col. 1:24 tells us that he did "fill up that which was behind," the remainders of the sufferings of Christ in His flesh. It is not as if Christ's sufferings were imperfect ("for by one offering He has perfected for ever them that are sanctified" [Heb. 10:14]), but in these two Scriptures Christ is considered in a twofold capacity; He suffered once in His own person, as Mediator; these sufferings are complete and full, and in that sense He suffers no more; He suffers also in His church and members, thus He still suffers in the sufferings of every saint for His sake, and though these sufferings in His mystical body are not equal to the other, either in their weight and value . . . nevertheless they are truly reckoned the sufferings of Christ, because the head suffers when the members do; and without this belief, Acts 9:5 is never to be understood, when Christ, the Head in heaven, cries out, "Saul, Saul, why persecutest thou me?" when the foot was trod upon earth. How does Christ sensibly feel our sufferings, or we His, if there be not a mystical union between Him and us?

> He suffers also in His church and members. Thus He still suffers in the sufferings of every saint for His sake.

Continuous Wonder

Jeremiah Burroughs

In heaven Christ shall be wonderful forever. Many things are wondered at for the present, but the wonder quickly ceases. We are used to saying of strange things, they are but of nine days wonder. But Jesus Christ is not only a wonder at first, when the soul first comes to embrace Him—it is true that poor sinners at their first embracing Jesus Christ, for the very novelty of those things they see in Him, do admire at them, for they never did understand such things before—but if that grace is true, you shall not only wonder when you come to Christ at first, at the excellency in Him, but the longer you continue a believer, the more you will wonder, and when you come to heaven, after a thousand millions of millions of years, you will wonder as much at Him as you did the first moment. Those that have made profession of religion, and seemed to come to Christ, they wonder at first hearing of the gospel, like the stony-ground that received the word with joy, oh how wonderfully are they affected at the first hearing of the glorious things of the gospel. But now their wonder quickly ceases and their joy ceases within a little while. They do not now see so great excellency to admire at it, neither have they so great joy, but where there is true faith, there the soul does not only wonder at Christ, at His first coming to Christ, but still more and more to all eternity.

Who is like unto thee, O LORD, among the gods?
Exodus 15:11a

> We are used to saying of strange things. They are but of nine days wonder.

To See God

Jeremiah Burroughs

I beseech thee, shew me thy glory.
Exodus 33:2b

The higher we see God to be, the lower we should be in our own eyes. There is nothing that will humble us more than the consideration of God. I dare say of every proud heart in the world, that such a one does not know God, never had a sight of the glory of God that he has to do withal. The sight of God will wonderfully humble the heart before Him. Job is very famous for this. He says, "With the hearing of the ear I have heard of thee, but now mine eyes have seen thee (what follows then upon that), wherefore I abhor myself, and repent in dust and ashes" (Job 42:5–6). Job was a holy man, yet he confessed that he had but only heard of God, he never had such a sight of God as God gave him at this time, and upon the sight that he had of God, though he was holy, and a gracious man, and could stand in his uprightness, yet he says, "Mine eyes have seen thee, wherefore I abhor myself, and repent in dust and ashes." Oh that God would give such a sight of Himself to all your souls, to those proud, stout, and rebellious sins that have gone on in ways of rebellion against Him. You have heard of God by the hearing of the ear, but have your eyes ever seen Him? If God would but give you a sight of what I have briefly spoken to you, you would certainly fall down before Him, and abhor yourself in dust and ashes.

> The sight of God will wonderfully humble the heart before Him.

To Love Sincere

Thomas Vincent

Christians ought to love Christ with sincerity of love: "Grace be with all them that love our Lord Jesus Christ in sincerity" (Eph. 6:24). It was the great sin of Judah that "she turned not to the Lord with her whole heart, but feignedly" (Jer. 8:10). So it is a great sin to love Christ with a feigned and hypocritical love. The love of Christians to Christ ought to be sincere, in regard of the habit and inward workings of it; they must love Him not only in show, word, and outward profession, but their love must be cordial, in the heart, and so a love indeed and in truth. The love of Christians to Christ must be sincere in regard of the object of it, they must love Christ for Himself, and not chiefly for what they get from Him. To love Christ only for temporal gain is hypocritical love; to love Christ chiefly for other gain, is not so spiritual, but to love Christ for His own excellencies and perfections, is most sincere and generous. This sincerity of love to Christ is everyone's duty.

O love the LORD, all ye his saints.
Psalm 31:23a

> They must love Christ for Himself, and not chiefly for what they get from Him.

Go to Christ

Jeremiah Dyke

In the last day, that great day of the feast, Jesus stood and cried, saying, If any man thirst, let him come unto me, and drink.

John 7:37

God commands us to come to Christ; "come, for all things are ready." We do not only have a commandment, which might have sufficed, but we have a promise, "Him that comes to me, I will in no wise cast out" (John 6:37), that is, I will with all hearty welcome embrace and receive those that come to and believe in Me. I see that "come" and the "welcome." The Christ that bids me, if I come at His bidding, will bid me welcome. Does my soul doubt it? Then consider what Christ is by what He was on earth. I find in the gospel that the poorest, and meanest, might come to Him. I see in Matt. 21:14 that the lame and the blind came to Him; they came, and they were welcome; they came to Him, and He healed them. If I come to Him, I shall find Him a healing Christ. And how much my soul needs healing! I see that a leper comes, a foul unclean leper, and yet he is not loathed for his leprosy, neither does Christ reprove him and tell him to keep off. He was welcome too and had his leprosy cleansed. I never find Christ displeased with any for coming to Him; never find Him complaining of any for coming. I see none refused, or forbidden to come. I hear Christ complain that men did not, would not, come. I find Christ displeased with His disciples for forbidding little ones to come: "Suffer little children to come; yes, and He embraces and blesses them" (Mark 10:16). Now I see that Christ bars none from coming. . . . I will go to Him; Lord Christ, I will come to Thee.

> I never find Christ displeased with any for coming to Him.

Divine Patience

John Collinges

f any of us has an appetite to our meat and drink, or a power to digest our food, it is the Lord that gives it. If we have power to move our tongue, our feet to walk, or any natural actions of our body, all is from the Lord, who is wonderful in working. Oh how patient is God with the drunkard, with the liar, the profane swearer, and with all sorts of sinners, who use their bodies to the profaning, abusing, and blaspheming of His holy Name, or in doing actions in the violation and contempt of His holy and righteous law. Why do they go on despising the riches of His goodness, and forbearance and longsuffering, not knowing that the goodness of God leads them to repentance? But after the hardness and impenitence of their hearts, they treasure to themselves wrath against the day of wrath, and the revelation of the righteous judgment of God, who will render to each according to their deeds (Rom. 2:3–5). Yea, and the Lord is not slack, as some count slackness, but is longsuffering towards us, not willing that anyone should perish, but that all should come to repentance. But the day of the Lord will come as a thief in the night.

And the LORD passed by before him, and proclaimed, The LORD, The LORD God, merciful and gracious, longsuffering, and abundant in goodness and truth.
Exodus 34:6

The Lord is not slack, as some count slackness.

Family Religion

Richard Alleine

Give unto the LORD the glory due unto his name; worship the LORD in the beauty of holiness.
Psalm 29:2

Do all you can that more immediately tends to the advancing of religion in those that have none. Be busy in your families to propagate religion there . . . O friends, if you will do any thing for God, be doing among your own; instruct them, teach them the way of the Lord, persuade and provoke them to Christ: Let religion be the top care and top business of your houses. Do what you can to make Christians of your children and friends; and this not so seldom, or sparely, or heartlessly, as some do, now a little, and a long time after never a word; but be constant, be instant with all yours to bring them to God, that there may be a face of serious religion appearing upon your whole families, that a spirit of religion may be the very temper and constitution of your houses. Some professors, whatever they be when among other professors, how much of religion there appears then, yet come into your houses, and there is no more to be seen or heard of God, than in the family of those that make no profession; there is ignorance, and carnality, and vanity, and barrenness, and unsavoriness, and emptiness of all that is good. You that come hither to the ordinances to kindle religion in your own heart, to fetch holy fire from the altar, what you get here, carry it home to your houses, instill it into the hearts of your children and servants. Here your holy activity must begin; he that is not busily doing for God with his own, is never likely to do much good to others.

> **Let religion be the top care and top business of your houses.**

Contentment

Thomas Watson

ontentment . . . is the best commentator upon providence; it makes a fair interpretation of all God's dealings. Let the providence of God be never so dark or bloody, contentment doth construe them ever in the best sense. I may say of it, as the apostle of charity, "it thinketh no evil" (1 Cor. 13:5). Sickness (says contentment) is God's furnace to refine His gold, and make it sparkle the more: the prison is an oratory, or house of prayer. What if God melts away the creature from it? He saw perhaps my heart grew so much in love with it; had I been long in that fat pasture I should have surfeited, and the better my estate had been, the worse my soul would have been. God is wise; He hath done this either to prevent some sin or to exercise some grace. What a blessed frame of heart is this! A contented Christian is an advocate for God against unbelief and impatience, whereas discontent takes everything from God in the worst sense; it doth impede and censure God: this evil I feel is but a symptom of greater evil; God is about to undo me; the Lord hath brought us hither into the wilderness to slay us. The contented soul takes all well; and when his condition is ever so bad, he can say, "truly God is good" (Ps. 73:1).

The LORD shall bless thee out of Zion: and thou shalt see the good of Jerusalem all the days of thy life.

Psalm 128:5

A contented Christian is an advocate for God against unbelief and impatience.

Growing to Relish

Robert Dingley

Let your heart there-fore be perfect with the LORD our God, to walk in his statutes, and to keep his com-mandments, as at this day.

1 Kings 8:61

Pray the Lord with Daniel, that He would avert your eyes from the world that they may not be taken with its glistering vanities. The world has many baits and snares forth, but hear Gregory, "You must not look upon that which it is a sin to covet." The world is a great sorcerer, and sets a spell on many; and at last shall be burnt for a witch. Now, by the eyes, often as by windows, death steals into the heart, as in the case of Eve and David. The eye is the soul's burning glass; if it fix too long it may endanger the burning of our affections. A world of mischief creeps into the heart by the eyes. Pray the Lord therefore to hold and guide the reins of that wandering sense, so that the world's vanity may be kept without us; or if our hearts must be the thoroughfare of vain thoughts, yet they may not lodge in us. Thus, if the world is a map of vanity, then expect not your rest in this life. Hope not to get full satisfaction till you get safe into heaven. Resolve to center and anchor in Jesus Christ. "As the needle in a compass trembles till it settles in the north-point, so the heart can have no rest but in Christ," said Augustine. And Bernard said, "When Christ begins to grow sweet, and we relish things spiritual, then the world will grow bitter, and we shall grow better." God is worthy of our loves, and we may safely put our trust in His Word, which cannot be affirmed of anything below God. Saints may well say and sing of Christ, "There is no beloved like this beloved!" Stand aside vanity, away with all the gilded glory and pomp of the world; here is a brightness that outshines it, and a glory that swallows it up! As the shining sun makes the stars to disappear, so the transcendent beauty and the matchless glory of Jesus Christ draws a veil upon the splendor of this world!

> If our hearts must be the thoroughfare of vain thoughts, yet they may not lodge in us.

Near to Christ

Thomas Watson

I t is a blessed thing to be with Christ. "I am ever with thee" (Ps. 73:13). What is it that the pious soul desires in this life, but to have the sweet presence of Christ? He cares for nothing but what has a liquid Christ, something of Christ in it. He loves duties only as they lead to Christ; why is prayer so sweet, but because the soul has private conference with Christ. Why is the Word precious, but because it is a means to convey Christ? He comes down to us upon the wings of the Spirit, and we go up to Him upon the wings of faith. An ordinance without Christ is but feeding upon the dish instead of the meat. Why does the wife love the letter, but because it brings her news of her husband? Here we enjoy Christ by letters, and that is sweet, but what will it be to enjoy His presence in glory? Here is that which may amaze us, we shall be with Christ; Christ is all that is desirable; nay, He is more than we can desire. If a man desires a little water to quench his thirst, bring him to the seas, and there is more than he can desire. In Christ there is not only a fullness of sufficiency, but a fullness of redundancy; it overflows all banks. A Christian that is most sublimated by faith, has neither a head to devise nor a heart to desire all that which is in Christ; only when we come to heaven God will enlarge the vessel of our desire, and will fill us as Christ did the water pots with wine, up to the brim.

Nevertheless I am continually with thee: thou hast holden me by my right hand.

Psalm 73:23

> **In Christ there is not only a fullness of sufficiency, but a fullness of redundancy.**

Swallowed in Glory

Thomas Manton

*Unto thee lift I up
mine eyes, O thou that
dwellest in the
heavens.*
Psalm 123:1

It teaches that the great work of prayer is to lift up the heart to God, to withdraw the heart from all created things which we see and feel here below, that we may converse with God in heaven. Prayer does not consist in a multitude and clatter of words, but in the getting up of the heart to God, that we may behave ourselves as if we were alone with God, in the midst of glorious saints and angels. There is a double advantage which we have by this getting the soul into heaven in prayer. It is a means to free us from distractions, doubts, and other intrusive thoughts. Until we get our hearts out of the world, as if we were dead and shut up to all present things, how easily is the heart carried away with the thoughts of earthly concerns! Until we can separate and purge our spirits, how do we intertwine our prayers with many ridiculous thoughts! It is too usual for us to deal with God as an unskillful person that wants to gather a posy for his friend, and puts in as many or more stinking weeds than He doth choice flowers. The flesh interposes, and our carnal hearts intertwine and interlace our prayers with vain thoughts and earthly distractions. When with our censer we come to offer incense to God, we mingle sulfur with our incense. Therefore we should labor all that we can to get the heart above the world into the presence of God and company of the blessed, that we may deal with Him as if we were by Him in heaven, and were wholly swallowed up of His glory. Though our bodies are on earth, yet our spirits should be with our Father in heaven. For want of practicing this in prayer, these distractions increase upon us. So for doubts, when we look to things below, even the very manifestations of God to us upon earth, we have many discouragements, dangers without and difficulties within: till we get above the mists of the lower world, we can see nothing of clearness and comfort; but when we can get God and our hearts together, then we can see that there is much in the fountain, though nothing in the stream; and though little on earth, yet we have a God in heaven.

Travelers

Richard Alleine

A traveler's eye is much towards his journey's end. Christians that are making their way heavenward are much and often looking heavenward. A Christian's heart is in his eye, and his eye is on his home. Their setting their faces there notes the bending of their courses there. It was said of Christ, "He set His face to go to Jerusalem" (Luke 9:51). Christians set their faces heavenward and there they bend their course. They are much in asking the way, "What must I do to be saved? Who shall ascend into the holy hill? What manner of persons must we be, that we may get there?" And they take the way that leads them there . . . they are set for another country, for another world; they are born from above, and they seek the things above, and there are they hastening. Whatever they have of this world's goods, for the support of their life, is not the scope and end of their life. They seek that glory, honor, and immortality which comes from God, and they are going on from strength to strength, till they come and appear before God in Zion. . . . In this a sincere Christian is differenced from all others in the world: he fixes his heart and his hope and aims upon an eternal happiness, and he bends his course towards the obtaining of it.

These all died in faith, not having received the promises, but having seen them afar off, and were persuaded of them, and embraced them, and confessed that they were strangers and pilgrims on the earth.

Hebrews 11:13

> They are born from above, and they seek the things above, and there are they hastening.

Father's Kindness

John Durant

For the Father himself loveth you, because ye have loved me, and have believed that I came out from God.

John 16:27

It was the Father's will that Christ should take the care of His flock, and that He should manage the care with much tenderness, especially towards the lambs. Look at Christ, though He had a singular care of all the flock (and therefore bid Peter feed them all), yet He had a special care of the weak of the flock, and therefore especially He commanded Peter to have a care of them. And as ever He would declare His love to Himself, He should tender over the lambs, and be sure to feed them (which might be another instance of the special care and tenderness of Christ to weak believers). In like manner, God the Father when He gave Christ His commission, in which He committed the whole flock to His care, did put in as it were a singular clause, that He should be very tender of, and very indulgent towards the weak members. . . . The Father charged Christ especially to carry kindly towards them. Indeed the great thing (next to the sweetness of His own nature, which set Him on to undertake the office) that moves Christ either to take freely any poor soul into His care, or to demean Himself sweetly in His carriage towards it, is His Father's will, which He came to fulfill (John 6:38). Now it was the Father's will that Christ should be very tender in His carriage towards the weak.

> Though he had singular care of all the flock, he had a special care of the weak.

Waiting for Peace

John Owen

The discovery of forgiveness in God . . . will produce a resolution of waiting on God for peace and consolation in His own time and way. "He that believeth shall not make haste" (Isa. 28:16). Not make haste to what? Not to the enjoyment of the thing believed. Haste argues precipitation and impatience; this the soul that has this discovery is freed from, resolving to wait until the time of God's appointment for peace and consolation. God, speaking of His accomplishment of His promises, says, "I the LORD will hasten it," (Isa. 60:22). Well, then, if God will hasten it, may not we hasten to it? "Nay," say He, "I will hasten it, but in its time." All oppositions and impediments considered, it shall be hastened, but in its time, its due time, its appointed time. And this the soul is to wait for; and so it will. As when Jacob had seen the beauty of Rachel, and loved her, he was content to wait seven years for the enjoyment of her to be his wife, and thought no time too long, no toil too hard, that he might obtain her; so the soul having discovered the beauty and excellency of forgiveness as it is with God, as it is in His gracious heart, in His eternal purpose, in the blood of Christ, in the promise of the gospel, is resolved to wait quietly and patiently for the time wherein God will clear up unto it its own personal interest therein. Even one experimental embracement of it, even at the hour of death, doth well deserve the waiting and obedience of the whole course of a man's life.

I have waited for thy salvation, O LORD.
Genesis 49:18

It shall be hastened, but in its time, its due time, its appointed time.

Promise of Pardon

John Shower

Who is a God like unto thee, that pardoneth iniquity, and passeth by the transgression of the remnant of his heritage? he retaineth not his anger for ever, because he delighteth in mercy.
Micah 7:18

As to sins after repentance and pardon, God has promised to multiply forgiveness, to heal backslidings, and therefore invites sinners to return, with a promise of pardon. "Return ye backsliding children, and I will heal your backslidings" (Jer. 3:22). In the early days of the Christian church, the Novatian doctrine spread, which denied repentance and pardon to sins after baptism, upon which account it is thought that many good souls delayed their baptism as long as they could, that they might not defile their garments after they were washed. It seemed to have taken its rise from the misunderstanding of Heb. 6. But any such doctrine as would discourage our repentance and return to God, after we have sinned, must be of a very dangerous consequence to our souls. I confess, it is a dismal symptom, to fall often into willful sin, to repent and then sin again, to repent and sin in a circle. This rather implies an intention of sinning again than a design of leaving it. But for such as have returned to God, and have been forgiven, and yet by the power of temptation have afterwards fallen, there is great encouragement for their return and ground to hope for forgiveness: "For if any man sin, we have an advocate with the Father, even Jesus Christ the righteous, who was a propitiation for our sins" (1 John 2:1–2). If any man sin; it is not to encourage to sin, but to prevent despair after the commission of it. And since we are to forgive one another, as God for Christ's sake has forgiven us, it would never have been made our duty to forgive our offending brother once and again, yes, unto seventy times seven, if there were no mercy with God for returning backsliders. You are allowed, and commanded in such a case, to return to God, and to sue out your pardon; and you ought to believe you shall find welcome, and that your backslidings shall be healed.

Repentance

Richard Stock

Repentance is the constant turning of a man in his whole life from all sin unto God, arising from true faith and the true knowledge of a man's own spiritual estate, ever joined with true humiliation. When I say it is a turning, I say it by the authority of the prophets in the Old Testament, and of Christ and His apostles in the New, which is manifest by their preaching and writings. . . . It is a turning of the whole life. In nature there are four kinds of turnings. One is the substance, called generation and corruption; the second is in quantity, either from the greater to the less, or from the more to the fewer, and contrary, called augmentation and diminution; a third in place, when things change places, called local change; a fourth in quality, when things change from one condition to another, called alteration. Now here is no change in substance, for the party sinning and repenting is the same, and has the same body and soul, the same faculties and powers both of soul and body; neither is there any change in quantity, for the change from greater sins to less, or from more to fewer, is not repentance. Nor is there any change of place, for sin, like a man's sickness, is carried with him, and change of place, as change of beds, does not free him, or make him whole. Being then none of these, it must be the change in quality, that is, when one and the same man is changed in the condition both of his soul and body, from iniquity to righteousness, from all sin to the living God, both in the inward man and outward conversation.

> *Come, and let us return unto the LORD: for he hath torn, and he will heal us; he hath smitten, and he will bind us up.*
>
> Hosea 6:1

> For the party sinning and repenting is the same and has the same body and soul.

The Holy Ghost

Richard Bernard

And when he had said this, he breathed on them, and saith unto them, Receive ye the Holy Ghost.
John 20:22

The Holy Ghost is the third person in the Trinity; He proceeds from the Father and from the Son. He works ever from both, together with both. He is Christ's vice-regent in His kingdom, His only general in His church. He rose up the prophets, He instructed the apostles, and now qualifies all of Christ's true messengers. The bad he makes good; in the good He increases grace. He reforms our ways, informs our judgment, and confirms our faith. He changes discord into duties of love, and turns all misdeeds into alms deeds; prattling into devout prayer, foolish prating into powerful and persuasive preaching; the preacher's tongue He makes the pen of a ready writer. Evil lusts, where He comes, He kills; the dead works of darkness, He expels. He is the Spirit sanctifying the elect; He is not partial, but deals measurably to all, without sinister favoritism. He is to the saints the blessed Comforter; He persuades them all, to call God "Father." He works repentance and gives thereupon true peace of conscience. Christ's church is His temple, and He is the safeguard of His sheep. . . . He helps us to incite, to frame our wills, to make our meditations, to moderate our affections, and to order all our actions. Our eyes by Him see into the Scriptures; He is the true commentary to understand the Word. . . . Here in this life He begins grace, sets on to goodness, persuades to holiness, urges to charitableness, presses to godly practice, and settles the soul in religious pureness.

> He works repentance and gives thereupon true peace of conscience.

Full to the Brim

Jeremiah Burroughs

Dear believer, you have found good already, that might make you say with David, "Surely it is good for me to draw near to God, and though I do meet with some troubles and temptations, yet let my soul say, It is good for me to draw near to God; it is good for me that I left such and such things, it is good for me that I have these ordinances, though it be with the loss of some outward comforts, and my estate be abated, and my trading less." Say as David in the seventy-third Psalm, "Truly God is good to Israel" (v. 1). However it be, yet God is good to Israel, though many things seem to the contrary. Therefore, conclude with your own heart, "Though I should never see a good day in the world, yet that comfort I have received in the ways of God is enough to make me prize them forever. If now I should die, and be annihilated, if God should deprive me of the joys of heaven, and turn me into nothing, yet that good that I have had already in God's ways should be enough to countervail all the troubles that I have met in the world, or ever shall meet. Though God should withdraw Himself in all the course of my life, and I should be in darkness, and have nothing but trouble, yet I have had enough in God already, to countervail all." Hath God thus spoken peace to your soul? Remember that text in Ps. 85:8, "Return not again to folly." The Lord has spoken peace already to your soul in afflictions, and therefore, God forbid that you should return to folly, but continue in your way. Go on constantly in your way to the end, and the Lord bless you in your way. This is for the encouragement of the hearts of God's people that have with Moses made this choice: rather to suffer affliction with the people of God, than to enjoy the pleasure of sin for a season.

And to know the love of Christ, which passeth knowledge, that ye might be filled with all the fulness of God.
Ephesians 3:19

> Go on constantly in your way to the end, and the Lord bless you in your way.

Saving Sight

Richard Baxter

To see thy power and thy glory, so as I have seen thee in the sanctuary.
Psalm 63:2

Suppose you saw the everlasting glory which Christ has purchased and prepared for His saints, that you had been once, with Paul, rapt up into the third heaven, and seen the things that are unutterable. Would you not after that have lived like Paul, and undergone his sufferings and contempt, than to have lived like the brainsick, brutish world? If you had seen what Stephen saw before his death . . . if you had seen the thousands and millions of holy, glorious spirits, that are continually attending the majesty of the Lord; if you had seen the glorified spirits of the just, that were once in flesh, despised by the blind, ungodly world, while waiting on God in faith, holiness, and hope, for that blessed crown which now they wear; if you had felt one moment of their joys; if you had seen them shine as the sun in glory, and made like unto the angels of God; if you had heard them sing the song of the Lamb, and the joyful Hallelujahs, and praise to their eternal King; what would you be, and what would you resolve on, after such a sight as this?

What would you resolve on after such a sight as this?

The Sands of Time

John Shower

The comparison of this life with the other, of time with eternity, whether in happiness or misery, is of so much moment and use, that it may serve so many excellent purposes, and produce such wise thoughts and reflections, that I wish we would consider the one and the other, more seriously and frequently. How little a while we are to abide here, and after death we must abide forever in Abraham's bosom, or in torments; with God in endless glory, or in everlasting fire, with the devil and his angels. Oh think a little, how inconsiderable a thing is the longest life of man on earth compared with an everlasting duration! The psalmist tells us, "Thou hast made my days as an hands breadth, and mine age (my life, my little time on earth) is as nothing unto thee" (Ps. 29:5–6), compared with God's duration, which is without beginning or end. Old Jacob, when he had passed one hundred and thirty years, said, "Few and evil are the days of the years of the life of my pilgrimage" (Gen. 47:9). What was that to Adam's nine hundred and thirty years, after his creation in full strength and maturity? Or to Methuselah's nine hundred and sixty years? But what a moment is that to the divine eternity! "A thousand years in thy sight, are but as one day; or as yesterday when it is past" (Ps. 90:5–6). If it had been said that a thousand millions of years are but as a minute, it would have been true. According to this computation, a thousand years as one day; suppose a man had been born above five thousand years ago, he is in God's sight as one born five days ago. If the first man were now alive, he would not be six days old, by that reckoning. And by the same account, he that has lived in the world sixty-two years has lived but an hour and a half. . . . How useful and awful it may be, to make the comparison between the longest life and eternity. Upon the whole, who would not pray with David, that God would teach him to number his days, and value his little time, so as to apply his heart to wisdom, that he may walk in the way of life?

So teach us to number our days, that we may apply our hearts unto wisdom.
Psalm 90:12

Christ's Support

John Durant

I can do all things through Christ which strengtheneth me.
Philippians 4:13

Christ gives ability and strength to perform whatsoever He calls any believer to. It is clear that His carriage is sweet to those that work. Christ gives power to do what ever He sets believers about. Ezekiel must stand on his feet; alas! he is weak, and cannot. Christ's Spirit therefore enters into him that he may. "Stand upon thy feet, son of man (says Christ) and the Spirit entered into him, and he stood up" (Ezek. 2:1). I thank our Lord Christ who has enabled me, says Paul to Timothy (1 Tim. 1:12). The apostles must preach to all nations and Christ gives them tongues to enable them so to do. Ah! says the poor soul, the work is weighty, and I am weak. True, but Christ will make you strong and able. If the burden is big, your back shall be strengthened. Christ will not lay a heavy burden upon weak shoulders. Doubtless He will strengthen your shoulders, O believing soul, according to the weight that He lays on it.

If the burden is big, your back shall be strengthened.

Delightful Bliss

Jeremiah Burroughs

I delight to do thy will, O my God: yes, thy law is within my heart.
Psalm 40:8

The ways of godliness are delightful ways, full of pleasure; yes, they are pleasantness itself. There is nothing that man's heart is set more upon than pleasure, and nothing hinders a man from the ways of godliness more than fear he shall not find pleasure in them. Therefore it is a matter of great concern for us to be thoroughly convinced that there is pleasantness in the ways of godliness. They are ways of pleasure, and I hope I speak unto those whose hearts close with the point as soon as it is named, who can say, "Yes, we find it so." The ways of wisdom are either ways of God's ordinances, ways of the exercise of grace, or ways of obedience, and all these are ways of pleasantness. "How amiable are thy tabernacles, O LORD of hosts!" (Ps. 84:1). "They shall be abundantly satisfied with the fatness of thy house; and thou shalt make them drink of the river of thy pleasures" (Ps. 36:8). "Give unto the LORD the glory due unto His name; worship the LORD in the beauty of holiness" (Ps. 29:2). These verses and many others like them speak of the ordinances of God. The exercises of the graces of the Spirit are the ways of wisdom and are full of delight and pleasure. Song 7:13 says, "The mandrakes give a smell, and at our gates are all manner of pleasant fruits, new and old, which I have laid up for thee, O my beloved." In the church of God the exercise of the graces of God's Spirit among them is pleasant. The duties of obedience are pleasant as found in these expressions of Scripture: "Oh how I love Thy Law!" (Ps. 119:97), "Thy Law is my delight!" (Ps. 119:77) and a hundred others.

> There is pleasantness in the ways of godliness.

Recreations

Henry Scudder

Whether therefore ye eat, or drink, or whatsoever ye do, do all to the glory of God.
1 Corinthians 10:31

A man, when he is weary, may be refreshed by a variety and interchange of the duties of his particular and general calling. And the best recreation to a spiritual mind, when it is weary of worldly employment, is to go into Christ's garden. There by reading and meditating, by singing of Psalms, and by holy conference, you may solace yourself with the sweet comforts of the Holy Spirit, and may work your hearts to joy in God, even to joy in the Holy Ghost, and to delight in the commandments and the Word of God. This is the most profitable, and most ravishing, and most lasting delights of all others. Now, by as much as the soul is of a better and of a more heavenly constitution, by so much it more contents and satisfies itself in these delights. . . . The matter of your other recreations must be of a common nature, and things of an indifferent use. Things holy are too good, and things vicious are too bad, to be sported or played with. Recreations must also be seasonable for time; not on the Lord's Day, in which time God forbids everyone to seek their own pleasures. Usually, diversions must be used, not before, but after the body or mind has been thoroughly employed in honest business. Not overly long, to the expense and loss of precious time, which you should study to redeem, and not trifle away. Your recreations must also be inoffensive, such as do no harm to yourself, or to your neighbor. . . . Whatever your leisurely activities are, you must engage them so that you are no worse, but rather better in the inward parts. For God has set such a blessed order in all lawful things, that even the smallest, lawfully used, shall not hinder but assist in the best things. In all recreations you must propose the right end . . . to revive your weary body and to quicken your mind. Your highest and principal end is that you may better serve and glorify God, that whether you eat or drink, or whatsoever you do, all may be done to the glory of God.

Safe Springs

Matthew Lawrence

All carnal joys have but their honey-moons. And though they do not presently sour, yet they grow flat and dull within a while. If they die not altogether, yet soon they come to the fall of the leaf. But the joys of God's people are as fresh and flourishing at the last as at the first: "His leaf also shall not wither" (Ps. 1:3). The bed of Jesus Christ is always green (Song 1:16). The poets fancy of a continual spring in the golden age of the world; here it is a reality. The joys of God's people are ever springing and budding forth new comforts. Further, it is a more wholesome and safe joy. The joy of the carnal is a destructive joy, and destructive to spiritual good. How hardly is that man reclaimed who makes sin the object of his joy? And it is destructive even to natural good. There is danger in excess of joy, as well as sorrow. And what the Apostle says of worldly sorrow may be said of worldly joy, "it worketh death" (2 Cor. 7:10). How many men have lost their wits, even their lives, in excessive joys? Such heights of joy have set the door of the heart so wide open that the spirits have run out of a sudden and returned no more. This is sometimes a fruit of carnal joy. But spiritual joy is safe and wholesome for the soul. It is a good means to concoct our knowledge, to love the truth, and rejoice in what we know, while otherwise the sweetest truths will lie raw and undigested upon the stomach of the soul. And, it is wholesome for the body. A cheerful spirit expels superfluities, helps inspiration, quickens the understanding, cheers the countenance, and in a word, "A merry heart doth good like a medicine" (Prov. 17:22).

All the days of the afflicted are evil: but he that is of a merry heart hath a continual feast.

Proverbs 15:15

> **Spiritual joy is safe and wholesome for the soul.**

Head Knowledge

Ralph Venning

Knowledge puffeth up, but charity edifieth.
1 Corinthians 8:1

We should all take heed and beware that we do not place our growth and advance in knowledge only (head and book learning), or only in gifts and parts; nor should we place it only in common graces, no, nor in going from one opinion to another, or one form of church government to another, or from one profession to another. This I fear has been a great mistake, as if it were a going on to, when it is a going from, perfection, for to be tossed to and fro with every wind of doctrine is but babyish (Eph. 4:13–16). Alas! What is it to be episcopal, presbyterian, or congregational? Our religion does not rest, much less our perfection, in these or any other opinions and forms of church government. I do not doubt that there are saints in all these churches, but I believe and affirm that none of these opinions makes them saints; a man may be in any of these and yet be but a babe, yes and not be a babe at all.

This is like them that go up and down the streets of London, crying, "Old satin and ends of gold and silver," by which they never grow rich, nor get any considerable estate.

I believe and affirm that none of these opinions makes them saints.

Faithful Steps

John Flavel

ow contented and well pleased should we be with our outward lot, however providence has cast it for us in this world? O do not repine, God has dealt bountifully with you; upon others He has bestowed the good things of this world; upon you, Himself in Christ. Secondly, how humble and lowly in spirit should you be under your great advancement! It is true, God has magnified you greatly by this mystical union with Christ, but yet do not swell. "You bear not the root, but the root you" (Rom. 11:18). You shine, but it is as the stars, with a borrowed light. Thirdly, how zealous should you be to honor Christ, who has put so many honors upon you! Be willing to give glory to Christ, though His glory should rise out of your shame. Never reckon that glory that goes to Christ, to be lost to you; when you lie at His feet, in the most particular heart-breaking confessions of sin, yet let this please you, that therein you have given Him glory. Fourthly, how exact and circumspect should you be in all your ways, remembering whose you are, and whom you represent! Shall it be said, that a member of Christ was convicted of unrighteousness and unholy actions! God forbid. "If we say, we have fellowship with Him, and walk in darkness, we lie" (1 John 1:6). Fifthly, how studious should you be of peace among yourselves, who are so nearly united to such a Head, and thereby are made fellow-members of the same body! The heathen world was never acquainted with such an argument as the Apostle urges for unity in Eph. 4:3–4. Sixthly, and lastly, how joyful and comfortable should you be to whom Christ, with all His treasures and benefits, is effectually applied in this blessed union of your souls with Him! This brings Him into your possession: O how great! how glorious a person do these little weak arms of your faith embrace!

And he that saith he abideth in him, ought also himself to walk even as he also walked.
1 John 2:6

How studious should you be of peace among yourselves.

To Be Thankful

Robert Dingley

There is a grateful and thanksgiving eye; an eye that on all occasions looks upward to bless and praise God for all His mercies, promises, and fatherly corrections. "Jesus lifted up His eyes, and said, 'Father I thank thee, that thou hast heard me' " (John 11:41). The little birds do not sip one drop of water, but they look up, as if they meant to give thanks, to shame all of a swinish disposition, that devours mercies but never looks up to the hand that gives them. Plato thanked God that he was a Grecian, an Athenian, and the scholar of Socrates. And Theodosius thanked God more that he was a member of Christ than the head of an empire. With Him and Paul we should especially lift up our eyes to God, and bless Him for all spiritual blessings in Christ. Yet there is no mercy so small but it requires thankfulness. At meals we must look up to God; so did Christ. "And when He had taken the five loaves, and two fishes, He looked up to heaven, and blessed, and brake the loaves, and gave them to His disciples" (Mark 6:41). Epictetus wished he were a nightingale, to be ever singing contentedly day and night. . . . This is the sure mark of a man unregenerate, to be earnest in craving mercies, but slow and dull in returning praises. Then the dumb devil possesses men. Pliny tells of some that have no mouths, but live on the smell of herbs and sweet flowers. You had better believe him, than go to disprove him. Sure I am, some have no mouths to praise the Lord. They greedily smell the fading flowers of earthly vanities. There is no grace but love, and not duty but thankfulness goes with us to heaven. A good man is not only grateful for blessings, but with holy Job, he lifts up his eyes, and sincerely blesses God for His fatherly corrections: "The Lord hath given, the Lord hath taken away, blessed be the Name of the Lord" (Job 8:21). For, says one, if the Lord whip His children, it is with sweet briar, He does it in faithfulness and mercy; and if He hides His face for a moment, with everlasting kindness He will embrace them. Every Christian knows how to bear afflictions, not only with patience, but also with thankfulness.

Downward Slope

Joseph Mede

he commission of one sin makes way to another. Agur thought if he were once brought to steal, he should not stay there but be carried further, even to forswear and take God's Name in vain: "Lest I steal and take the Name of my God in vain" (Prov. 30:9). Peter first denied Christ, but the devil would not let him stay there, but made him curse and forswear Him. David once committed adultery with the wife of Uriah, and the devil took the advantage to make him commit murder too. Sin is like a serpent; if it can but once get ahead, it will draw the whole train after. While there is no rift in a block, it is hard for the wedge or axe to enter; but if a rift be once made, it will enter all with a little driving, and so will sin. The reason is, because he that commits sin puts himself, more or less, into the devil's power, who is not so negligent as to lose or not to ply his advantage. The devil is the prince of death (Heb. 2:14). Now death comes by sin; therefore sin gives the devil a title; it first brought, and still brings, man into the devil's jurisdiction. Hence those who are converted to God, and acquainted with their sins, are said "to be delivered from the power of the devil" (Acts 26:18). But sin makes them again obnoxious to his power; it allows him a new hold of us, which though (perhaps) it is not so much as he may quite pull us from God, yet it will serve him to pull us into many transgressions, and cost us much work and a great deal of sorrow before we get free again.

Then when lust hath conceived, it bringeth forth sin: and sin, when it is finished, bringeth forth death.
James 1:15

> **Sin is like a serpent; if it can but once get ahead, it will draw the whole train after.**

Be Careful

William Jenkyn

Watch ye and pray,
lest ye enter into
temptation.
Mark 14:38

Let us be eminently careful, lest our deliverance obtained by Christ be perverted to looseness of life. Let that which was a pledge of His love be a spur to our duty. Though some abuse this grace to a wrong end, let us use it to a right end. To this end: first, to admire and study the excellency of this grace, in its fullness and sufficiency. Do not abuse that which is able to help you. Who but a madman would throw away a cabinet of pearls and purest gold? But we were not redeemed with such "corruptible things, but with the precious blood of Christ" (1 Pet. 1:18), the blood of God. Secondly, admire its freeness. God's bestowing it upon you when you did not deserve it, when you had no other merit but misery to call for it, aggravates your sin in abusing and condemning it. Thankfulness becomes the distressed rather than scornfulness. Get an experiential taste of this grace. Grace has no enemy but the ignorant. Those who abuse it show that they never found benefit by it. A notional professor may condemn that grace which an experimental partaker will highly esteem. Grace is never good in the soul's valuation till it be possessed. Those who love it but do not know why will soon disrespect it, though they know not how.

Grace is never good in the soul's valuation till it be possessed.

Tender Fingers

Henry Smith

We must seek Christ alone because there is no one so willing to help as He. It is a great courage to us to make suit when we are persuaded of the willingness of Him to whom we make suit; and I ask you, who was ever more careful for our salvation, and more watchful over us than the Lord? Who ever put their trust in Him and was confounded? In this respect He is called a "Father," because as the father tenders his son, so the Lord pities all those that put their trust in Him. Can there be any more willing to help us than Christ, whose whole head was sick, and whose heart was heavy for our sakes? Yea, in whose body, from the sole of the foot to the crown of the head, was nothing but wounds, and swellings, and sores? But, alas, this was nothing to what He suffered for our sakes. He was compassed about with fear and horrors till His sweat was drops of blood, and His bones bruised in the flesh; He was whipped, and scourged, and chastised with sorrows, till He cried out in bitterness of soul, "O Lord, if it be possible, let this cup pass from me" (Matt. 26:39). The heavy hand of God was so grievous upon Him that He bruised His very bones, and rent His reins asunder. He could find no health in His flesh, but was wounded, yes, wounded to the death, even the most bitter death upon the cross. His tender fingers were nailed to the cross; His face was wrinkled with weeping and wailing; His sides imbrued and gored with His own blood, spurting and gushing fresh from His ribs; the shadow of death was upon His eyes. Oh what a grief could be like this, or what condemnation could be so heavy, since there was no wickedness in His hands . . . Oh that my head were a well of water, and a fountain of tears, that I might weep day and night at the remembrance of this!

And they clothed him with purple, and platted a crown of thorns, and put it about his head.
Mark 15:17

> Who ever put their trust in Him and was confounded?

But One God

Richard Stock

*Have we not all one
father? hath not one
God created us?*
Malachi 2:10

The world continues, and is not destroyed, not only because there is a God, but because there is but one God, and He always preserves it. Saint Chrysostom says, "As it is with the body, if God forsakes it, it cannot continue, so it is with the world, if God did not uphold it, it would come to nothing." He says further, "the world is like unto a ship, the mariners are the men, the sails are the heaven; why does this ship never perish? Because there is but one governor; if there were two governors, the ship must necessarily perish, for while the one would hoist up sail, the other would cast anchor, and so there would be confusion." Saint Athanasius says, "If there were as many governors and colonels in one army as soldiers, the army would soon be confounded; this is the safety of an army, that there is but one general, and so all are preserved; so it is of the world, that there is but one God."

This is the safety
of an army, that
there is but one
general.

Desire Pure Milk

Robert Bolton

t is the property of all those who have become new creatures, who are washed from their sins, sanctified, and newborn by the immortal seed of the Word, and the Spirit of grace; to long after, and earnestly desire the sincere milk of the Word, that they may grow thereby in knowledge, comfort, and new obedience. A newborn babe will be pleased and satisfied with nothing but the pap, not gold, pearls, or anything else will content it; even so a new-renewed soul does ever hunger and thirst after the sacred and sincere milk of God's holy Word, as Saint Peter calls it, that it may daily gather strength in grace; otherwise, as the child, so it would languish, pine away, and die. He that grows not, and goes not forward in grace, had never true grace. He that does not labor to feed his soul with spiritual food never passed the new birth. "The way of the righteous (says Solomon) shines as the light, that shines more and more unto the perfect day" (Prov. 4:18). For if the Daystar of saving knowledge once appears to us, if the Sun of Righteousness arises in our hearts, we never set until we are brought to that glorious light above, that no one can attain unto. Whoever proceeds and profits in the great mystery of godliness, in faith, repentance, and sincerity, he grows from virtue to virtue, from knowledge to knowledge, from grace to grace, until he become a perfect man in Christ Jesus (Eph. 4:13). It may be, as the fairest sun may sometimes be overcast, and darkened with clouds, and mists; so the holiness of a godly man may be over-clouded and disgraced sometimes, by falls into a sin, upon infirmities, ignorance, heedlessness, or the like; but, if he be so overtaken, after his passing through sorrow and grief of heart for the same, and his rising again by repentance, he shines far more brightly and pleasantly both to God and man, in sincerity and all holy graces; he afterwards runs a more swift and settled course in the race of sanctification.

As newborn babes, desire the sincere milk of the word, that ye may grow thereby.
1 Peter 2:2

Commit to Memory

Nicholas Byfield

Thou hast put gladness in my heart, more than in the time that their corn and their wine increased.
Psalm 4:7

When we come to the promises, we must renounce our own merits, and all opinion of our own worthiness, and acknowledge from our hearts that all the grace we find in the promises is in and through Jesus Christ. All the promises are yes and amen through Him, and only in Him. When we have the promises laid open before us, we must believe them and apply them to ourselves or else they will do us no good. We must be further careful to hide them in our hearts, and to commit them to memory, that we may be often thinking of them, and musing upon them. It will not serve the turn that we have them written in the Bible, or in our notebooks, but we must get them written in our hearts too. We must be at pains to acquaint ourselves distinctly with them, and to fill our heads with stores of them. When anything ails us, we must flee to God for refuge and cast the anchor of our hope upon them that God Himself may see that our hearts are bent to trust upon His Word. We must never cast away our confidence in them, but wait with patience and not limit God to the time, or manner, or means of accomplishment, but hold fast to His promise and leave the rest to God, as Scripture says in many places, especially Heb. 10:36 and Rom. 4:22. In short, we must look to it that we are not slothful and idle, and such as will not be at pains to study and commit to memory, and rest upon these glorious comforts; but we must follow them which through faith and patience did inherit the promises (Heb. 6:22).

> It will not serve that we have them written in the Bible, but we must get them written in our hearts too.

One Foundation

John Owen

A foundation must be hidden and out of sight unto all those that outwardly look upon the house. They cannot perceive it, though every part of the house rests upon it. And this has occasioned many mistakes in the world. An unwise man coming to a great house, seeing the antics and pictures crouching under the windows and sides of the house, may chance to think that they bear up the weight of the house, when indeed they are for the most part painted posts. They bear not the house; the house bears them. By their bowing and outward appearance, the man thinks the burden is on them, and supposes it would be an easy thing, at any time, by taking them away, to demolish the house itself. But when he sets himself to work, he finds these things of no value. There is a foundation in the bottom, which bears up the whole that he thought not of. Men looking upon the church do find that it is a fair fabric indeed, but cannot imagine how it should stand. A few supporters it seems to have in the world, like crouching antics under the windows that make some show of under propping it. Here you have a magistrate, there an army or so. Think the men of the world, "Can we but remove these people, the whole would quickly topple to the ground." Yea, so foolish have I been myself, and so void of understanding before the Lord, as to take a view of some goodly appearing props of this building and to think, How shall the house be preserved if these be removed—when lo! Suddenly some have been manifested to be held up by the house, and not to hold it up. I say then, Christ, as the foundation of this house, is hidden to the men of this world; they see it not, they believe it not. There is nothing more remote from their apprehension than that Christ should be at the bottom of them and their ways, whom they so much despise.

As the whirlwind passeth, so is the wicked no more: but the righteous is an everlasting foundation.
Proverbs 10:25

> Men, looking upon the church, find that it is a fair fabric, but cannot imagine how it should stand.

Providence

William Bates

The sun applies its quickening influences for the production and growth of a single plant as particularly as if there were no other things in the world to receive them; yet at the same time it passes from sign to sign in the heavens, changes the scenes of the elements, produces new seasons, and its active and prolific heat forms and transforms whatsoever is changed in nature. This is a fit resemblance of the universal and special operations of divine providence; what a strong security doth this give to a Christian in the midst of all trouble in this corrupt and changeable world? How will it clear the mind from those miserable perplexities, and quiet those improvident, precipitant passions that so often afflict the afflicted? Whatever evils befall the saints, are with the knowledge and will, and by the efficiency of God, materially considered; and is he defective in wisdom, power, or goodness, that what he does either might or ought to be better otherwise? Indeed, sometimes the special ends of his afflicting providence are in such deep obscurity, that our line is too short to fathom, and the manner how God shall result from evil is unknown; but then we may conclude with evidence, it is for the best. When Cesarius, a primitive saint, was arguing in himself, how that scripture could be true, that the earth was founded on the waters; how the weightier element should not sink, and be overwhelmed by the other: he stopped the course of his thoughts by this reflection, "I forgot myself when I said to God, how can this be?" He admires that which he could not comprehend.

I forgot myself when I said to God, "How can this be?"

Inner Conflicts

John Shower

Where God bestows forgiveness, He communicates the Spirit of grace for the mortification of sin. And though that work is not perfect, it shall be progressive, and the remainders of corruption in the soul will not prove that your sin is not forgiven. The flesh will war against the spirit, and the spirit will strive against the flesh; but you cannot conclude that you are not forgiven from the opposition that sin makes against the grace of God in the soul. Would you judge of yourselves? Consider what opposition you make against sin; would you have relief? Apply to the fountain open, to the blood and Spirit of Christ, for new strength from day to day, to crucify the flesh, to continue the warfare, and maintain the conflict. That sin yet remains in the soul is consistent with your reconciliation to God, and your sense of this with His acceptance of you. Yea, I am persuaded that there is never such a discovery of corruption as after forgiveness, when the grace of God has enlightened the soul. But which part do you side with? Do you condemn, bewail, oppose, resist, strive, watch, pray, fight, and endeavor the mortification of that corruption that yet remains, after the hopes of pardon? You shall then by the grace of Christ hold on, and be more than a conqueror. You should apply to Him, and exalt His power, as able to destroy the works of the devil. He has promised, and undertakes it, that no iniquity shall be charged to your condemnation. No old stories shall be repeated, no latter displeasure harbored, no former quarrel revived. If you return to God with all your heart, He will never upbraid you with your former sins, though others may. But if you can hope that God forgives you, you will easily bear that and little mind it. Can you doubt of this fullness of pardon when God has said He will hide and blot out our sins, so as "when sought for they shall not be found" (Jer. 50:20), and that He will "put them as far from us, as the east is from the west" (Ps. 103:12), that none of them shall be mentioned again to us?

For the flesh lusteth against the Spirit, and the Spirit against the flesh: and these are contrary the one to the other: so that ye cannot do the things that ye would.

Galatians 5:17

The Trinity

Richard Stock

And there are three that bear witness in earth, the spirit, and the water, and the blood: and these three agree in one.
1 John 5:8

The mystery of the Trinity is only to be found in the Word of God, and so only known by the church of God, which has the true Word of God. And the church has endeavored to speak as plain as it can in such a mystery. I remember a speech of Saint Augustine, who wrote a book on the Trinity, on this great and excellent point: "We must speak with modesty, and fear, we ought to hear with great attention; for where unity of the Trinity is to be showed, men err most dangerously, and nothing is enquired with more difficulty, nor found with more profit." We must have great care to endeavor to understand it, so far as it is revealed; God has revealed it, and it is sinful, and damnable negligence not to seek after that which is revealed by God. But let us labor for humility, that we look not into this mystery further than is needful. The weakness of man can look on the beams of the sun, but not on the body of the sun; so man in this case, if he look too far, may lose his eyes. The men of Beth Shemesh had the hand of God upon them when they looked into the ark of God; will it not therefore follow that we must be sober in this, seeing God has really manifested His anger against them in that manner?

> But let us labor for humility, that we look not into this mystery further than is needful.

Heavenly Happiness

Richard Bernard

eaven is the haven of rest, desired of all and hoped for by many. But it is only enjoyed by the best. It is the highest place, the seat and throne of God, the habitation of angels, and the harbor for the just. It is the court of the great King, the mighty Creator. It is the Lord's tabernacle, the faithful man's receptacle, the region resplendent, the comfortable continent, the city of safety, and the sacred sanctuary of peace and prosperity. All in it are without misery, never subject to calamity. It is a paradise for pleasure, a city for beauty, and a kingdom for state. Here is life temporal, there is life eternal; here are the beginnings of grace, there is the perfection of goodness. There is God in His fullness of glory, yet to none dreadful; there He reigns in justice, and yet without wrath. . . . This heavenly happiness cannot be imagined; the blessings are so many that they cannot be numbered, and so innumerable that they cannot be equaled. This heaven is of such value that it cannot be prized; it is so great that it cannot be measured, and of such eternity, as it never can be ended. Its inhabitants are joyful in an ever-rejoicing joy; they cry aloud Hosanna, and sing cheerfully Hallelujah. . . . There is flowering youth, never decaying, and strength never abating . . . the name of heaven is to all lovely.

Heaven is my throne, and earth is my footstool: what house will ye build me? saith the Lord: or what is the place of my rest?

Acts 7:49

> ꟶere are the beginnings of grace; there is the perfection of goodness.

Sister Duties

Samuel Slater

Give unto the LORD the glory due unto his name: bring an offering, and come before him: worship the LORD in the beauty of holiness.

1 Chronicles 16:29

It is both a wicked and miserable thing for any to be without God in the world (Eph. 2:12). He is so great, so necessary a good, that nothing can possibly supply the want of Him. Notwithstanding the moon and all the stars, it is night with us when once the sun is departed off our horizon. God is absolutely necessary for us, and our all is due to Him. Single persons must know it to be their duty and interest to serve and worship God in their capacities, as publicly in the gates of Zion, which God loves, in the assemblies of the saints, unto which they ought to join themselves as followers of the same Lord, and members of the same body; so singly and alone, let their chambers and closets be witnesses for them that they do not live in an ungrateful and wicked forgetfulness of God. Let children begin bedtimes with God. Let young men and women have early converse with God, waiting upon Him, and walking with Him. And when they have come to alter their condition, and to have yokefellows and families, let them be careful to set up the worship of God in them. . . . It is not enough for them to worship God in their families, but they ought to do it in their chambers too. Nor is it enough to worship God in their chambers, but they ought to do it in their families too. Let not these jostle nor exclude one another, but as sister duties live sweetly together under the same roof.

God is absolutely necessary for us, and our all is due to Him.

To Value Heaven

Richard Baxter

A sound belief in things unseen will cause practical estimation of them, and that above all earthly things. A glimpse of the heavenly glory as in a glass will cause the soul deliberately to say, "This is the chief desirable felicity; this is the crown, the pearl, the treasure; nothing but this can serve my turn." It will debase the greatest pleasures, or riches, or honors of the world in your esteem. How contemptible will they seem while you see God stand by, and heaven as it were set open to your view; you will see there is little cause to envy the prosperity of the servants of the world; you will pity them, as miserable in their mirth, and bound in the fetters of their folly and concupiscence, and as strangers to all solid joy and honor. You will be moved with some compassion to them in their misery, when they are braving it among men, and domineering for a little while; and you will think, "Alas! Poor man! Is this all your glory? Do you have no better wealth, no higher honor, no sweeter pleasures than these husks?" With such a practical judgment as you value gold above dirt, and jewels above common stones, you will value heaven above all the riches and pleasures of this world, if you have indeed a living, saving faith.

The tongue of the just is as choice silver: the heart of the wicked is little worth.
Proverbs 10:20

> As you value gold above dirt you will value heaven above all the riches and pleasures of this world.

Sincere Milk

Ralph Venning

As newborn babes, desire the sincere milk of the word, that ye may grow thereby.
1 Peter 2:2

ilk is the food of babes; and therefore it is necessary that we come to know what this milk is. . . . In the general, all the Word of God (the gospel) is called "milk." "As new-born babes desire the sincere milk of the word, that you may grow thereby" (1 Pet. 2:2). This milk is for growth; the Word is not only for begetting, as in 1 Pet. 1:23, but for nourishing and bringing up also, even to a perfect stature (Eph. 4:11–16). It is observable that Peter does not speak merely of the Word written in the Bible, but of the Word preached. But then this Word preached must be sincere milk of the Word, not mixed with and corrupted by the devices of invention, glosses and comments; this the Apostle Paul disclaims against: "We are not as many, who are corrupt, or deal deceitfully with the word of God, but as of sincerity, but as of God, in the sight of God speak we in Christ" (2 Cor. 2:17). . . . As the Word must not be mixed with and corrupted by false doctrine and base ends, so this milk must not be made luscious and fulsome with the sugar and honey of men's wisdom and eloquence, for this the Apostle no less disowns and disallows. . . . So then it is not a sound of words, but sound and sincere doctrine or milk of the Word by which we grow and thrive.

> **The Word must not be mixed with and corrupted by false doctrine and base ends.**

Christ's Return

William Greenhill

he Lord Jesus Christ shall appear eminently in His greatness and glory. Previously, Christ appeared like a servant in a state of humiliation; but when He comes He shall appear eminently, in greatness and in glory.... Christ shall come with power and great glory. It will be a day of glory indeed, for the world shall be filled with the glory of Christ. Scripture says that "they shall see the sign of the Son of Man in heaven" (Matt. 24:30). What is the sign of the Son of Man? Not the cross . . . but as you can gather out of Matt. 24:27, "For as the lightning cometh out of the east, and shineth even unto the west, so shall also the coming of the Son of Man be." He shall come with lightning; the brightness of Christ shall fill the world with the glory of Christ. Christ is glorified, and Christ's coming now shall be so shining and glorious that its luster shall be seen in the world. In Acts 26:13, Paul said that he saw a light "brighter than the sun at noonday." Christ is so glorious, so bright, that when He comes He will fill the world with glory, and that will make it an eminent day indeed, a day of great concern.

And to wait for his Son from heaven, whom he raised from the dead, even Jesus, which delivered us from the wrath to come.
1 Thessalonians 1:10

> He shall come with lightning; the brightness of Christ shall fill the world with the glory of Christ.

Circle of Love

Peter Sterry

O love the LORD, all ye his saints: for the LORD preserveth the faithful, and plentifully rewardeth the proud doer.

Psalm 31:23

This is the circle of heavenly love: first, God loves you in eternity with that love with which He loves the Lord Jesus, for He beholds you in the light of the same loveliness in which He beholds Jesus Christ. Then He brings down the treasure of this love and loveliness, which is His beloved Son, into you, and sows Him, as the seed of the divine nature and sonship. He springs up in you, transforms you into His own likeness, and grows up in an inseparable union and fellowship with you. Now God has another son, in which He sees His Son in conjunction on earth, as He saw them before in conjunction in heaven. Lastly, God embraces this son on earth, in whom He sees His Son. He gives him the kiss of a father, with all the joys of a father. He takes Him into His arms, carries him up into heaven changing him still, as He carries him up, till this union begun below, be at last made perfect in, and swallowed up into that union, which was at first in eternity. Then shall the Lord Jesus see Himself in a saint after the same manner, in which a saint is seen in the Lord Jesus; both being made perfect in each, and all made perfect in one. Follow on to know the Lord, and His love, and you shall know this love of the Lord.

Then shall the Lord Jesus see Himself in a saint as a saint is seen in the Lord Jesus.

Harvest of Promise

William Spurstowe

A bide and continue in a holy waiting upon God, until He who is the maker of the promises becomes the fulfiller of them. "Our eyes wait upon the Lord our God, until that He have mercy upon us" (Ps. 123:2). Some promises are like the almond tree which puts out upon the first approach of the spring, and brings forth an early fruit; they are not long pleaded, before they are fulfilled, and have their blessings like ripe fruit to drop in the mouth of the eater. Others are like the mulberry tree, which is slow and backward in the imparting of its sap unto the branches; they are long before they bud forth into any appearances which may disclose any step and progress to be made toward their future accomplishment. So that they who are the inheritors of them, though they need not fear their failing the appointed time, yet they need patience to expect and wait for their fulfilling. The great promise which God made to Abraham of multiplying his seed like the stars of heaven did for twenty-five years continue its motion like a slow-placed planet, having in all that tract of time gone little of that course which it was to finish. Abraham was seventy-five years old when the promise was made, and a hundred years old when Isaac, who was the first blossom of that promise, was born. . . . Seeing therefore that there is often a long interval between the seedtime and the harvest of the promise, between its making and fulfilling, it is necessary for believers to wait upon God, who is the one that can best date and time His own promises, and to expect with patience the appointed time of the promise, which at the end shall speak and not lie.

Though it tarry, wait for it.
Habakkuk 2:3

> There is often a long interval between the seedtime and the harvest of the promise.

Precious Knowledge

John Durant

And to know the love
of Christ, which
passeth knowledge,
that ye might be filled
with all the fulness of
God.
Ephesians 3:19

Of all divine knowledge, the knowledge of Jesus Christ in the light of love is most precious, as tending most to the perfection of our souls. As there are degrees of luster in the heavenly lights, so there are degrees of glory in divine truths. Every star in the firmament has a glorious light; but yet the light of the sun exceeds them all in glory. And every truth (which is as a star in the heaven of divinity) has a peculiar excellency in it, and the knowledge thereof is precious, yet Jesus Christ (who is the sun in divinity's heaven) has a transcendent excellency in Him. And to know Him far more tends to the perfecting of our souls than the knowledge of any, or all divine truths besides. Therefore it is that Paul accents this knowledge with an excellency, Phil. 3:8, "Yea doubtless, I count all things but loss, for the excellency of the knowledge of Christ Jesus my Lord." And certainly Paul might well say thus; for although he had attained the knowledge of other things, yet without this he had been at a loss in point of soul-sacred perfection. So that however other knowledge (as being some way perfecting and precious) be desirable; yet there is no knowledge which is so to be desired (at least by saints) as the knowledge of Jesus Christ.

As there are degrees of luster in the heavenly lights, so there are degrees of glory in divine truths.

Matchless Mercy

John Flavel

That God should be reconciled after such a dreadful breach as the fall of man made, is wonderful; no sin, all things considered, was ever like to this sin: other sins, like a single bullet, kill particular persons, but this, like a chain-shot, cuts off multitudes as the sand upon the seashore, which no man can number. If all the posterity of Adam in their several generations should do nothing else but bewail and lament this sin of his, whilst this world continues, yet would it not be enough lamented; for a man so newly created out of nothing, and admitted the first moment into the highest order, crowned a king over the works of God's hands (Ps. 8:5), a man perfect and upright, without the least inordinate motions, or sinful inclination: a man whose mind was most clear, bright, and apprehensive of the will of God, whose will was free, and able to have easily put by the strongest temptation: a man in a paradise of delights, where nothing was left to desire for advancing the happiness of soul or body: a man understanding himself to be a public, complete person, carrying not only his own, but the happiness of the whole world in his hand: so soon, upon so slight a temptation, to violate the law of his God, and involve himself and all his posterity with him, in such a gulf of guilt and misery; all which he might so easily have prevented! O wonderful amazing mercy, that ever God should think of being reconciled, or have any purposes of peace towards so vile an apostate creature as man.

Who is a God like unto thee, that pardoneth iniquity, and passeth by the transgression of the remnant of his heritage? he retaineth not his anger for ever, because he delighteth in mercy.
Micah 7:18

> This, like a chain-shot, cuts off multitudes as the sand upon the seashore.

Radiant Morning

Samuel Lee

*Wherefore he saith,
Awake thou that
sleepest, and arise
from the dead, and
Christ shall give thee
light.*

Ephesians 5:14

Moses and Xerxes took a view of their puissant armies, the first from a mountain in the plains of Moab, the other in the plains of Abydus. One rejoiced to see the land of Canaan, and the goodly range of Lebanon, extending forty miles in length, which Israel was now ready to possess. The other wept that his burdensome bulk of barbarous nations, within a hundred years, would raise so many heaps of bones, whereon death might stand and blow his trumpet of triumph. Saints have but Jordan's Valley to pass through into eternal joys, while others wasting their precious time in vain signs suddenly slip into eternal woe. Saints militant after many a sharp combat enter victoriously into paradise. And although some may encounter with fainting, drooping qualms, yes it may be, set in a cloud, yet what an ecstasy of spirit will surprise them, who after many labyrinths and mazes of trouble unexpectedly enter the ravishing glories of heaven! The best may labor under fears and tears, but one hour there makes amends for all, when these mists will be scattered in that radiant morning, and all tears washed away in those rivers of pleasure, which run through the streets of New Jerusalem.

Saints, militant after many a sharp combat, enter victoriously into paradise.

Without Price

William Spurstowe

The freeness of God's grace in the promises is exceedingly useful to succor and relieve the perplexing fears of the weak and tempted Christian, who though he has eyes to see the unspeakable worth and excellency of the promises, yet has not the confidence to put forth the hand of faith and to apply them to his necessities. He wants forgiveness of sins, but doubts the promise of blotting out iniquities belongs not to him; he is naked, and gladly would that Christ might spread the skirt of His righteousness over him to hide his deformities; but alas! What has a leper to do with a royal robe? He is sick and diseased, but the physic that must cure him, the least drop of it is of more worth than a world, and he is viler than the dust. How then can he expect that he should ever be the patient of such a physician, who will be both at the cost to buy the physic and at the pains to administer it? If he had a heart to love God as David, if talents to glorify God as Paul, if he were but an Israelite without guile as Nathanael, then he might have hopes together with them, to have his person accepted, his services rewarded, and his imperfections pardoned. But his heart with which he should love God is carnal and not spiritual; his talents and abilities with which he should glorify God are few or none; his sincerity which should be the evangelical perfection of all his duties, has more than ordinary tincture of hypocrisy and self-ends mixed with it. With what confidence therefore can such a person draw near to Christ, or ever expect to be welcomed by Him? Now to put to silence these reasonings, and to allay these fears, which unless checked and bounded, do often terminate in the blackness of despair; there is not a more effectual remedy than the consideration of the freeness of the grace of God and Christ in the promise, which are not made to such as deserve mercy, but to such as want it; not to righteous persons, but to sinners, not the whole, but to the sick.

Ho, every one that thirsteth, come ye to the waters, and he that hath no money; come ye, buy, and eat; yes, come, buy wine and milk without money and without price.
Isaiah 55:1

Infinite Wisdom

Thomas Watson

God sees, in His infinite wisdom, that the same condition is not convenient for all; that which is good for one, may be bad for another; one season of weather will not serve all men's occasions, one needs sunshine, another rain; one condition of life will not fit every man, no more than one suit of apparel will fit every body; prosperity is not fit for all, nor yet adversity. If one man be brought low, perhaps he can bear it better; he has a greater stock of grace, more faith and patience; he can gather grapes of thorns, pick some comfort out of the cross: every-one cannot do this. Another man is seated in an eminent place of dignity; he is fitter for it; perhaps it is a place that requires more parts of judgment, which everyone is not capable of; perhaps he can use his estate better, he hath a public heart as well as a public place. The wise God sees that condition to be bad for one, which is good for another; hence it is He places men in different orbs and spheres—some higher, some lower. One man desires health. God sees sickness is better for him. God will work health out of sickness by consuming the body of death. Another man desires liberty. God sees restraint better for him. He will work his liberty by restraint; when his feet are bound, his heart shall be most enlarged. Did we believe this it would give a check to the sinful disputes and cavils of our hearts: shall I be discontented at that which is enacted by a decree, and ordered by providence? Is this to be a child or a rebel?

> That which is good for one, may be bad for another.

Sensibility

Nathaniel Vincent

They that would pray must be sensible of their sins, their needs, and their unworthiness, to have those needs supplied; they must also be sensible that none can help them, but the God they are praying to. 1. They must be sensible of their sins. "I acknowledge my iniquities," says David, "and my sin is ever before me" (Ps. 51:3); so Isa. 59:12, "For our transgressions are multiplied before thee, and our sins testify against us, for our transgressions are with us, and as for our iniquities we know them." Sin must be acknowledged with shame and sorrow; else it will separate between God and us, and prove a cloud through which our prayers will never pass. There must be such a sense of sin as implies a hatred and weariness of it; for if the heart out of love and liking of it, has a regard to sin, God will be deaf, and His mercies restrained. "If I regard iniquity in my heart, the Lord will not hear my prayer" (Ps. 66:18). 2. They that pray must be sensible of their needs. All the posterity of Adam is needy, however rich and full they conceive themselves. The first man being a public person had the whole stock in his own hand, and having lost it, has lost his whole progeny; we are all come short of the glory of God, as descended from Adam; we are flesh, and in our flesh dwells no good thing. This must be understood and believed: poverty of spirit Christ commends, and pronounces those that are thus poor, blessed (Matt. 5:3). For they that perceive they are wretched, and miserable, and empty, and naked, will cry the louder to the Lord for gold tried in the fire to enrich them, and white raiment that they may be clothed. . . . And were we but better acquainted with our wants, oh what strong cries would come from us, that sin might be forgiven, that grace might be wrought, that peace might be spoken; what spiritual maladies might be healed! . . . Therefore David lays this charge upon his soul to wait only upon God, and to have all this expectation from Him. God will be seriously sought unto, when we are under the power of this conviction, that no other helper can be found.

Hear my prayer, O LORD, and give ear unto my cry; hold not thy peace at my tears: for I am a stranger with thee, and a sojourner, as all my fathers were.
Psalm 39:12

Read the Scriptures

Robert Dingley

And Philip ran thither
to him, and heard him
read the prophet
Esaias, and said,
Understandest thou
what thou readest?
Acts 8:30

The Scriptures are God's epistle to us. Christ has honored reading with His own example. For coming to Nazareth, as His custom was, He stood up and read the Scriptures. And the same Christ has charged us that we also search the Scriptures; and for so doing the Bereans were styled noble. Sabellicus says that the Virgin Mary spent the third part of her time in reading the Scriptures. Timothy was trained up in them from a child, and so was Origen. And although the Word preached is the ordinary means of conversion, yet some have been converted in reading of the Scriptures, as Augustine and Fulgentius. Junius was converted by reading the first chapter of John. Reading the Scriptures shuts out worldly cares, dulls carnal delights, and enflames divine love. It steers the judgment, clears the memory, cheers the conscience, and sweetly composes the affections. Let your eyes be on the Scriptures daily, they will make you perfect in the doctrines of faith and the rules of life. . . . The Rabbis say that on every syllable and tittle of the law hangs a mountain of sense and holy doctrine. It is a dreadful thing that so many slight and neglect reading of the Scripture . . . Those of highest attainments and endowments may find much delight in the Word, for in the Scriptures we find variety of learning, that the eyes of no reader depart unsatisfied. There are histories for the historian, philosophy for the philosophical, ethics for the moralist, mysteries for the artist, and tongues for the linguist; there is flood for elephants, food for lambs, milk for babes, and meat for adults. Let us then delight to have our eyes on the Scriptures into which angels pry; read, though you understand not; in God's time a Philip comes to the eunuch. Mingle meditations and prayers with your reading; confer with the judicious, which are dead by their comments, but are living by their conference. Finally, live up to the light you have received; so shall you mind, understand, remember, and delight in the Scriptures, above thousands of gold and silver.

Look after Peace

Jeremiah Burroughs

Take heed therefore, that you never maintain peace with any sin. "Great peace have they that love thy Law, and nothing shall offend them" (Ps. 119:165). Oh, how many of you have broken your peace with God! At least the comfort of it is exceedingly darkened; you would fain have outward ease and peace, but you have neglected the comforts of this peace, and that is the reason you have no strength to suffer anything for the truth. Nehemiah 8:10 says, "The joy of the Lord is your strength." That joy comes from this inward peace, but where this is not, there is nothing to sweeten sorrows, and therefore they are very bitter. That time therefore, that God gives you yet respite from afflictions, let it be spent in making up your peace with God more than ever, and getting clearer evidence and sense of His love. If you ever knew what peace with God meant, I appeal to you: when at any time the sense of it has enlarged your heart with joy, have you not found yourselves willing to suffer anything for God? You could then go through fire and water. Your spirits could triumph with the Apostle; "I am persuaded that neither life, nor death, nor principalities, nor powers, nor things present, nor things to come, shall ever be able to separate me from the love of God in Christ Jesus" (Rom. 8:38–39).

Thou wilt keep him in perfect peace, whose mind is stayed on thee: because he trusteth in thee. Trust ye in the LORD for ever: for in the LORD JEHOVAH is everlasting strength.
Isaiah 26:3–4

> That joy comes from this inward peace, but where this is not, there is nothing to sweeten sorrows.

Breath of Prayer

Henry Scudder

Create in me a clean heart, O God; and renew a right spirit within me.
Psalm 51:10

If in your meditations and in your prayers you find dullness and want of spirituality, I would have you to be humbled in the sense of your impotency and infirmity; yet, be not discouraged nor give them over, but rather betake yourself to these duties with more diligence and earnestness. When you are out of water, your pump being dry, by pouring in a little water and much laboring in pumping, can fetch water. So, too, by laboring the heart in preparation and prayer, you may recover the gift of prayer. And, as when your fire is out, by laying on fuel and blowing the spark remaining, you kindle it again, so by meditation you stir up the grace that is in you and by the breath of prayer you may revive and inflame the spirit of grace and prayer in you. Yet if you find that you have not time to prepare by meditation, or having done so, if you find a confusion and distraction in your meditation, then it will be best to break through all hindrances and without further preparation attend to the duty of prayer, only with premeditation of God, to whom, and of Christ, by whom, through the Spirit, you must pray.

Break through all hindrances and without further preparation attend to the duty of prayer.

Acceptable Time

John Shower

ow or never is the season to prepare for eternity, seeing that your states are unchangeable after death. The gulf will then be fixed; there is no possibility for repentance, or hope of pardon beyond the grave. It will be in vain to cry with the foolish virgins, "Lord open to us," when the door is shut (Matt. 25:11). Now you are encouraged to pray for mercy, earnestly invited and entreated to work out your own salvation; and warned of your danger. Now is your time to hearken to good counsel. Many of you have misspent a great part of your life; you shall not live it over again. You are not certain of the future. You may be in an unchangeable state before you are aware. So that to defer it one week or day longer may be your undoing. You have now a promise of forgiveness, if you repent, and the hopes of God's grace, if you seek it. You have yet an opportunity to make peace with God. This is your accepted time, the day of salvation. The door of mercy and of hope is yet open, but before long it will be shut, and your state immutable. Whatever is to be done in preparation for eternity must be now or never. Now quickly or it will be too late; now presently, and without delay, or it may be too late.

For he saith, I have heard thee in a time accepted, and in the day of salvation have I succoured thee: behold, now is the accepted time; behold, now is the day of salvation.
2 Corinthians 6:2

> **Whatever is to be done in preparation for eternity must be now or never.**

Spiritual Music

William Fenner

And Hannah answered and said, No, my lord, I am a woman of a sorrowful spirit: I have drunk neither wine nor strong drink, but have poured out my soul before the LORD.

1 Samuel 1:15

mportunate prayer is assurance-getting prayer, a prayer that will not be quiet until it has assurance that God has heard it. Wicked men pray, and presume that God hears them, but God hears them not; nay, many of God's dear children pray many times, and are not heard. "How long wilt thou be angry with thy people that prayeth?" (Ps. 80:4), not only with their persons, but with their prayers also. How then, do you think, is the prayer of such as live in their sins taken? They pray, but their prayers vanish away in the air like clouds. These may pray and pray, but they get nothing. "Behold he [Saul] prays," says the voice to Ananias (Acts 9:11). What, did he not pray before? Yes, he had made many a long prayer, else he could not have been a Pharisee; but now he did not only pray, but he prayed unto God as David did, who did lift up his heart to God, or else his heart could not have prayed. . . . Our hearts are just like a bell, which so long as it lies on the ground will make no music, until it is lifted up. Our hearts are not like the bell of Rochea, which (they say) will ring of its own accord, but our hearts must be lifted up, otherwise they will make no delightful music in the ears of God. Wherefore, if you pray and labor not to bring your hearts home to God, that He may hear them in mercy, He will hear them, but it will be to your condemnation, as He hears the prayers of the wicked; therefore, if you pray, pray fervently.

> Our hearts are just like a bell, which so long as it lies on the ground will make no music.

To Meet Christ

Christopher Nesse

Excite and quicken all your faculties; the affections (those handmaids of the soul) should give attendance to meet Christ (the mystical David) just as the virgins of Israel met the literal David in their singings and dancing (1 Sam. 18:6–8). Everyone singing their part appointed them accordingly is sent out to wait for this King of glory (and if He come not, desire is sent out to fetch Him), and love, delight, and joy receive and entertain Him. All these virgins go out to meet this blessed bridegroom (Matt. 25:1), having first swept the house clear and cast all the filth in the brook Kidron, and bring forth their best bravery (Arras hangings, Persian carpets, rich stools, all their plate and jewels), to wit, all the graces of the Spirit (far surpassing Aaron's rich garments that were for glory and beauty), all to prepare a large upper room for entertaining the King of glory. Even so, all the faculties of the soul must be stirred up, to improve their interest in such a blessed guest as 1. Your understanding must look round about him, and behold him altogether lovely from this sycamore tree, as Zacchaeus. 2. Your will must offer up both sword and keys, as the major does to his prince at his entertainment. 3. Your memory must be ready to register every act of love to your soul, remembering His loves more than wine. In a word Christ must be led into every room of your heart; and lastly, all your graces must be excited, and made ready to receive each their alms from Christ's fullness, as saving knowledge, justifying faith, sincere repentance, fervent love. All come to touch Him for healing virtue, well knowing that Christ comes with a royal heart in the soul to give abundantly; and like himself, no mean gift can come from so noble a hand and heart, and that all this may be done you must use the third thing required, that is, strong invocation, coming as a prince to Him and begging His grace with your whole heart.

And at midnight there was a cry made, Behold, the bridegroom cometh; go ye out to meet him.

Matthew 25:26

In a Manger

Thomas Adams

And she brought forth her firstborn son, and wrapped him in swaddling clothes, and laid him in a manger; because there was no room for them in the inn.

Luke 2:7

It is evident in St. Luke's Gospel that the shepherds found the Christ-child lying in a cradle. He who sits on the right hand of the Majesty on high was lodged in a stable. He that measures the waters in His fist, and heaven with a span, was now crowned in a manger, and swaddled with a few rags. Here they find neither guard to defend Him, nor tumults of people thronging to see Him, neither crown on His head, nor scepter in His hand, but a young child in a cradle. They saw a child, who, having so little external glory, they might have saved their pain and seen many in their own country far beyond Him. Our instruction in this is that God does often strangely and strongly exercise the faith of His people, that their persuasion may not be guided by their sight, but by His Word. The eye of true faith is so quick sighted that it can see through all the mists and fogs of difficulties. Hereon these shepherds did confidently believe that this poor child, lying in so base a manner, is the great King of heaven and earth. Thus faith that is grounded in the promises of God must believe that in prison there is liberty, in trouble peace, in affliction, comfort, in death life, in the cross a crown, and in a manger, the Lord Jesus.

> In prison there is liberty, in trouble peace, in affliction, comfort, in death life.

Practice God's Will

William Gouge

othing is sufficient without practice. I say nothing, because neither knowledge of God's will, nor a good disposition thereto, nor profession thereof, without doing it, is anything. All these are in their kind needful; for practice without knowledge can not but be very preposterous. Without a good disposition, life is mere hypocrisy, and without a free profession, it is too afraid. So knowledge of God's will is as light to give direction unto practice. A good disposition thereto is as salt, to season it. A free profession is as wine to make it quick and cheerful. But yet all those without practice are as nothing: "he that knoweth his Master's will and doth not according to it shall be beaten with many stripes" (Luke 12:47). He that has a good mind and disposition to God's will, and yet does it not, condemns himself in that which he allows. And he that makes a fair profession of it, but yet does it not, is like to a fig-tree which Christ cursed. And he has this doom denounced against him by the judge of all, "depart from me, thou worker of iniquity" (Matt. 7:23). I may therefore well say to them that know, like, and profess God's will, "blessed are ye if ye do it" (John 13:17). But without doing, all is in vain.

For whosoever shall do the will of God, the same is my brother, and my sister, and mother.
Mark 3:35

> Practice without knowledge can not but be very preposterous.

Scripture Beauties

Robert Bolton

Thy word is very pure:
therefore thy servant
loveth it.
Psalm 119:140

There is nothing proposed and handled in the Word of God but things of greatest weight and highest excellency; things such as the infinite majesty, power, and mercy of God; the unspeakable love and strange sufferings of the Son of God, for our sakes; the mighty and miraculous working of the Holy Spirit upon the souls of men. There is nothing in this treasury, but oriental pearls and rich jewels such as promises of grace, spiritual comfort, the thwarting of sin, the triumph of godliness, refreshing of wearied souls, the beauty of angels, the holiness of saints, the state of heaven, salvation for sinners, and everlasting life. What fools are they that neglecting these precious pearls, root only in the earth, wallow in worldly pleasures, feed upon vanities, transitory trash, and vanishing riches, which in their greatest need will take them to their wings, like an eagle, and fly into the heavens? Besides, the Word of God is only able to prepare us for true happiness in this world, and to possess us of it, in the world to come. It only begets in us a true, entire, and universal holiness, without which none shall ever see the face of God or the glory of heaven; for it is impossible hereafter to live the life of glory in blessedness in heaven, if we live not here in the life of grace and sincerity in all our ways.

What fools are they that neglect these precious pearls.

Pray for Grace

Thomas Manton

All our prayers should carry a correspondence with our great aim. What is our great aim? To be with God in heaven, as remembering that is the center and place of our rest, to which we are all tending: "If ye then be risen with Christ, seek those things which are above, where Christ sitteth on the right hand of God" (Col. 3:1). We come to our Father which is in heaven. He will have His residence there that our hearts might be there. Therefore the main things we should seek of God from heaven are saving graces, for these "come down from above, from the Father of lights" (Jas. 1:17). We have liberty to ask supplies for the outward life, but chiefly we should ask spiritual and heavenly things: "Your heavenly Father knoweth that ye have need of all these things" (Matt. 6:32–33). What then? First seek the kingdom of God. If we have to do with a heavenly Father, our first and main care should be to ask things suitable to His being and His excellency. If children should ask of their parents such a thing as is pleasing to their palate, possibly they might give it them; but when they ask instruction, and desire to be taught, that is far more acceptable to them. When we ask supplies of the outward life, food and raiment, God may give it us; but it is more pleasing to Him when we ask for grace. In every prayer we should seek to be made more heavenly by conversing with our heavenly Father.

Grace be with all them that love our Lord Jesus Christ in sincerity.
Ephesians 6:24

> If we have to do with a heavenly Father, our first and main care should be to ask things suitable to His being.

Heaven on Earth

Thomas Watson

He maketh me to lie down in green pastures: he leadeth me beside the still waters.

Psalm 23:2

A contented Christian carries heaven about him: for, what is heaven, but that sweet repose and full contentment that the soul shall have in God? In contentment there are the first fruits of heaven. There are two things in a contented spirit, which make it like heaven. God is there; something of God is to be seen in that heart. A discontented Christian is like a rough tempestuous sea; when the water is rough you can see nothing there; but when it is smooth and serene, then you may behold your face in the water. When the heart rages through discontent, it is like a rough sea, you can see nothing there, unless passion and murmuring; there is nothing of God, nothing of heaven in that heart: but by virtue of contentment, it is like the sea when it is smooth and calm, there is a face shining there; you may see something of Christ in that heart, a representation of all the graces. Rest is there. O what a Sabbath is kept in a contented heart! What a heaven! A contented Christian like Noah in the ark: though the ark were tossed with waves, Noah could sit and sing in the ark. The soul that is gotten into the ark of contentment, sits quiet, and sails above all the waves of trouble; he can sing in this spiritual ark; the wheels of the chariot move, but the axle-tree stirs not; the circumference of the heavens is carried about the earth, but the earth moves not out of its center. When we meet with motion and change in the creatures round about us, a contented spirit is not stirred nor moved out of its center. The sails of a mill move with the wind, but the mill itself stands still, an emblem of contentment; when our outward estate moves with the wind of providence, yet the heart is settled through holy contentment; and when others are like quicksilver, shaking and trembling through disquiet, the contented spirit can say, as David, "O God my heart is fixed" (Ps. 57:7), what is this but a piece of heaven?

Heaven's Joy

Christopher Love

Live in the meditation and contemplation of the joy and glory of heaven. And this will be a great means to keep out worldly sorrow; the glory and happiness of heaven will so transport a Christian's soul with spiritual joy, that he will not easily be overwhelmed with worldly sorrow. I have read one of the schoolmen that was of the opinion, that the reason why Adam in innocency was not sensible of his nakedness, was because he was so taken up with immediate converse and communion with God. So now, if you were more taken up with conversing with God, and apprehensions of glory, though you had nothing here below, yet you would think you wanted nothing. The condition of heaven and glory and happiness would make you overlook all worldly crosses and afflictions. It is said of Paul, that he was rapt up into the third heaven, and saw things ineffable; but whether in the body or out of the body, he could not tell; that is, he saw so much glory, and was so taken up with the joys of heaven, that he could not tell whether he was in the body or not; it made him to forget all his troubles and miseries here below. I remember I have read in Jerome, what advice he gives a young man in his time that was overmuch pressed with sorrow and grief for worldly crosses. "Do but now and then take a turn or two in paradise, and then you will never think of a wilderness or be troubled at the miseries of a desert," he said. Oh beloved, that your souls had once this art of divine sight and contemplation, that you might have an experimental knowledge of the joys of heaven, and this would keep you from mourning any more for worldly crosses.

Look unto the heavens, and see; and behold the clouds which are higher than thou.

Job 35:5

> Take a turn or two in paradise, and then you will never think of a wilderness.

An Abiding Plant

Edmund Calamy

Let not mercy and truth forsake thee: bind them about thy neck; write them upon the table of thine heart.

Proverbs 3:3

Integrity is like an abiding plant, a plant that will live under the most severe storm and abide the hottest summer and the coldest winter. . . . it will hold out in the hottest persecution, and in the greatest defection. An upright heart abides in the truth, and the truth abides in it. "The upright do hold on his way" (Job 17:9). A hypocrite may profess the truth, and go far in the profession of it for a time, but he will not always abide in it. Sooner or later he will fall away from it . . . but an upright heart will hold on its way, and hold out upright in crooked times; it will hold fast its integrity whatever it part with else, as God and an upright man affirms (Job 2:3, 27:5–6). As a hypocrite will not abide in the truth, no more will the truth abide in him. Truth may be in a hypocrite for a time, but it will not abide in him. God does sooner or later take it quite from him. But truth in an upright heart abides there, or so says the apostle: "The anointing which ye have received of God abideth in you" (1 John 2:27). Truth in an upright heart is in its proper element, and therefore abides there.

It will hold out in the hottest persecution and in the greatest defection.

Sources of Readings

JANUARY 1

Moses His Choice, with His Eye Fixed upon Heaven: Discovering the Happy Condition of a Self-Denying Heart (London: Printed by M. F. for R. D., 1641), 44–45.

JANUARY 2

The Wells of Salvation Opened: Or a Treatise Discovering the Nature, Preciousness, Usefulness of Gospel Promises, and Rules for the Right Application of Them (London: Printed by E. M. for Ralph Smith, 1659), 77–79.

JANUARY 3

A Profitable Exposition of the Lord's Prayer, by Way of Questions and Answers for Most Plainness: Together with Many Fruitful Applications to the Life and Soul, as Well for the Terror of the Dull and Dead, as for the Sweet Comfort of the Tender Hearted (London: Printed by Thomas Orwin for Thomas Charde, 1588), 26–28.

JANUARY 4

A Discovery of Glorious Love or the Love of Christ to Believers Opened in the Truth, Transcendency, and Sweetness Thereof, Together with the Necessity that Lies Upon Every Believer to Strive after the Spiritual and Experimental Knowledge of It (London: Printed for R. I., 1655), 36–37.

JANUARY 5

The Mourner's Directory, Guiding Him to the Middle Way betwixt the Two Extremes: Defect and Excess of Sorrow for His Dead, to Which Is Added The Mourner's Soliloquy (London: Printed for J. A. for Thomas Cockerill, 1693), 6–9.

JANUARY 6

The Humbled Sinner Resolved What He Should Do to Be Saved: Or Faith in the Lord Jesus Christ, the Only Way of Salvation for Sensible Sinners (Printed for Adoniram Byfield, 1656), 101–3.

JANUARY 7

The Guard of the Tree of Life: Or a Sacramental Discourse (London: Printed by M. Simmons for A. Kembe, 1644), 5–7.

JANUARY 8

The Duty and Blessing of a Tender Conscience: Plainly Stated and Earnestly Recommended to All That Regard Acceptance with God, and the Prosperity of Their Souls (London: Printed by J. R. for J. Salisbury, 1691), 31–32.

JANUARY 9

The Rise, Race, and Royalty of the Kingdom of God in the Soul of Man (London: Printed for Thomas Cockerill, 1683), 33.

JANUARY 10

The Saint's Nearness to God: Being a Discourse upon Part of the CXLVIII Psalm, Written at the Request of a Friend (London: Printed by A. M. for Francis Tyron, 1662), 117–21.

JANUARY 11

Mr. Jenkins's Dying Thoughts, Who Departed This Life on Monday the 19th of This Instant January, in the Prison of Newgate (London: Printed for Edward Goldwin, 1683), 1.

JANUARY 12

The Saint's Nearness to God: Being a Discourse upon Part of the CXLVIII Psalm, Written at the Request of a Friend (London: Printed by A. M. for Francis Tyron, 1662), 63–64.

JANUARY 13

The Mystery of Self-Deceiving: Or a Discourse and Discovery of Deceitfulness of Man's Heart (London: Printed by Thomas Snodham, 1617), 240–41.

JANUARY 14

A Plain and Familiar Exposition of the Ten Commandments (London: Printed by Thomas Man, Paul Man, and Jonah Man, 1632), 20.

JANUARY 15

Communion with God in Two Sermons, Preached at St. Paul's: The First, September 3, 1654; the Second, March 25, 1655 (London: Printed by Evan Tyler, 1655), 4–5.

JANUARY 16

A Plain Discourse upon Uprightness (London: Printed for F. Calvert, 1672), 7–8.

JANUARY 17

The Day of Grace, in Which the Chief of Sinners May Be Turned and Healed (London: Printed for Thomas Parkhurst, 1669), 20.

JANUARY 18

A Christian's Walk and Work on Earth until He Attain to Heaven (London: Printed for Dorman Newman, 1678), 65–66.

JANUARY 19

Gospel-Revelation in Three Treatises: Viz., the Nature of God, the Excellency of Christ, and the Excellency of Man's Immortal Soul (London: Printed for Nathan Brook 1660), 9–10.

JANUARY 20

The Doctrine of Faith, Wherein Are Practically Handled Twelve Principal Points Which Explain the Nature and Use of It (London: Printed by John Dawson for Joan Newbury and Henry Overton, 1638), 198–200.

JANUARY 21

God's Thoughts and Ways Above Ours, Especially in the Forgiveness of Sins (London Printed by the Widow Astwood, 1699), 40–41.

JANUARY 22

A Plea for the Godly, Wherein Is Shown the Excellency of a Righteous Person (London Printed by A. Maxwell for Thomas Parkhurst, 1672), 11.

JANUARY 23

The Works of the Late Reverend and Pious Mr. Thomas Gouge (London: Printed by Thomas Braddyll, 1706), 218–19.

JANUARY 24

The Spiritual Taste Described and a Glimpse of Christ Discovered (London: Printed by Matthew Simmons, 1649), 42–43

JANUARY 25

A Cordial for a Fainting Soul: Or Some Essays for the Satisfaction of Wounded Spirits Laboring under Several Burdens (London: Printed for Richard Tomlins, 1649), 8–9.

JANUARY 26

Adam Abel: Or Vain Man (London: Printed for Thomas Parkhurst, 1692), 1–2.

JANUARY 27

The True Christian's Love of the Unseen Christ: Or a Discourse Chiefly Tending to Excite and Promote the Decaying Love of Christ in the Hearts of Christians (London: Printed by J. Atwood for Samuel Sprint, 1689), 55–56.

JANUARY 28

The Christian's Labour and Reward: Or a Sermon, Part of Which Was Preached at the Funeral of the Right Honourable the Lady Mary Vere, Relict of Sir Horace Vere, Born of Tilbury, on the 10th of January, 1671, at Castle Heviningham in Essex (London: Printed by J. M. for Ralph Smith, 1672), 47–49.

JANUARY 29

Christian Constancy Crowned by Christ (London: Printed by John Haviland for William Bladen, 1614), 22–23.

JANUARY 30

Christ's Power over Bodily Diseases (London: Printed by J. C. for Francis Tyton, 1672), 126–27.

JANUARY 31

Temptations: Their Nature, Danger, Cure (London: Printed by E. B. for John Bartlett, 1655), 153–54.

FEBRUARY 1

The Promises: Or a Treatise Showing How a Godly Christian May Support His Heart with Comfort Against All the Distresses Which by Reason of Any Afflictions or Temptations Can Befall Him in This Life (London: Printed by G. P. for Ralph Rounthwaite, 1619), 32–35.

FEBRUARY 2

The Cure of Distractions in Attending upon God: In Several Sermons (London: Printed for Brabazon Aylmer, 1695), 26–27.

FEBRUARY 3

Christ's Victory over the Dragon, or Satan's Downfall: Showing the Glorious Conquests of Our Saviour for His Poor Church, against the Greatest Persecutors (London: Printed by M. F. for R. Dawlman, 1633), 125–26.

FEBRUARY 4

A Funeral Sermon Occasioned by the Sudden Death of the Rev. Nathaniel Vincent (London: Printed for John Lawrence, 1697), 4.

FEBRUARY 5

Divine Opticks: Or a Treatise of the Eye, Discovering the Vices and Virtues Thereof as Also How That Organ May Be Tuned, Chiefly Grounded on Psalm 119:37 (London: Printed by J. M. for H. Cripps, 1655), 7–8.

FEBRUARY 6

A Key of Heaven: The Lord's Prayer Opened, and So Applied, That a Christian May Learn How to Pray, and to Procure All Things Which May Make for the Glory of God, and the Good of Himself, and of His Neighbor (London: Printed by Thomas Harper, 1633), 102–4.

FEBRUARY 7

Sermons and Discourses on Several Divine Subjects (London: Printed for Thomas Parkhurst, 1696), 637.

FEBRUARY 8

A Treatise of Love, Written by John Rogers, Minister of God's Word at Dedham in Essex (London: Printed by Mary Dawson for Joan Newberry, 1637), 19–20.

FEBRUARY 9

Heaven and Hell: Or the Unchangeable State of Happiness or Misery for All Mankind in Another World (London: Printed by J. Heptinstall for John Sprint, 1700), 10–11.

FEBRUARY 10

Instructions about Heart-Work (London: Printed by J. F. for Thomas Cockerill, 1684), 310.

FEBRUARY 11

A Guide to Go to God: Or an Explanation of the Perfect Pattern of Prayer, the Lord's Prayer. Second Edition (London: Printed by G. M. for Edward Brewster, 1636), 13–14.

FEBRUARY 12

Moses His Choice, with His Eye Fixed upon Heaven (London: Printed by M. F. for R. D., 1641), 400–401.

FEBRUARY 13

Jacob's Seed: Or the Generation of Seekers and David's Delight or the Excellent on Earth (Cambridge: Printed by Roger Daniel, 1643), 11–12.

FEBRUARY 14

Looking Unto Jesus: A View of the Everlasting Gospel or the Soul's Eyeing of Jesus, as Carrying on the Great Work of Man's Salvation, from First to Last (London: Printed for Richard Chiswel, Benjamin Tooke, and Thomas Sawbridge, 1680), 22.

FEBRUARY 15

A Worthy Communicant: Or a Treatise Showing the Due Order of Receiving the Sacrament of the Lord's Supper (London: Printed by J. Raworth for Luke Fawn, 1645), 446–47.

FEBRUARY 16

The Ninth, Tenth, and Eleventh Books of Mr. Jeremiah Burroughs (London: Printed by Peter Gale, 1654), 74–75.

FEBRUARY 17

Helps to Humiliation (London: Printed by T. Cotes for Peter Whaly, 1630), 3–8.

FEBRUARY 18

The Doctrine of Zeal Explained and the Practice of Zeal Persuaded (London: Printed by A. M. for George Sanbridge, 1655), 2–3.

FEBRUARY 19

The Godly Man's Ark: Or the City of Refuge in the Day of His Distress (London: Printed for Thomas Parkhurst and for John Hancock, 1693), 2.

FEBRUARY 20

The Christian's Daily Walk in Holy Security and Peace (London: Printed for William Miller, 1690), 11–12.

FEBRUARY 21

The Works of the Right Reverend Father in God, Gervase Babington (London: Printed for Miles Flesher, 1637), 30.

FEBRUARY 22

Evidence for Heaven: Containing Infallible Signs and Real Demonstrations of Our Union with Christ and Assurance of Salvation (London: Printed for Simon Miller, 1657), 7.

FEBRUARY 23

A Practical Exposition of the Lord's Prayer (London: Printed by J. D., 1684), 109.

FEBRUARY 24

Defensive Armor Against Four of Satan's Most Fiery Darts (London: Printed for Benjamin Alsop, 1680), 212–13.

FEBRUARY 25

A Commentary or an Exposition upon the Divine Second Epistle General Written by the Blessed Apostle St. Peter (London: Printed by Richard Badger for Jacob Bloome, 1633), 14.

FEBRUARY 26

Communion with God in Two Sermons, Preached at St. Paul's: The First, September 3, 1654; the Second, March 25, 1655 (London: Printed by Evan Tyler, 1655), 16.

FEBRUARY 27

The Works of the Late Reverend and Learned William Bates (London: Printed for B. Aylmer, 1700), 927.

FEBRUARY 28

Prima, Media, and Ultima: Or the First, Middle, and Last Things (London: Printed by T. M. for Rowland Reynolds, 1674), 3–4.

FEBRUARY 29

Autarkeia: Or the Art of Divine Contentment (London: Printed for Ralph Smith, 1682), 144–46.

MARCH 1

Heaven upon Earth: Or the Best Friend in the Worst of Times (London: Printed by L. Dilbourn, 1673), 20–21.

MARCH 2

A Treatise of Love, Written by John Rogers, Minister of God's Word at Dedham in Essex (London: Printed by Mary Dawson for Joan Newberry, 1637), 15–16.

MARCH 3

Gospel-Revelation in Three Treatises: Viz., the Nature of God, the Excellency of Christ, and the Excellency of Man's Immortal Soul (London: Printed for Nathan Brook, 1660), 4–5.

MARCH 4

The Works of the Right Reverend Father in God, Gervase Babington (London: Printed for Miles Flesher, 1637), 284.

MARCH 5

Practical Divinity: Or Gospel-Light Shining Forth in Several Choice Sermons on Divers Texts of Scripture (London: Printed by T. R. and E. M. for John Stafford, 1650), 87–89.

MARCH 6

The Spiritual Taste Described and a Glimpse of Christ Discovered (London: Printed by Matthew Simmons, 1649), 55–56.

MARCH 7

A Worthy Communicant: Or a Treatise Showing the Due Order of Receiving the Sacrament of the Lord's Supper (London: Printed by J. Raworth for Luke Fawn, 1645), 348–49.

MARCH 8

The Righteous Man's Hope at Death, Considered and Improved for the Comfort of Dying Christians and the Support of Surviving Relations (London: Printed for Thomas Cockerill, 1693), 28–29.

MARCH 9

The Method of Grace in Bringing Home the Eternal Redemption (London: Printed by M. White, 1681), 12–13.

MARCH 10

The Conversion of the Soul: Or a Discourse Explaining the Nature of that Conversion Which Is Sincere, and Directing, and Persuading All to Cease Their Loving Sin and Death, and to Turn to God and Live (London: Printed by J. Astwood for Thomas Parkhurst, 1688), 1–2.

MARCH 11

God's Thoughts and Ways above Ours, Especially in the Forgiveness of Sins (London: Printed by the Widow Astwood, 1699), 35–36.

MARCH 12

A Communicant Instructed: Or Practical Directions for Worthy Receiving of the Lord's Supper (London: Printed by T. R. and E. M. for George Calvert, 1651), 47–48.

MARCH 13

The Use and Practice of Faith: Or Faith's Universal Usefulness and Quickening Influence into Every Kind and Degree of the Christian Life (London: Printed by A. Maxey, 1657), 13.

MARCH 14

The Works of George Swinnock (vol. 1; London: Printed by James Nichol, 1868), 97–98.

MARCH 15

The Soul's Conflict with Itself and Victory over Itself by Faith (London: Printed for R. D., 1658), 365–66.

MARCH 16

A Key of Heaven: The Lord's Prayer Opened, and So Applied, That a Christian May Learn How to Pray, and to Procure All Things Which May Make for the Glory of God, and the Good of Himself, and of His Neighbor (London: Printed by Thomas Harper, 1633), 216–18.

MARCH 17

Looking Unto Jesus: A View of the Everlasting Gospel or the Soul's Eyeing of Jesus, as Carrying on the Great Work of Man's Salvation from First to Last (London: Printed for Richard Chiswel, Benjamin Tooke, and Thomas Sawbridge, 1680), 18–19.

MARCH 18

Moses His Choice, with His Eye Fixed upon Heaven (London: Printed by M. F. for R. D., 1641), 357–58.

MARCH 19

A Plain and Familiar Exposition of the Ten Commandments (London: Printed by Thomas Man, Paul Man, and Jonah Man, 1632), 1–2.

MARCH 20

The Christian's Directory, Tending to Guide Him in Those Several Conditions Which God's Providence May Cast Him Into (London: Printed for John Rothwell, 1653), 9–10.

MARCH 21

The Godly Man's Ark: Or a City of Refuge in the Day of His Distress (London: Printed for Thomas Parkhurst, 1693), 89–90.

MARCH 22

A Discourse of Closet (or Secret) Prayer from Matthew VI:6 (London: Printed for Jonathan Robinson and Thomas Cockerill, 1691), 36–38.

MARCH 23

The True Christian's Love of the Unseen Christ: Or a Discourse Chiefly Tending to Excite and Promote the Decaying Love of Christ in the Hearts of Christians (London: Printed by J. Atwood for Samuel Sprint, 1689), 1–3.

MARCH 24

A Rebuke to Backsliders and a Spur for Loiterers (London: Printed by J. Astwood for John Hancock, 1684), 69–70.

MARCH 25

Moses His Choice, with His Eye Fixed upon Heaven (London: Printed by M. F. for R. D., 1641), 57–58.

MARCH 26

The Saints' Sure and Perpetual Guide: Or a Treatise Concerning the Word (London: Printed by E. Purstowe for Rapha Harford, 1634), 45–46.

MARCH 27

A Guide to Go to God: Or an Explanation of the Perfect Pattern of Prayer, the Lord's Prayer. Second Edition (London: Printed by G. M. for Edward Brewster, 1636), 76–77.

MARCH 28

Eighteen Sermons Preached upon Several Texts of Scripture (London: Printed for Thomas Parkhurst, 1674), 51–52.

MARCH 29

The Nature and Principles of Love as the End of the Commandment (London, 1673), 40–41.

MARCH 30

The Conversion of the Soul: Or a Discourse Explaining the Nature of That Conversion Which Is Sincere, and Directing, and Persuading All to Cease Their Loving Sin and Death, and to Turn to God and Live (London: Printed by J. Astwood for Thomas Parkhurst, 1688), 55–56.

MARCH 31

The Christian's Charter: Showing the Privileges of a Believer (London: Printed for Ralph Smith, 1665), 111–13.

APRIL 1

Looking Unto Jesus: A View of the Everlasting Gospel: Or the Soul's Eyeing of Jesus, as Carrying on the Great Work of Man's Salvation from First to Last (London: Printed for Richard Chiswel, Benjamin Tooke, and Thomas Sawbridge, 1680), 317.

APRIL 2

The Spiritual Taste Described and a Glimpse of Christ Discovered (London: Printed by Matthew Simmons, 1649), 69–70.

APRIL 3

A Worthy Communicant: Or a Treatise Showing the Due Order of Receiving the Sacrament of the Lord's Supper (London: Printed by J. Raworth for Luke Fawn, 1645), 365–67.

APRIL 4

Heaven upon Earth: Or the Best Friend in the Worst of Times (London: Printed by L. Dilbourn, 1673), 73–75.

APRIL 5

Sips of Sweetness: Or Consolation for Weak Believers (London: Printed for R. I., 1652), 1–3.

APRIL 6

The True Christians' Love of the Unseen Christ: Or a Discourse Chiefly Tending to Excite and Promote the Decaying Love of Christ in the Hearts of Christians (London: Printed by J. Atwood for Samuel Sprint, 1689), 11–13.

APRIL 7

The Wells of Salvation Opened: Or a Treatise Discovering the Nature, Preciousness, Usefulness of Gospel Promises, and Rules for the Right Application of Them (London: Printed by E. M. for Ralph Smith, 1659), 62–63.

APRIL 8

The Works of the Late Reverend and Pious Mr. Thomas Gouge (London: Printed by Thomas Braddyll, 1706), 191–92.

APRIL 9

Christ's Famous Titles and a Believer's Golden Chain (London: Printed for the Use of Private Families, Especially His Friends in Devon, 1687), 1–2.

APRIL 10

A Treatise of Love, Written by John Rogers, Minister of God's Word at Dedham in Essex (London: Printed by Mary Dawson for Joan Newberry, 1637), 5–7.

APRIL 11

The Lord's Last-Sufferings Showed in the Lord's Supper: Or an Historical Account of Christ's Sorrows in the Garden, Trial in the Ecclesiastical, Political Court, Execution at Golgotha, Practically Improved (London: Printed for John Dunton, 1682), 287–88.

APRIL 12

The Christian's Charter: Showing the Privileges of a Believer (London: Printed for Ralph Smith, 1665), 29–30.

APRIL 13

Several Discourses Concerning the Actual Providence of God (London: Printed by Thomas Parkhurst, 1678), 617.

APRIL 14

Three Divine Sisters (London: Printed by Thomas Purfoot for Clement Knight, 1616), 6–7.

APRIL 15

The Dead Saint Speaking to Saints and Sinners Living (London: Printed by Robert Ibbitson for Thomas Parkhurst, 1657).

APRIL 16

The Use and Practice of Faith: Or Faith's Universal Usefulness and Quickening Influence into Every Kind and Degree of the Christian Life (London: Printed by A. Maxey, 1657), 364.

APRIL 17

The Complete Works of William Bates (vol. 3; London: Printed for James Black, 1815), 14–15.

APRIL 18

The Spiritual Taste Described and a Glimpse of Christ Discovered (London: Printed by Matthew Simmons, 1649), 76–77.

APRIL 19

The Works of George Swinnock (vol. 1; London: James Nichol, 1868), 105.

APRIL 20

The True Christian's Love of the Unseen Christ: Or a Discourse Chiefly Tending to Excite and Promote the Decaying Love of Christ in the Hearts of Christians (London: Printed by J. Atwood for Samuel Sprint, 1689), 104–5.

APRIL 21

The Righteous Man's Hope at Death, Considered and Improved for the Comfort of Dying Christians and the Support of Surviving Relations (London: Printed for Thomas Cockerill, 1693), 97–98.

APRIL 22

The Spiritual Taste Described and a Glimpse of Christ Discovered (London: Printed by Matthew Simmons, 1649), 39.

APRIL 23

The Wells of Salvation Opened: Or a Treatise Discovering the Nature, Preciousness, Usefulness of Gospel Promises, and Rules for the Right Application of Them (London: Printed by E. M. for Ralph Smith, 1659), 81–83.

APRIL 24

A Plain and Familiar Exposition of the Ten Commandments (London: Printed by Thomas Man, Paul Man, and Jonah Man, 1632), 14.

APRIL 25

A Guide to Go to God: Or an Explanation of the Perfect Pattern of Prayer, the Lord's Prayer. Second Edition (London: Printed by G. M. for Edward Brewster, 1636), 106.

APRIL 26

Moses His Choice, with His Eye Fixed upon Heaven (London: Printed by M. F. for R. D., 1641), 62–63.

APRIL 27

A Key of Heaven: The Lord's Prayer Opened, and So Applied, that a Christian May Learn How to Pray, and to Procure All Things Which May Make for the Glory of God, and the

Good of Himself, and of His Neighbor (London: Printed by Thomas Harper, 1633), 132–36.

APRIL 28

Looking unto Jesus: A View of the Everlasting Gospel: Or the Soul's Eyeing of Jesus, as Carrying on the Great Work of Man's Salvation from First to Last (London: Printed for Richard Chiswel, Benjamin Tooke, and Thomas Sawbridge, 1680), 20.

APRIL 29

The Conversion of the Soul: Or a Discourse Explaining the Nature of That Conversion Which Is Sincere, and Directing, and Persuading All to Cease Their Loving Sin and Death, and to Turn to God and Live (London: Printed by J. Astwood for Thomas Parkhurst, 1688), 62–63.

APRIL 30

A Key of Heaven: The Lord's Prayer Opened, and So Applied, That a Christian May Learn How to Pray, and to Procure All Things Which May Make for the Glory of God, and the Good of Himself, and of His Neighbor (London: Printed by Thomas Harper, 1633), 233–35.

MAY 1

A Treatise of Love, Written by John Rogers, Minister of God's Word at Dedham in Essex (London: Printed by Mary Dawson for Joan Newberry, 1637), 13–15.

MAY 2

Gospel-Revelation in Three Treatises: Viz., the Nature of God, the Excellency of Christ, and the Excellency of Man's Immortal Soul (London: Printed for Nathan Brook, 1660), 145.

MAY 3

Divine Opticks: Or a Treatise of the Eye, Discovering the Vices and Virtues Thereof as Also How That Organ May be Tuned, Chiefly Grounded on Psalm 119:37 (London: Printed by J. M. for H. Cripps, 1655), 10–11.

MAY 4

A Key of Heaven: The Lord's Prayer Opened, and So Applied, That a Christian May Learn How to Pray, and to Procure All Things Which May Make for the Glory of God, and the Good of Himself, and of His Neighbor (London: Printed by Thomas Harper, 1633), 136–38.

MAY 5

The Sound-Hearted Christian: Or a Treatise of Soundness of Heart (London: Printed for Nathaniel Crouch, 1670), 55–56.

MAY 6

The Christian's Charter: Showing the Privileges of a Believer (London: Printed for Ralph Smith, 1665), 68–69.

MAY 7

A Rebuke to Backsliders and a Spur for Loiterers (London: Printed by J. Astwood for John Hancock, 1684), 4–5.

MAY 8

The Works of the Late Reverend and Pious Mr. Thomas Gouge (London: Printed by Thomas Braddyll, 1706), 303.

MAY 9

A Practical Exposition of the Lord's Prayer (London: Printed by J. D., 1684), 89.

MAY 10

The Lord's Last-Sufferings Showed in the Lord's Supper: Or an Historical Account of Christ's Sorrows in the Garden, Trial in the Ecclesiastical, Political Court, Execution at Golgotha, Practically Improved (London: Printed for John Dunton, 1682), 13–16.

MAY 11

Christ All in All: Or Several Significant Similitudes by Which the Lord Jesus Christ is Described in the Scriptures (London: Printed for John Rothwell, 1660), 82–83.

MAY 12

The Works of the Late Reverend and Learned William Bates (London: Printed for B. Aylmer, 1700).

MAY 13

Works of George Swinnock (vol. 1; London: James Nichol, 1868), 109–10.

MAY 14

Of Communion with God the Father, Son, and Holy Ghost, Each Person Distinctly in Love, Grace, and Consolation: Or the Saints' Fellowship with the Father, Son, and Holy Ghost Unfolded (London: Printed for William Marshall, 1700), 31–32.

MAY 15

Defensive Armor against Four of Satan's Most Fiery Darts (London: Printed for Benjamin Alsop, 1680), 115–16.

MAY 16

Divine Opticks: Or a Treatise of the Eye, Discovering the Vices and Virtues Thereof as Also How That Organ May Be Tuned, Chiefly Grounded on Psalm 119:37 (London: Printed by J. M. for H. Cripps, 1655), 83–85.

MAY 17

Moses His Choice, with His Eye Fixed upon Heaven (London: Printed by M. F. for R. D., 1641), 171–72.

MAY 18

A Rebuke to Backsliders and a Spur for Loiterers (London: Printed by J. Astwood for John Hancock, 1684), 7–8.

MAY 19

Autarkeia: Or the Art of Divine Contentment (London: Printed for Ralph Smith, 1682), 98–99.

MAY 20

The Works of That Eminent Servant of Christ, Mr. John Bunyan, Late Minister of the Gospel and Pastor of the Congregation at Bedford (London: Printed and Are to Be Sold by William Marshall, 1692), 600.

MAY 21

How to Live, and That Well in All Estates and Times, Especially When Helps and Comforts Fail (Cambridge: Printed by John Legat, 1601), 13–15.

MAY 22

The Nature and Principles of Love as the End of the Commandment (London, 1673), 39–40.

MAY 23

The Method of Grace in Bringing Home the Eternal Redemption (London: Printed by M. White, 1681), 1–2.

MAY 24

Moses His Choice, with His Eye Fixed upon Heaven (London: Printed by M. F. for R. D., 1641), 311–12.

MAY 25

The Works of the Late Reverend and Learned William Bates (London: Printed for B. Aylmer, 1700), 287.

MAY 26

The Way to True Happiness (London: Printed for John Bartlet, 1632), 89–90.

MAY 27

The Promises: Or a Treatise Showing How a Godly Christian May Support His Heart with Comfort Against All the Distresses Which by Reason of Any Afflictions or Temptations Can Befall Him in This Life (London: Printed by G. P. for Ralph Rounthwaite, 1619), 155–56.

MAY 28

A Christian's Walk and Work on Earth until He Attain to Heaven (London: Printed for Dorman Newman, 1678), 1–2.

MAY 29

The Works of That Eminent Servant of Christ, Mr. John Bunyan, Late Minister of the Gospel and Pastor of the Congregation at Bedford (London: Printed and Are to Be Sold by William Marshall, 1692), 601.

MAY 30

The Christian's Charter: Showing the Privileges of a Believer (London: Printed for Ralph Smith, 1665), 36–38.

MAY 31

Looking unto Jesus: A View of the Everlasting Gospel: Or the Soul's Eyeing of Jesus, as Carrying on the Great Work of Man's Salvation from First to Last (London: Printed for Richard Chiswel, Benjamin Tooke, and Thomas Sawbridge, 1680), 47.

JUNE 1

A Treatise of Love, Written by John Rogers, Minister of God's Word at Dedham in Essex (London: Printed by Mary Dawson for Joan Newberry, 1637), 28–30.

JUNE 2

Communion with God in Two Sermons Preached at Paul's: The First, September 3, 1654; the Second, March 25, 1655 (London: Printed by Evan Tyler, 1655), 25–26.

JUNE 3

The Spiritual Taste Described and a Glimpse of Christ Discovered (London: Printed by Matthew Simmons, 1649), 208–9.

JUNE 4

Defensive Armor Against Four of Satan's Most Fiery Darts (London: Printed for Benjamin Alsop, 1680), 312–14.

JUNE 5

A Rebuke to Backsliders and a Spur for Loiterers (London: Printed by J. Astwood for John Hancock, 1684), 10–11.

JUNE 6

Evidence for Heaven: Containing Infallible Signs and Real Demonstrations of Our Union with Christ and Assurance of Salvation (London: Printed for Simon Miller, 1657), 23–24.

JUNE 7

A Plea for the Godly, Wherein Is Shown the Excellency of a Righteous Person (London: Printed by A. Maxwell for Thomas Parkhurst, 1672), 15–17.

JUNE 8

Works of George Swinnock (vol. 1; London: James Nichol, 1868), 141.

JUNE 9

Of Communion with God the Father, Son, and Holy Ghost, Each Person Distinctly in Love, Grace, and Consolation: Or the Saints' Fellowship with the Father, Son, and Holy Ghost Unfolded (London: Printed for William Marshall, 1700), 33.

JUNE 10

Moses His Choice, with His Eye Fixed upon Heaven (London: Printed by M. F. for R. D., 1641), 48–50.

JUNE 11

The Way to True Happiness (London: Printed for John Bartlet, 1632), 160–61.

JUNE 12

A Christian's Walk and Work on Earth until He Attain to Heaven (London: Printed for Dorman Newman, 1678), 17–18.

JUNE 13

The Duty and Blessing of a Tender Conscience: Plainly Stated and Earnestly Recommended to All that Regard Acceptance with God, and the Prosperity of Their Souls (London: Printed by J. R., 1691), 23–24.

JUNE 14

The Works of That Eminent Servant of Christ, Mr. John Bunyan, Late Minister of the Gospel and Pastor of the Congregation at Bedford (London: Printed and Are to Be Sold by William Marshall, 1692), 603.

JUNE 15

A Practical Exposition of the Lord's Prayer (London: Printed by J. D., 1684), 124–25.

JUNE 16

Divine Opticks: Or a Treatise of the Eye, Discovering the Vices and Virtues Thereof as Also How That Organ May Be Tuned, Chiefly Grounded on Psalm 119:37 (London: Printed by J. M. for H. Cripps, 1655), 89–91.

JUNE 17

The Christian's Charter: Showing the Privileges of a Believer (London: Printed for Ralph Smith, 1665), 61–63.

JUNE 18

The Works of the Late Reverend and Learned William Bates (London: Printed for B. Aylmer, 1700), 278.

JUNE 19

Divine Opticks: Or a Treatise of the Eye, Discovering the Vices and Virtues Thereof as Also How That Organ May Be Tuned, Chiefly Grounded on Psalm 119:37 (London: Printed by J. M. for H. Cripps, 1655), 47–48.

JUNE 20

The Method of Grace in Bringing Home the Eternal Redemption (London: Printed by M. White, 1681), 23–24.

JUNE 21

Christ's Famous Titles and a Believer's Golden Chain (London: Printed for the Use of Private Families, Especially His Friends in Devon, 1687), 10–11.

JUNE 22

A Discovery of Glorious Love or the Love of Christ to Believers Opened in the Truth, Transcendency, and Sweetness Thereof, Together with the Necessity That Lies Upon Every Believer to Strive after the Spiritual and Experimental Knowledge of it (London: Printed for R. I., 1655), 85–86.

JUNE 23

Practical Divinity: Or Gospel-Light Shining Forth in Several Choice Sermons on Diverse Texts of Scripture (London: Printed by T. R. and E. M. for John Stafford, 1650), 174–75.

JUNE 24

The Golden Book of John Owen (London: Printed by Hodder and Stoughton, 1904), 101.

JUNE 25

The Godly Man's Ark: Or a City of Refuge in the Day of His Distress (London: Printed for Thomas Parkhurst, 1693), 44–45.

JUNE 26

The Duty and Blessing of a Tender Conscience: Plainly Stated and Earnestly Recommended to All That Regard Acceptance with God, and the Prosperity of Their Souls (London: Printed by J. R., 1691), 48–49.

JUNE 27

Heaven and Hell: Or the Unchangeable State of Happiness or Misery for All Mankind in Another World (London: Printed by J. Heptinstall for John Sprint, 1700), 9–10.

JUNE 28

Moses His Choice, with His Eye Fixed upon Heaven (London: Printed by M. F. for R. D., 1641), 173–74.

JUNE 29

A Rebuke to Backsliders and a Spur for Loiterers (London: Printed by J. Astwood for John Hancock, 1684), 15.

JUNE 30

A Key of Heaven: The Lord's Prayer Opened, and So Applied, That a Christian May Learn How to Pray, and to Procure All Things Which May Make for the Glory of God, and the Good of Himself, and of His Neighbor (London: Printed by Thomas Harper, 1633), 158–61.

JULY 1

A Rebuke to Backsliders and a Spur for Loiterers (London: Printed by J. Astwood for John Hancock, 1684), 32–33.

JULY 2

A Practical Exposition of the Lord's Prayer (London: Printed by J. D., 1684), 92–93.

JULY 3

The Works of the Late Reverend and Learned William Bates (London: Printed for B. Aylmer, 1700), 559.

JULY 4

Works of George Swinnock (vol. 1; London: James Nichol, 1868), 163–64.

JULY 5

The Way to True Happiness (London: Printed for John Bartlet, 1632), 202–3.

JULY 6

A Christian's Walk and Work on Earth until He Attain to Heaven (London: Printed for Dorman Newman, 1678), 66–67.

JULY 7

Christ's Famous Titles and a Believer's Golden Chain (London: Printed for the Use of Private Families, Especially His Friends in Devon, 1687), 15–16.

JULY 8

The Works of That Eminent Servant of Christ, Mr. John Bunyan, Late Minister of the Gospel and Pastor of the Congregation at Bedford (London: Printed and Are to Be Sold by William Marshall, 1692), 218.

JULY 9

A Plea for the Godly, Wherein Is Shown the Excellency of a Righteous Person (London: Printed by A. Maxwell for Thomas Parkhurst, 1672), 20–21.

JULY 10

Of Communion with God the Father, Son, and Holy Ghost, Each Person Distinctly in Love, Grace, and Consolation: Or the Saint's Fellowship with the Father, Son, and Holy Ghost Unfolded (London: Printed for William Marshall, 1700), 38–39.

JULY 11

God's Thoughts and Ways above Ours, Especially in the Forgiveness of Sins (London: Printed by the Widow Astwood, 1699), 9–11.

JULY 12

Instructions about Heart-Work (London: Printed by J. R. for Thomas Cockerill, 1684), 274.

JULY 13

The Spirit of Prayer: Or a Discourse Wherein the Nature of Prayer Is Opened, the Kinds of Prayer are Handled, and the Right Manner of Praying Discovered (London: Printed for Thomas Parkhurst, 1674), 1–3.

JULY 14

Eleothriambos: Or the Triumph of Mercy in the Chariot of Praise (London: Printed for John Hancock, 1677), 1, 2, 11.

JULY 15

The Christian's Charter: Showing the Privileges of a Believer (London: Printed for Ralph Smith, 1665), 75–76.

JULY 16

Divine Opticks: Or a Treatise of the Eye, Discovering the Vices and Virtues Thereof as Also How That Organ May Be Tuned, Chiefly Grounded on Psalm 119:37 (London: Printed by J. M. for H. Cripps, 1655), 57–59.

JULY 17

Evidence for Heaven: Containing Infallible Signs and Real Demonstrations of Our Union with Christ and Assurance of Salvation (London: Printed for Simon Miller, 1657), 19–20.

JULY 18

The Wells of Salvation Opened: Or a Treatise Discovering the Nature, Preciousness, Usefulness of Gospel Promises, and Rules for the Right Application of Them (London: Printed by E. M. for Ralph Smith, 1659), 222–23.

JULY 19

A Rebuke to Backsliders and a Spur for Loiterers (London: Printed by J. Astwood for John Hancock, 1684), 41.

JULY 20

Moses His Choice, with His Eye Fixed upon Heaven (London: Printed by M. F. for R. D., 1641), 569–70.

JULY 21

Armilla Catechetica: Or a Chain of Principles: An Orderly Concatenation of Theological Aphorisms and Exercitations, Wherein the Chief Heads of Christian Religion Are Asserted and Improved (Cambridge: Printed by John Field, 1659), 32–33.

JULY 22

The Shepherd of Israel: Or God's Pastoral Care Over His People (London: Printed by D. Maxwell, 1658), 15–16.

JULY 23

The Sound-Hearted Christian: Or a Treatise of Soundness of Heart (London: Printed for Nathaniel Crouch, 1670), 40.

JULY 24

The Spiritual Armor (London: Printed by H. L. for R. Milbourn, 1620), 21–23.

JULY 25

The Duty and Blessing of a Tender Conscience: Plainly Stated and Earnestly Recommended to All That Regard Acceptance with God, and the Prosperity of Their Souls (London: Printed by J. R., 1691), 62–66.

JULY 26

The Christian's Daily Walk in Holy Security and Peace (London: Printed for William Miller, 1690), 23–24.

JULY 27

Heaven upon Earth: Or the Best Friend in the Worst of Times (London: Printed by L. Dilbourn, 1673), 31–32.

JULY 28

A Cordial for a Fainting Soul: Or Some Essays for the Satisfaction of Wounded Spirits Laboring Under Several Burdens (London: Printed for Richard Tomlins, 1649), 1–2.

JULY 29

Heaven and Hell: Or the Unchangeable State of Happiness or Misery for All Mankind in Another World (London: Printed by J. Heptinstall for John Sprint, 1700), 29–30.

JULY 30

The Godly Man's Ark: Or a City of Refuge in the Day of His Distress (London: Printed for Thomas Parkhurst, 1693), 58–59.

JULY 31

A Key of Heaven: The Lord's Prayer Opened, and So Applied, That a Christian May Learn How to Pray, and to Procure All Things Which May Make for the Glory of God, and the Good of Himself, and of His Neighbor (London: Printed by Thomas Harper, 1633), 298–301.

AUGUST 1

Prima, Media, and Ultima: Or the First, Middle, and Last Things (London: Printed by T. M. for Rowland Reynolds, 1674), 80.

AUGUST 2

CVIII Lectures upon the Fourth of John (London: Printed for Edward Brewster, 1656), 97.

AUGUST 3

Moses His Choice, with His Eye Fixed upon Heaven (London: Printed by M. F. for R. D., 1641), 283–84.

AUGUST 4

A Rebuke to Backsliders and a Spur for Loiterers (London: Printed by J. Astwood for John Hancock, 1684), 45.

AUGUST 5

A Plea for the Godly, Wherein Is Shown the Excellency of a Righteous Person (London: Printed by A. Maxwell for Thomas Parkhurst, 1672), 32–33.

AUGUST 6

The Taming of the Tongue (London: Printed by Thomas Purfoot for Clement Knight, 1616), 31.

AUGUST 7

Christian Behavior: Or the Fruits of True Christianity (London: Printed for F. Smith, 1663), 22–23.

AUGUST 8

A Practical Exposition of the 130th Psalm (London: Printed for Nathanial Ponder, 1680), 74–75.

AUGUST 9

Practical Divinity: Or Gospel-Light Shining Forth in Several Choice Sermons on Divers Texts of Scripture (London: Printed by T. R. and E. M. for John Stafford, 1650), 59–60.

AUGUST 10

The Rise, Race, and Royalty of the Kingdom of God in the Soul of Man (London: Printed for Thomas Cockerill, 1683), 159.

AUGUST 11

Armilla Catechetica: Or a Chain of Principles: An Orderly Concatenation of Theological Aphorisms and Exercitations, Wherein the Chief Heads of Christian Religion Are Asserted and Improved (Cambridge: Printed by John Field, 1659), 73–74.

AUGUST 12

Christ's Famous Titles and a Believer's Golden Chain (London: Printed for the Use of Private Families, Especially His Friends in Devon, 1687), 188–89.

AUGUST 13

A Practical Exposition of the Lord's Prayer (London: Printed by J. D., 1684), 130–31.

AUGUST 14

A Key of Heaven: The Lord's Prayer Opened, and So Applied, That a Christian May Learn How to Pray, and to Procure All Things Which May Make for the Glory of God, and the Good of Himself, and of His Neighbor (London: Printed by Thomas Harper, 1633), 311–15.

AUGUST 15

The Wells of Salvation Opened: Or a Treatise Discovering the Nature, Preciousness, Usefulness of Gospel Promises, and Rules for the Right Application of Them (London: Printed by E. M. for Ralph Smith, 1659), 37–39.

AUGUST 16

A Rebuke to Backsliders and a Spur for Loiterers (London: Printed by J. Astwood for John Hancock, 1684), 57–58.

AUGUST 17

Of Communion with God the Father, Son, and Holy Ghost, Each Person Distinctly in Love, Grace, and Consolation: Or the Saints' Fellowship with the Father, Son, and Holy Ghost Unfolded (London: Printed for William Marshall, 1700), 56–57.

AUGUST 18

The Way to True Happiness (London: Printed for John Bartlet, 1632), 283–84.

AUGUST 19

Moses His Choice, with His Eye Fixed upon Heaven (London: Printed by M. F. for R. D., 1641), 64–65.

AUGUST 20

Divine Opticks: Or a Treatise of the Eye, Discovering the Vices and Virtues Thereof as Also How That Organ May Be Tuned, Chiefly Grounded on Psalm 119:37 (London: Printed by J. M. for H. Cripps, 1655), 12–14.

AUGUST 21

A Christian's Walk and Work on Earth until He Attain to Heaven (London: Printed for Dorman Newman, 1678), 103–4.

AUGUST 22

God's Thoughts and Ways above Ours, Especially in the Forgiveness of Sins (London: Printed by the Widow Astwood, 1699), 26–27.

AUGUST 23

A Stock of Divine Knowledge, Being a Lively Description of the Divine Nature: Or the Divine Essence, Attributes, and Trinity Particularly Explained and Profitably Applied (London: Printed by T. H. for Philip Nevill, 1641), 1–3.

AUGUST 24

The Christian's Charter: Showing the Privileges of a Believer (London: Printed for Ralph Smith, 1665), 107–8.

AUGUST 25

Eighteen Sermons Preached upon Several Texts of Scripture (London: Printed for Thomas Parkhurst, 1674), 221–22.

AUGUST 26

The Progress of Saints to Full Holiness in Sundry Apostolical Aphorisms or Short Precepts Tending to Sanctification (London: Printed by W. I. for John Bartlett, 1630), 20–21.

AUGUST 27

Temptations: Their Nature, Danger, Cure (London: Printed by E. B. for John Bartlett, 1655), 358–59.

AUGUST 28

The Use and Practice of Faith: Or Faith's Universal Usefulness and Quickening Influence into Every Kind and Degree of the Christian Life (London: Printed by A. Maxey, 1657), 348–49.

AUGUST 29

Sermons of Christ: His Last Discovery of Himself (London: Printed by R. I. for Livewell Chapmen, 1657), 47–48.

AUGUST 30

Eleothriambos: Or the Triumph of Mercy in the Chariot of Praise (London: Printed for John Hancock, 1677), 14–15.

AUGUST 31

A Treatise of Love, Written by John Rogers, Minister of God's Word at Dedham in Essex (London: Printed by Mary Dawson for Joan Newberry, 1637), 7–8.

SEPTEMBER 1

A Treatise of Love, Written by John Rogers, Minister of God's Word at Dedham in Essex (London: Printed by Mary Dawson for Joan Newberry, 1637), 103–5.

SEPTEMBER 2

Evidence for Heaven: Containing Infallible Signs and Real Demonstrations of Our Union with Christ and Assurance of Salvation (London: Printed for Simon Miller, 1657), 10–11.

SEPTEMBER 3

Prima, Media, and Ultima: Or the First, Middle, and Last Things (London: Printed by T. M. for Rowland Reynolds, 1674), 79.

SEPTEMBER 4

The Conversion of the Soul: Or a Discourse Explaining the Nature of That Conversion Which Is Sincere, and Directing, and Persuading All to Cease Their Loving Sin and Death, and to Turn to God and Live (London: Printed by J. Astwood for Thomas Parkhurst, 1688), 64.

SEPTEMBER 5

The True Christian's Love of the Unseen Christ: Or a Discourse Chiefly Tending to Excite and Promote the Decaying Love of Christ in the Hearts of Christians (London: Printed by J. Atwood for Samuel Sprint, 1689), 13–15.

SEPTEMBER 6

Heaven upon Earth: Or the Best Friend in the Worst of Times (London: Printed by L. Dilbourn, 1673), 38–39.

SEPTEMBER 7

A Rebuke to Backsliders and a Spur for Loiterers (London: Printed by J. Astwood for John Hancock, 1684), 64–65.

SEPTEMBER 8

A Plea for the Godly, Wherein Is Shown the Excellency of a Righteous Person (London: Printed by A. Maxwell for Thomas Parkhurst, 1672), 35–37.

SEPTEMBER 9

Christ's Famous Titles and a Believer's Golden Chain (London: Printed for the Use of Private Families, Especially His Friends in Devon, 1687), 269–70.

SEPTEMBER 10

A Guide to Go to God: Or an Explanation of the Perfect Pattern of Prayer, the Lord's Prayer. Second Edition (London: Printed by G. M. for Edward Brewster, 1636), 92–93.

SEPTEMBER 11

A Christian's Walk and Work on Earth until He Attain to Heaven (London: Printed for Dorman Newman, 1678), 136–37.

SEPTEMBER 12

A Practical Exposition of the Lord's Prayer (London: Printed by J. D., 1684), 206–7.

SEPTEMBER 13

The Way to True Happiness (London: Printed for John Bartlet, 1632), 322–23.

SEPTEMBER 14

The Duty and Blessing of a Tender Conscience: Plainly Stated and Earnestly Recommended to All that Regard Acceptance with God, and the Prosperity of Their Souls (London: Printed by J. R., 1691), 70–71.

SEPTEMBER 15

Moses His Choice, with His Eye Fixed upon Heaven (London: Printed by M. F. for R. D., 1641), 66–67.

SEPTEMBER 16

The Sacrifice of Thankfulness (London: Printed by Thomas Purfoot for Clement Knight, 1616), 5.

SEPTEMBER 17

Sips of Sweetness: Or Consolation for Weak Believers (London: Printed for R. I., 1652), 28–30.

SEPTEMBER 18

A Plain and Familiar Exposition of the Ten Commandments (London: Printed by Thomas Man, Paul Man, and Jonah Man, 1632), 16–17.

SEPTEMBER 19

Divine Opticks: Or a Treatise of the Eye, Discovering the Vices and Virtues Thereof as Also How That Organ May Be Tuned, Chiefly Grounded on Psalm 119:37 (London: Printed by J. M. for H. Cripps, 1655), 30–31.

SEPTEMBER 20

Heaven and Hell: Or the Unchangeable State of Happiness or Misery for All Mankind in Another World (London: Printed by J. Heptinstall for John Sprint, 1700), 32–33.

SEPTEMBER 21

Instructions about Heart-Work (London: Printed by J. R. for Thomas Cockerill, 1684), 176–77.

SEPTEMBER 22

A Practical Exposition of the Lord's Prayer (London: Printed by J. D., 1684), 484–85.

SEPTEMBER 23

God's Thoughts and Ways above Ours, Especially in the Forgiveness of Sins (London: Printed by the Widow Astwood, 1699), 159–60.

SEPTEMBER 24

The Works of Henry Smith (vol. 2; London: Printed by James Nichol, 1867), 87.

SEPTEMBER 25

A Discovery of Glorious Love: Or the Love of Christ to Believers Opened in the Truth, Transcendency, and Sweetness Thereof, Together with the Necessity That Lies upon Every Believer to Strive after the Spiritual and Experimental Knowledge of It (London: Printed for R. I., 1655), 164–66.

SEPTEMBER 26

Evidence for Heaven: Containing Infallible Signs and Real Demonstrations of Our Union with Christ and Assurance of Salvation (London: Printed for Simon Miller, 1657), 56–57.

SEPTEMBER 27

The Conversion of the Soul: Or a Discourse Explaining the Nature of That Conversion Which Is Sincere, and Directing, and Persuading All to Cease Their Loving Sin and Death, and to Turn to God and Live (London: Printed by J. Astwood for Thomas Parkhurst, 1688), 69–70.

SEPTEMBER 28

A Plea for the Godly, Wherein Is Shown the Excellency of a Righteous Person (London: Printed by A. Maxwell for Thomas Parkhurst, 1672), 70–72.

SEPTEMBER 29

Moses His Choice, with His Eye Fixed upon Heaven (London: Printed by M. F. for R. D., 1641), 216–17.

SEPTEMBER 30

The Works of the Late Reverend and Pious Mr. Thomas Gouge (London: Printed by Thomas Braddyll, 1706), 23–24.

OCTOBER 1

Moses His Choice, with His Eye Fixed upon Heaven (London: Printed by M. F. for R. D., 1641), 114–15.

OCTOBER 2

A Rebuke to Backsliders and a Spur for Loiterers (London: Printed by J. Astwood for John Hancock, 1684), 86.

OCTOBER 3

Autarkeia: Or the Art of Divine Contentment (London: Printed for Ralph Smith, 1682), 27–28.

OCTOBER 4

The Saints' Sure and Perpetual Guide: Or a Treatise Concerning the Word (London: Printed by E. Purstowe for Rapha Harford, 1634), 23–24.

OCTOBER 5

A Christian's Walk and Work on Earth until He Attain to Heaven (London: Printed for Dorman Newman, 1678), 173–75.

OCTOBER 6

A Practical Exposition of the 130th Psalm (London: Printed for Nathanial Ponder, 1680), 195–96.

OCTOBER 7

Divine Opticks: Or a Treatise of the Eye, Discovering the Vices and Virtues Thereof as Also How That Organ May Be Tuned, Chiefly Grounded on Psalm 119:37 (London: Printed by J. M. for H. Cripps, 1655), 37–39.

OCTOBER 8

The Christian's Charter: Showing the Privileges of a Believer (London: Printed for Ralph Smith, 1665), 96–97.

OCTOBER 9

A Stock of Divine Knowledge, Being a Lively Description of the Divine Nature: Or the Divine Essence, Attributes, and Trinity Particularly Explained and Profitably Applied (London: Printed by T. H. for Philip Nevill, 1641), 16–17.

OCTOBER 10

Contemplative Pictures with Wholesome Precepts (London: Printed by William Hall for William Welbie, 1610), 1–11.

OCTOBER 11

Venning's Remains: Or Christ's School (London: Printed for John Hancock, 1675), 19–20.

OCTOBER 12

God's Thoughts and Ways above Ours, Especially in the Forgiveness of Sins (London: Printed by the Widow Astwood, 1699), 125–26.

OCTOBER 13

Armilla Catechetica: Or a Chain of Principles: An Orderly Concatenation of Theological Aphorisms and Exercitations, Wherein the Chief Heads of Christian Religion Are Asserted and Improved (Cambridge: Printed by John Field, 1659), 156–57.

OCTOBER 14

A Discourse of Closet (or Secret) Prayer from Matthew VI:6 (London: Printed for Jonathan Robinson and Thomas Cockerill, 1691), 8–10.

OCTOBER 15

Venning's Remains: Or Christ's School (London: Printed for John Hancock, 1675), 23–24.

OCTOBER 16

Moses His Choice, with His Eye Fixed upon Heaven (London: Printed by M. F. for R. D., 1641), 203–5.

OCTOBER 17

The Way to True Happiness (London: Printed for John Bartlet, 1632), 325.

OCTOBER 18

The Duty and Blessing of a Tender Conscience: Plainly Stated and Earnestly Recommended to All That Regard Acceptance with God, and the Prosperity of Their Souls (London: Printed by J. R., 1691), 82–84.

OCTOBER 19

CVIII Lectures upon the Fourth of John (London: Printed for Edward Brewster, 1656), 165.

OCTOBER 20

Instructions about Heart-Work (London: Printed by J. R. for Thomas Cockerill, 1684), 195–96.

OCTOBER 21

R. A. Bertram, *A Homiletic Encyclopedia* (New York: Printed by Funk and Wagnalls, 1889), 4602.

OCTOBER 22

Eleothriambos: Or the Triumph of Mercy in the Chariot of Praise (London: Printed for John Hancock, 1677), 21–22.

OCTOBER 23

Sermons and Discourses on Several Divine Subjects (London: Printed for Thomas Parkhurst, 1696), 675.

OCTOBER 24

An Exposition upon the Epistle of Jude (London: Printed by James Sherman, 1839), 169.

OCTOBER 25

A Key of Heaven: The Lord's Prayer Opened, and So Applied, That a Christian May Learn How to Pray, and to Procure All Things Which May Make for the Glory of God, and the Good of Himself, and of His Neighbor. (London: Printed by Thomas Harper, 1633), 122–23.

OCTOBER 26

Meditations and Disquisitions upon Seven Consolatory Psalms of David (London: Printed by John Dawson, 1640), 100–103.

OCTOBER 27

A Discourse about True Happiness (London: Printed by Felix Kingston, 1611), 51–52.

OCTOBER 28

Contemplative Pictures with Wholesome Precepts (London: Printed by William Hall for William Welbie, 1610), 107–13.

OCTOBER 29

The Progress of Saints to Full Holiness in Sundry Apostolical Aphorisms or Short Precepts Tending to Sanctification (London: Printed by W. I. for John Bartlett, 1630), 183.

OCTOBER 30

The Method of Grace in Bringing Home the Eternal Redemption (London: Printed by M. White, 1681), 29.

OCTOBER 31

Gospel-Revelation in Three Treatises: Viz., the Nature of God, the Excellency of Christ, and the Excellency of Man's Immortal Soul (London: Printed for Nathan Brook, 1660), 147.

NOVEMBER 1

Gospel-Revelation in Three Treatises: Viz., the Nature of God, the Excellency of Christ, and the Excellency of Man's Immortal Soul (London: Printed for Nathan Brook, 1660), 34–35.

NOVEMBER 2

The True Christian's Love of the Unseen Christ: Or a Discourse Chiefly Tending to Excite and Promote the Decaying Love of Christ in the Hearts of Christians (London: Printed by J. Atwood for Samuel Sprint, 1689), 17–18.

NOVEMBER 3

A Worthy Communicant: Or a Treatise Showing the Due Order of Receiving the Sacrament of the Lord's Supper (London: Printed by J. Raworth for Luke Fawn, 1645), 373–75.

NOVEMBER 4

Several Discourses Concerning the Actual Providence of God (London: Printed by Thomas Parkhurst, 1678), 81–82.

NOVEMBER 5

A Rebuke to Backsliders and a Spur for Loiterers (London: Printed by J. Astwood for John Hancock, 1684), 95.

NOVEMBER 6

Autarkeia: Or the Art of Divine Contentment (London: Printed for Ralph Smith, 1682), 108–9.

NOVEMBER 7

Divine Opticks: Or a Treatise of the Eye, Discovering the Vices and Virtues Thereof as Also How That Organ May Be Tuned, Chiefly Grounded on Psalm 119:37 (London: Printed by J. M. for H. Cripps, 1655), 15–17.

NOVEMBER 8

The Christian's Charter: Showing the Privileges of a Believer (London: Printed for Ralph Smith, 1665), 105–6.

NOVEMBER 9

A Practical Exposition of the Lord's Prayer (London: Printed by J. D., 1684), 117–18.

NOVEMBER 10

Vindiciae Pietatis: Or a Vindication of Godliness, in the Greatest Strictness and Spirituality of It, from the Imputations of Folly and Fancy (London: Printed for Peter Parker, 1676), 8–9.

NOVEMBER 11

Sips of Sweetness: Or Consolation for Weak Believers (London: Printed for R. I., 1652), 38–39.

NOVEMBER 12

A Practical Exposition of the 130th Psalm (London: Printed for Nathanial Ponder, 1680), 118.

NOVEMBER 13

God's Thoughts and Ways above Ours, Especially in the Forgiveness of Sins (London: Printed by the Widow Astwood, 1699), 44–45.

NOVEMBER 14

The Doctrine and Use of Repentance Necessary to Be Practiced and Used of All Who Look to Sing the Song of Moses and the Song of the Lamb Beyond the Glassy Sea (London: Printed by Felix Kingston, 1610), 1–3.

NOVEMBER 15

Contemplative Pictures with Wholesome Precepts (London: Printed by William Hall for William Welbie, 1610), 37–42.

NOVEMBER 16

Moses His Choice, with His Eye Fixed upon Heaven (London: Printed by M. F. for R. D., 1641), 154–55.

NOVEMBER 17

The Life of Faith as It Is the Evidence of Things Unseen (London: Printed by R. W. and A. M. for Francis Tyton and Jane Underhill, 1660), 42.

NOVEMBER 18

Heaven and Hell: Or the Unchangeable State of Happiness or Misery for All Mankind in Another World (London: Printed by J. Heptinstall for John Sprint, 1700), 83–86.

NOVEMBER 19

Sips of Sweetness: Or Consolation for Weak Believers (London: Printed for R. I., 1652), 78–79.

NOVEMBER 20

Moses His Choice, with His Eye Fixed upon Heaven (London: Printed by M. F. for R. D., 1641), 182–83.

NOVEMBER 21

The Christian's Daily Walk in Holy Security and Peace (London: Printed for William Miller, 1690), 35–36.

NOVEMBER 22

The Use and Practice of Faith: Or Faith's Universal Usefulness and Quickening Influence into Every Kind and Degree of the Christian Life (London: Printed by A. Maxey, 1657), 327.

NOVEMBER 23

Venning's Remains: Or Christ's School (London: Printed for John Hancock, 1675), 383.

NOVEMBER 24

The Method of Grace in Bringing Home the Eternal Redemption (London: Printed by M. White, 1681), 44–45.

NOVEMBER 25

Divine Opticks: Or a Treatise of the Eye, Discovering the Vices and Virtues Thereof as Also How That Organ May Be Tuned, Chiefly Grounded on Psalm 119:37 (London: Printed by J. M. for H. Cripps, 1655), 69–70.

NOVEMBER 26

The Works of the Pious and Profoundly Learned Joseph Mede, B.D., Sometime Fellow of Christ's College in Cambridge (London: Printed by Roger Norton for Richard Royston, 1677), 135.

NOVEMBER 27

An Exposition upon the Epistle of Jude (London: Printed by James Sherman, 1839), 97.

NOVEMBER 28

The Works of Henry Smith (vol. 2; London: Printed by James Nichol, 1867), 338–39.

NOVEMBER 29

A Stock of Divine Knowledge, Being a Lively Description of the Divine Nature: Or the Divine Essence, Attributes, and Trinity Particularly Explained and Profitably Applied (London: Printed by T. H. for Philip Nevill, 1641), 58–59.

NOVEMBER 30

The Saints' Sure and Perpetual Guide: Or a Treatise Concerning the Word (London: Printed by E. Purstowe for Rapha Harford, 1634), 37–39.

DECEMBER 1

The Promises: Or a Treatise Showing How a Godly Christian May Support His Heart with Comfort Against All the Distresses Which by Reason of Any Afflictions or Temptations Can Befall Him in This Life (London: Printed by G. P. for Ralph Rounthwaite, 1619), 19–21.

DECEMBER 2

The Branch of the Lord, the Beauty of Sion: Or the Glory of the Church, in Its Relation unto Christ (Edinburgh: Printed by Evan Tyler, 1650), 14–15.

DECEMBER 3

The Works of the Late Reverend and Learned William Bates (London: Printed for B. Aylmer, 1700), 285.

DECEMBER 4

God's Thoughts and Ways above Ours, Especially in the Forgiveness of Sins (London: Printed by the Widow Astwood, 1699), 38–39.

DECEMBER 5

A Stock of Divine Knowledge, Being a Lively Description of the Divine Nature: Or the Divine Essence, Attributes, and Trinity Particularly Explained and Profitably Applied (London: Printed by T. H. for Philip Nevill, 1641), 257–58.

DECEMBER 6

Contemplative Pictures with Wholesome Precepts (London: Printed by William Hall for William Welbie, 1610), 87–102.

DECEMBER 7

An Earnest Call to Family Religion: Or a Discourse Concerning Family Worship, Being the Substance of Eighteen Sermons (London: Printed for Thomas Parkhurst, 1694), 7–8.

DECEMBER 8

The Life of Faith as It Is the Evidence of Things Unseen (London: Printed by R. W. and A. M. for Francis Tyton and Jane Underhill, 1660), 32–33.

DECEMBER 9

Venning's Remains: Or Christ's School (London: Printed for John Hancock, 1675), 67–68.

DECEMBER 10

Sermons of Christ: His Last Discovery of Himself (London: Printed by R. I. for Livewell Chapmen, 1657), 94–95.

DECEMBER 11

The Rise, Race, and Royalty of the Kingdom of God in the Soul of Man (London: Printed for Thomas Cockerill, 1683), 319.

DECEMBER 12

The Wells of Salvation Opened: Or a Treatise Discovering the Nature, Preciousness, Usefulness of Gospel Promises, and Rules for the Right Application of Them (London: Printed by E. M. for Ralph Smith, 1659), 86–87.

DECEMBER 13

A Discovery of Glorious Love or the Love of Christ to Believers Opened in the Truth, Transcendency, and Sweetness Thereof, Together with the Necessity That Lies upon Every Believer to Strive after the Spiritual and Experimental Knowledge of It (London: Printed for R. I., 1655), 1–2.

DECEMBER 14

The Method of Grace in Bringing Home the Eternal Redemption (London: Printed by M. White, 1681), 51.

DECEMBER 15

Eleothriambos: Or the Triumph of Mercy in the Chariot of Praise (London: Printed for John Hancock, 1677), 158–59.

DECEMBER 16

The Wells of Salvation Opened: Or a Treatise Discovering the Nature, Preciousness, Usefulness of Gospel Promises, and Rules for the Right Application of Them (London: Printed by E. M. for Ralph Smith, 1659), 49–51.

DECEMBER 17

Autarkeia: Or the Art of Divine Contentment (London: Printed for Ralph Smith, 1682), 35–36.

DECEMBER 18

The Spirit of Prayer: Or a Discourse wherein the Nature of Prayer Is Opened, the Kinds of Prayer Are Handled, and the Right Manner of Praying Discovered (London: Printed for Thomas Parkhurst, 1674), 12–14.

DECEMBER 19

Divine Opticks: Or a Treatise of the Eye, Discovering the Vices and Virtues Thereof as Also How That Organ May Be Tuned, Chiefly Grounded on Psalm 119:37 (London: Printed by J. M. for H. Cripps, 1655), 71–73.

DECEMBER 20

Moses His Choice, with His Eye Fixed upon Heaven (London: Printed by M. F. for R. D., 1641), 83–84.

DECEMBER 21

The Christian's Daily Walk in Holy Security and Peace (London: Printed for William Miller, 1690), 27.

DECEMBER 22

Heaven and Hell: Or the Unchangeable State of Happiness or Misery for All Mankind in Another World (London: Printed by J. Heptinstall for John Sprint, 1700), 55–57.

DECEMBER 23

Practical Divinity: Or Gospel-Light Shining Forth in Several Choice Sermons on Divers Texts of Scripture (London: Printed by T. R. and E. M. for John Stafford, 1650), 90–91.

DECEMBER 24

A Christian's Walk and Work on Earth until He Attain to Heaven (London: Printed for Dorman Newman, 1678), 189–90.

DECEMBER 25

Christ His Star: Or the Wise-Men's Oblation (London: Printed by Thomas Purfoot for Clement Knight, 1616), 92–93.

DECEMBER 26

A Guide to Go to God: Or an Explanation of the Perfect Pattern of Prayer, the Lord's Prayer. Second Edition (London: Printed by G. M. for Edward Brewster, 1636), 74.

DECEMBER 27

The Saints' Sure and Perpetual Guide: Or a Treatise Concerning the Word (London: Printed by E. Purstowe for Rapha Harford, 1634), 43–44.

DECEMBER 28

A Practical Exposition of the Lord's Prayer (London: Printed by J. D., 1684), 119–20.

DECEMBER 29

Autarkeia: Or the Art of Divine Contentment (London: Printed for Ralph Smith, 1682), 92–93.

DECEMBER 30

The Christian's Directory, Tending to Guide Him in Those Several Conditions Which God's Providence May Cast Him Into (London: Printed for John Rothwell, 1653), 47–48.

DECEMBER 31

Evidence for Heaven: Containing Infallible Signs and Real Demonstrations of Our Union with Christ and Assurance of Salvation (London: Printed for Simon Miller, 1657), 119–20.

More about the English Puritans

Thomas Adams (c. 1583–c.1656) Adams was called "the prose Shakespeare of the Puritan theologians." He was born five years before the Spanish Armada sailed for England. He was trained in the finest schools, served as a preacher in Willington, Bedfordshire, and two years later, became vicar of Wingrave, Bucks. His most sustained effort, and largest work, was *A Commentary; Or, Exposition upon the Divine Second Epistle General, Written by the Blessed Apostle St. Peter.* The original commentary spanned 1,656 pages.

Richard Alleine (1611–1691) The author of *A Vindication of Godliness,* a sustained defense of personal piety, Alleine was the rector of Batcombe in Somersetshire, where he ministered for more than twenty years. He was zealous for the work of the Lord, but was ejected from his pulpit in 1662. He is often construed as the brother of Joseph Alleine, but in reality was his uncle. Alleine's works are probing, convicting, and edifying. He is best known for his practical writings, which normally appeared under the insignia "R. A."

Isaac Ambrose (1604–1664) Ambrose was the son of the clergyman Richard Ambrose, and was probably descended from the Ambroses of Lowick in Furness, a well-known Roman Catholic family. He graduated from Brazen-Nose College, Oxford, in 1624. He ministered in Lancashire for the rest of his life, married, and had several daughters. His most famous work is *Looking unto Jesus.* As a religious writer, Ambrose has a vividness and freshness of imagination equaled by few others. Many who have no love for Puritan doctrine or sympathy with Puritan experience have appreciated the pathos and beauty of his writings.

Samuel Annesley (c. 1620–1696) The father of Susanna Wesley, Annesley was born in Warwick around 1620. He received both his Bachelor and Master of Arts from Queen's College, Oxford. He was a chaplain at sea for a time, and upon returning to England ministered in Kent. He served at St. Gile's Cripplegate for several years but was ejected in 1662.

Annesley had a large family and cared for them with great zeal and learning. His few surviving sermons show him to have been a highly cultured and eminently pious Christian. He also wrote the preface to Richard Alleine's *Instructions about Heart-work,* and another to Elisha Coles's *Discourse on Divine Sovereignty.*

John Arrowsmith (1602–1659) Born near Newcastle-on-Tyne, Arrowsmith received a classical education at St. John's College, Cambridge. He sat as a member of the Westminster Assembly in 1643 and became master of St. John's in 1644. In 1647 he was vice-chancellor of Cambridge University, in 1651 Regius Professor of Divinity at Cambridge, and in 1658 became master of Trinity College. His best known work, *A Chain of Principles,* discusses six theological aphorisms. Benjamin Whichcote, the Cambridge philosopher, said of Arrowsmith: "He is my friend of choice, a companion of my special delight, whom in former years I have acquainted with all my heart."

Simeon Ashe (d. 1662) Ashe was a Presbyterian divine educated at Emmanuel College, Cambridge. He first settled in Staffordshire and then in London, where he ministered for twenty-three years. He was one of the deputies who went to congratulate Charles II at Breda. Aside from miscellaneous sermons, Ashe's primary literary achievement rests in having collected, edited, and published several farewell sermons by eminent divines. *An Exact Collection of Farewell Sermons Preached by the Late London Ministers* was printed in 1662 and contains farewells from Edmund Calamy, Thomas Manton, William Jenkyn, Thomas Watson, and others.

Gervase Babington (1550–1610) Gervase Babington was born in Nottingham. He studied at Trinity College under the tutelage of William Whitgift, Archbishop of Canterbury and an English Reformer. He later became a fellow at Trinity and there earned his Doctor of Divinity degree. He served as chaplain to the Earl of Pembroke and became bishop of Llandaff in Wales. In 1595, Queen Elizabeth appointed him to the bishopric in Exeter. Babington was revered as "a true pattern of piety to the people."

Sir Richard Baker (1568–1645) Richard Baker was a man of eminent piety but gross misfortune. At the pinnacle of his career, he even entertained Queen Elizabeth at the Baker family seat of Sissinghurst. But when he was reported to be a debtor to the crown, his estate was seized and, facing insurmountable debt, he was placed in the Fleet prison. His imprisonment turned out for the better as it was there that Baker began his literary career. His *Meditations and Disquisitions* are full of evangelical sense and piety. Baker is best known for his *Chronicle of the Kings of England from the Time of the Romans' Government unto the Death of King James*. He died in prison on February 18, 1645.

William Bates (1625–1699) Bates was educated at Cambridge and admitted Doctor of Divinity in 1660. After the restoration of the Stuart monarchy, he was appointed chaplain to Charles II and was, for a time, minister of St. Dunstan's. He was ejected from that post in 1662. The latter part of his life was spent in Hackney, where he died on July 19, 1699. Bates is affectionately known as "The Queen's Puritan." His works were eagerly read by William and Mary, King and Queen of England. When Mary died from smallpox in 1694, Bates preached *A Sermon Preached upon the Much Lamented Death of Our Late Gracious Sovereign, Queen Mary*.

Richard Baxter (1615–1691) Baxter was one of the most prolific Puritan authors. He penned almost two hundred works, an amazing achievement for one largely self-educated. Baxter was ordained in the Church of England and served a congregation in Kidderminster, near the Welsh border. During the Civil War, he served as a chaplain to a regiment in Cromwell's forces. For years following the Great Ejection of 1662, Baxter was a leading spokesman for the nonconformists. His criticisms of the English church, however, brought him into serious trouble with the authorities. He was thus silenced from preaching but continued to minister through the written word. While most of the Puritans admired Baxter's godly life, they seriously questioned his unorthodox doctrine of justification. Baxter maintained that some element of sanctification preceded final justification, an idea abhorrent to the Puritan mainstream.

Paul Baynes (d. 1617) Baynes was born in London and educated at Christ's College, Cambridge. For some time Baynes lived unrepentantly. His father took strict measures to ensure that he would not receive the family fortune unless he was to "forsake his evil ways and become steady." Shortly after his father's death, Baynes became an heir of heaven and several years afterward was chosen successor to William Perkins at St. Andrew's, Cambridge. Baynes was a powerful Puritan and gave sound counsel to those who sought it. His *Christian Letters* are full of sage advice. Baynes is best known for his commentary on Ephesians.

Richard Bernard (1568–1641) Bernard was born in Epworth, Lincolnshire (where Samuel Wesley later ministered, and where John Wesley was born). He received his Master of Arts degree from Christ's College, Cambridge, in 1598. When young, two daughters of Sir Christopher Wray, Lord Chief-Justice of England, took notice of Bernard and paid for his education. He mentioned their kindnesses to him in several of the dedicatory epistles to his books. Bernard ministered as vicar in Worksop, Nottinghamshire, until 1613, when he was called to Batcombe in Somersetshire. Bernard's best work is *The Faithful Shepherd,* in which he details the excellency, necessity, and duty of the pastoral ministry.

Robert Bolton (1572–1631) Bolton was born at Blackbourne in Lancashire, on Whitsunday in 1572. He was educated at Lincoln College and Brazen-Nose College. For some time he was a teaching fellow at Brazen-Nose, where he excelled in logic and philosophy. Considered one of the best scholars of his time, Bolton wrote works on casuistry, Christian living, and the four last things (death, judgment, heaven, hell). *A Discourse on Happiness* was Bolton's most popular work, which went through at least six editions in his lifetime. The seventeenth-century diarist John Ward wrote of him: "Nazianzen's commendation of Basil might be Bolton's: 'He thundered in his life and lightened in his conversation.' "

Samuel Bolton (c. 1606–1654) Samuel Bolton was educated at Christ's College, Cambridge, and held several pastorates in London. He was nominated one of the additional members of the Westminster Assembly. He later served as master of Christ's College, Cambridge. Even with no ministerial charge of his own, he preached every Lord's Day for many years in various pulpits. Bolton died in 1654 and was buried at St. Martin's Church in London. Though a man of great learning, he said that he "hoped to rise in the Day of Judgment and appear before God not as a doctor, but as a humble Christian." His best work is a compilation of shorter treatises he wrote for the press. *The Dead Saint Speaking to Saints and Sinners Living* was published in 1657 and includes discussions on sin, faith, love, sincerity, and the power of God.

John Bunyan (1628–1688) John Bunyan is probably the best known and most loved of the English Puritans. His *Pilgrim's Progress* has been reprinted hundreds of times and has been the constant companion of many children. Known as the "immortal dreamer," Bunyan was imprisoned several times for preaching the gospel. He considered it his greatest honor to suffer for Christ's cause. He suffered from a severe case of what we now call obsessive-compulsive disorder. His struggles are recorded in his autobiographical work *Grace Abounding to the Chief of Sinners.* Remarkably, Bunyan did not know the original languages of the Scriptures, but made do with a few lexicons and dictionaries. His prose material is some of the best of the period. Admired by secular as well as religious scholars, Bunyan made an indelible mark on English history.

Jeremiah Burroughs (1599–1647) Burroughs, another of the prolific Puritans, was a popular and successful preacher in London. He represented the Independent cause at the Westminster Assembly, and spent six years preaching at a small country church. For a time he ministered in the English church at Rotterdam, and upon returning to London he became the "morning star" of the church in Stepney. Burroughs was one of the best Puritan orators of his time; he had a special love for the church fathers and Christian history. Cotton Mather remarked that Burroughs's *Moses His Choice* "will not make you complain that you have lost your time in conversing with it."

Nicholas Byfield (1579–1622) A native of Warwickshire, Byfield entered Exeter College, Oxford, in Lent term 1596. He spent four years at the college but did not graduate. He intended to enter the ministry in Ireland but was prevailed upon to preach in Chester. His sermons at St. Peter's Church made him extremely popular. For fifteen years before his death he suffered from a stone in the bladder, which caused great pain. He died on September 8, 1622. During his lifetime he published eight works; six more were published posthumously. He is best known for *An Exposition upon the Epistle to the Colossians*, the compilation of seven years' worth of daily sermons.

Edmund Calamy (1600–1666) Calamy was educated at Pembroke Hall, Cambridge. He was successively bishop's chaplain at Ely, vicar of St. Mary, vicar of Swaffham Prior, and lecturer at Bury St. Edmunds. At first, Calamy was indifferent to high church ceremonies, but later opposed the strict policies of William Laud. Calamy was a prominent member of the Westminster Assembly. He was chosen by Oliver Cromwell to be one of his counselors, but opposed the Protector's desire for total power. Calamy was instrumental in restoring Charles II to the English throne, and preached before Parliament the day prior to the vote to invite Charles to return. He was ejected for nonconformity in 1662, and spent his remaining years in quiet retirement.

Richard Capel (1586–1656) Capel was descended from an ancient Herefordshire family. He was born at Gloucester and became a commoner of St. Alban Hall, Oxford, in 1601. He received his Master of Arts degree from Magdalen College. While in the university he was much consulted by his peers on theological matters. His favorite pupil was William Pemble. When James I enforced the "Book of Sports," Capel refused to read it from the pulpit. He willingly resigned his ministry and obtained a license to practice medicine from the bishop of Gloucester. He then settled in Pitchcombe, Brook, where he had an estate. Benjamin Book wrote that Capel "was sometimes a Boanerges, the son of thunder; but more commonly a Barnabas, the son of consolation." He died on September 21, 1656. His principal work was *Temptations: Their Nature, Danger, and Cure.*

Joseph Caryl (1602–1673) Joseph Caryl was born in London and educated at Exeter College, Oxford. He preached at Lincoln's Inn for several years. He was appointed a member of the Westminster Assembly in 1643. Ejected by the Act of Uniformity of 1662, he began a private congregation in his neighborhood that totaled 136 members at the time of his death. Caryl is best known for his commentary on Job. He preached on the book of Job for more than twenty-five years, averaging three sermons a month.

David Clarkson (1622–1686) Clarkson was born at Bradford, Yorkshire, where he was baptized on March 3, 1622. He became a fellow of Clare Hall, Cambridge, where he tutored many individuals. The famous John Tillotson was among his students and eventually succeeded him in the fellowship. Clarkson ministered at Mortlake, Surrey, until 1662 when he was ejected for nonconformity. For some time he was an assistant to John Owen in London. He succeeded the "Prince of Puritans" after Owen's death in 1683. Clarkson published several works during his lifetime. These were collected and printed in the nineteenth century in three volumes.

John Collinges (1623–1690) John Collinges was the son of Edward Collinges, a famous clergyman. Collinges spent his early years under the ministry of John Rogers of Dedham, the "fiery" Puritan. Collinges, a Presbyterian, wrote several works of controversy early in his ministry; later his writings turned more to pastoral matters. He is best known for his sermons on the Song of Solomon.

Timothy Cruso (1656–1697) Timothy Cruso was born in Middlesex. He was educated at Newington Green Academy, where his tutor was Charles Morton, later vice president of Harvard College. One of his classmates was Daniel Defoe. Cruso ministered in London, where he strived to "preach all in practicals." His most famous work is *Sermons on the Rich Man and Lazarus.*

Robert Dingley (1619–1660) Dingley was educated at Magdalen College, Oxford. Though at first a staunch Anglican, he became a Puritan and rejected Anglican worship. He was rector of Brightstone on the Isle of Wight, where he had a reputation as a great practical preacher. His opposition to ignorant and scandalous ministers, caused him to be censured. He died in 1660, and was buried in the chancel of his church.

John Dod (c.1549–1645) John Dod was educated at Jesus College, Cambridge. While there, he debated so well that the faculty of Oxford invited him to join them, an offer Dod declined. He continued at Cambridge for sixteen years as a student, and then as a teaching fellow. In 1579, he was installed as the pastor of Hanwell, Oxfordshire, a position he held for twenty years. The famous Puritan casuist Richard Greenham was his father-in-law. Dod is most famous for his *Exposition upon the Ten Commandments,* which he wrote with Robert Cleaver.

Samuel Doolittle (c. 1673–c. 1730) The son of Thomas and Mary Doolittle, Samuel was raised in a godly Puritan home with several sisters. Little is known about his life. He printed two sermons before 1700: *The Righteous Man's Hope at Death,* which he preached on the occasion of his mother's death on December 16, 1692, and *A Sermon Occasioned by the Late Earthquake,* which refers to the September 8, 1692, earthquake that devastated many areas in and about London. Doolittle seems to have inherited his father's ability to paint striking verbal portraits of eternal truths.

Thomas Doolittle (1630–1707) Thomas Doolittle was born at Kidderminster in 1630. Richard Baxter's work *The Saints' Everlasting Rest* was instrumental in his conversion. Doolittle was educated at Pembroke Hall, Cambridge. Baxter later encouraged Doolittle to enter the ministry, and Doolittle served as Baxter's assistant. He took his first pastorate in London in 1653, and later began a boarding school, which soon had so many students that larger facilities were needed. After the plague raged through London in 1665, Doolittle opened a meeting house near Bunhill Fields. He preached twice every Lord's Day, and on Wednesdays lectured on the Westminster Assembly's smaller catechism. He was assisted in this ministry by Thomas Vincent. Doolittle died in 1707; he was the last of the ejected ministers to be buried at Bunhill Fields.

John Durant (c. 1620–c. 1660) Little is known about Durant. He was a preacher at Sandwich in Kent in 1644. Two years later he moved to Canterbury, where he preached at first in a church and then in a private room, and afterwards in the Canterbury Cathedral. After the Restoration he was ejected from the cathedral. Durant published seven works, mostly of a consolatory nature.

William Dyer (d. 1696) Dyer was a nonconformist divine, minister of Chesham, and later of Cholesbury, Buckinghamshire. He was a preacher at St. Anne's Aldersgate Street in London around 1666. One record states that Dyer joined the Quakers, but the evidence is suspect. A more accurate statement would be that Dyer inclined toward Quaker sentiments. He was buried in the Quaker burial ground at Southwark. His works have been compared stylistically to Bunyan's.

Daniel Dyke (d. 1614) Dyke was born at Hempstead, where his father was silenced for nonconformity. He received his education at Cambridge, and became a fellow of Sussex College in 1606. He soon afterward became the minister of Coggeshall, Essex, but was suspended for nonconformity. He moved to St. Albans and became the preacher there, where he met with great success. Over the next few years Dyke had conflicts with Bishop Aylmer, who suspended, restored, and suspended Dyke again. Many appeals were made to Lord Treasurer Burghley (William Cecil), but his pleas on Dyke's behalf were ineffectual. Dyke died in 1614. The place of his burial is unknown. Dyke's masterpiece, *The Mystery of Self-Deceiving,* is a work of unusual depth and candor. It was used by many eminent divines for insight into the heart's deceitfulness.

Jeremiah Dyke (d. 1620) Jeremiah was Daniel Dyke's brother. He shared his brother's nonconformist sentiments, but does not seem to have been suspended for them. He was the minister of Epping in Essex from 1609 until his death in 1620. While Dyke published several discourses of his own, he is best known for editing his brother's manuscripts and sending them to the press.

William Fenner (1600–1640) William Fenner was educated at Pembroke College, Cambridge. He was forced to leave his first pastorate because of his puritanical principles. He was much appreciated as a spiritual physician, and was sought after for advice by the nobility. Though he died at a rather early age, his writings filled a small folio volume. Among other works, Fenner published *Christ's Alarm to Drowsy Saints* in two parts.

John Flavel (c.1627–1691) The son of a minister, John Flavel was educated at University College, Oxford. He received Presbyterian ordination at Salisbury in 1650, and ministered in Devonshire. The majority of his ministry was at Dartmouth in South Devon. He was one of the ejected ministers of 1662 and preached in his own house for ten years. Flavel's works have been highly regarded since their first publication, and even today enjoy a wide readership.

Thomas Gataker (1574–1654) Gataker was born on September 4, 1574, in the rectory house of St. Edmund's, Lombard Street, in London. In 1590 he entered St. John's College, Cambridge, where he gained a scholarship and graduated with a Master of Arts degree. In 1596 Gataker became one of the first fellows of Sidney Sussex College. He subsequently served the rectory of Rotherhithe, Surrey, and was a member of the Westminster Assembly. He preached at St. Mary's, Cambridge, on one occasion, the day after the death of Queen Elizabeth. He died of a fever on July 27, 1654, revered as a godly patriarch in the Puritan cause. His printed works varied greatly, from devotional pieces and sermons, to a controversial work on the nature and use of casting lots.

Thomas Gouge (1609–1681) Gouge was the eldest son of William Gouge (see below). He was born in London on September 29, 1609. He received a good education at Eton, and was admitted as a scholar at King's College, Cambridge, on August 16, 1625. Gouge ministered at St. Sepulchre's, London, for most of his life. He gave liberally to all, but especially to the poor. Inspired by Joseph Alleine's "Life," Gouge traveled to Wales to do missionary work. He readily made Welsh books available to the poor and even financed a Welsh translation of the Bible. He died in his sleep on October 29, 1681.

William Gouge (1578–1653) William Gouge was the nephew of Samuel and Ezekiel Culverwell, both noted Puritans. He was educated first at St. Paul's School and then at the grammar school of Felstead, Essex, where his uncle Ezekiel was vicar. He then studied at Eton and from there was admitted to King's College, Cambridge. Gouge advanced greatly in logic and defended the new philosophy of Peter Ramus (a watered-down Aristotelian system). On the recommendation of Arthur Hildersam, Gouge was appointed minister of St. Anne's, Blackfriars. In 1643, Gouge served at the Westminster Assembly, and it was said that "no one was more assiduous in attendance." Gouge, known as the gentle scholar, was most famous for his *Commentary on the Epistle to the Hebrews*, which was nearly finished at his death. Posthumously published, the Hebrews commentary filled two large folios and consisted of almost a thousand sermons preached at Blackfriars.

William Greenhill (1591–1677) Greenhill was born in Oxfordshire in 1591. When he was thirteen years old he entered Magdalen College, Cambridge. Eight years later he received his Master of Arts degree, and for thirteen years, ministered in New Shoreham in Sussex. Greenhill was called "the evening star" of Stepney because he preached at three in the afternoon. His most important contribution to Christian literature is his commentary on Ezekiel. He also published two collections of sermons.

His messages focused on the beauty and grandeur of Christ's person, and the inheritance of the saints.

William Gurnall (1617–1679) Gurnall was born in the parish of Walpose St. Peter, near Lynn, Norfolk, in 1617. He received early training in the Lynn grammar school and entered Emmanuel College, Cambridge, in 1631. In 1644 he obtained the living of Lavenham, Suffolk, and there spent his days. Gurnall is best known for *The Christian in Complete Armor*, the substance of sermons he preached at Lavenham.

Robert Harris (1581–1658) Harris, the president of Trinity College, was born at Broad Campden, Gloucestershire, in 1581. Harris was educated at the free schools of Chipping Campden and Worcester. He entered Magdalen Hall, Oxford, on June 10, 1597. His parents were poor and could not pay for his education, thus he taught Greek and Hebrew to advance in academics. Harris preached in several different places and earned a reputation as a great Puritan and scholar. He printed a large number of sermons.

Arthur Hildersam (1563–1631) Arthur Hildersam was descended from a branch of the royal family that settled in Cambridgeshire, where he was born on October 6, 1563. His father, a staunch Roman Catholic, disinherited him for embracing Protestantism. Thrown upon his own resources, Hildersam found favor with Henry, Earl of Huntingdon, who provided financial support to the "orphaned" boy. After a time as a fellow at Trinity Hall, Cambridge, Hildersam was appointed to preach at Ashby-de-la-Zouch in Leicestershire. He remained in the Church of England, and opposed separation. He labored for reformation from within, but met with severe persecution. As a cousin of Queen Elizabeth, however, Hildersam was spared from the most severe punishments. His persecutors were content to silence him.

James Janeway (1636–1674) James Janeway was born in Hertfordshire, the son of a minister, at the end of 1636. He was educated at Christ's College, Oxford, and spent time as a private tutor. He is listed as one of the ejected ministers of 1662. In 1672 his admirers built a large meeting house for him near London, where it is said that "he had a very numerous auditory, and a great reformation was wrought amongst many." Janeway's popularity so enraged high church officials that several times they threatened to shoot him, which they attempted to do on at least two occasions. Janeway contracted tuberculosis and died in his thirty-eighth year. He is best known for *A Token for Children*, in which he collected personal accounts of the conversions of a number of children in his parish. He also wrote *Invisible Realities*, a spiritual biography of his older brother John.

William Jenkyn (1612–1685) Jenkyn was educated at Cambridge, and placed under the tutelage of the great Anthony Burgess at Emmanuel College. After receiving his Master of Arts degree, he ministered in London and Colchester until 1641, when he was chosen vicar of Christ Church, Newgate Street, and some months later, lecturer of St. Ann's, Blackfriars. Along with others, he was imprisoned during the Commonwealth for attempting to raise funds for Charles's Scottish army. Jenkyn was one of the ejected ministers in 1662. He retired to his house in Hertfordshire, where he preached privately. He was restored once more to his pulpit and then ejected again. After preaching privately, he was caught and imprisoned, and declined in health. He died in prison on January 19, 1685. Mourners in more than 150 coaches attended his funeral.

Edward Lawrence (1623–1695) Lawrence was born at Moston in Shropshire. He was educated first in the school at Whitchurch, and then was admitted to Magdalen College, Cambridge, as a work-study scholar on June 8, 1644. Four years later he was made vicar of Baschurch in Shropshire. He was ejected from that post in 1662 for nonconformity. Penniless, Lawrence was asked how he planned to support his wife and children. He answered, "We must all live on Matt. 6." Lawrence spent his last days in London. He died in November 1695. His most famous work was *Christ's Power over Bodily Diseases*, published in 1662.

Matthew Lawrence (d. 1645) All that is known about Matthew Lawrence is that he served as pastor of Ipswich and wrote *The Use and Practice of Faith*.

Samuel Lee (1625–1691) Lee was born in London and educated at St. Paul's School. He entered Magdalen Hall, Oxford, in 1647, and was elected fellow of Wadham College on October 3, 1648. Several other fellowships were offered to him but he declined and stayed at Wadham. Near the close of his life, he emigrated to New England and started a church there. On the return voyage to England, his ship was seized by French pirates and he lost his wife and daughter. Overcome with grief, Lee died at St. Malo of a fever about Christmas 1691. Lee was known as a universal scholar, especially in the field of languages.

Christopher Love (1618–1651) Christopher Love served in London as a Presbyterian minister and member of the Westminster Assembly of divines (though his impact seems to have been relatively small). He was imprisoned by Oliver Cromwell on charges of treason, and was convicted and beheaded, leaving a wife and three children. Love never denied his involvement in efforts to restore the monarchy. Curiously, just prior to his death, he made many predictions about the future after studying the books of Daniel and Revelation. Love was a historicist, believing that events described in Revelation are actual events in the history of the world. Love's many manuscripts, which were published posthumously by his friends, contain none of these ideas, and are, instead, prime examples of evangelical depth and piety.

Thomas Manton (1620–1677) Thomas Manton was educated at Wadham College, Oxford. He graduated in 1639 and was ordained by Joseph Hall, Bishop of Norwich. Manton, the leading Puritan in London, was near Christopher Love when the latter was executed. He was a member of the Westminster Assembly, and succeeded Obadiah Sedgwick as the minister at St. Paul's in Covent Garden. Manton was arrested on several occasions for preaching after he had been silenced in 1662. In the nineteenth century, a complete edition of Manton's works was published in twenty-two volumes. He is best known for his commentaries and expository sermons on the books of James and Jude.

Joseph Mede (1586–1638) Mede was born at Burdon in Essex, descended from a respectable family in that county. He received his early education at Hoddesdon in Hertfordshire, then at Wethersfield in Essex. In 1602, he was sent to Christ's College, Cambridge, where he tutored Daniel Rogers. Mede earned a great reputation as a scholar and disputant. When Archbishop James Ussher was compiling his *Sacred Chronology*, he asked Mede's advice on several occasions. It was Mede's custom to ask his students whether they doubted what they had read—contending that those who do not doubt, inevitably do not understand. Though Mede made a small living, he was nevertheless generous toward others. He loved peace, unity, and good order, and worked to advance the reformation of the church.

Christopher Nesse (1621–1705) Christopher Nesse was born in 1621 in Yorkshire. He was educated first at a private school under the Puritan Lazarus Seaman, and later at St. John's College, Cambridge. In 1644 he became pastor of an independent church. In 1656 he became a preacher in Leeds, but was ejected in 1662. For several years, the local authorities harried Nesse for his Puritan principles. Near the close of his life, Nesse preached to a private congregation in London, where he died in his eighty-fourth year. His best known book, often reprinted, is *An Antidote against Arminianism*.

John Owen (1616–1683) Known as the "Prince of Puritans," John Owen was born in 1616, the second son of Henry Owen, a Puritan minister. He was such a capable student that at the age of twelve, he was admitted to Queen's College, Oxford. For several years, he allowed himself only four hours of sleep each night so that he might devote more of his time to his studies. Originally a Presbyterian, Owen became convinced that congregationalism most agreed with New Testament principles. He was a close associate of Oliver Cromwell, who insisted that Owen become head of the college in Dublin, Ireland. Owen reluctantly agreed to hold that position for eighteen months; then soon returned to London. He was called by the House of Commons to be the vice chancellor of Christ Church, Oxford. Owen was also invited to become the president of Harvard College, but declined in order to remain in his native England.

William Perkins (1558–1602) William Perkins was born in Warwickshire and educated at Christ's College, Cambridge. He was a teaching fellow there until 1595, and then a lecturer at Great St. Andrews in Cambridge until he died in 1602. He is known as the "father of English Puritanism," because of his great influence on succeeding generations. Perkins had a ministry to prisoners, and on at least one occasion, tearfully pleaded with an inmate to receive the gospel of Christ.

Francis Roberts (1609–1675) Roberts was born at Methley, near Leeds. He entered Trinity College, Oxford, early in 1625. At the outbreak of the English Civil War, he joined the Presbyterians, and subscribed to "The Solemn League and Covenant." In 1643 he became pastor of St. Augustine's, Watling Street, and in 1649, rector of Wrington, Somerset. Roberts also served as Lord Essex's first chaplain in Dublin, Ireland. Roberts's best contribution to Christian literature is *The Mystery and Marrow of the Bible,* the most extensive Puritan work on the covenants between God and humanity.

Ralph Robinson (1614–1655) Born at Heswall, Cheshire, Robinson received a fine education at Katharine Hall, Cambridge. He was ordained as a Presbyterian minister at St. Mary's Woolnoth, Lombard Street, in London, in 1642. Robinson was sent to the Tower of London on charges of high treason, but was released several months later. He died on June 15, 1655 and was buried in the chancel of St. Mary's, Woolnoth. His best known work is *Christ All in All.*

John Rogers (c.1572–1636) John Rogers was born near Essex about 1572. His longest pastorate was in the town of Dedham, where he became well-known for his lively sermons. There is an anecdote about Rogers's ministry that is too popular to omit here. On one occasion, Rogers was chiding his people for their neglect of the Bible, and began a dramatized dialogue between God and His people, Rogers playing both parts. He personified the people, pleading with God for his Bible to remain with them, and ended on God's behalf, "Say you so? Well, I will try you a while longer; and here is my Bible for you. I will see how you use it, whether you will love it more . . . observe it more . . . practice it more, and live more according to it." And he walked out of the church carrying the Bible, got on his horse, and would have left had not the crowd stopped him.

Henry Scudder (d. 1659) Little is known about Scudder. He was educated at Christ's College, Cambridge, in 1606, and ministered in Drayton, Oxfordshire, until 1633. In 1643, he was chosen as one of the Presbyterian members of the Westminster Assembly. His best known work, *The Christian's Daily Walk in Security and Peace,* was highly recommended by John Owen and Richard Baxter.

Obadiah Sedgwick (1600–1658) Obadiah Sedgwick was the son of a clergyman. He received his degrees from Magdalen Hall, Oxford. In 1626 he tutored Matthew Hale, who became one of the most respected lawyers of his time. Sedgwick was a Presbyterian, and a member of the Westminster Assembly. He was one of several ministers who petitioned Parliament for the release of Christopher Love. In 1646 he was appointed to pastor St. Paul's in Covent Garden, in London. Sedgwick's works are numerous, but his best known is *The Bowels of Tender Mercy Sealed in the Everlasting Covenant.* There he sets forth the nature, excellency, and benefits of the covenant relation between God and his people.

Samuel Shaw (1635–1696) The son of a blacksmith, Shaw was born at Repton, Derbyshire. He entered St. John's College, Cambridge, in 1650. Six years later he became the schoolmaster at Tamworth, Warwickshire. In 1658 he was ordained as a Presbyterian and served the parish of Long Watton, Leicestershire, but Shaw was ejected in 1662. In 1665, he lost two daughters to the plague. At the end of 1666, he moved to Ashby-de-la-Zouch, where Arthur Hildersam had ministered. Shaw obtained a license to preach, but would only preach privately. He died in 1696. His most famous work is *Immanuel; Or, A Discovery of True Religion.*

John Shower (1657–1715) Brother of Bartholomew Shower, John Shower served as an assistant to Vincent Alsop, lived in Holland for some time, and lectured at the English church in Rotterdam. His last twenty-four years were spent ministering to a variety of London parishes. He wrote several treatises on subjects including the forgiveness of sins, the day of grace, heaven and hell, and time and eternity.

Richard Sibbes (1577–1635) Sibbes was one of the greatest Puritans of his age. He greatly influenced the direction and content of Puritan preaching, theology, and writing in both England and America. He was born in Sudbury, in Suffolk, in 1577, and was educated at St. John's College, Cambridge. Sibbes was a lecturer at Trinity Church, Cambridge, and pastored that church during the last two years of his life. He was chosen master of Katharine Hall, Cambridge, where, although a Puritan, he was permitted to retain until his death. He died on July 5, 1635. He is most famous for *The Bruised Reed,* which went through numerous editions.

Samuel Slater (d. 1701) Slater was educated at Emmanuel College, Cambridge. After ordination, he was first appointed a minister at Nayland, Suffolk, and afterward at Bury St. Edmunds. He was ejected in 1662 for nonconformity. He moved to London and there succeeded the great Stephen Charnock in Crosby Square, Bishopsgate Street. He is known for a work of poetry that is sometimes attributed to his father; in the preface, Slater wrote that his inspiration was Milton's *Paradise Lost,* but that he sought to present his work in plainer clothing.

Henry Smith (1560–1591) Smith was known as "silver-tongued Smith," for his great oratorical skills. He was the most popular Puritan lecturer during Elizabeth's reign in England. Smith's practical and experiential sermons were used for family devotions for over a century after his death, and went through numerous editions. He combined force of language with force of thought and preached the gospel in its primitive power. Descended from an honorable family in Leicestershire, Smith spent most of his ministry as a lecturer at St. Clement Danes. Due to scruples about Prayer Book ceremonies, Smith never sought to be a full parish minister, though he was ordained. His works were collected and published by Thomas Smith in the late seventeenth century, and reprinted in the nineteenth.

William Spurstowe (c. 1605–1666) William Spurstowe was born around 1605, the eldest son and heir, of William Spurstowe, Sr., a London merchant, and grandson of Thomas Spurstowe, of Shrewsbury. His mother, Damoris Parkhurst, of Gilford, had many ties to Puritan families in both England and New England. Spurstowe was sent to Emmanuel College, Cambridge, in 1623. He was incorporated at Oxford in 1628. He became a fellow of St. Catherine's in 1638 and a master of the college in 1645. He was approved master of Clare on April 22, 1645, but the appointment was given to Ralph Cudworth. From St. Catherine's, a budding Puritan institution that was then under the mastership of Richard Sibbes, Spurstowe accepted a call to the rectory of Great Hampden, Buckinghamshire. John Hampden, a great parliamentary leader, was a member there. Spurstowe was deprived of his ministry after the Restoration, but continued to preach as the times allowed. His best known work, *The Wells of Salvation,* is probably the finest Puritan treatise on God's promises.

Richard Steele (1629–1692) Richard Steele was the son of a farmer. He received his Master of Arts degree from Oxford in 1656. A Presbyterian, he was part of the ordination classis for both Philip and Matthew Henry. Steele was ejected in 1662 but continued to preach in private homes. He moved to London, where he was granted a license to preach, and gathered a small congregation. He died suddenly in 1692. Steele was the author of several practical discourses.

Peter Sterry (d. 1672) Best known as Cromwell's chaplain, Sterry was born in Surrey, and entered Emmanuel College, Cambridge, in 1629. He became a preacher in London, and was one of fourteen divines nominated for the Westminster Assembly by the House of Lords. Sterry was somewhat mystical and obscure in his preaching, but has been likened to Milton in subject matter and style.

Richard Stock (c.1569–1626) Well-versed in the church fathers, Richard Stock was born in York, and educated at St. John's College, Cambridge. He was highly esteemed by his teacher, the renowned William Whitaker. He was a lecturer at several churches in London. Stock was a fervent advocate for the poor. He died in 1626 and was buried in St. Paul's Cathedral. A monument was dedicated to his memory, but was destroyed in the great fire of 1666.

George Swinnock (1627–1673) Relatively little is known about the life of George Swinnock. He was born in Maidstone, Kent, and raised in the home of his uncle, Robert Swinnock, sometime mayor of Maidstone. George Swinnock was educated at Cambridge and served as a chaplain at New College, Oxford, until his appointment as a fellow of Balliol College in 1648. He also served pastorates in Rickmansworth, Hertfordshire, and Great Kemble, Buckinghamshire. He was ejected in 1662 and then served as a chaplain in the family of Richard Hampden. Swinnock's works are among the easiest and most profitable to read.

Nathanael Taylor (d. 1702) Taylor was fluent in ancient languages, and preached the funeral sermons of at least two noted Puritans. Otherwise, little is known about him. Taylor's principal work seems to have been *A Preservative against Deism,* published in 1698, in which he showed the advantage of revelation over reason in two areas: the pardon of sin and the future state of happiness.

Thomas Taylor (1576–1633) Taylor was born in 1576 at Richmond, Yorkshire, where his father, a man of good family, was known as a friend to Puritans. Taylor distinguished himself at Christ's College, Cambridge. He was only twenty-one years old when he preached at St. Paul's Cross before Queen Elizabeth. He was zealous for reformation, and was chosen minister of St. Mary's Aldermanbury, London. There he preached until 1630 when, in failing health, he retired to Isleworth in the country. He died three years later. Taylor authored more than seventeen works.

Ralph Venning (c. 1621–1674) Ralph Venning, born in Devon, was educated at Emmanuel College, Cambridge. He was a lecturer in St. Olave's Church, Southwark, until he was forced to leave in 1662 for nonconformity. He later served as co-pastor of an independent congregation in London. His best known work is *The Plague of Plagues,* a treatise on the nature and danger of sin. Venning also published several collections of short sayings; of these, the most notable is *Milk and Honey,* which contains such statements as "the fear of the faithful should be a faithful fear."

Nathaniel Vincent (1639–1697) Nathaniel Vincent was born in Cornwall and graduated from Christ Church, Oxford, in 1656. He was appointed chaplain of Corpus Christi College, and later to a pastorate in Buckinghamshire. After the Great Ejection of 1662, Vincent spent three years as a private chaplain before moving to London in 1666. He was fined and mistreated, and literally dragged from his pulpit for preaching. Vincent spent several months in prison, and was actually banished from the country, but a flaw in his indictment prevented that sentence from being carried out. Weakened by imprisonment, Vincent died in 1697. He published several practical discourses during his lifetime.

Thomas Vincent (1634–1678) Little is known about Thomas Vincent, a brother of Nathaniel Vincent, who ministered in London during the 1665 plague. His most famous work is *The True Christian's Love to the Unseen Christ.*

Richard Vines (1600–1656) Vines was born at Blaston, Leicestershire. He was educated at Magdalen College, Cambridge, where he excelled as a Greek scholar. Vines lectured for some time at Nuneaton, where Samuel Clarke was among his listeners. He was elected to the Westminster

Assembly and the rectory of St. Clement Danes. Vines was among the drafters of the Westminster Confession of Faith. On the morning of Charles I's execution, Vines offered him religious counsel, which the king gladly accepted. Vines published only individual sermons during his lifetime. Several of his works were printed posthumously, most notably *The Saint's Nearness to God.*

Thomas Watson (d. 1686) Little is known about Watson's early life. He earned a Master of Arts degree from Emmanuel College in Cambridge, and subsequently began a long pastorate at St. Stephen's Walbrook in London. With Christopher Love, William Jenkyn, and others, he was imprisoned in 1651 for his part in a plot to reestablish the monarchy. He was released on the promise of good behavior. In 1662, Watson was ejected for nonconformity. Watson retired to Essex in 1686 and died there.

William Whittaker (1629–1672) Born at Oakham, Rutland, Whittaker was the son of Jeremiah Whittaker. He entered Emmanuel College, Cambridge, in his fifteenth year, excelling there in the classical and oriental languages. He succeeded his father at St. Mary Magdalen, Bermondsey, in 1645. Whittaker was ejected in 1662; after his ejection he preached in small meeting house in Long Walk, Bermondsey. For many years his house was full of candidates in divinity, and he had many foreign divines under his care. Whittaker's sermons were published posthumously as *Eighteen Sermons Preached upon Several Texts of Scripture.* In a sketch of Whittaker's character, Thomas Jacombe wrote: "How much have we lost in one Whittaker! And shall we not be sensible of our loss?"

BIBLIOGRAPHY

Brook, Benjamin. *The Lives of the Puritans.* 3 vols. Morgan: Soli Deo Gloria, 1996.

Reid, James. *Memoirs of the Westminster Divines.* Edinburgh: The Banner of Truth Trust, 1982.

Stephen, Leslie and Sidney Lee, eds. *Dictionary of National Biography.* 22 vols. Oxford: Oxford University Press, 1993.